THE FIX-POINT APPROACH TO INTERDEPENDENT SYSTEMS

CONTRIBUTIONS TO ECONOMIC ANALYSIS

132

NORTH-HOLLAND PUBLISHING COMPANY

AMSTERDAM · NEW YORK · OXFORD

THE FIX-POINT APPROACH TO INTERDEPENDENT SYSTEMS

HERMAN WOLD

Editor

NORTH-HOLLAND PUBLISHING COMPANY
AMSTERDAM · NEW YORK · OXFORD

ISBN: 0 444 85451 7

Publishers:

NORTH-HOLLAND PUBLISHING COMPANY
AMSTERDAM · NEW YORK · OXFORD

Sole distributors for the U.S.A. and Canada:

ELSEVIER NORTH-HOLLAND INC.
52 VANDERBILT AVENUE
NEW YORK, N.Y. 10017

Library of Congress Cataloging in Publication Data
Main entry under title:

The Fix-point approach to interdependent systems.

(Contributions to economic analysis ; 132)
Bibliography: p.
Includes indexes.
1. Fix-point estimation--Addresses, essays, lectures.
2. Econometrics--Addresses, essays, lectures.
I. Wold, Herman. II. Series.
HB139.F59 330'.01'51 80-39934
ISBN 0-444-85451-7

PRINTED IN THE NETHERLANDS

INTRODUCTION TO THE SERIES

This series consists of a number of hitherto unpublished studies, which are introduced by the editors in the belief that they represent fresh contributions to economic science.

The term "economic analysis" as used in the title of the series has been adopted because it covers both the activities of the theoretical economist and the research worker.

Although the analytical methods used by the various contributors are not the same, they are nevertheless conditioned by the common origin of their studies, namely theoretical problems encountered in practical research. Since for this reason, business cycle research and national accounting, research work on behalf of economic policy, and problems of planning are the main sources of the subjects dealt with, they necessarily determine the manner of approach adopted by the authors. Their methods tend to be "practical" in the sense of not being too far remote from application to actual economic conditions. In addition they are quantitative rather than qualitative.

It is the hope of the editors that the publication of these studies will help to stimulate the exchange of scientific information and to reinforce international cooperation in the field of economics.

THE EDITORS

FOREWORD BY HARALD CRAMÉR

My friend Herman Wold has asked me to write a preface to the volume on Fix-Point methods written by him and a number of his collaborators. Although the subject of this work is somewhat distant from the field where I have been mostly engaged in the course of my own research work, I will do my best to write down some appropriate introductory remarks.

In modern econometric research, an important part is played by the discussion of systems of linear relations assumed to hold between various quantities characteristic of the economic life of a community. Some of these quantities have predetermined values, while others are regarded as observed values of stochastic variables with unknown mean values, sometimes assumed to have a multinormal distribution. At least some of the coefficients occurring in the linear relations are unknown.

Given a set of statistical observations on the variables entering into such a system, it is required to estimate the unknown coefficients and mean values. This may be performed by different methods. In order that a proposed method of estimation should be regarded as satisfactory, the requisite numerical work should not be too cumbersome, and the resulting estimates should satisfy some convenient tests of consistency and accuracy.

In the present volume, the family of estimation methods known as the Fix-Point (FP) methods introduced by Herman Wold in 1965 is closely studied.

The FP methods work with a system of linear relations of the form known as *structural*, where each of the stochastic (endogenous) variables under investigation is expressed as a linear combination of the other (explanatory) stochastic variables, the predetermined variables, and a residual. The residuals are assumed to be uncorrelated with all the predetermined variables. In general such a system is called a system of interdependent (ID) relations. The direct application of ordinary least squares (OLS) regression to such a system has been criticized, as it does not give a consistent forecast of the variables occurring in the time series under investigation.

In order to obtain an estimation method capable of giving forecasts in the form of conditional mean values of the relevant variables, Wold introduced in 1963 a transformation of the system of equations in the structural form referred to above, each explanatory variable being replaced by the sum of its mean value and a residual of zero mean value. The transformed system is of a type called a reformulated interdependent (REID) system. Each endogenous variable now becomes expressed as a conditional mean value, relative to given values of the other variables, and the transformed system may thus be applied for predictionary use.

The original FP method as introduced in 1965 consists in a sequence of iterated estimations of the coefficients and mean values in a REID system, starting from a more or less arbitrary sequence of initial values, and proceeding by successive steps of OLS regression. It is assumed that the stochastic variables concerned have finite variances, but no further assumptions about their distributions have to be made. The requisite numerical work is fairly easily performed by an electronic computer.

As explained in detail in this volume, the sequence of iterated estimations will, under appropriate conditions, converge to a unique limit which constitutes a consistent system of estimates for the unknown coefficients and mean values. The conditions that have to be imposed in order to establish convergence, uniqueness and consistency are fully discussed in several chapters of the volume. In particular interesting conditions for convergence are given, in terms of the eigenvalues of the coefficient matrix. The analysis of the uniqueness problem shows that, although the case of multiple solutions is theoretically possible, in all cases actually encountered in practical applications the resulting estimate has been found to be unique.

An important generalization of the REID class of equations is made possible by the observations that, in the majority of cases occurring in practical applications, the number of explanatory and predetermined variables entering into each particular equation is fairly small. The FP method will then work under the more general assumption that each residual is uncorrelated only with those explanatory variables that appear in the same equation. This implies that only a smaller number of assumptions on uncorrelatedness have to be made. It is shown by examples that the reduction of the necessary number of assumptions may be very substantial. For such a system of generalized independent (GEID) relations, the FP method will work in the same way and yield the same estimates as in the REID case.

Various modified forms of the FP method are fully discussed, and their properties are compared with the original FP method. A large number of important recent statistical examples are discussed, and extensive comparisons are made between the results obtained by the various FP methods and other possible methods of estimation. It is remarkable to find that, in the great majority of cases given, the FP methods seem to give more accurate results than the various classical estimation methods.

It should be clear from these brief remarks that the present Volume constitutes an important contribution to some of the main problems of current econometric research.

HARALD CRAMÉR

Stockholm, January 1979

PREFACE BY THE EDITOR

When initiating in the early 1960's the Fix-Point method for the estimation of interdependent systems, my main incentive was to establish the behavioural relations as the conceptual and operative basis of the systems. The reformulation of the system (REID) and the ensuing generalization (GEID) opened up a new problem area, new vistas that were explored in theory and practice in several doctoral dissertations and other studies. By good luck of timing the early studies obtained generous support from the first distributions of grants from the newly established Tercentenary Fund of the Bank of Sweden. In the mid-1970's, as the applied work accumulated, the FP approach showed off favourably in comparative studies with current estimation methods.

In Chapter 1, Section 4 is a joint statement on the FP family of methods by the authors of this volume. Six chapters draw from four Doctoral Dissertations sponsored by myself: Chapters 2 and 8 by Lennart Bodin (1974), Chapter 3 by Anders Ågren (1972), Chapters 5 and 7 by Reinhold Bergström (1974), Chapter 6 by David Edgerton (1973). Simulation experiments on the robustness of FP estimation are reported in Chapter 10 by Anders Westlund (robustness against specification errors) and in Chapter 11 by Sydney May (invariance to the start of the FP iterations).

Ejnar Lyttkens, to whom I am indebted for innumerable consultations on theoretical aspects of the FP approach, presents in Chapter 4 his parametric and algebraic versions of FP estimation. Jan Selén in Chapter 9, drawing from his Doctoral Dissertation (1973) sponsored by Ejnar Lyttkens, adapts the FP method to deal with autocorrelated residuals. Like Ejnar Lyttken's method of IIV (Iterative Instrumental Variables) for the estimation of interdependent systems, Jan Selén adopts the assumption that the behavioural relations are deterministic, subject to superimposed 'errors in equations'. This classical assumption is conceptually different from the predictor specification of the FP approach, and is more stringent (see 4.2 in Chapter 1).

The developments have placed the FP family of methods between two chairs in the mainstream of contemporary econometrics. On the one side are the large macroeconomic forecasting systems with hundreds or thousands of variables and structural relations, systems too large for interpretation and operative use of the structural parameters; cf.

Mosbaek (1968). On the other side are the refined estimation methods for interdependent systems that are based on very stringent assumptions, notably that all structural residuals are uncorrelated with all predetermined variables. While the FP methods have been in play less than 15 years, it is only recently that their intermediate position has begun to show off as a useful compromise.

The international dissipation of the FP approach having been rather limited, we authors appreciate so much the more the opportunity to publish this volume in the CEA series. I wish to express my thanks and appreciation to the co-authors for helpful collaboration in the planning and editing of the volume.

HERMAN WOLD

Uppsala, June 1980

CONTENTS

Chapter 1

THE FIX-POINT APPROACH TO INTERDEPENDENT SYSTEMS
Review and Current Outlook

HERMAN WOLD

1. Challenges of Simultaneous Equations Systems: Operative Interpretation and Statistical Estimation

1.1. Introductory

1.1.1. The research background of the present volume can be seen as evolving in three periods or stages. First, the simultaneous equations systems introduced by Trygve Haavelmo in 1943 were subject to a lively discussion in the 40's and 50's, as highlighted in *Econometrica* 1960[1] in the prestigeous symposium: "Simultaneous equations: Any verdict yet?" The crucial issue is the causal–predictive interpretation of the structural equations that define the simultaneous equations. Making distinction between simultaneous equations of *recursive* and *non-recursive* type, Bentzel and Wold (1946) showed that Haavelmo's wholesale dismissal of OLS (Ordinary Least Squares) estimation of the structural equations is to the point for non-recursive systems, but not for recursive systems. In several papers [Wold (1947, 1954, 1955)] the clearcut causal interpretation of recursive systems (later called *causal chain systems*) was emphasized and the obscurity around the causal aspects of non-recursive systems (later called *interdependent*, briefly ID, *systems*) was stressed. Bentzel and Hansen (1954) gave a causal interpretation of one type of ID systems, the argument being that if the system is a causal chain when observed over sufficiently short periods, say weekly or monthly or quarterly observations, then the system appears to be interdependent when the data are aggregated over longer periods, say one year.

1.1.2. In the second period, from the late 50's to the mid-70's, the material of this volume took shape. Shifting the focus from causation to prediction, I started to explore econometric models from the point of view of *predictor specification*, assuming that the systematic part of the predictor relation is the conditional expectation of the predictand for given values of

[1] Christ et al. (1960); see also Klein (1960).

the predictor(s); Wold (1960). Two features of predictor specification at fundamental level:

(i) Predictor specification defines the relation at issue as a *stochastic relationship*, not as a *deterministic equation* subject to *superimposed* "errors".

(ii) OLS regression as applied to a predictor relation will under mild supplementary conditions give parameter estimates that are consistent in the large-sample sense; Wold (1963a).

As to simultaneous equations systems, predictor specification led to an array of new insights; Wold (1960, 1964a). The structural relations of simultaneous equations system do or do not allow predictor specification according as the system is a causal chain or an ID system. The structural relations of an ID system will allow predictor specification if they are reformulated so that each explanatory variable that is endogenous and interdependent is replaced by its predictor (conditional expectation) as given by the reduced form. The REID (Reformulated ID) systems thus defined involve no change in the parameters. The predictor specification of the structural relations of REID systems sets the stage for estimation by OLS regression, but the requisite regressions cannot be formed directly since some or all regressors are reformulated and thereby unknown. This difficulty was overcome by the iterative device called Fix-Point (FP) estimation, each iteration giving new proxies for the unknown regressors; Wold (1965, 1966).

At the outset the FP algorithm for the estimation of REID systems was based on the classical assumption of simultaneous equation systems, namely that the residual of each structural relation is independent of all predetermined (exogenous or lagged endogenous) variables in the system. In overdetermined systems the classical assumption imposes more zero correlations on the residuals than there are parameters to estimate. Almost at the outset it was realized that the predictor specification of the structural relations of ID systems implies an extension of the FP algorithm so as to give consistent estimates when applied to GEID (Generalized ID) systems; these are formally the same as REID systems, but the residual of each structural relation is assumed to have zero correlation only with the explanatory variables of that same relation. In other words, GEID systems honour the "parity principle" that just as many zero correlations are imposed on the structural residuals as there are parameters to estimate.

The FP algorithm for the estimation of simultaneous equations systems attracted a circle of researchers interested in developing the FP approach in theory and practice. The FP algorithm was soon generalized in several directions; applications of the FP family of methods to real-world models and data were reported; using simulated or real-world data as basis for the analysis, emphasis was placed on comparative studies of the FP methods versus the various classical methods. Specific reference is made to the systematic work of Reinhold Bergström (1974, 1976) on the performance in real-world applications of the FP methods as compared with the classical methods.

1.1.3. The third phase or period of FP evolution began in the mid-70's as the real-world applications of FP estimation accumulated, and FP showed off favourably in comparison with the classical methods. Then I felt that the time had come to bring together the various contributions in the FP approach in theoretical and applied work, and very soon the ensuing discussions with the co-authors led to the planning of the present volume.

Now let me briefly refer to an important point in the continuing research on the FP approach. Already when contemplating on the earliest comparisons of FP and classical estimates I had noticed an intriguing regularity, namely that when the estimates of a parameter are plotted along a line the classical estimates except FIML tend to lie in a cluster, whereas the FP and FIML estimates usually lie at a distance from the cluster, with FP on one side or the other, and FIML on the same or the other side. It seems plausible to conjecture that the two features have a common cause, and that large part of the explanation is given by the parity principle (see above): in contrast to FP estimation the classical methods have to cope with more zero correlation assumptions on the residuals than there are parameters to estimate. To put it otherwise, the parity principle sets FP apart from the classical methods, which become intercorrelated in their vain efforts to cope with the supernumerous correlation assumptions on the structural residuals.

1.2. The Research Material of the Present Volume

1.2.1. After the monograph by Mosbaek and Wold et al. (1970) the continued development of the FP family of methods has mainly been a Swedish affair. The following chapters of this volume summarize the doctoral dissertations of Ågren (1972a), Edgerton (1973c), Bodin (1974), Bergström (1974), Selén (1975), Westlund (1975) and report further contributions by these authors as well as contributions by Lyttkens (Chapter 4) and May (Chapter 11).

Readers of the volume are assumed to have a working knowledge of current econometric methods of multirelational modelling as given in leading textbooks; see Johnston (1972), Klein (1974), Madansky (1976), Malinvaud (1964).

Section 2 of this introductory chapter gives a formal briefing of FP estimation of ID systems. Section 3 reviews the FP approach to ID systems with special regard to conceptual and operative aspects of the formal analysis. The focus is in particular on predictive and causal inference from the behavioural relations of ID systems. As compared with the first chapter in Mosbaek and Wold et al. (1970), Section 3 is more outspoken about cases of formalism in the current econometric methods. Section 4 is a joint statement by the authors of the volume. The current outlook on the field of applications is briefly discussed, with special regard to the incentives for the volume.

1.2.2. Incentives for the FP approach to ID systems. The FP method was conceived in 1963, at the Econometric Week of the Vatican Academy of Sciences and shortly thereafter; cf. Wold (1963b, 1964a). By this time the FIML method had been developed so it could estimate simultaneous equations systems with up to 12 structural relations; Klein (1964). Already at such moderate size the FIML method becomes intractable: In large or moderately large systems other classical estimation methods become inoperative since all of the predetermined variables enter in each relation of the reduced form, with result that the OLS regressions of the reduced form tend to give vanishing residuals and to give an illusory reproduction of the endogenous variables.

Hence for some time I had tried to design an estimation method that stays in the structural form, where each relation usually involves only some few explanatory variables. This idea seemed so much the more natural as I had shown that the structural form can be reformulated so as to allow predictor specification, thereby providing an operative interpretation of the structural relations, and at the same time paving the way for Least Squares estimation of the structural form; Wold (1960). This clue led to the FP method, an iterative procedure involving a sequence of OLS regressions on the structural form; Wold (1965, 1966).

1.3. Background: On the Evolution of Simultaneous Equations Systems

1.3.1. With Jan Tinbergen's multirelational models in the mid- and late 1930's a new era begins in quantitative economics.[2] Designed as macroeconomic tools for business cycle analysis and policy, his models were pioneering in their bold raise of aspiration levels, as well as in the introduction of new empirical concepts and operative devices.

[2] Tinbergen (1937, 1939).

Tinbergen's models being too large to be quoted here, we give the following very simple model for illustration:

$$y_{1t} = \alpha_1 \qquad\qquad + \gamma_{11} y_{2,t-1} + \delta_{1t}, \tag{1.1a}$$

$$y_{2t} = \alpha_2 + \beta_{21} y_{1t} + \gamma_{22} y_{3,t-1} + \delta_{2t}, \tag{1.1b}$$

$$y_{3t} = \alpha_3 + \beta_{32} y_{2t} + \gamma_{33} x_{1t} \quad + \delta_{3t}. \tag{1.1c}$$

The model has three behavioral relations, three endogenous variables $y = (y_1, y_2, y_3)$, and three predetermined variables, of which $y_{2,t-1}$ and $y_{3,t-1}$ are lagged endogenous variables and x_1 is exogenous. Figure 1 shows the Tinbergen arrow schemes for this model.

In conjunction with behavioral relations, Tinbergen's models involve a number of identities; that is, exact relations with prescribed numerical coefficients. Until further notice we shall consider multirelational models of Tinbergen's and other types that involve no identities.

To estimate the parameters of his models, Tinbergen applied OLS regression to each separate behavioral relation. In current terminology the behavioral relations and the identities constitute the *structural form* of the model. The *reduced form* of the models is obtained by solving for the endogenous variables. The reduced form of system (1.1a–c) reads

$$y_{1t} = \alpha_1 + \gamma_{11} y_{2,1-t} + \delta_{1t}, \tag{1.2a}$$

$$y_{2t} = \beta_{21}\alpha_1 + \alpha_2 + \beta_{21}\gamma_{11} y_{2,t-1} + \gamma_{22} y_{3,t-1} + \beta_{21}\delta_{1t} + \delta_{2t}, \tag{1.2b}$$

$$\begin{aligned} y_{32} = {} & \beta_{31}\beta_{21}\alpha_1 + \beta_{32}\alpha_2 + \alpha_3 + \beta_{32}\beta_{21}\gamma_{11} y_{2,t-1} \\ & + \beta_{32}\gamma_{22} y_{3,t-1} + \gamma_{33} x_{1t} + \beta_{32}\beta_{21}\delta_{1t} + \beta_{32}\delta_{2t} + \delta_{3t}. \end{aligned} \tag{1.2c}$$

In vector and matrix notation the structural form (1.1a–c) is written

$$\underset{3\times 1}{y_t} = \underset{3\times 3}{\beta}\ \underset{3\times 1}{y_t} + \underset{3\times 4}{\Gamma}\ \underset{4\times 1}{z_t} + \underset{3\times 1}{\delta_t}, \tag{1.3a}$$

where β and Γ are given by

$$\beta = \begin{bmatrix} 0 & 0 & 0 \\ \beta_{21} & 0 & 0 \\ 0 & \beta_{32} & 0 \end{bmatrix}, \tag{1.3b}$$

$$\Gamma = \begin{bmatrix} \gamma_{10} & \gamma_{11} & 0 & 0 \\ \gamma_{20} & 0 & \gamma_{22} & 0 \\ \gamma_{30} & 0 & 0 & \gamma_{33} \end{bmatrix}, \tag{1.3c}$$

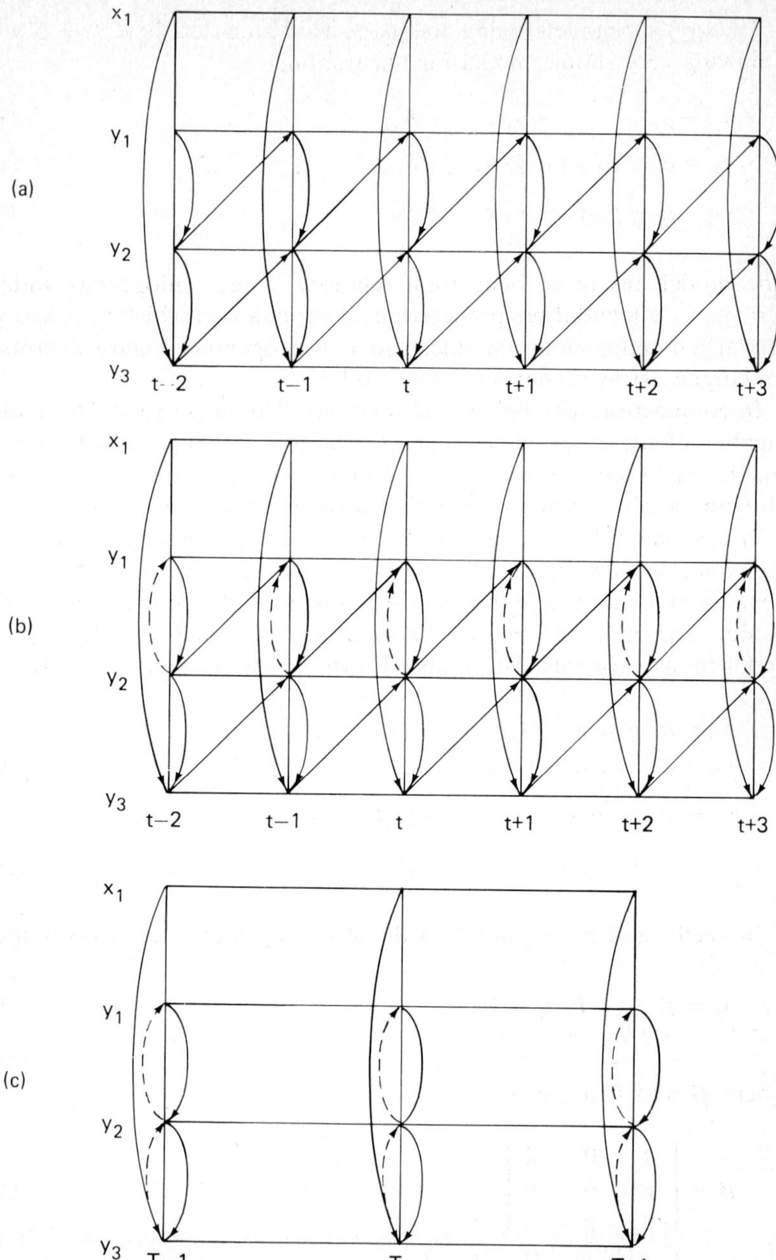

FIGURE 1. Tinbergen arrow schemes for Model (1.1a–c): (a) six time periods of the model; (b) one time period of the model as modified by (1.12); (c) the model when aggregated over time [see 1.3.4 with reference to Bentzel and Hansen (1954)].

and z_t is the column vector of predetermined variables,

$$z_t = (z_{0t}, z_{1t}, z_{2t}, z_{3t}) = (1, y_{2,t-1}, y_{3,t-1}, x_t), \tag{1.3d}$$

where the exogenous dummy variable $z_{0t} = 1$ has been introduced to cover the constant terms $\alpha_i = \gamma_{i0}$ $(i = 1, 3)$. For the reduced form (1.2a–c) we write in matrix notation

$$\underset{3\times 1}{y_t} = \underset{3\times 4}{\Omega}\ \underset{4\times 1}{z_t} + \underset{3\times 1}{\varepsilon_t}, \tag{1.4a}$$

where $\Omega = [\omega_{ik}]$ is the 3×4 matrix of coefficients, and ε_t is the 3×1 vector of residuals. For example,

$$\omega_{22} = \beta_{21}\gamma_{11}, \tag{1.4b}$$

$$\varepsilon_{2t} = \beta_{21}\delta_{1t} + \delta_{2t}. \tag{1.4c}$$

Generally, we shall write n and m for the number of endogenous and predetermined variables, respectively. Dropping the time subscripts, the structural form of Tinbergen's model is written as

$$\underset{n\times 1}{y} = \underset{n\times n}{\beta}\ \underset{n\times 1}{y} + \underset{n\times m}{\Gamma}\ \underset{m\times 1}{z} + \underset{n\times 1}{\delta}, \tag{1.5}$$

and the reduced form

$$\underset{n\times 1}{y} = \underset{n\times m}{\Omega}\ \underset{m\times 1}{z} + \underset{n\times 1}{\varepsilon}, \tag{1.6a}$$

where the coefficient matrix Ω and the residual vector ε are given by

$$\Omega = [I - \beta]^{-1}\Gamma, \tag{1.6b}$$
$$\varepsilon = [I - \beta]^{-1}\delta. \tag{1.6c}$$

For the ith structural relation we shall write

$$y_i = \beta_i y + \gamma_i z + \delta_i, \tag{1.7a}$$

where β_i, γ_i denote the ith rows of matrices β and Γ. Equivalently, we write the ith structural relation (1.7a) as

$$y_i = \beta_{(i)} y_{(i)} + \gamma_{(i)} z_{(i)} + \delta_i, \tag{1.7b}$$

where $\beta_{(i)}$, $\gamma_{(i)}$ are the non-zero entries of vectors β_i, γ_i, and $y_{(i)}$, $z_{(i)}$ are the corresponding entries of y_i, z_i. The *positions* (i, j), (i) of matrix β and row vector β_i are the subscripts of their non-zero entries, and similarly for Γ, γ_i. Thus in system (1.1a–c) the positions of matrices β and Γ are (2, 1), (3, 2) and, respectively, (1, 1), (1, 2), (2, 1), (2, 3), (3, 1), (3, 4).

1.3.2. Trygve Haavelmo's seminal works (1943, 1949) started with a wholesale dismissal of OLS regression as applied to the structural form of simultaneous equations models. Haavelmo used a stochastic definition of the model, namely by solving the structural form for the endogenous variables, and assuming the reduced form to provide the conditional joint probability distribution for the endogenous variables, conditioned by the predetermined variables. Then Haavelmo gives explicit examples where OLS estimation of the structural form is systematically biased. For the parameter estimation of simultaneous equations systems, Haavelmo proposes the Maximum Likelihood method.

In symbols, Haavelmo defines the structural form by

$$\beta^* y + \Gamma^* z = \delta, \tag{1.8}$$

where we have used notations that correspond to (1.5),

$$\beta^* = I - \beta, \tag{1.9a}$$

$$\Gamma^* = -\Gamma. \tag{1.9b}$$

Solving the structural form (1.8) gives the reduced form of the system,

$$y = \Omega z + \varepsilon, \tag{1.10}$$

where Ω and ε are the same as in (1.6), or equivalently,

$$\Omega = -(\beta^*)^{-1}\Gamma^*, \tag{1.11a}$$

$$\varepsilon = (\beta^*)^{-1}\delta. \tag{1.11b}$$

The estimation problem as posed by Haavelmo thus is to estimate the parameters β^*, Γ^* from (1.10), subject to the restriction (1.11a).

To illustrate a special case, we modify system (1.1a–c) by adding $\beta_{12}y_{2t}$ to the right in (1.1a), thus replacing (1.1a) by

$$y_{1t} = \alpha_1 + \beta_{12}y_{2t} + \gamma_{11}y_{2,t-1} + \delta_{1t}. \tag{1.12a}$$

For the modified system the matrices β, β^* are

$$\beta = \begin{bmatrix} 0 & \beta_{12} & 0 \\ \beta_{21} & 0 & 0 \\ 0 & \beta_{32} & 0 \end{bmatrix}, \tag{1.12b}$$

$$\beta^* = \begin{bmatrix} 1 & -\beta_{12} & 0 \\ -\beta_{21} & 1 & 0 \\ 0 & -\beta_{32} & 1 \end{bmatrix}. \tag{1.12c}$$

In what follows the simultaneous equations models of Haavelmo's type will be written either in the form (1.8) or in the equivalent form

$$y = \beta y + \Gamma z + \delta, \tag{1.13}$$

using relations (1.9a–b) to transform from (1.5) to (1.13) or conversely.

1.3.3. Bentzel and Wold (1946) showed that if a simultaneous equations system (1.8) is *recursive* in the sense of Wold (1938, 1955), ML estimation on the classical assumptions of multinormal distribution and mutually independent residuals will be numerically equivalent to OLS regression as applied to the structural relations. In consequence, Haavelmo's dismissal of OLS estimation of the structural form can only apply to non-recursive systems, not to recursive systems.

This result was very much to my relief, for in my earlier work I had used OLS regression extensively for the estimation of consumer demand relations [Wold (1940), Wold and Juréen (1953)], and since any demand relation can be conceived of as being part of a multirelational model, I was quite disturbed by Haavelmo's dismissal of OLS estimation as applied to simultaneous equations models.

By the definition referred to, system (1.8) is recursive if the endogenous variables y_n can be ordered so that the matrix β is *subdiagonal*; that is, has all its positions below the main diagonal,

$$\beta_{ij} = 0 \quad \text{for all} \quad i \leq j. \tag{1.14}$$

In discussing Tinbergen's multirelational macroeconomic models I had pointed out that they are recursive in this sense. In accordance with Tinbergen's operative procedures, the reduced form of a recursive system is obtained from the structural form by consecutive elimination of the explanatory (right-hand) endogenous variables.

The distinction recursive vs. non-recursive systems is synonymous to the current terms *causal chain systems* vs. *interdependent systems*.

1.3.4. Uni- vs. multirelational models: Causal and predictive aspects. This is a much-discussed and partly controversial topic. It will suffice for our purpose to review some causal–predictive arguments that had a bearing on the initiation of the FP approach. Key features are the distinctions between causal vs. predictive relations, and between experimental vs. non-experimental situations.

The stimulus–response relationships of controlled experiments are subject to general consensus with respect to causal interpretation and operative use, as well as with respect to statistical estimation. Let us suppose that (1.1c) is a relation that has been established by a controlled experiment with x_1 and y_2 as stimulus variables, and y_3 as response variable. As to causal interpretation and operative use, β_{32} then is the average or expected change of y_3 if the experimenter increases y_2 by one unit while x_1 and other controlled variables are kept constant, and similarly for $\gamma_{33}x_1$. As to statistical estimation, the ML estimates of α_3, β_{32}, γ_{33} are, on the classical assumptions, numerically equivalent to the estimates given by OLS regressian of the response variable y_3 on the stimulus variables x_1 and y_2; R.A. Fisher (1925).

More or less approximately, the statements of the previous paragraph carry over to non-experimental relations. A number of supplementary explanatory variables then have to be included in the OLS regression to cope with the *ceteris paribus* clause. In practice the main problem is the appropriate selection of the supplementary variables. Another point of general consensus is that the causal and operative interpretation of unirelational models extends to simultaneous equations systems, both in structural form and reduced form, provided the structural form is recursive. This is so since cause–effect relations are transitive in the sense that if an endogenous variable in one relation occurs as effect variable explained by predetermined variables, and in another relation as cause variable, it can be eliminated from the second relation by substitution from the first.

In non-recursive (interdependent) systems the joint causal interpretation of the structural and reduced forms breaks down. This is so since in non-recursive systems the transformation from structural to reduced form requires the reversion of one or more structural relations, and in the real world there are very few cause–effect relationships that are causally reversible, and then only under ideal conditions; cf. Wold (1954).

In the literature on non-recursive simultaneous equations systems there is a general lack of consensus as regards the conceptual interpretation of the structural form, including a lack of consensus as regards the need for such an interpretation. This much is clear from prestigeous discussions on the rationale of simultaneous equations systems; see Christ et al. (1960) and Klein (1960). Part of the story is that Haavelmo in his definition of simultaneous equations systems (see 1.3.2) uses the structural form only for the formal deduction of the reduced form, which then is used to define the model as a stochastic process. This feature goes a long way to explain why the causal–operative aspects of the structural form is more or less ignored in the literature on simultaneous equations systems. This state of things is however not satisfactory, for the behavioral relations of the structural form belong to the conceptual foundations of simultaneous equations systems. However, having seen that the cause–effect interpretation of the behavioral relations and their parameters does not carry over from recursive to non-recursive systems, what is then their conceptual meaning in simultaneous equations systems, if any?

Bentzel and Hansen (1954) shed new light on the situation by the argument that if a recursive (causal chain) system is aggregated over time, the aggregate system will approximately form a non-recursive (interdependent) system. For an illustration of their argument, on aggregation over time the causal chain system (1.1a–c) will approximate an interdependent system with arrow scheme as in Figure 1c; thus if the time period t in system (1.1a–c) and Figure 1a is one month, and the aggregation is over 6 months, the aggregate time period T in Figure 1c is 6 months.

While Bentzel and Hansen interpreted interdependency as a matter of aggregation over time, their argument did not cover the interdependency that has its source in the assumption of "instantaneous equilibrium". For example, demand and supply over a given period are conceptually and observationally different; then if the model builder equates demand and supply to "quantity bought and sold", the demand and supply equations become interdependent. There is the difference from the previous situation that one and the same variable occurs on the left-hand sides of the two relations (that is, it is explained by both relations), and this type of interdependence remains the same for aggregation and disaggregation.

Again with reference to the lack of consensus as regards the conceptual interpretation of the structural form of interdependent systems, the controversial debate is partly due to the philosophical obscurity around the concept of causality. To explore the general rationale of causal inference, I had in the early 1950's begun to explore the notion of cause–effect relationship, with a view to clarify the definition and meaning of causality; see Wold (1954, 1958, 1964b, 1969b). This led to the following interpretation, which uses two steps to define the notion of cause–effect relationship:

(i) In controlled experiments of the stimulus–response type, the relation between stimulus and response is a special case of cause–effect relationships.

(ii) Let us consider a non-experimental relation, say (1.1c), which is part or the whole of a hypothetical model. Suppose the model includes the hypothesis that the variables can be subjected to a fictitious stimulus–response experiment, with x_1 and y_2 as stimulus variables and y_3 as response variable. The investigator then may or may not include, as part of the model, the hypothesis that the result of the controlled experiment will be in accordance with (1.1c), with parameters α_3, β_{32}, γ_{33}. If the model does include this hypothesis, then (1.1c) is a cause–effect relation, with x_1 and y_2 as cause variables, and y_3 as effect variable.

* Well to note, the notions of *definition* and *validation* must be kept apart. (i)–(ii) is a definition of causality, stating what is meant when we say that there is a cause–effect relationship between two phenomena, say A and B. The question whether A in actual fact has a causal influence on B is a different matter, is a matter of validation. Much of the confusion around causal concepts is due to vain attempts to give definitions of causation that at the same time provide validation of causation; cf. Wold (1969b).

1.3.5. While Bentzel and Hansen's argument was in the nature of a reconciliation between causal chain systems and interdependent systems, there remained other important questions to be explored about the rationale of interdependent systems. Can the structural form of interdependent systems be used operatively for predictive purposes? If yes, to what extent is the operative use the same as for unirelational models?

To explore the rationale of predictive inference, I had in the late 1950's begun to study predictive relations that are specified as *conditional expectations*, or briefly as *predictors*; see Wold (1960). Given any linear relation, say (1.7b), it is called a predictor if

$$E(y_i \mid y_{(i)}, z_{(i)}) = \beta_{(i)} y_{(i)} + \gamma_{(i)} z_{(i)}. \tag{1.15}$$

Whether (1.7b) constitutes a unirelational model or is part of a multirelational model, the assumption (1.15) is in accordance with the customary use of (1.7b) to predict y_i in terms of the variables $y_{(i)}$ and $z_{(i)}$; the prediction will be unbiased in the sense of (1.15).

General rules are readily established for various operative procedures with predictor relations, among those the transformation from structural to reduced form in simultaneous equations models. Reference is made to the following implications of predictor relations; cf. Wold (1961b, 1963a).

(i) In recursive systems (1.1) the structural and reduced forms are jointly amenable to predictor specification, provided the residual of each structural relation is uncorrelated with all predetermined variables.

(ii) In non-recursive systems the structural and reduced forms are not jointly amenable to predictor specification. This is so since in predictor relations (1.15) the predicted and predicting variables cannot be reversed; the only exceptional case is when the residual is identically zero.

(iii) For any predictor relation (1.7b) in conjunction with (1.15), OLS regression of y_i on $y_{(i)}$, $z_{(i)}$ will under mild supplementary conditions be consistent in the large-sample sense. Sufficient conditions are:
(a) All variables y_i, $y_{(i)}$, $z_{(i)}$ have finite variances.

(b) The explanatory variables $y_{(i)}$, $z_{(i)}$ are not collinear.

(c) The residuals δ_{it} $(t = 1, T)$ are not too strongly intercorrelated.

Letting (1.16a) denote the residual autocorrelations, it suffices that the residual autocorrelations have zero mean (1.16b) in the sense of the law of large numbers,

$$\rho_s = r(\delta_{it}, \delta_{i,t-s}), \tag{1.16a}$$

$$\lim_{S\to\infty} \frac{1}{S} \sum_{s=1}^{S} \rho_s = 0. \tag{1.16b}$$

1.3.6. Comments on 1.3.5(i–iii). We see that Theorems 1.3.5(i–iii) extend the scope of the Bentzel and Wold results 1.3.3. On the one hand, the consistency of OLS regression as applied to the structural form of recursive systems follows from 1.3.4(i) in conjunction with 1.3.4(iii), without making distributional assumptions on the variables and the residuals. Similarly, and in line with Haavelmo's dismissal of OLS regression (see 1.3.2), Theorem 1.3.4(ii) combined with 1.3.4(iii) implies that OLS is inconsistent as applied to the structural form of ID (interdependent) systems, again irrespective of distributional assumptions.

Speaking broadly, causal relations are predictive, but predictive relations are not necessarily causal. Having seen in 1.3.4 that the structural relations of ID systems do not allow causal interpretation, and knowing from 1.3.5(ii–iii) that they are not even predictive, the question about the conceptual interpretation of the structural relations becomes all the more pressing: what is the operative use, if any, of the structural relations of ID systems and their parameters?

Pondering on this question I found that a positive answer is provided by the following reformulation of ID system (1.13),

$$y_t = \beta\eta_t^* + \Gamma z_t + \beta(y_t - \eta_t^*) + \delta_t, \tag{1.17a}$$

$$y_t = \beta\eta_t^* + \Gamma z_t + \varepsilon_t, \tag{1.17b}$$

where the parameters β, Γ are the same as in (1.13), and η^* denotes the systematic part of the endogenous variables y as given by the reduced form

$$y_t = \eta_t^* + \varepsilon_t, \tag{1.18a}$$

$$\eta_t^* = [I - \beta]^{-1}\Gamma z_t, \tag{1.18b}$$

with

$$\eta_t^* = E(y_t \mid z_{1t}, \cdots, z_{mt}). \tag{1.18c}$$

Under the classical assumptions of simultaneous equations (see 1.3.2) the system (1.17b) with (1.18c) is called a REID (Reformulated ID) system; Wold (1965).

First of all, we see that REID systems in structural form (1.17b) have the following obvious interpretation: Each endogenous variable y_i is assumed to depend upon the predetermined variables $z_{(i)}$, just as in (1.13), and upon the *expected* values $\eta_{(i)}$ of other endogenous variables $y_{(i)}$, not as in (1.13) upon the observed values $y_{(i)}$ of these variables.

Second, we see that the residuals in (1.17a–b) are identically the same; in fact, (1.9a), (1.11b) and (1.18a) imply

$$\beta(y - \eta^*) + \delta = \beta\varepsilon + \delta = \beta\varepsilon + (I - \beta)\varepsilon = \varepsilon. \tag{1.19}$$

We are now in a position to show that the structural and reduced forms of systems allow joint specification as predictors; in symbols,

$$E(y_i \mid \eta_{(i)}^*, z_{(i)}) = \beta\eta_{(i)}^* + \Gamma z_{(i)}, \tag{1.20a}$$
$$E(y_i \mid \Omega_i z) = \Omega_i z, \tag{1.20b}$$

where the left-hand notation in (1.20b) indicates that the conditional expectation is formed for known parameters $\Omega = [I - B]^{-1}\Gamma$. First we see that (1.17b) and (1.18) imply

$$\eta_i^* = \beta_i \eta^* + \gamma_i z, \tag{1.21a}$$
$$\eta_i^* = ([I - \beta]^{-1}\Gamma)_i z, \tag{1.21b}$$
$$\eta_i^* = \Omega_i z. \tag{1.21c}$$

Second, the distribution of the variables y_i $(i = 1, n)$ is multivariate normal; each residual δ_i is uncorrelated with all predetermined variables z; since η_i^* by (1.21c) is linear in the variables z, each residual δ_i is uncorrelated with all η^*; hence

$$\eta^* = E(y_i \mid \eta_{(i)}^*, z_{(i)}) = \beta_{(i)} y_{(i)}^* + \gamma_{(i)} z_{(i)}, \tag{1.22a}$$
$$\eta^* = E(y_i \mid z) = \Omega_i z \tag{1.22b}$$

where the notation in (1.22b) indicates that the conditional expectation is formed by parameters Ω_i that are given by the unrestricted reduced form.

For REID systems (1.17b), formulas (1.20a–b) establish the joint specification of the structural and reduced forms as predictors, η_i^* being the conditional expectation of y_i for known values of $\eta_{(i)}^*$ and $z_{(i)}$. Formulas (1.20b) and (1.21b–c) show that the reduced form of REID system can be interpreted and estimated either by estimating the parameters β, Γ of the structural form, or by direct estimation of the parameters Ω of the reduced form.

The reformulation (1.17b) of Classical ID systems has the double purpose to make for an operative use of the structural form, and to make for consistent estimation of the parameters β, Γ by OLS regression as applied to the structural form. Now this second purpose is in accordance with Theorem 1.3.5(iii), but there is the snag that the expectations η_t^* are unknown ($t = 1, T$), and have to be estimated as part of the estimation procedure. The FP method is an iterative approach to this last problem.

1.3.7. Before turning to the FP method, let us consider the reformulation (1.17) from an operative point of view. For illustration we shall use the ID system defined by (1.1b–c) and (1.12). We repeat that the reformulation (1.17) has dissolved the difficulty that (1.1b–c) and (1.12) cannot be interpreted as predictors jointly with the reduced form.

* The point I wish to make is that, while the structural equations (1.1b) and (1.12) *exist* jointly, it is not meaningful to *use* them jointly, nor is it meaningful to use these structural equations jointly after the reformulation (1.17). We see that (1.12) gives a prediction for y_{1t} when y_{2t} and $y_{2,t-1}$ are known. Then it is not meaningful to ask at the same time what prediction (1.1b) gives for y_{2t} when y_{1t} and $y_{2,t-1}$ are known.

As we shall see in 3.2.3(ii) the argument extends to reformulated ID systems.

1.3.8. As designed for the estimation of REID systems, the FP method is based on the classical assumptions of ID systems. Accordingly, the ensuing parameter estimates, without numerical change, can be seen as estimates for the unmodified ID systems (1.8) or (1.13). At the same time we see that for OLS regression as applied to the structural form (1.17b) to give consistent estimates of the parameters β, Γ, the classical assumptions are unnecessarily stringent. It will suffice that the structural form (1.17b) satisfies the predictor specification (1.20a). Note that (1.20a) implies the predictor specification (1.20b) of the reduced form. Further note that the predictor specification (1.20a) implies that in the structural relation for y_i ($i = 1, n$) the residual ε_i is uncorrelated with the explanatory variables $\eta_{(i)}^*$, $z_{(i)}$ in the same relation. Hence the FP estimation method will be applicable to REID systems on the generalized condition that the reformulated structural relations (1.17b) are subject to the predictor specification (1.20a). REID systems (1.17a) thus generalized are called GEID (General ID) systems; Wold (1965). It will be noted that both predictor specifications (1.20b) and (1.22b) are satisfied by the reduced form of REID systems, whereas only (1.20b) is satisfied by the reduced form of a GEID system.

1.3.9. The FP method for the estimation of Classical ID systems, REID systems, and GEID systems, has been improved and generalized in several respects. Chapter 2 of this volume gives a technical exposition of the ensuing family of FP methods. We proceed to give in Section 2 of this introductory chapter the basic formulas for the FP method.

2. The FP Method: Groundwork

2.1. The Basic Estimation Formulas for the FP Method

We consider a REID–GEID system (1.17b) which is subject either to the classical ID assumptions 1.3.2 or to the predictor specification (1.20). The FP estimation procedure is iterative, say with steps $s = 1, 2, \cdots$. For the FP estimates of the unknowns β, Γ and η_{it} we shall write

$$B = [b_{ij}] = \text{est } \beta = \lim_{s\to\infty} B^{(s)}, \tag{2.1a}$$

$$G = [g_{ij}] = \text{est } \Gamma = \lim_{s\to\infty} [g_{ij}^{(s)}], \tag{2.1b}$$

$$y_{it}^* = \text{est } \eta_{it}^* = \lim_{s\to\infty} y_{it}^{(s)}. \tag{2.1c}$$

2.1.1. Start, $s = 1$. Starting values are needed for the proxies $y_{it}^{(s)}$. As is usually the case in iterative procedures, the starting values are largely arbitrary. We note the following options for the start:

$$y_{it}^{(1)} = y_{it}, \tag{2.2a}$$
$$y_{it}^{(1)} = 0, \tag{2.2b}$$
$$y_{it}^{(1)} = \text{any } z_{jt}, \qquad j = 1, m, \tag{2.2c}$$
$$y_{it}^{(1)} = y_{it}^{\text{TSLS}}, \tag{2.2d}$$

where $i = 1, n$ and $t = 1, T$ throughout, and TSLS refers to Theil–Basmann's two-stage least-squares method, y_{it}^{TSLS} thus being the systematic part of y_{it} as given by OLS estimation of the reduced form (1.10).

2.1.2. The general step from s to s + 1. The proxies in step $s+1$ are obtained in two substeps:

(i) Using the proxies $y_{it}^{(s)}$ computed in step s, keeping $i = 1, n$ fixed, and computing the OLS regression of y_{it} on $y_t^{(s)}$ and z_t, say

$$y_{it} = b_i^{(s+1)} y_t^{(s)} + g_i^{(s+1)} z_t + e_{it}^{(s+1)}, \tag{2.3a}$$

we obtain the parameter proxies in step $s+1$, that is $b_i^{(s+1)} = (b_{i1}^{(s+1)}, \cdots, b_{in}^{(s+1)})$ and $g_i^{(s+1)} = (g_{i1}^{(s+1)}, \cdots, g_{im}^{(s+1)})$. Equivalently, using the notation (1.7b), the OLS regression (2.3a) can be written

$$y_{it} = b_{(i)}^{(s+1)} y_{(i)t}^{(s)} + g_{(i)}^{(s+1)} z_{(i)t} + e_{it}^{(s+1)}. \tag{2.3b}$$

(ii) In this second substep the proxy $y_{it}^{(s+1)}$ for the systematic part η_{it}^* of y_{it} is computed for every $i = 1, n$ and $t = 1, T$. The substep has two versions, the first of which computes $y_{it}^{(s+1)}$ from the structural form (1.7) by omitting the residual $e_{it}^{(s+1)}$ in (2.3a) or (2.3b), say

$$y_{it}^{(s+1)} = b_i^{(s+1)} y_t^{(s)} + g_i^{(s+1)} z_t. \tag{2.4a}$$

The second version uses the reduced form (1.21b),

$$y_{it}^{(s+1)} = [I - B^{(s+1)}]^{-1} G^{(s+1)} z_t. \tag{2.4b}$$

Version (2.4a) is the original FP method; Wold (1965). Version (2.4b) is called Solved system FP (SFP), earlier called Reduced Form FP (RFFP); Wold (1966).

2.2. *Identities*

Dropping the assumption that all relations of the structural form are behavioural, and denoting identities by subscript 2, we write

$$\beta = (\beta_1, \beta_2) = \begin{bmatrix} \beta_1 \\ \beta_2 \end{bmatrix}, \tag{2.5a}$$

$$\Gamma = (\Gamma_1, \Gamma_2) = \begin{bmatrix} \Gamma_1 \\ \Gamma_2 \end{bmatrix}, \tag{2.5b}$$

and reformulate behavioural relations and identities:

$$y_1 = \beta_1 \eta^* + \Gamma_1 z + \varepsilon_1, \tag{2.6a}$$
$$y_2 = \beta_2 y + \Gamma_2 z = \beta_2 \eta^* + \Gamma_2 z + \beta_2 \varepsilon. \tag{2.6b}$$

This gives

$$\varepsilon_2 = \beta_2 \varepsilon. \tag{2.6c}$$

Assuming predictor specification (1.20) on the behavioural relations, the system (1.17) remains formally the same, with or without identities.

2.2.1. Comments. (i) Having adopted predictor specification (1.20a) for the behavioural relations, we shall assume predictor specification also for the identities; in symbols,

$$E(y_{2t} \mid \eta_t^*, z_t) = \beta_2 \eta_t^* + \Gamma_2 z_t. \tag{2.7}$$

This is an additional requirement, needed when a structural prediction of the variables y_{2t} is needed; see Lyttkens (1973a, p. 365).

(ii) The restrictions (2.6c) will be automatically fulfilled by the parameters β and the residuals e_2, given by the FP procedure (2.2)–(2.4) as applied to the system (2.6a–b).

(iii) The restrictions (2.6c) and (2.7) are formally equivalent. Note that (2.6c) is an assumption in terms of the systematic parts of the observables, while (2.7) is in terms of the residuals.

2.3. Computer Programs for the FP Estimation Procedure

The two steps (2.3) and (2.4) of the iterative FP procedure are simple matter on the computer, (2.3) being a set of OLS regressions and (2.4) a set of linear aggregations. In their computational work with FP estimation as applied to real-world or simulated data, the authors of the subsequent chapters have used workshop computer programs that they have compiled for the purpose. These workshop programs can be obtained from the authors at nominal cost. A library computer program is being prepared, and is planned to be available at the same time as this volume; Bergström (1979).

2.4. Basic Requirements for the FP Estimation Method to Work in Practice

Three basic requirements are: (i) convergence of the passage to the limit $s \to \infty$ in (2.1a–c); (ii) consistency of the ensuing parameter estimates; (iii) uniqueness of the ensuing estimates as a solution to the estimation problem. The favourable results of my first array of applications of the FP procedure led me to the erroneous thought and claim that the requirements (i) and (iii) are always fulfilled; Wold (1965, 1966) for claim and disclaimer. We shall briefly discuss the situation in the light of the subsequent chapters.

2.4.1. Convergence. (i) The conditions for convergence of the iterative FP estimation procedure (2.3)–(2.4) have been explored by Ågren (Chapter 3) and Bodin (Chapter 5). As shown by Ågren (1970) a necessary condition for convergence is that the matrix β to be estimated has all of its eigenvalues lying inside the unit circle of the complex plane.

(ii) The same eigenvalue condition occurs in a related context. If $y_t^{(1)}$ is the starting proxy (2.2) of the FP procedure (2.3)–(2.4), we see from (2.4a) that if $y_t^{(1)}$ lies in the linear space L_z spanned by the predetermined variables z_j $(j = 1, m)$, then L_z will include all proxies $y_t^{(s)}$ $(s = 2, 3, \cdots)$ as well as the limiting estimate y_t^*. Now if we ask whether y_t can be used as starting proxy, it has been shown by Ågren (1972a) that a necessary condition for the FP procedure (2.3)–(2.4) to converge with $y_t^{(1)} = y_t$ as starting proxy is that all eigenvalues of β are inside the unit circle.

2.4.2. Coherence. (i) In each step of the iterative procedure of FP estimation the various structural relations are estimated separately, proxy estimates for the coefficients of each relation being obtained in terms of proxy estimates for the expectations of some of the endogenous variables. An array of LS optimizations being in play in each step, the question arises whether the limiting estimates of the unknowns are *coherent* in the sense that they satisfy all of the structural relations. The answer is in the affirmative: the relations are fulfilled at each finite step of the FP procedure; hence if the procedure converges the relations must remain fulfilled in the limit.

The structural relations are estimated on different optimization criteria, namely the minimization of the residual variances. The coherence raises the question whether the FP estimation is ruled by some overall, total optimization criterion. A discussion of this question follows.

(ii) From the general point of view of LS estimation we are concerned with the problem of minimizing the residual variances $\text{var}(\varepsilon_i)$ in (1.17b), subject to the conditions or "restrictions" (1.21a) or, equivalently, (1.21b). The classical approach to this problem is to minimize the variances $\text{var}(\varepsilon_i)$ simultaneously, taking the restrictions (1.21a) into account by as many Lagrange multipliers. Comparing the Lagrange estimation with the FP approach, we see that FP honours the conditions (1.21a) in each step of the iterative procedure, and therefore also in the limit when the procedure has converged. Well to note, this does not imply that the two estimation methods are equivalent. In fact, in the system of relations that determine the Lagrange estimates of the parameters the derivatives of the unknowns y_i^* with regard to the parameters yield an array of terms, and these terms do not occur in the corresponding FP system.[3]

(iii) As is clear from (ii), Lagrange estimation gives the same parameter estimates whether the residual variances are minimized separately for the structural relations or are subject to joint, total minimization. Further it is clear that this invariance is not present in FP estimation.[4] Thus while Lagrange estimation is ruled by a total optimization criterion, there is in general no corresponding total criterion for FP estimation. Full Information Maximum Likelihood (FIML) being a total optimization principle, it is interesting to note that under appropriate conditions the FP estimates can be given a FIML interpretation; see Lyttkens (1973a, pp. 165–168).

(iv) Reference is made to "soft modeling", i.e., the PLS (Partial Least Squares) procedure for the estimation of path models with (latent) variables indirectly observed by multiple indicators; cf. Wold (1979a, b). In the PLS procedure each latent variable is explicitly estimated by a weighted aggregate of its indicators, with weights iteratively determined by the PLS procedure.

With regard to coherence and total criteria of optimization, the FP and PLS procedures are similar. To put it otherwise, FP estimation can be seen as a special case of PLS estimation, if we define PLS estimation as an iterative procedure of OLS regressions subject to constraints, be it that the constraints take form as in FP estimation, or in soft modeling, or take some other form.

2.4.3. Consistency. Theorem 1.3.5(iii) on the consistency of OLS regression as applied to predictors carries over to the iterative FP procedure (2.3)–(2.4). The crucial point is the reversion of the two passages to the limit; that is $t \to \infty$, $s \to \infty$. By a general theorem of calculus, the reversion is admissible for every point β, Γ in the parameter space that is a point of continuity for the parameters.

[3] The derivatives of y_i^* at issue are technically complicated. The fact that these derivatives have no counterpart in FP estimation is a main reason for the technical simplicity of the FP algorithm.

[4] The total estimation criterion at issue has a counterpart in the approach of Morriss Brown (1960), where ID systems of the original form (1.13) are estimated by the LS principle, using the sum total of the residual variances as optimization criterion. Brown's estimation method involves the derivatives of the reduced form coefficients Ω with respect to the structural coefficients β, Γ. FP estimation is much simpler than Brown's approach, since the derivatives at issue are technically complicated, and have no counterpart in the FP algorithm.

2.5. *Multiple Solutions*

If the structural relations (1.17b) are seen as regression relations subject to the side conditions (1.20), the least squares estimation of the parameters leads to a system of nonlinear normal equations. Solving for the parameters by algebraic method, it was shown by Lyttkens (1967, 1970a) that there are cases when the problem has multiple solutions, giving several sets of parameter estimates B, G. If the multiple solutions are known, the total square sum of the ensuing residuals in the sample period provides a criterion for choosing the solution with the best prediction accuracy. If only the limiting FP parameter estimates are known, as is the case in practice, the question arises whether there exist other solutions with higher prediction accuracy.

The possibility of multiple solutions has been something of a dark cloud over the FP family of methods. As the experience of applied work has accumulated, however, the evidence points in the direction that multiple solutions can occur mainly in small systems, and then mainly when the residuals are large. Hence it is the consensus of the authors of this volume that the question about multiple solutions should be toned down. In moderately large systems with small residuals there seems to be little or no risk of multiple solutions. This is so even in Classical ID systems if the residuals are small. Thus in attempts to find multiple solutions Bodin (1974) explored all of the simulated data of Classical ID systems in Mosbaek and Wold et al. (1970); in Classical ID systems there are no multiple solutions in the population, but the individual samples of length 20 could perhaps give rise to multiple solutions since the sample correlations between residuals and exogenous variables have a sizeable range (often up to ± 0.40); for each sample the FP parameter estimates were computed by the algebraic method, and in every sample the FP estimates were found to be unique. Reference is further made to the experiments on a ten-relation GEID model reported by May in Chapter 11 of this volume; the various starting points scattered over the space of exogenous variables show no trace of multiple solutions. Furthermore, see 4.3(ii).

3. Comparison of FP versus Classical Estimation Methods for ID Systems

3.1. *Background: The Advent of Econometrics*

With forerunners in the first decades of the 20th century and earlier, Econometrics was born under the star of Modern Mathematical Statistics. Defined as economic science developed by mathematical and statistical methods, econometrics was institutionalized around 1930 by the new journal *Econometrica.* By this time modern mathematical statistics had been established by the trail-blazing work of Sir R.A. Fisher and his followers. As is clear already from the first volumes of *Econometrica,* econometrics was greatly influenced by the Fisherian methods, in raising the aspiration levels of statistical analysis, and in a corresponding refinement of the methods.

3.1.1. Fisher's pioneering statistical methods were primarily intended for the design and analysis of controlled experiments; R.A. Fisher (1925, 1935). Of principal relevance in the present context are his methods for controlled experiments of the stimulus–response type. Considering the simplest linear case, say

$$y = \alpha + \beta x + \varepsilon, \tag{3.1}$$

the stimulus variable x takes numerical values specified in the design of the experiment; the residual ε is a random variable that covers disturbances and extraneous variables not under experimental control; by randomization of the stimulus x in the replications of the experiment the residual is assumed to be independent of x.

The general aspiration of Fisherian methods is to achieve *optimal accuracy* in the statistical analysis, including

(i) efficient estimation methods, and
(ii) powerful tests of hypothesis.

As to (ii), reference is made to R.A. Fisher's principle of the self-contained experiment; that is, the same data used for estimating the parameters of the model should also be used for testing the hypotheses that constitute the model.

3.1.2. The main technical tool of the Fisherian methods is the ML (Maximum Likelihood) principle. In the ML approach, the observables are assumed to be generated by a specified joint distribution, usually one of two types:

(i) multivariate normal distribution of the observables, with independent replications,
(ii) the stimulus variables are assumed to be non-stochastic; the residuals are assumed to have normal distribution with independent replications.

Under assumption (ii), as is well known, ML estimation will be numerically equivalent to OLS regression; R.A. Fisher (1925).

3.1.3. ML versus Least Squares (LS) estimation. ML and LS estimation are fundamentally different as regards the technical implementation. This is so in consequence of differences in the basic principles and assumptions. Usually, however, the differences will only to a limited extent carry over to the numerical values of ensuing parameter estimates.

(i) *Basic principles*: ML maximizes the probability that the model generates the data as observed. As applied to predictive relations, LS maximizes the prediction accuracy (minimizes the variance of the prediction error).

(ii) *Differences in assumptions*: ML requires distributional assumptions on variables and/or residuals; see 3.1.2. In linear models, LS requires only the existence of first- and second-order moments; otherwise, LS is distribution-free.

(iii) *Aspiration levels*: In line with (ii), the estimation accuracy aimed at is higher for ML than for LS estimation. ML estimates aim at *optimality* in the sense of efficiency (smallest possible standard errors). LS estimates aim at *consistency* in the large-sample sense.

(iv) *Comment*: Under supplementary assumptions of type 3.1.2, LS estimates will gain in accuracy, and may even be numerically equivalent to ML estimates; see 1.3.2 and 3.1.2.

3.1.4. Experimental versus non-experimental data. Econometrics carried over Fisher's high aspiration levels of statistical analysis from controlled experiments to the non-experimental data of economics. In the present context the focus is on the econometric methods of time series analysis, and in particular on the dualism between the macroeconomic forecasting models called simultaneous equations systems, estimated by classical methods, versus the formally similar interdependent (ID) systems, estimated by FP methods. Specific reference is made to the fundamental work of T.C. Koopmans on the rationale of simultaneous equations systems; see Koopmans et al. (1950) and Hood and Koopmans (1973).

Two basic features of simultaneous equations systems will be noted:

(a) the distinction between endogenous and exogenous variables, and
(b) the data are assumed to measure the observables without measurement errors.

The following assumptions are classical and customary in simultaneous equations systems:

(i) The model is assumed to form a *complete system*. External variables and disturbances are assumed to be covered by the residuals, subject to simplifying assumptions.

(ii) In accordance with Haavelmo's design 1.3.2, the observables are subject to assumptions in line with 3.1.2(ii), the exogenous variables being non-stochastic, and the residuals generating a multivariate normal distribution for the endogenous variables.

(iii) All residuals are assumed to be uncorrelated with all exogenous (or predetermined) variables.

3.2. FP versus the Classical Approach to Simultaneous Equations Systems

3.2.1. In the FP approach, simultaneous equations systems are re-specified as REID systems (1.17) or GEID systems (see 1.3.8). To repeat from 1.1.2 and 1.2.2 the key incentives for the FP approach and REID–GEID systems are:

(i) to make for operative use of the structural form, and

(ii) to design an estimation method that stays in the structural form (objectives (i)–(ii) were met by the design of REID systems and their FP estimation); as stated in 1.3.8 this device led to a third result, namely:

(iii) the generalization from REID to GEID systems, a generalization that involves no formal change in the system, nor in the FP estimation procedure.

3.2.2. REID–GEID versus classical specification of simultaneous equations systems. The REID–GEID versions of simultaneous equations systems share the basic features 3.1.4(a–b). As compared with the classical assumptions 3.1.4(i–iii), the REID–GEID versions involve both conceptual and operative generalizations.

(i) GEID systems allow the interpretation that the residuals of a structural relation may partly be due to disturbances related to explanatory variables of other structural relations. Otherwise stated, GEID systems are open models, are not assumed to be closed in the sense of complete systems 3.1.4(i).

(ii) In this second aspect, we note that REID and GEID models differ from the classical approach in three ways.

First, while the Haavelmo design 1.3.2 of simultaneous equations systems specifies only the reduced form for operative use, REID and GEID systems specify both the structural form and the reduced form for causal–predictive inference. The key feature is here, of course, that REID and GEID systems are designed for predictive interpretation and use of the behavioural relations, the conceptual basis of the model.

Second, REID and GEID systems impose no restrictions on the distributional properties of the observables; not only the endogenous but also the exogenous variables can be assumed to be stochastic variables.

Third, as indicated by the name "simultaneous *equations* systems" the classical approach assumes the structural relations to be deterministic equations subject to "errors in the equations"; that is, behind the disturbances there are functionally exact relationships between the observables. In REID and GEID systems the "equations" are specified as predictor relations of type (1.15); that is, each predictor gives the *conditional expectation* of an endogenous variable as an exact linear function of the explanatory variables, but between the observables themselves there is no functionally exact relation. In the classical models the deterministic specification is needed to make the transformation from structural form to reduced form meaningful in the sense of solving a linear system of equations; in REID and GEID systems the corresponding stochastic transformation is stochastic, and is established by the predictor relations (1.20a) and (1.20b).

(iii) Classical ID systems (1.8) are subject to the assumption that all residuals are uncorrelated with all predetermined variables; in symbols,

$$r(\delta_i, z_j) = 0, \qquad i = 1, n, \quad j = 1, m. \tag{3.2}$$

Hence in Classical ID systems there are $n \times m$ non-correlation assumptions.

Assumption (3.2) is shared by REID systems, but in GEID systems it is generalized by the predictor specifications (1.20a–b) of the structural and reduced forms. Hence in GEID systems there are just as many zero correlations between residuals on the one hand and variables η^* and z on the other as there are positions in the parameter matrices β, Γ; this is the *parity principle* of GEID systems.

For an example, in the Classic ID system (1.1a–c) with (1.1a) replaced by (1.12) there are $3 \times 3 = 9$ zero correlations between the residuals and the predetermined variables, whereas there are only six right-hand variables y, z, and as many positions, and accordingly only six zero intercorrelations in the corresponding GEID system. In larger systems the classical zero intercorrelations usually are far more numerous than in the corresponding GEID systems.[5]

[5] The larger the system, the more the classical assumptions violate the parity principle. Summers' model has two behavioural relations, four predetermined variables, and six multiplicative parameters for the explanatory variables; the classical assumptions impose eight zero correlations between the residuals and the predetermined variables, whereas the corresponding GEID model involves six zero correlations between residuals and explanatory variables. Klein–Goldberger's model has 11 behavioural relations with 10 predetermined variables and 24 multiplicative parameters; hence there are 110 zero correlations on the classical assumptions, and 24 in the GEID model. In the large Polish model FP-estimated by Reinhold Bergtröm (1980), the 228 structural relations contain a block of 40 interdependent behavioural relations with 58 predetermined variables and 148 multiplicative parameters; hence there are 2320 against 148 zero correlations on the classical and GEID assumptions.

The parity principle, of course, is greatly to the advantage for the prediction accuracy of GEID systems and FP estimation as applied to real-world models and data. For every position of the β, Γ matrices the FP procedure yields a parameter estimate that minimizes the prediction error as measured by the residual variance.[6] The classical estimation methods for ID systems try to make each residual uncorrelated with all of the predetermined variables; in other words, they seek for the parameter estimates in a narrower space, with the result that the residual variances must necessarily be larger.

3.2.3. Further comments on REID–GEID systems and FP estimation. (i) As shown by Lyttkens (1970c), FP and FIML estimation of GEID systems are asymptotically equivalent in the large-sample sense. Thus far, however, FP estimation is the only known method for numerical computation of consistent parameter estimates for GEID systems.

(ii) *On the operative use of REID–GEID systems in structural form.* To repeat, a main incentive for the REID–GEID approach is to make the structural form and thereby the behavioural relations of the model amenable to operative use for prediction. Thus (1.20a) provides an unbiased prediction of the endogenous variable y_{it} for given values of the explanatory variables in that same relation; that is, the predetermined variables $z_{(i)t}$ and the expectations $y^*_{(i)t}$ of the endogenous variables $y_{(i)t}$. At the same time, by the very logic of predictive inference, the interdependence implies that interdependent behavioural relations can be used separately for prediction, but not simultaneously. As noted in 1.2.7, this is so since the very question to be answered by one of the interdependent relations assumes that the answer is known to the question posed to the other relation.

For an example we refer again to the interdependent system of three relations, (1.1b–c) and (1.12), all behavioural. When y^*_{2t}, $y_{2,t-1}$ and x_{1t} are known, relation (1.12) allows us to predict y_{1t}, and relation (1.1c) allows us to predict y_{3t}. Now when y_{1t} is subject to prediction, assuming that y^*_{2t} is known, it is not meaningful to ask for a simultaneous prediction of y_{2t}.

REID and GEID systems thus have the paradoxical feature that while their behavioural relations constitute a simultaneous set of predictors, any two of the interdependent relations cannot be used simultaneously, only separately. As we have seen in 1.3.8, the classical form (1.8) or (1.13) of ID systems is subject to the same paradox, except that the predictions given by

[6] The estimation method of Morriss Brown (1960) is conceptually related in this respect; cf. 2.4.2 and footnote 4.

the separate behavioural relations are not unbiased in the sense of predictors (1.15). The lack of simultaneous applicability, and the bias in separate predictive application, are perhaps sufficient to explain the ambiguity and lack of consensus about the conceptual meaning of Classical ID systems in structural form; see 1.3.4.

(iii) *ID systems with latent (indirectly observed) variables.* Causal chains and interdependent systems are often called path models, a term originating from genetics; Wright (1934). Around 1960, path models with latent variables were introduced [by Duncan (1966)] and have gained momentum in the social sciences in the 60's and 70's. As to causal chain systems with latent variables, a PLS (Partial Least Squares) approach has been developed for the design and statistical estimation of the model; Wold (1979a, b).

In the PLS approach the observables are grouped into blocks, which form the structural unit of the model; in each block the observables are seen as indicators of a latent (indirectly observed) variable; the latent variables are assumed to be related by a system of "inner" relations that form a causal chain system; causal–predictive relations for the indicators of the endogenous blocks are obtained by combined use of the block structure and the inner relations. Each latent variable is estimated by a weighted aggregate of its indicators; the weights are determined by a system of weight relations. The PLS estimation procedure has two phases. The first phase is iterative and estimates the latent variables and the weights of the indicators by alternating between the weighted aggregates and the weight relations. The second phase is a non-iterative array of OLS regressions, using the observables and the estimated latent variables to estimate the block structure, the inner relations, and the causal–predictive relations.

In the first phase of the estimation, interdependency between the inner relations brings a slight change in the weight relations. Then the inner relations are estimated by the FP method, and in other respects there is no change in the second phase of the estimation.

The FP approach to ID systems with latent variables has been implemented and developed by Hui (1978, 1979). Drawing from his work, Figure 2 shows the arrow schemes for two ID systems with latent variables. As is convenient for path models with latent variables the arrow scheme is of Wright's type (1934). The arrow scheme illustrates the model in structural form. Figure 2 refers to a psychological–educational application with four latent variables: Achievement (A), Motivation (M), Self-esteem (S), and Perceived expectation of others (P), with S, P as exogenous variables, and A, M as endogenous variables.

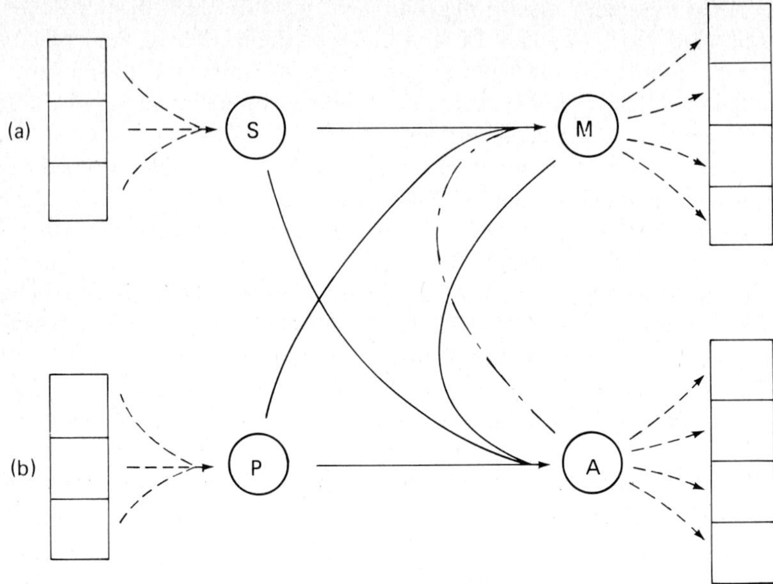

FIGURE 2. Wright arrow schemes for two PLS models with four latent variables: (a) omitting the dashed arrow from A to M (—·—·→), the latent variables form a causal chain system with two relations; (b) including the dashed arrow, the latent variables form an interdependent system; from Hui (1978).

3.3. FP versus Classical Estimation of Simultaneous Equations Systems

In a large part of this volume the focus is on the performance of FP estimation as compared with other estimation methods. In the present section the ways and means of such comparisons will be briefly discussed. The limited purpose is to outline the criteria of comparison, and to warn against biases, handicaps, and other pitfalls in the ensuing evaluations.

3.3.1. Comparison of models, and comparison of estimation methods. The comparison of different estimation methods as applied to the same model and the same data is essentially a matter of statistical technique, as distinct from subject-matter considerations. In contrast, the comparison between different models for the analysis of one and the same set of data is to some extent a statistical matter, but must essentially be based on subject-matter considerations.

In the comparison of models as applied to non-experimental data, R.A. Fisher's principle of the self-contained experiment is too narrow; the decisive criterion is how the models perform when confronted with fresh evidence. When comparing the performance of estimation methods, on the other hand, it is appropriate to base the comparison on the data used in the estimation, in accordance with the principle of the self-contained experiment. The performance outside the data used in the estimation, such as in prediction one time period beyond the data under analysis, will necessarily be influenced by the quality of the model estimated, and this introduces an element of spuriousness in the comparison of estimation methods.

When the estimation methods under comparison are designed for different types of models, predictive tests beyond the data used in the estimation are appropriate, in spite of potential handicaps associated with the quality of the models. Such is the case when it comes to GEID systems and FP estimation on the one hand, and the classical methods for the estimation of simultaneous equations systems on the other. We proceed to elaborate this statement.

3.3.2. Models and data in the comparison of estimation methods. In the comparison of estimation methods, their performance is measured using either

(i) real-world models and data, or

(ii) formal models and simulated data.

Both strategies have their advantages and disadvantages.

Real-world models and data are of course the ultimate test for the performance of estimation methods. Formal models and simulated data, on the other hand, can be designed to demonstrate features of estimation methods that are of specific relevance for their evaluation.

In the present context the real-world models under consideration are simultaneous equation systems and ID systems for macroeconomic forecasting. Speaking broadly, we may distinguish between short-range forecasting models with a prediction horizon from some few months up to two years; medium-range models that forecast from two to five years, and long-range models with a horizon from five years and upwards. Modern short-range models usually are large, involving hundreds or more of equations and variables; medium- and long-range models are smaller, often with some 20 structural relations. In short-range models the residuals usually are quite small, their variance in the estimation period keeping within some few percent of the variance of the endogenous variable to be forecast. In medium- and long-range models the residuals are larger, often much larger, as is only natural with regard to the wider diversity of uncertainties.

In large-scale models with small residuals, OLS regression is approximately consistent; see 1.2.5(iii). Hence in the present volume the real-world models of primary interest for comparative evaluation of estimation methods are not the large-size models for short-range forecasting, but rather the small or moderately large models for medium- and long-range forecasting.

Formal models designed for the production of simulated data usually are quite small, for the most part from two to five structural relations. With its ten structural relations, the GEID model used in Sydney May's experiments thus is on the large side of its kind.

May's experiments in Chapter 11 are designed to test whether the FP estimates are invariant for different choices of the starting values (2.2) of the iterative estimation procedure. This invariance shows off very distinctly in his experiments.

When the data is simulated in accordance with the GEID specification, the estimation methods perform in accordance with the large-sample consistency of FP estimation, and the inconsistency of the classical estimation methods. In May's experiments the simulated data are generated by a procedure that exploits the bias of the classical estimation methods for ID systems as applied to GEID systems. It is not the purpose of the experiments to illustrate this bias, however, and so it is only natural that the bias in these experiments turns out to be quite small.

The bias of the classical estimation methods when they are applied to GEID models is influenced by the size of the residuals and the size of the model. If other conditions are the same, the bias will be small when the residuals are small, and the bias tends to increase with the size of the model, since the parity principle then tends to be more violated; see 3.2.2(iii).

Reports on the comparison of estimation for simultaneous equations systems are only in some few cases based on simulated data generated from GEID models. So much the more common are comparisons based on data generated from Classical ID systems. The classical estimation methods as well as FP estimation are then consistent in the large-sample sense. It will be noted, however, that the data simulated from Classical ID systems has a built-in handicap in favour of the classical estimation methods. In fact, the simulated data honours the classical assumptions 3.1.4(iii) of zero intercorrelation between residuals and predetermined variables; the design of the classical estimation methods makes operative use of these stringent classical assumptions; FP estimation is designed on the parity principle (see 3.2.2) and thereby on less stringent intercorrelation assumptions; hence when using such data for the comparison it cannot be expected that FP estimation will perform with quite the same accuracy as the classical estimation methods. However, see 4.4(i).

3.3.3. Criteria in the comparison of estimation methods. In the comparison of estimation methods for simultaneous equations systems, two main types of criteria are in common use for evaluating the performance of the methods. To specify, using hats (^) to denote estimated values:

(i) Criteria on prediction accuracy, say

$$\Sigma|\hat{y} - y| \quad \text{or} \quad \Sigma(\hat{y} - y)^2. \tag{3.3}$$

(ii) Criteria on estimated versus true parameters, say

$$\Sigma|\hat{p} - p| \quad \text{or} \quad \Sigma(\hat{p} - p)^2. \tag{3.4}$$

In simulated data 3.3.2(ii) the numerical parameters of the formal model are the true parameters of the comparison. In real-world models and data 3.3.2(i) the parameters to be estimated are hypothetical, and numerically unspecified, unknown. Hence criteria of type (i) can be used both with real-world models and formal models, whereas criteria of type (ii) can be used only with formal models and simulated data.

Whether it is criterion (i) or (ii) that is being used for the evaluation, the results of the comparison are usually given by ranking the performance of the various estimation methods. When working with simulated data, the rankings that result from the two criteria (i)–(ii) may or may not be unanimous. If the ranking orders differ, say R_1 and R_2, it is desirable to report both rankings. It is also desirable to report a third ranking that combines R_1 and R_2 into an aggregate ranking R, say

$$R = R_1 + R_2, \tag{3.5a}$$

$$R = R_1^2 + R_2^2. \tag{3.5b}$$

Interpreted by way of loss functions, formula (3.5a) gives equal weight to good and bad performances. Using formula (3.5b), good performance of the estimation is at a premium, and bad performances drag down the aggregate rank. Aggregate ranks (3.5b) or similar loss functions are appropriate if the model builder is satisfied with estimation methods which usually perform rather well, without often giving top results, but which stay away from the bottom ranks.

3.3.4. Comparing the robustness of estimation methods. Anders Westlund in Chapter X of this volume reports comparative studies of FP versus other estimation methods with regard to robustness against errors in the model specification. As regards the choice of comparison criteria when dealing with simulated data, most or all of the considerations in 3.3.1–3.3.3 carry over. It turns out that the good performance of FP estimation extends to the comparison of robustness against mis-specification.

4. Incentives for the Present Volume: Joint Statement of the Authors

Although the FP approach to simultaneous equations (interdependent systems) only dates back to the mid-60's, most of the contributions are scattered in hard-to-come-by periodicals, Festschrifts, and doctoral dissertations. In the large monograph by Mosbaek and Wold et al. (1970), many simulation experiments have an inappropriate design with too large residual variances. Accordingly, we believe that time is due for a fresh exposition that summarizes the rationale of the FP family of methods, and reports about the developments in the 1970's.

4.1. The basic rationale of the FP approach has two corner stones:

(i) Reformulation of the system in structural form so as to allow causal–predictive inference from the system both in structural form and reduced form; see (1.20a–b) and (1.22b).

(ii) Parameter estimation in accordance with the parity principle: for each parameter to be estimated, the FP estimation gives zero correlation between the residual and the corresponding explanatory variable; see 3.2.2(iii).

4.1.1. Points 4.1(i–ii) are in distinct contrast to Classical ID systems, i.e., the traditional theory of simultaneous equations. In most real-world models, 4.1(ii) involves a drastic generalization relative to the correlation assumptions of Classical ID systems; see 3.2.2(iii) and footnote 5.

Note that the reformulation 4.1(i) does not interfere with the parameters of the system. Hence if the model builder wants to retain the classical version of the structural form, the FP parameter estimates can be regarded as referring to the classical version of the system.

4.2. In addition to 4.1(ii), the FP approach involves the following fundamental generalizations relative to Classical ID systems:

(i) The structural relations are specified as stochastic, not as deterministic relations subject to superimposed disturbances; see 3.2.2(ii).

(ii) The FP procedure (2.3)–(2.4) is distribution free; that is, it involves no distributional assumptions on the variables and/or residuals.

4.2.1. While the reformulation in 4.1(i) implies that the structural and reduced form relations of the system can be specified as conditional expectations (predictors), point 4.2(i) emphasizes the stochastic aspect of the reformulation.

As to 4.2(ii), substep (2.3) is an OLS regression, (2.4) is a linear aggregation, and both operations are distribution free.

4.3. The basic design 2.1–2.2 of the FP approach has been consolidated, improved, and generalized in several ways.

(i) Modified versions of the FP estimation procedure 2.1–2.2 are available that make for safe and speedy convergence, without numerical change in the resulting estimates; hereunder: Fractional FP (FFP), see Ågren (1972a); and Recursive FP (RFP), see Bodin (1974).

In the RFP method it makes for rapid convergence of the iterative procedure if the structural relations are ordered so as to have few interdependencies. Bodin gives an algorithm for finding a reordering that is optimal in this respect; see Chapter 8.

(ii) In the early stages the FP research mainly focused on small ID systems. The iterative procedure 2.1–2.2 can then be replaced by Algebraic FP (AFP), see Lyttkens (1967, 1970a, b) which makes possible a detailed analysis, including the checking for multiple sets of solution to the estimation problem. Multiple solutions in general are not equivalent on the Least Squares criterion; cf. 2.5.

When it comes to larger systems and real-world models the residuals are small. In our experience the case of multiple solutions then is virtually non-existent. Even in small systems it seems to be quite exceptional that multiple solutions occur when the residuals are small or moderately large; see 2.5. Sydney May's experiment with a ten-relation model with fairly substantial residuals (Chapter 11) shows no trace of multiple parameter estimates.

(iii) Edgerton (1973c) has extended the FP approach so as to cover ID systems with nonlinearities in the variables, linearizing the endogenous variables by Taylor expansions around their conditional expectations; see Chapter 6.

(iv) Selén (1975) and Bergström (1975b, c) have extended the FP method so as to cover ID systems with autocorrelated residuals; see Chapters 8 and 9.

4.4. As earlier, much of the recent research on the FP family of estimation methods has focused on the performance of FP in applied work as compared with other estimation methods. Applications to theoretical models and simulated data serve to study, test, and demonstrate specific features of the estimation methods under comparison. Applications to real world models and data are the ultimate test of performance.

(i) FP is the only known method of consistent estimation of GEID systems; that is, ID systems subject to the parity principle 4.1(ii). For GEID systems the FP estimates are asymptotically equivalent to FIML estimates; Lyttkens (1970d).

Thus far only some few simulation experiments with GEID systems have been reported. In the present volume, as earlier, most of the simulation experiments for comparing FP and other estimation methods are based on Classical ID systems; see Chapters 5–10. In Classical ID systems, however, FP is somewhat handicapped relative to TSLS and other classical estimation methods since FP honours the parity principle 4.1(ii), and therefore, in contrast to the classical estimation methods, cannot use to the full the classical assumption of zero intercorrelation between all residuals and all predetermined variables; see 3.1.4. Hence it is perhaps somewhat surprising that FP shows off fairly well relative to the classical estimation methods in simulation experiments with Classical ID systems. The explanation may be that the handicap just referred to is offset by FP being favoured by the criterion of comparison: prediction performance in the sample is the criterion of comparison, and since FP is based on the Least Squares principle it tends to give small prediction errors.

Sydney May's simulation experiment in Chapter 11 is based on a GEID system. The consistency of FP estimation is not in focus in his experiment, however, but rather the invariance of the iterative procedure (2.3)–(2.4) relative to the starting values (2.2), and thereby the absence of multiple solutions; see 4.3(ii).

(ii) In the real-world applications of simultaneous equations systems, macroeconomic forecasting models dominate the scene. In the last two decades the trend is toward ever larger systems, with variables and structural relations in the hundreds or thousands. Such large systems are always estimated by OLS regression. This is so since FP and other estimation methods for ID systems become intractable with increasing size of the system. And if the residuals of the structural relations are small the OLS estimates are approximately consistent; for a proximity theorem to this effect, see Wold and Juréen (1953, p. 251).

For the estimation of small or moderately large systems the FP family of methods can offer itself as appropriate. This statement is a summarizing conclusion of the reports in the subsequent chapters on FP estimation of real-world models. In most of the comparisons with classical estimation methods, FP scores among the top results. Specific reference is made to the broad array of comparisons reported by Reinhold Bergström (Chapters 5 and 7). A striking case in point is the Czech model, where the FP estimates rank as No. 1 in 20 of 25 comparisons.

Three chapters in this volume report generalizations of the FP approach; namely estimation methods for nonlinear ID systems, David Edgerton (Chapter 6), and for ID systems with autocorrelated residuals, Jan Selén (Chapter 9) and Reinhold Bergström (Chapter 7). In comparisons based on simulated data the generalized methods score higher than the ordinary FP methods, as could be expected. Since the generalized methods involve more parameters it is a question to what extent the advantage of the more elaborate methods carries over when it comes to applications to real-world models and data. Of specific interest is here the analysis of Bergström (Chapter 7), who reports several applications to real-world data, and finds that at least some of the advantage carries over, again as could be expected.[7]

The FP family of methods being of recent date, it is only natural that the applications have been limited to small or not so small systems. However, even in large systems the structural relations often involve only some few explanatory variables, and then the residuals may be sizable and bring a tangible bias into the OLS estimates. Now in a very recent project the FP methods are being applied to a rather large real-world model, namely a

[7] The autocorrelation in the residuals is removed by a corresponding "prewhitening" transformation of the variables under analysis. Well to note, the improvement relative to the ordinary FP estimation is usually measured on the prewhitened variables, not on the "dark" variables actually observed. This may clearly be to the disadvantage of the ordinary FP method in the comparison.

It will further be noted that the rationale of "prewhitening" belongs under "errors in variables", and is thereby radically different from "errors in equations" and from the predictor specification that is the conceptual basis of the FP method; cf. 1.1.2(i). Let us consider the simple case

$$y_t = \alpha + \beta x_t + e_t, \qquad e_t = 0.5 e_{t-1} + \Delta_t. \tag{1a,b}$$

"Errors in variables" assumes: (*) the residual-free relation $\eta_t = \alpha + \beta\xi_t$ is deterministic, functionally exact, and (**) the residual e_t is uncorrelated with ξ_s and η_s for all s. The prewhitening takes the form

$$y_t - 0.5 y_{t-1} = 0.5\alpha + \beta^*(x_t - 0.5 x_{t-1}) + \Delta_t \quad \text{with} \quad \beta^* = \beta. \tag{2}$$

As it should be, OLS regression of (2) gives a consistent estimate of $\beta^* = \beta$. If $x_t = y_{t-k}$ it is well-known that assumption (**) is necessary for the OLS regression of (2) to be consistent for all k. If x_t is purely exogenous relative to y_t, assumption (**) remains radically different from the predictor specification. The difference is less radical if we assume $r(\eta_s, e_t) = 0$ for all $s < t$, but if $r(\eta_s, e_t) \neq 0$ for $s \geq t$ the prewhitening will not work. For example, of $r(\eta_{t+1}, e_t) \neq 0$ we see that OLS regression of (2) will give an inconsistent estimate of β^* and thereby of β.

Polish model with 228 structural relations; Bergström (1980). This is not the place to say anything about the results, but to judge from this application the ID systems of such size are technically within the reach of the FP methods.

4.5. Part of the incentive for the present volume is to report about FP estimation as a problem area at the research frontier. First of all, more applications to real-world models and data are needed to explore the reach and limitation of FP estimation in practice. If the residuals are not too large, FP estimation converges rapidly and is not much more expensive than OLS estimation; if the residuals are not too small, the difference between the FP and OLS estimates may be relevant. To put it in another way, more research is needed to establish the area where FP estimation is at a premium, an area intermediate between small systems with large residuals, and large systems with not too small residuals.

Chapter 2

ITERATIVE ALGORITHMS FOR FIX-POINT ESTIMATION, THEIR DESIGN AND CONVERGENCE PROPERTIES

LENNART BODIN

1. Introduction

The Fix-Point (FP) method was developed by Wold (1965) as an iterative estimation method for interdependent systems which are subject either to the classical ID assumptions 3.2 or the predictor specification (1.20a–b) in Chapter 1. An extensive Monte Carlo simulation of the FP method and its properties was performed and reported by Mosbaek and Wold et al. (1970). Although the method performed very well in most of the investigated models, it was found that in a few cases convergence difficulties appeared. Modifications and improvements of the iterative estimation techniques have therefore been developed. Extensive studies are reported by Ågren (1972a), Bodin (1974) and Bergström (1974). The methods developed and investigated in these studies are the Fractional Fix-Point (FFP) method, the Recursive Fix-Point (RFP) method and the Solved System Fix-Point (SFP) method.[1] The analysis includes theoretical developments, Monte-Carlo simulations and applications on medium-sized real-world models.

The following exposition will partly be based on results first given by the above-mentioned authors and it will cover the designs, convergence properties and other computational aspects of the different methods. Summarizing results concerning comparisons of the iterative efficiency of the Fix-Point algorithms will give conclusions for the choice of method in different applications.

2. The Model and the GEID Estimator

We will consider Wold's reformulation of the interdependent system and write the model in its estimated (sample) structural form (SF) as

[1] The Solved System Fix-Point (SFP) method has earlier been called the Reduced Form Fix-Point (RF-FP) method; see Bergström (1974), Bodin (1973a) and Chapter 1 of this monograph.

$$y_t = By_t^* + Gz_t + e_t, \tag{2.1}$$

with

$$y_t^* = By_t^* + Gz_t. \tag{2.2}$$

The matrix $(I - B)$ is assumed to be non-singular and the reduced form (RF) of the system is written

$$y_t = (I - B)^{-1} Gz_t + e_t. \tag{2.3}$$

It is a specific feature of the reformulation that the residuals of the reduced form are identical to those of the structural form.

By $b_{(i)}$ and $g_{(i)}$ we denote the set of non-zero parameters of row i of the B and G matrices, and by $y_{(i)}$ and $z_{(i)}$ those variables present on the right-hand side of relation i of the reformulated system. We assume that the system consists of n relations of which p are behavioural and subject to estimation of their structural parameters; $n - p = q$ relations are identities.

The GEID estimator is defined by Ågren (1972a) as the set of real solutions, such that $I - B$ is non-singular, to the nonlinear equation system

$$(b_{(i)} \,\vdots\, g_{(i)}) = (y_i y_{(i)}^{*\prime} \,\vdots\, y_i z'_{(i)}) \begin{pmatrix} y_{(i)}^* y_{(i)}^{*\prime} & y_{(i)}^* z'_{(i)} \\ z_{(i)} y_{(i)}^{*\prime} & z_{(i)} z'_{(i)} \end{pmatrix}^{-1}, \tag{2.4}$$

with (2.2) fulfilled. The nonlinear system may produce multiple parameter sets.

The definition of the GEID estimator does not imply a computational algorithm suitable to produce the parameter sets of the model (2.1)–(2.3). In a few small models it has been possible to obtain an explicit, non-iterative computational scheme based on the GEID estimator, see Ågren (1972a). The Algebraic Fix-Point (AFP) method, first developed by Lyttkens (1967) and reviewed in Chapter 4 of this volume, is another device for an explicit determination of the parameter sets of small ID systems. In actual econometric work the estimation of the reformulated system must be based on different iterative algorithms. These algorithms are reviewed in Section 4.

3. Framework for the Analysis

The conceptual framework for the analysis and the evaluation of the iterative estimation methods is outlined in Figure 1 taken from Bodin (1974). The figure illustrates a case where k different parameter sets are

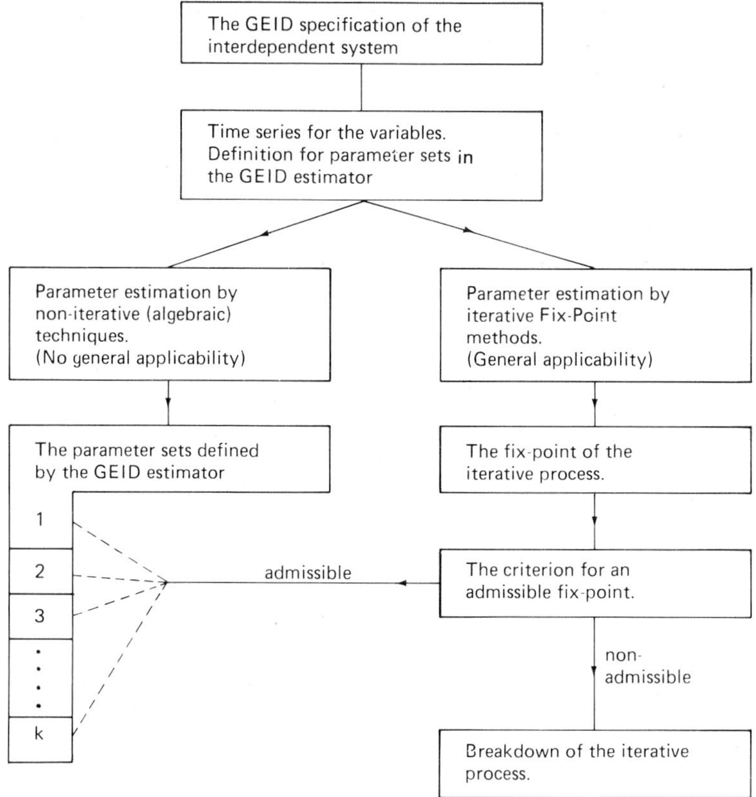

FIGURE 1. The principal design of the convergence evaluation of the iterative Fix-Point estimation methods of GEID systems, cf. Section 9.

defined by the GEID estimator. In each realization of the iterative estimation the Fix-Point algorithm may, in the normal case, produce one of these parameter sets. Through apparent convergence, discussed in Section 6 of this chapter, more than one parameter set can be recognized in a single estimation.

A fix-point of the iterative process is defined as admissible if and only if it satisfies the defining nonlinear system of the GEID estimator. The criterion for the classification of the fix-points as admissible or non-admissible utilizes the fact that the residuals of the RF should be identical to those of the SF, or

$$e_t^{\mathrm{RF}} = y_t - (I - B^{(s)})^{-1} G^{(s)} z_t = y_t - y_t^{(s)} = e_t^{\mathrm{SF}}, \tag{3.1}$$

where $B^{(s)}$, $G^{(s)}$ and $y_i^{(s)}$ are the iterates obtained in step 's' of the iterative procedure, and where these proxies should fulfill the convergence criterion employed for the iterative process.

It is indicated in the figure that the iterative process may fail to produce the parameter sets of the GEID estimator. This is of course the case if no convergence is obtained. Other cases described as a breakdown of the iterative process have been reported but it must be emphasized that they have occurred very seldom.[2]

For practically all econometric models the algebraic estimations indicated in the left-hand column of Figure 1 are impossible to accomplish. This implies that questions concerning the uniqueness of the parameter set can in general not be solved. In this matter we must rely on results and conclusions derived from the analysis of the small models where the complete evaluation scheme of Figure 1 can be carried through. It is reported in Section 9 of this chapter that for conditions which occur in many econometric models, such as small residual variances and a low degree of interdependence, the empirical investigations strongly support the hypothesis of a unique parameter set.

4. The Design of the Iterative Algorithms

With reference to the basic formulas for the FP method given in Section 2 of Chapter 1 we define the computations leading from iteration step s to $s+1$ as consisting of two substeps or phases. The first phase consists of a least squares regression where new proxies $b_i^{(s+1)}$ and $g_i^{(s+1)}$ are computed in an OLS regression using y_i as regressand and $y_{(i)}^{(s)}$ and $z_{(i)}$ as regressors. Two alternative formulations of the OLS regression will be used, and in component form they will read as follows.

Phase 1

OLS regression for FP, FFP and SFP:

$$y_i = \sum_{j=1}^{n} b_{ij}^{(s+1)} y_j^{(s)} + \sum_{j=1}^{m} g_{ij}^{(s+1)} z_j + e_i^{(s+1)}, \qquad i = 1, \cdots, p, \tag{4.1}$$

OLS regression for RFP:

[2] Bodin (1974) reports on singular solutions where the obtained $(I - B)$ matrix is singular.

$$y_i = \sum_{j=1}^{i-1} b_{ij}^{(s+1)} y_j^{(s+1)} + \sum_{j=i+1}^{n} b_{ij}^{(s+1)} y_j^{(s)} + \sum_{j=1}^{m} g_{ij}^{(s+1)} z_j + e_i^{(s+1)}, \quad i = 1, \cdots, p. \tag{4.2}$$

The OLS regression works entirely within the structural form (2.1), the systematic part $y^*_{(i)}$ of the structural and reduced forms being substituted for components of $y_{(i)}^{(s)}$ and $y_{(i)}^{(s+1)}$.

The OLS regressions are performed for the behavioural relations only since the identities of the system are not subject to estimation of structural parameters.

In the second phase of the general step from s to $s+1$ the new proxies $y^{(s+1)}$ are calculated by one of three different formulas. Two of these formulas are extensions of the formulas (2.4a–b) in Chapter 1, the extension being the inclusion of a relaxation parameter α, $0 < \alpha < 2$.

Phase 2

Computation of $y^{(s+1)}$, FFP:

$$y_i^{(s+1)} = (1-\alpha) y_i^{(s)} + \alpha \left\{ \sum_{j=1}^{n} b_{ij}^{(s+1)} y_j^{(s)} + \sum_{j=1}^{m} g_{ij}^{(s+1)} z_j \right\}, \quad i = 1, \cdots, n, \tag{4.3}$$

Computation of $y^{(s+1)}$, RFP:

$$y_i^{(s+1)} = (1-\alpha) y_i^{(s)} + \alpha \left\{ \sum_{j=1}^{i-1} b_{ij}^{(s+1)} y_j^{(s+1)} + \sum_{j=i+1}^{n} b_{ij}^{(s+1)} y_j^{(s)} + \sum_{j=1}^{m} g_{ij}^{(s+1)} z_j \right\}, \quad i = 1, \cdots, n. \tag{4.4}$$

Computation of $y^{(s+1)}$, SFP:

$$y_i^{(s+1)} = (1-\alpha) y_i^{(s)} + \alpha \sum_{j=1}^{m} W_{ij}^{(s+1)} z_j, \qquad i = 1, \cdots, n, \tag{4.5}$$

where

$$W^{(s+1)} = (I - B^{(s+1)})^{-1} G^{(s+1)}. \tag{4.6}$$

The computation of $y^{(s+1)}$ in FFP and RFP works entirely within the structural form, but for SFP the reduced form must be utilized. Another difference between FFP and RFP on the one hand and SFP on the other hand is manifested in the fact that the new iterate $y_i^{(s+1)}$ of the former methods is a weighted average of the systematic part of the OLS regression and the preceding iterate $y_i^{(s)}$. This is not the case for SFP.

The calculations of (4.3)–(4.5) are carried through for all n relations of the system. For the q identities the parameters of B and G that are specified *a priori* are used. This way of handling the identities has been suggested by Ågren (1972a).

A very important difference between the computational schemes for FFP and SFP and the computational scheme for RFP lies in the different principles used for the shift between the OLS regression and the computation of new proxies $y^{(s+1)}$. For FFP and SFP the OLS regression is completed for all p behavioural relations before the calculation of $y^{(s+1)}$ starts. In RFP an alternating scheme is used. The OLS regression of relation i is immediately followed by the calculation of $y_i^{(s+1)}$. Then the OLS regression proceeds to relation $i + 1$, provided this is not an identity. The principles are illustrated in Figure 2.

The sequential principle employed for the RFP method implies that the order in which the relations are processed will be of great importance for the convergence properties of the method. For the simultaneous principle used in FFP and SFP estimations the order in which the relations are processed does not influence the convergence of the methods.

Relation	$B^{(s+1)}, G^{(s+1)}$	$y_i^{(s+1)}$	$B^{(s+1)}, G^{(s+1)}$	$y_i^{(s+1)}$
1	x	x	x →	x
2	x	x	x →	x
3	x	x	x →	x
•	x	•	•	•
•	•	•	•	•
p	x	x	x →	x
p+1		x		x
•		•		•
p+q=n		x		x
	FFP and SFP		RFP	

FIGURE 2. Arrow scheme of the computations in the step from 's' to '$s + 1$' for the FFP, SFP and RFP methods in an ID system with n relations of which q are identities; } = simultaneous computations, → = sequential computations.

The dependence of the RFP method on the order in which the relations are processed is one reflection of the fact that the method is based on the principles of the Gauss–Seidel iterative method for solving linear systems of equations. The FFP method on the other hand resembles the Jacobi iterative method. The similarity is spelled out more clearly if the iterative schemes (4.1)–(4.6) are rewritten in matrix formulations. To this end a decomposition of the B matrix will be given as

$$B = E + F, \tag{4.7}$$

where E is a strictly lower triangular matrix and F a strictly upper triangular matrix.

The two alternative formulations of the OLS regressions are now written

$$y_t = B^{(s+1)} y_t^{(s)} + G^{(s+1)} z_t + e_t^{(s+1)}, \tag{4.8}$$

for the FP, FFP and SFP methods, and

$$y_t = E^{(s+1)} y_t^{(s+1)} + F^{(s+1)} y_t^{(s)} + G^{(s+1)} z_t + e_t^{(s+1)}, \tag{4.9}$$

for the RFP method.

The computation of $y_t^{(s+1)}$ is formulated in three different versions:

$$y_t^{(s+1)} = (\alpha B^{(s+1)} + (1-\alpha)I) y_t^{(s)} + \alpha G^{(s+1)} z_t, \tag{4.10}$$

for the FFP method,

$$\begin{aligned} y_t^{(s+1)} = {} & (I - \alpha E^{(s+1)})^{-1}((1-\alpha)I + \alpha F^{(s+1)}) y_t^{(s)} \\ & + \alpha (I - \alpha E^{(s+1)})^{-1} G^{(s+1)} z, \end{aligned} \tag{4.11}$$

for the RFP method, and

$$y_t^{(s+1)} = (1-\alpha) y_t^{(s)} + \alpha (I - B^{(s+1)})^{-1} G^{(s+1)} z_t, \tag{4.12}$$

for the SFP method.

The formulas (4.10) and (4.11) are completely equivalent to the iteration formulas for the Jacobi Overrelaxation (JOR) method and the Successive Overrelaxation (SOR) method given by Young (1971) provided that the subscripts $s + 1$ are dropped as concerns the parameter matrices B and G. The nonlinear character of the Fix-Point algorithms can be thought of as depending on the fact that the B and G matrices are not constant, as in the linear methods, but subject to a continuous revision by the use of least squares regression.

Before we turn to analysis of convergence we should point out that it can easily be demonstrated that the iterative estimation methods in case of convergence to a fix-point, classified as an admissible fix-point, give a parameter set that satisfies the defining equations of the GEID estimator. A proof is found in Bodin (1974).

5. Exact Convergence Theorems for Local Convergence

The formal background for the convergence analysis of the Fix-Point algorithms can be described with reference to a general nonlinear iterative algorithm of the form

$$X^{(s+1)} = F(X^{(s)}), \tag{5.1}$$

where F is a nonlinear function or mapping with domain D in R^{nT} and range in $R^{nT}, F: D \subset R^{nT} \to R^{nT}$.

In the convergence analysis of this process distinction is made between local and global convergence:

Definition 1: The local convergence analysis is an analysis of the iterative process (5.1) for start values $X^{(0)}$ in the neighbourhood of the fix-point $X^* = F(X^*)$.

Definition 2: The global convergence analysis is an analysis of the iterative process for arbitrary start values $X^{(0)}$.

In this section only local convergence will be considered. The following theorem by Ostrowski (1960) is the basic reference for this analysis:

Theorem 1: Given that the nonlinear function $F: D \subset R^{nT} \to R^{nT}$ has a fix-point $X^* \in \text{int}(D)$ and is Fréchet-differentiable at X^*, the iterative process (5.1) will converge to X^* for any $X^{(0)}$ in a neighbourhood of X^* if $\rho(F'(X^*)) < 1$ where $F'(X)$ is the Jacobian of F and ρ is the spectral radius.

In order to determine the rate of convergence of (5.1) the following definitions are introduced:

Definition 3: The asymptotic rate of convergence for the nonlinear process (5.1), defined for a neighbourhood of X^*, is given by

$$r(F'(X^*)) = -\ln \rho(F'(X^*)). \tag{5.2}$$

Definition 4: The nonlinear process (5.1) is iteratively faster, in a neighbourhood of X^*, than the nonlinear process $X^{(s+1)} = H(X^{(s)})$, with the same fix-point X^*, if

$$\rho(F'(X^*)) < \rho(H'(X^*)), \tag{5.3}$$

or equivalently

$$r(F'(X^*)) > r(H'(X^*)). \tag{5.4}$$

Comment: The definition is also suitable for an analysis of the iterative performance of (5.1) at different fix-points,

$$X^* = F(X^*) \text{ and } X^{**} = F(X^{**}).$$

After the reformulation of the iterative algorithms (4.8)–(4.12) into the general form (5.1), which essentially means that the least squares regression and the computation of new proxies $y_t^{(s+1)}$ is rewritten in one equation, the criterion of Theorem 1 can be applied and determined.

Based on the results of Ågren (1972a), Bodin (1974) and Bergström (1974) the following table summarizes the Jacobians of the different Fix-Point algorithms. Local convergence for the different Fix-Point algorithms will occur if

$$\rho(J_i) < 1, \tag{5.5}$$

where J_i is given by the appropriate line of Table 1.

In the definition of J_1 and J_4 the following notations, given by Bergström (1974), are used:

$$R = \begin{pmatrix} R_1 & 0 & \cdots & \cdots & 0 \\ 0 & R_2 & 0 & \cdots & 0 \\ \vdots & & \ddots & & \vdots \\ 0 & & & \cdots & R_n \end{pmatrix}, \tag{5.6}$$

TABLE 1

The Jacobians of the local convergence theorems for the Fix-Point algorithms.

Method	Jacobian[a]
FP	$J_1 = (I - R)B \otimes I + D$
FFP	$J_2 = (1 - \alpha)I + \alpha J_1$
RFP	$J_3 = (I - aG)^{-1}((1 - a)I + aH)$
SFP, $\alpha = 1$	$J_4 = (I - B)^{-1} \otimes I(D - RB \otimes I)$
SFP	$J_5 = (1 - \alpha)I + \alpha J_4$

[a] The definitions of R, D, G and H are given in the text.

with

$$R_i = I - (b_{(i)}(I - y^{*\prime}_{(i)}\{y^*_{(i)}b_{(i)}y^{*\prime}_{(i)}\}^{-1}y^*_{(i)}b_{(i)})), \tag{5.7}$$

and

$$D = \quad (D_{ij}), \qquad i,j = 1,\cdots,n, \tag{5.8}$$

with

$$\begin{aligned} D_{ij} &= x_j e_i, \quad \text{when } j \text{ is an index in } (i), \\ &= 0, \qquad \text{otherwise,} \end{aligned} \tag{5.9}$$

and

$$x_i = b_{(i)}y^*_{(i)}\{y^*_{(i)}b_{(i)}y^{*\prime}_{(i)}\}^{-1}. \tag{5.10}$$

G and H are defined by a decomposition of J_1 equivalent to that of B in (4.7), that is,

$$J_1 = G + H, \tag{5.11}$$

with G a strictly lower triangular matrix and H a strictly upper triangular matrix.

It follows from the results given in Table 1 that the spectral radii of the Jacobians J_2, J_3 and J_5 are dependent on the value of the relaxation parameter α. By changing the parameter value α the rate of convergence for the Fix-Point algorithms can be optimized and an optimal value of α, α_{opt}, specified.

It also follows from the results of Table 1 that the ordering in which the relations are processed has influence on the spectral radius of J_3. The crucial point is that different orderings will have a direct effect on which elements of J_1 should belong to G and which should belong to H in the decomposition (5.11). It is thus possible to define an optimal ordering of the relations.

The formal definition of the optimal α for FFP and SFP is based on the inequality

$$\rho(J_i(\alpha_{opt})) \leq \rho(J_i(\alpha)), \qquad i = 2 \text{ for FFP, } 4 \text{ for SFP.} \tag{5.12}$$

The definition of the optimal α and the optimal ordering for RFP rests on the double inequality

$$\rho(J_3(\alpha_{opt}, v_{opt})) \leq \rho(J_3(\alpha_{opt}, v)) \leq \rho(J_3(\alpha, v)), \tag{5.13}$$

where v is used to symbolize the impact of different orderings on the Jacobian J_3.

The basis for the analysis of optimal orderings given by Bodin (1974) is the definition of an ordering vector

$$(i_1, i_2, i_3, \cdots, i_n), \tag{5.14}$$

which specifies the order in which the relations are processed. The natural ordering vector is defined as

$$(1, 2, 3, \cdots, p, p+1, \cdots, p+q), \tag{5.15}$$

which is an ordering as close as possible to that specified by the model builders and if necessary rewritten to define the behavioural relations as the first p relations, the identities as the next q relation.[3] It is shown by Bodin (1974) that there exist $(n-1)!$ different orderings that affect $\rho(J_3(\alpha, v))$.[4]

The mathematical analysis of the Jacobians of Table 1 is difficult even for small models. This is partly due to the fact that the order of the Jacobians is $nT \times nT$, and partly due to the fact that the partial derivatives are rather complicated expressions. In order to facilitate the understanding of the basic convergence properties of the Fix-Point algorithms other approaches have therefore been tried. One approach is based on Lyttkens' device of Parametric Fix-Point (PFP) estimation, reviewed in Chapter 4 of this monograph. In the next section this approach is discussed and related to the empirical analysis of the notion 'apparent convergence'.

A second approach is the establishment of approximate convergence conditions based on simpler mathematical expressions. This approach, first initiated by Ågren (1967), will be discussed in the section next to follow.

6. Apparent Convergence and Decompositions of the Exact Convergence Theorems

Early investigations of the FP method reported by Bodin (1968, 1970) made it clear that in the analysis of the empirical performance of the FP method it was necessary to distinguish between two kinds of convergence. In Bodin (1970) these two concepts are defined as true and apparent

[3] In the form presented here the Fix-Point algorithms require that the endogenous variables appear once and only once as a left-hand variable in each relation, including the identities. The natural ordering is based on this one-to-one correspondence between the endogenous variables and the relations. Extensions of the Fix-Point methods based on relaxations of these restrictions have been developed; see e.g. Lyttkens (1970c) and Edgerton (1974).

[4] Extensive investigations of different orderings of the relations of the interdependent system including analysis of different ways of decomposing the system into blocks are reported by Bodin (1974). A review of some of these investigations is given in Chapter 8 of this monograph.

convergence. They are defined with reference to the convergence test utilized in the computer programs,

$$\max_{i,j} |(a_{ij}^{(s+1)} - a_{ij}^{(s)})/a_{ij}^{(s+1)}| < 10^{-k}, \tag{6.1}$$

where $a_{ij}^{(s+1)}$ denotes the estimated parameters and proxies of step $s+1$, $B^{(s+1)}, G^{(s+1)}$ and $y^{(s+1)}$.

Definition 1: True convergence implies that (6.1) is satisfied for all s larger than s_0, and as s increases (6.1) will be satisfied for larger values of k until the accuracy of the computer puts a limit on k.

Definition 2: Apparent convergence implies that (6.1) is satisfied only for a limited sequence of $s > s_0$, that is $s_0, s_0+1, \cdots, s_0+\nu$. When s increases (6.1) will not be satisfied for some $s > s_0 + \nu$ and the iterations will diverge.

Extensive empirical investigations of the occurrence of apparent convergence, based on the use of the evaluation scheme of Figure 1 and reported by Bodin (1968, 1970, 1974), have shown two major findings:

(i) The parameter sets obtained in the case of apparent convergence, that is $B^{(s_0)}, G^{(s_0)}$ and $y_t^{(s_0)}$, satisfy the defining equations of the GEID estimator. These parameter sets are thus true FP parameter sets.
(ii) Apparent convergence occurred frequently in many of the Monte-Carlo simulations performed by Mosbaek and Wold et al. (1970). In all these estimations the start value $y_t^{(0)}$ was defined as a linear combination of the predetermined variables,

$$y_t^{(0)} = Pz_t. \tag{6.2}$$

Re-estimations of these cases using start values which were not restricted to being of the form (6.2), did not result in apparent convergence but immediate divergence. One example of this kind of start value is defined as OLS-start, i.e., $y_t^{(0)} = y_t$.

The final divergence in those cases where apparent convergence was present was explained by Lyttkens (1968) as due to the accumulation of rounding errors orthogonal to the space spanned by the predetermined variables, the z-space. When the iterations start from the z-space, which is the case if (6.2) is satisfied, the iterations may lead to the FP parameter set if certain convergence conditions are satisfied. These conditions refer strictly to iterations in the z-space. Perturbations introduced through lack of computational accuracy may under certain other conditions accumulate and cause $y_t^{(s)}$ to contain components not included among the predetermined variables. The iterations then drift away from the FP parameter set and diverge.

This observation led to the derivation of the Parametric Fix-Point (PFP) method, a method which corresponds to the FP method but every iterate is now forced to be a linear combination of the predetermined variables. The PFP method and its convergence properties are discussed in detail in Chapter 4. We shall here relate the method and the convergence analysis of the method to the apparent convergences and to a decomposition of the exact convergence theorems of Section 5.

The computations of the PFP method are the least squares regression of (4.8) and the calculation of new proxies through

$$y_t^{(s+1)} = W^{(s+1)} z_t, \tag{6.3}$$

with

$$W^{(s+1)} = B^{(s+1)} W^{(s)} + G^{(s+1)}. \tag{6.4}$$

With reference to the general convergence analysis of (5.1) and Theorem 1 in Section 5 we obtain

$$W^{(s+1)} = f(W^{(s)}), \tag{6.5}$$

and the convergence condition

$$\rho\left(\frac{\delta f}{\delta W^{(s)}}\right)_{W^{(s)}=W^*} < 1, \tag{6.6}$$

with

$$W^* = BW^* + G, \tag{6.7}$$

or

$$W^* = (I - B)^{-1} G. \tag{6.8}$$

The Jacobian of (6.6) is of the order $nm \times nm$ with m the number of predetermined variables.

Starting from the empirical analysis of apparent convergence and Lyttkens' analysis of the PFP method alternative expressions of the Jacobians J_1–J_3 have been derived by Bodin (1974). In this analysis each iterate $y_t^{(s)}$ of the FP method is written

$$y_t^{(s)} = W^{(s)} z_t + v_t^{(s)} = u_t^{(s)} + v_t^{(s)}, \tag{6.9}$$

where $u_t^{(s)}$ are the iterates of PFP according to (6.3) and (6.4), and $v_t^{(s)}$ are vectors in the orthogonal complement of the space spanned by the predetermined variables. In order to obtain convergence for the $y_t^{(s)}$ process the iterates $u_t^{(s)}$ must converge towards the fix-point

$$u_t = W^* z_t = (I - B)^{-1} G z_t. \tag{6.10}$$

The iterates $v_t^{(s)}$ must converge towards the zero vector since they constitute a process of perturbations introduced either through start values which are not of the form (6.2) or originating from rounding errors.

For the FP method we obtain in the transition from step 's' to step '$s+1$'

$$u_t^{(s+1)} = B^{(s+1)} u_t^{(s)} + G^{(s+1)} z_t, \tag{6.11}$$

and

$$v_t^{(s+1)} = B^{(s+1)} v_t^{(s)}. \tag{6.12}$$

Under certain assumptions, including the assumption that $u_t^{(s)}$ and $v_t^{(s)}$ are orthogonal processes, the convergence condition of the FP method, originally formulated by (5.5) can be decomposed as

$$\rho\left(\begin{array}{c|c} \delta f/\delta W & 0 \\ \hline 0 & B \end{array}\right) < 1. \tag{6.13}$$

The characteristic equation of (6.13) is

$$|(\delta f/\delta W - \lambda I_{n+m})(B - \lambda I_n)| = 0, \tag{6.14}$$

with I as identity matrices of order $n+m$ and n, respectively.

The roots of (6.14) yield eigenvalues corresponding to both eigenvectors contained in the z-space and eigenvectors contained in the orthogonal complement of the z-space. The former eigenvectors relate to the $u_t^{(s)}$ process, the latter to the $v_t^{(s)}$ process.

Apparent convergence occurs if the following conditions are satisfied:

(i) the start value is of the form (6.2),

(ii) the $u_t^{(s)}$ process converges, that is, the convergence conditions of PFP are satisfied, and

(iii) the $v_t^{(s)}$ process diverges, that is, accumulation of rounding errors is causing a final divergence.

The theoretical analysis has been confirmed by several empirical investigations in Monte-Carlo simulations. It should be observed that for larger models where $T > m$ the iterates $y^{(s)}$ cannot contain components outside the z-space which implies that the apparent convergence discussed in the preceding paragraphs cannot occur.

The convergence approach resulting in (6.13) and (6.14) has been extended to the FFP and RFP methods. For the RFP method Bodin (1974) obtains $\rho(J_3)$ expressed as

$$\rho\begin{pmatrix} (I-\alpha f^{E})^{-1}((1-\alpha)I+\alpha f^{F}) & 0 \\ 0 & (I-\alpha E)^{-1}((1-\alpha)I+\alpha F) \end{pmatrix} < 1, \tag{6.15}$$

with

$$\delta f/\delta W = f^{E} + f^{F}, \tag{6.16}$$

that is, a decomposition of $\delta f/\delta W$ analogous to that of B in (4.7).

One main advantage of the decomposition (6.9) is that the resulting Jacobians (6.13) and (6.15) can sometimes, in small models, be determined analytically. As an illustration a model presented by Girshick and Haavelmo (1947) will be used. The reformulated B matrix of this model is written

$$B = \begin{pmatrix} 0 & b_{12} & b_{13} & 0 & 0 \\ b_{21} & 0 & 0 & b_{24} & 0 \\ 0 & 0 & 0 & 0 & 0 \\ 0 & 0 & 0 & 0 & b_{45} \\ 0 & b_{52} & 0 & 0 & 0 \end{pmatrix}. \tag{6.17}$$

The characteristic equation of the matrix (6.15) is

$$((1-\alpha-\lambda)^{3}+\alpha^{3}\lambda^{v}b_{24}b_{45}b_{52}) \times ((1-\alpha-\lambda)^{3}-(1-\alpha-\lambda)\alpha^{2}\lambda b_{12}b_{21}+\alpha^{3}\lambda^{v}b_{24}b_{45}b_{52}) = 0, \tag{6.18}$$

with $v = 1$ or 2 depending on which ordering of the relations has been used.

The convergence analysis of the SFP method can sometimes be facilitated through an analysis similar to the analysis of the PFP method. Illustrations are given by Bergström (1974). As the SFP method in its original formulation forces the $y^{(s)}$ iterates to be linear combinations of the predetermined variables no analogy of the decomposition (6.9) is meaningful for the SFP method. No cases of apparent convergence in the sense of the preceding paragraphs have been reported.

7. Approximate Convergence Conditions

Ågren (1967) suggested and analysed an approximate convergence condition for the FFP method. Ågren's criterion is based on an analysis of the eigenvalues of the matrix $K(\alpha)$ defined as

$$K(\alpha) = (1-\alpha)I + \alpha B, \tag{7.1}$$

B given by the fix-point parameter set. With this criterion a straightforward analogy with the convergence analysis of the linear iterative scheme of the Jacobi type is obtained.

Ågren (1972a) stated that

$$\rho(K(\alpha)) < 1 \tag{7.2}$$

is a necessary condition for the FFP method to converge. Extensive investigations of the usefulness of the suggested convergence criterion on many models, both real-world models and models of Monte-Carlo simulations, indicate that the criterion is a very good approximation to the exact local convergence condition given in Section 5.

Bodin (1968), in analogy with Ågren's criterion, analysed an approximate convergence criterion for the RFP method based on the matrix $L(\alpha, v)$ defined as

$$L(\alpha, v) = (I - \alpha E)^{-1}((1-\alpha)I + \alpha F), \tag{7.3}$$

with E and F defined by (4.7). This criterion is a straightforward application of the analysis of linear iterative algorithms, in this case of the algorithms of the Gauss–Seidel family.

Bergström (1972) developed an approximate criterion for the SFP method. In this case it is not possible to rely on a direct analogy with the linear iterative scheme. The criterion is instead suggested on the basis of investigations of the exact local convergence criterion and of empirical indications. It is based on the matrix $R(\alpha)$ defined as

$$R(\alpha) = (1-\alpha)I - \alpha(I - B)^{-1}B_0, \tag{7.4}$$

with B_0 obtained by setting the elements in all rows of B that correspond to the identities equal to 0.

The definitions of the optimal α and the optimal ordering, introduced in Section 5 with respect to the analysis of the Jacobians J_i of the exact convergence theorems, can be applied directly on the matrices of the approximate criteria. Hence we have

$$\rho(K(\alpha_{\text{opt}})) \leq \rho(K(\alpha)), \tag{7.5}$$

$$\rho(R(\alpha_{\text{opt}})) \leq \rho(R(\alpha)), \tag{7.6}$$

$$\rho(L(\alpha_{\text{opt}}, v_{\text{opt}})) \leq \rho(L(\alpha_{\text{opt}}, v) \leq \rho(L(\alpha, v)). \tag{7.7}$$

The influence of different orderings is indicated by v, $K(\alpha)$ and $R(\alpha)$ not being dependent on different orderings.

Empirical investigations have shown that in many small models there is a very close correspondence between the optimal α of the exact convergence theorems and the optimal α given by the approximate criteria. The same result has been found with respect to the optimal orderings of $J_3(\alpha, v)$ and $L(\alpha, v)$, respectively.

Summarizing it can be stated that the approximate convergence criteria can be applied as necessary conditions for convergence. They are however not sufficient conditions, since it has been found that the relation between the exact condition and the approximate condition is

$$\rho(J_i) \geqslant \rho(A(\alpha)), \tag{7.8}$$

with J_i of the exact condition and $A(\alpha)$ of the approximate. In almost every investigated real-world model it has been found, however, that the approximate criterion can serve both both as a necessary and as a sufficient condition.

8. On the Significance of the *B* Matrix for the Convergence Analysis

The mathematical expressions involved in the convergence theorems are in most cases difficult to calculate and also difficult to interpret in terms of the parameters of the interdependent system. An exception to this rule is given by the coefficient matrix of the endogenous variables, the B matrix. The B matrix is involved in the convergence analysis and the convergence theorems in several aspects, some of which deserve additional comments:

(i) All of the approximate convergence conditions are based on the B matrix or transformations of the B matrix.

(ii) The B matrix has been used to explain the convergence of the perturbation process $v_t^{(s)}$ of (6.9), thus giving a foundation for the analysis of apparent convergence.

(iii) The B matrix and parameters of the B matrix form an essential part of the exact local convergence conditions in the form given by Table 1. In (6.18) an example is shown where the convergence condition is expressed exclusively with the use of the parameters of the B matrix.

(iv) The decomposition of the B matrix, introduced in (4.7), has an exact analogy in the decomposition (5.11) of the Jacobian J_1 of the exact local convergence condition of the RFP method. Introducing a position matrix $P(b)$ of the B matrix as

$$\begin{aligned} P(b)_{ij} &= 1, \quad b_{ij} \neq 0 \quad \textit{a priori}, \\ &= 0, \quad \text{otherwise}, \end{aligned}$$

it can be found that the $P(b)$ matrix serves as a position matrix for zero and non-zero submatrices of the J_1 matrix; see Bodin (1974).

9. Convergence to Multiple Parameter Sets

The defining nonlinear system of the GEID estimator may possess multiple solutions, the estimation problem thus giving rise to multiple parameter sets. In an extensive investigation of the simulated models of the Mosbaek and Wold et al. (1970) study, Bodin (1974) showed that multiple parameter sets did not exist in any of the investigated models. By changing the sample size to extremely small values or by using new generating designs based on Lyttkens' original examples where multiple solutions were first found, cases of multiple parameter sets could be investigated with respect to the convergence analysis.

The general results of this analysis indicate that the local convergence theorems can be applied on each one of the multiple parameter sets. In this way it is possible to obtain a theoretical basis for the convergence evaluations. Actual estimations have shown that convergence can be obtained to different parameter sets for (i) different start values, (ii) different values of the relaxation parameter α of the FFP, RFP and SFP algorithms. For the RFP method changes in the order in which the relations are processed may lead to convergence to different parameter sets.

Cases have been found where apparent convergence has been obtained to one parameter set whereas continued iterations lead to true convergence to another parameter set. In this way the iterative method in one and the same estimation results in two (or more) parameter sets. A principal illustration of the iterative behaviour in such a case is given by Figure 3.

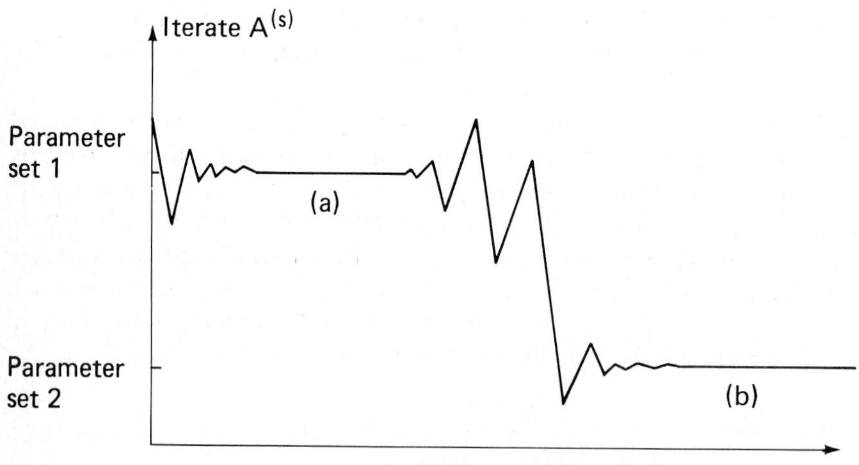

FIGURE 3. Illustration of (a) apparent convergence to parameter set 1 and (b) true convergence to parameter set 2.

The summarizing results on multiple parameter sets show that they seem to occur very seldom. For those cases where they exist the Fix-Point algorithms can be applied with an expected iterative performance about equivalent to that obtained for unique parameter sets. One new feature concerns the possibility of detecting new parameter sets through reestimations using different designs of the iterative computations.

10. Applications

The preceding sections have focussed on a general description of the Fix-Point algorithms, their designs and the foundation for the convergence analysis. The concluding section of this chapter is devoted to comparisons of the iterative performance of the different algorithms. Illustrations will be taken both from mathematical analysis and from estimations of a number of interdependent systems used in applied econometric work.

10.1. The One-Loop Model

One class of models much used in the evaluation of the Fix-Point methods is labelled by Mosbaek and Wold et al. (1970) as the one-loop model. In this class of models the number of equations is unspecified but there are two current endogenous variables per equation. The number of predetermined variables can be specified in various ways. The design of the one-loop model used here is the following:

$$y_1 = b_{12} y_2 + g_{11} z_1 + d_1, \qquad (10.1)$$

$$y_2 = b_{23} y_3 + g_{22} z_2 + d_2, \qquad (10.2)$$

$$\vdots \quad \vdots \quad \vdots \quad \vdots$$

$$y_n = b_{n1} y_1 + g_{nn} z_n + d_n. \qquad (10.3)$$

In our analysis different assumptions concerning the number of identities, q, were employed. In general q is allowed to vary in the interval $0 \leq q \leq n-1$.

One feature of the one-loop model that is characteristic for many large econometric models is the sparse B matrix of the system. On the other hand the one-loop model shows an unbroken direct causal loop between all the endogenous variables

$$\circlearrowright y_1 \rightarrow y_n \rightarrow y_{n-1} \rightarrow \cdots \rightarrow y_2 \circlearrowleft, \qquad (10.4)$$

a property which seldom is found in applied models.

The one-loop model will now be analysed with respect to the approximate convergence conditions of (7.1), (7.3) and (7.4).[5] Two different aspects of the convergence analysis will be particularly evaluated, that is, the importance of using the optimal ordering vector when applying the RFP method and the impact of the different number of identities of the model for the convergence of SFP.

The characteristic equations of the matrices $K(\alpha)$, $L(\alpha, v)$, $R(\alpha)$ read

$$(\lambda + \alpha - 1)^n - \alpha^n P = 0, \tag{10.5}$$

$$(\lambda + \alpha - 1)^n - \alpha^n \lambda^{n-v} P = 0, \qquad v = 1, \cdots, n-1, \tag{10.6}$$

$$(\lambda + \alpha - 1)^q \left[(\lambda + \alpha - 1)^{n-q} - (\lambda - 1)^{n-q} P\right] = 0, \qquad q = 0, \cdots, n-1, \tag{10.7}$$

respectively, with

$$P = \prod_{ij} b_{ij}, \tag{10.8}$$

The equation $|K(\alpha) - \lambda I| = 0$ is not influenced by the number of identities or the order in which the relations are estimated.

The equation $|L(\alpha, v) - \lambda I| = 0$ is not influenced by the number of identities but is influenced by the ordering in which the relations are estimated. In the equation (10.6) v denotes the impact of different orderings. It has been shown that one optimal ordering vector of this model is

$$(n, n-1, \cdots, 2, 1) \tag{10.9}$$

For all optimal orderings of the one-loop model the number of non-zero parameters above the main diagonal of B is equal to one. These orderings are obtained for $v = n - 1$ in the equation (10.6).

The equation $|R(\alpha) - \lambda I| = 0$ is not influenced by the ordering in which the relations are estimated but it is influenced by the number of identities, q, of the model.

The first investigation of (10.5)–(10.7) concerns the case $q = 0$, that is, the case with no identities. It was demonstrated by Bodin (1973a) that for the ranges of P given in Table 2 the roots of (10.5)–(10.7) are all less than unity in absolute value. In Table 2 only the optimal ordering is analysed, that is, $L(\alpha, n-1)$ is analysed. We notice that the convergence region for $L(\alpha, n-1)$ is much larger than that of $K(\alpha)$ and $R(\alpha)$. In the same analysis it has been shown that

[5] In Bodin (1974) it is shown that the main results of the analysis of the approximate convergence criteria are valid in the application of the exact convergence theorems on the one-loop model.

TABLE 2
Convergence regions, expressed in $P = \prod b_{ij}$, for different values of n, the number of relations of the one-loop model.

Matrix	$3 \leq n < \infty$	Limit value, $n \to \infty$
$K(1.0)$	$-1 < P < 1$	$-1 < P < 1$
$R(1.0)$	$-(\frac{1}{2})^n (\cos^n \pi/n)^{-1} < P < (\frac{1}{2})^n$	$P = 0$
$K(\alpha)$, $R(\alpha)$	$-(\cos^n \pi/n)^{-1} < P < 1$	$-1 < P < 1$
$L(\alpha, n-1)$	$-n^n (n-2)^{-n} < P < 1$	$-e^2 < P < 1$

$$\rho(L(\alpha_{opt}, n-1)) < \rho(K(\alpha_{opt})) = \rho(R(\alpha_{opt})), \tag{10.10}$$

and

$$\begin{aligned} \lim_{n\to\infty} \alpha_{opt} &= 1, \quad \text{for } K(\alpha) \text{ and } L(\alpha, n-1), \\ &= 0, \quad \text{for } R(\alpha), \end{aligned} \tag{10.11}$$

In this analysis the $L(\alpha, n-1)$ matrix shows convergence properties that are superior to those of $K(\alpha)$ and $R(\alpha)$. Analysis of the exact local convergence criterion for the FFP, RFP and SFP methods and actual estimations firmly indicate that for the one-loop model, with no identities, application of RFP with optimal ordering is the optimal Fix-Point estimation. Analysis of RFP applied with the natural ordering of the model (10.1)–(10.3), that is the ordering vector (5.15), indicates convergence properties that are only slightly better than those of FFP and SFP.

The second investigation concerns an analysis of the impact of an increasing number of identities in the model. The analysis will be restricted to the case where $\alpha = 1.0$, but $L(1.0, v)$ will be analysed for $1 \leq v \leq n-1$.

The three characteristic equations (10.5)–(10.7) will now read

$$\lambda^n - P = 0, \tag{10.12}$$

$$\lambda^v - P = 0, \qquad v = 1, 2, \cdots, n-1, \tag{10.13}$$

$$\lambda^{n-q} - (\lambda - 1)^{n-1} P = 0, \qquad q = 0, 1, \cdots, n-1. \tag{10.14}$$

for the matrices $K(1.0)$, $L(1.0, v)$ and $R(1.0)$, respectively.

By defining a transformation

$$z = \lambda/(\lambda - 1), \tag{10.15}$$

(10.14) can be rewritten as

$$z^{n-q} - P = 0, \qquad q = 0, 1, \cdots, n-1. \tag{10.16}$$

As a result the following relations between $\rho(R(1.0))$, $\rho(K(1.0))$ and $\rho(L(1.0, v))$ can be established:

$$\rho(R(1.0)) = |\rho(K(1.0))/(\rho(K(1.0)) - 1)|, \qquad q = 0, \tag{10.17}$$

$$= |\rho(L(1.0, v))/(\rho(L(1.0, v)) - 1)|, \qquad q = v = 1, \cdots, n-1. \tag{10.18}$$

It follows that $\min \rho(R(1.0))$ is obtained for $q = n - 1$, that is, the maximum number of identities specified for this class of models.

Based on the results of this analysis we conjecture that SFP will perform better in the models with relatively many identities than in those models where the number of the behavioural relations is relatively large.

10.2. *The Klein Model I*

The interdependent system formulated by Klein (1950) as a model of the U.S. economy 1921–41 has been much used in the analysis of different econometric techniques. The model is here referred to as the Klein I model and is analysed in the slight modification of the original form given by Ăgren (1972a). The B matrix of the system is

$$B = \begin{bmatrix} 0 & 0 & 0 & 0 & b_{15} & 0 & b_{17} & 0 \\ 0 & 0 & 0 & 0 & b_{25} & 0 & 0 & 0 \\ 0 & 0 & 0 & 0 & 0 & 0 & 0 & b_{38} \\ 1 & 1 & 0 & 0 & 0 & 0 & 0 & 0 \\ 0 & 0 & -1 & 1 & 0 & 0 & 0 & 0 \\ 0 & 1 & 0 & 0 & 0 & 0 & 0 & 0 \\ 0 & 0 & 1 & 1 & 0 & 0 & 0 & 0 \\ 0 & 0 & 0 & 1 & 0 & 0 & 0 & 0 \end{bmatrix}. \tag{10.19}$$

In this section the approximate convergence criteria are applied on this matrix.

Two different ordering vectors will be used, the original ordering vector (5.15) and an anticipated optimal ordering vector,[6]

$$(8, 3, 5, 2, 7, 1, 4, 6). \tag{10.20}$$

The two orderings will be referred to as original and optimal orderings, respectively.

[6]The ordering is produced by the computer routine available for selecting orderings with optimal convergence properties, cf. footnote 4 and Chapter 8 of this monograph.

With the introduction of the two expressions

$$c_1 = b_{15} + b_{25}, \tag{10.21}$$

$$c_2 = b_{15}\,b_{38} + b_{25}\,b_{38} - b_{17}\,b_{38}, \tag{10.22}$$

the characteristic equations for $K(1.0)$, $L(1.0, \text{original})$, $L(1.0, \text{optimal})$ and $R(1.0)$ are

$$\lambda^5 - c_1\lambda^2 + c_2 = 0, \tag{10.23}$$

$$\lambda^2 - c_1\lambda + c_2 = 0, \tag{10.24}$$

$$\lambda - c_1 + c_2 = 0, \tag{10.25}$$

$$\lambda^2 + (1-\lambda)c_1 + (1-\lambda)^2 c_2 = 0, \tag{10.26}$$

respectively.

Using the transformation (10.15), equation (10.26) can be rewritten as

$$z^2 - c_1 z + c_2 = 0, \tag{10.27}$$

and the analogy with (10.24) is established. For the spectral radii of $R(1.0)$ and $L(1.0, \text{original})$, we obtain

$$\rho(R(1.0)) = |\rho(L(1.0, \text{original}))/(\rho(L(1.0, \text{original})) - 1)|. \tag{10.28}$$

In the next step of the analysis the fix-point estimates of B are used to evaluate the optimal value of α and the corresponding spectral radius. For $R(\alpha)$ it has been possible to perform an analytical determination since the characteristic equation of $R(\alpha)$ reads

$$(1-\alpha-\lambda)^6[(1-\alpha-\lambda)^2 - (1-\alpha-\lambda)(1-\lambda)c_1 + (1-\lambda)^2 c_2] = 0. \tag{10.29}$$

For

$$c_3 = 1 - c_1 + c_2, \tag{10.30}$$

we can derive α_{opt} as

$$\alpha_{\text{opt}} = -2c_3/(c_1 - 2) = 0.6513, \tag{10.31}$$

and

$$\rho(R(\alpha_{\text{opt}})) = (c_1^2 - 4c_2)^{1/2} \cdot (2 - c_1)^{-1} = 0.5571. \tag{10.32}$$

For $K(\alpha)$ and $L(\alpha, v)$ a numerical evaluation has been performed. The results are summarized in Table 3.

We thus have

$$\begin{aligned}\rho(L(\alpha_{\text{opt}}, \text{optimal})) &< \rho(L(\alpha_{\text{opt}}, \text{original})) \\ &< \rho(R(\alpha_{\text{opt}})) < \rho(K(\alpha_{\text{opt}})),\end{aligned} \tag{10.33}$$

TABLE 3
Convergence characteristics of $K(\alpha)$, $L(\alpha, v)$ and $R(\alpha)$ for the Klein I model.

Matrix	Optimal α	Spectral radius
$K(1.0)$	1.0	0.8089
$K(\alpha)$	1.014	0.8062
$R(1.0)$	1.0	1.3912
$R(\alpha)$	0.6513	0.5571
$L(1.0$, original)	1.0	0.5818
$L(\alpha_{opt}$, original)	1.024	0.5552
$L(1.0$, optimal)	1.0	0.3847
$L(\alpha_{opt}$, optimal)	1.045	0.1448

that is, the approximate convergence criterion based on the B matrix is in favour of the RFP method.

10.3. Models of National and Regional Economies

Our third study consists of a comparison of the iterative estimation of 8 models. The comparisons consist of an analysis of the approximate convergence criteria and actual estimation results. The models and the basic references are given in Table 4, and in Table 5 some characteristics of the models are given.

The Fix-Point estimations have been carried through using either start values denoted by OLS-start,

$$y_t^{(0)} = y_t, \tag{10.34}$$

or by TSLS-start,

$$y_t^{(0)} = Pz_t. \tag{10.35}$$

TABLE 4
Models and references.

Model	Reference
US I	Christ (1966)
US II (Klein I)	Klein (1950)
Greece	Pavlopoulos (1966)
US III	Klein and Goldberger (1955)
Taiwan	Yu (1970)
Ohio	L'Esperance et al. (1969)
Czechoslovakia	Sujan and Tkáč (1972)
Puerto Rico	Dutta and Su (1969)

TABLE 5
Characteristic features of the models.

Model	Number of Relations	Identities	*B* parameters	Time points
US I	7	4	11	27
US II	8	3	11	21
Greece	17	12	26	11
US III	23	11	34	29
Taiwan	24	18	46	18
Ohio	27	14	39	10
Czechoslovakia	35	17	64	16
Puerto Rico	36	23	61	17

In the convergence test (6.1) we used 10^{-5} or in some cases 10^{-6} as the required accuracy. For every estimation the number of iterations necessary to fulfil the convergence test (*NOIT*) was recorded. As the estimations were repeated with systematic changes in the values of the relaxation parameter α it was possible to determine an optimal value of α for the estimation. In Table 6 this value is denoted a_{opt}. Once the Fix-Point estimates had been obtained they were used in evaluations of the approximate convergence criteria.

Table 6 summarizes the results of the analysis. Some of the results of this table are taken from Bergström (1976) and Bodin (1974). All RFP estimations and analysis are based on the use of an optimal ordering of the investigated model.

One of the main conclusions of the results of Table 6 is the very close correspondence between the approximate convergence criteria, the spectral radii of the $K(\alpha)$, $L(\alpha, v)$ and $R(\alpha)$ matrices, and the actual estimation results. The demonstrated correspondence is also evident in the work by Ågren (1972a), Bodin (1974) and Bergström (1974).

Another main conclusion concerns the ranking of RFP as the fastest iterative method. In seven out of the eight models RFP is faster than the other two methods provided that the evaluation is based on *NOIT*. SFP is the second best method. It has been demonstrated by Bodin (1974) that RFP scores even better if the relaxation parameter α is more accurately specified. Table 7, derived for the Klein model, US II, is an example.

A few computational points will conclude the evaluation of the eight models. The first point concerns the need for computer memory storage during the computations. In the FFP method we need the simultaneous storage of both $y^{(s)}$ and the new iterate $y^{(s+1)}$, whereas this is not the case for RFP and SFP. For SFP we need to reserve memory space for the

TABLE 6
Convergence characteristics for FFP, SFP and RFP in eight models of national and regional economies.

Model	FFP				SFP				RFP			
	α_{opt}	$\rho(K(\alpha))$	a_{opt}	$NOIT$	α_{opt}	$\rho(R(\alpha))$	a_{opt}	$NOIT$	α_{opt}	$\rho(L(\alpha, v))$	a_{opt}	$NOIT$
US I	0.9	0.73	0.9	73	0.7	0.46	0.7	17	1.1	0.22	1.1	19
US II	1.0	0.81	1.0	61	0.6	0.59	0.6	27	1.1	0.29	1.0	15
Greece	0.9	0.84	0.9	76	1.0	0.46	1.0	21	1.0	0.21	0.9	17
US III	0.9	0.67	0.8	43	0.9	0.34	0.9	14	1.0	0.17	1.0	12
Taiwan	0.7	0.67	0.8	37	0.8	0.43	0.9	16	1.0	0.09	1.0	9
Ohio	0.9	0.83	0.9	66	0.7	0.56	0.7	23	1.0	0.23	1.0	11
Czechoslovakia	1.0	0.82	1.0	101	0.6	0.62	0.6	25	1.0	0.36	1.0	16
Puerto Rico	0.8	0.88	0.8	152	0.4	0.73	0.6	45	1.0	0.46	1.0	31

TABLE 7
Optimal α and spectral radius for different accuracy in α for the US II model.

	Accuracy of $\alpha = 0.1$		Accuracy of $\alpha = 0.001$	
Matrix	α	$\rho(A(\alpha))$	α	$\rho(A(\alpha))$
$K(\alpha)$	1.0	0.8089	1.014	0.8062
$L(\alpha, \text{optimal})$	1.1	0.2943	1.045	0.1448
$R(\alpha)$	0.6	0.5919	0.651	0.5571

(repeated) calculation of the inverse of the $(I - B)$ matrix, whereas this is not needed for FFP and RFP.

The inversion of $(I - B)$ is one factor which disfavours the SFP method if the iterative performance is based on comparison of required central processor time. For the estimation of the Klein–Goldberger model of the US economy, the US III model of Tables 4–6, a complete RFP estimation was carried through in 4 seconds on the IBM 370/155 of the University Computer Center, Uppsala, the FFP estimation in 16 seconds and the SFP estimation in 27 seconds. Thus the ranking between FFP and SFP is reversed if we base the comparison on time rather than number of iterations.

The RFP method, based on the Gauss–Seidel principle, constitutes a simple and straightforward iterative technique that is easy to adapt to different models. The good results obtained with this method are similar to the results reported in the analysis of the Brookings model where Gauss–Seidel programming has been developed for dynamic simulation of nonlinear econometric models; see Klein (1975). The Gauss–Seidel principle is described by Fromm and Klein (1969) as "extremely fast, simple to understand and easy to program". The same conclusion can be emphasized with respect to Recursive Fix-Point estimation of reformulated interdependent systems.

Chapter 3

THE GEID SPECIFICATION

An Interpretation and Some of its Consequences

ANDERS ÅGREN

1. Introduction and Summary

The specification of a linear interdependent system usually involves the assumption that the disturbances are uncorrelated with the predetermined variables. The GEID specification proposed by Wold (1965, 1966) relaxes this assumption considerably by allowing the disturbance of any structural equation to be correlated with the predetermined variables that occur in other structural equations. The GEID specification is based on the REID specification, the latter being a reformulation of a classically specified system. In Section 2 the REID and GEID specifications are reinterpreted, and some implications are discussed of the interpretation adopted.

The traditional estimators (e.g. 2SLS, 3SLS, LIML, etc.) are all consistent when applied to REID systems but inconsistent when applied to GEID systems, a consequence of the correlations that may exist between the disturbances and the predetermined variables. Wold's Fix-Point (FP) method, however, yields consistent estimates for REID as well as for GEID systems; Wold (1965). Instead of defining this estimator as the operative result of an iterative procedure which might not converge, Ågren (1972a) proposes the GEID estimator. This is defined as the solution of a system of equations, and when the FP method converges, it converges to a solution of this system. In Section 3 the GEID estimator is presented and it is shown that under a normality assumption the maximum-likelihood estimator and the GEID estimator coincide for GEID specified systems. This simplifies the discussion of the asymptotic properties of the GEID estimator when applied to GEID systems.

In the final section the possibility of testing whether a system should be REID- or GEID-specified is discussed. Since the REID system is obtained by putting restrictions on certain parameters of a GEID system, the likelihood ratio test is considered. We also consider the question whether two GEID systems, based on the same set of endogenous and predetermined variables can be discriminated by using the likelihood. In the latter case the likelihoods will be the same and cannot be used to separate between structures that differ in the positions of the ensuing parameters. Another approach to overcome the difficulties with the choice of a GEID-structure is based on the sum of squares of the residuals, the R^2-criterion. However, the distributional properties of this criterion have not been investigated.

2. Specification of the Model

2.1. REID Systems

We consider the model as defined by the equations in Chapter 1. Of specific relevance for this section are the following implications of the REID specification:

(i) The disturbances δ_{it} and ε_{jt} are uncorrelated with the predetermined variables z_{kt}, all i, j, k, t.

(ii) The structural form is an unbiased predictor, i.e.,

$$E(Y_{it} \mid \eta^*_{(i)t}, Z_{(i)t}) = \beta_{(i)}\eta^*_{(i)t} + \gamma_{(i)}Z_{(i)t}. \tag{2.1}$$

(iii) The systematic part of the restricted and unrestricted reduced forms coincide, i.e.,

$$E(Y_t \mid Z_t) = (I - \beta)^{-1}\Gamma Z_t = \Omega Z_t. \tag{2.2}$$

2.2. GEID Systems

In his seminal paper on the Fix-Point method, Wold proposes a generalized specification of an ID system. After the reformulation of the SF as shown in the previous sub-section, Wold assumes that ε_{it} is uncorrelated with those components of η^*_t and z_t which occur in the right-hand side of the ith equation. This specification is somewhat modified in Wold (1966) and in Ågren and Wold (1969), where it is assumed that

$$Y_{it} = \beta_{(i)}\eta^*_{(i)t} + \gamma_{(i)}Z_{(i)t} + \varepsilon_{it}, \tag{2.3a}$$

with

$$i = 1, \cdots, n.$$

$$E(Y_{it} \mid \eta^*_{(i)t}, Z_{(i)t}) = \beta_{(i)}\eta^*_{(i)t} + \gamma_{(i)}Z_{(i)t}, \tag{2.3b}$$

The GEID specification is here defined as the reformulated system (2.3a) together with the predictor specification (2.3b). The difference between the REID and GEID specifications lies in the assumptions implied by (2.3b) and the corresponding assumption for a REID system. In a REID system the disturbances ε_{it} are all uncorrelated with the components of z_t, whereas (2.3b) only implies that ε_{it} is uncorrelated with the components of $\eta^*_{(i)t}$ and $z_{(i)t}$. It has been pointed out by Wold (1969a) that the GEID specification fulfills the parity principle since the number of zero correlations implied by (2.3b) equals the number of unknown parameters in β and Γ.

We have earlier stated that the RRF and the URF coincide for REID systems. For GEID systems this is in general not the case. Consider the regression of y_t on z_t which may be written as

$$E(Y_t \mid Z_t) = \Omega Z_t + E(\varepsilon_t \mid Z_t). \tag{2.4}$$

Since ε_t may be correlated with z_t in a GEID system, the last term in general is not equal to zero. We shall restrict our analysis to ID systems that are subject to the additional linearity assumptions that

$$E(\varepsilon_t \mid Z_t) = \Lambda Z_t \quad \text{or} \quad \varepsilon_t = \Lambda Z_t + u_t, \tag{2.5}$$

where Λ is a matrix of order $n \times m$. Defining $\Pi = \Lambda + \Omega$, we obtain the URF

$$Y_t = \Pi Z_t + u_t, \tag{2.6}$$

which is different from the RRF whenever a non-zero element occurs in Λ.

Next we show that the structural form can be obtained as a reformulation of the URF; cf. Lyttkens (1970d). Using (2.3a) and (2.5) the structural form may be written as

$$Y_{it} = \beta_{(i)}\eta^*_{(i)t} + \gamma_{(i)}Z_{(i)t} + \lambda_i Z_t + u_{it}, \qquad i = 1, \cdots, n, \tag{2.7}$$

where λ_i denotes the ith row of Λ. It follows from (2.3b) that the covariance between the linear expression $\lambda_i z_t$ in z_t and any component of $\eta^*_{(i)t}$ or $z_{(i)t}$ is zero. In general this implies that there are $m_i + n_i$ linear restrictions on the coefficient vector λ_i. Hence (2.7) may be transformed as follows (by eliminating $m_i + n_i$ coefficients in λ_i):

$$Y_{it} = \beta_{(i)}\eta^*_{(i)t} + \gamma_{(i)}Z_{(i)t} + \alpha_i\varphi_{it} + u_{it}, \qquad i = 1, \cdots, n. \tag{2.8}$$

Here α_i consists of the $m - (m_i + n_i)$ coefficients remaining in λ_i, and φ_{it}

consists of $m-(m_i+n_i)$ linear functions of the predetermined variables whose coefficients in general are non-linear expressions of the elements of β and Γ. Hence (2.8) may be written as

$$Y_{it}=\sum_{j=1}^{m}\Pi_{ij}(\beta,\Gamma,\alpha_i)Z_{jt}+u_{it},\qquad i=1,\cdots,n. \tag{2.9}$$

The functions $\Pi_{ij}(\beta,\Gamma,\alpha_i)$ are identical to the URF parameters Π_{ij}. We observe that the number of URF parameters equals the total number of SF parameters. Under general conditions of regularity on the functions relating $\Pi^*=(\Pi_{11},\cdots,\Pi_{nm})$ to the vector of $\theta=(\beta_{(1)},\gamma_{(1)},\alpha_1,\cdots,\beta_{(n)},\gamma_{(n)},\alpha_n)$, we may solve for θ to obtain

$$\theta=f(\Pi^*). \tag{2.10}$$

However, due to nonlinearities in the function $\Pi_{ij}(\beta,\Gamma,\alpha_i)$, the solution set in (2.10) may not be unique; Lyttkens (1970d). This multiplicity is a difficulty connected with the GEID specification. Conditions under which unique solutions are obtained have only been studied under very restrictive assumptions on the size of the system; see Bodin (1974), Lyttkens (Chapter 4) and May (Chapter 11).

Comment: Equation (2.10) can be derived under two different assumptions, namely (i) assuming that the population moments of the second order are given, or (ii) assuming that the sample moments of the second order are given.

In Section 3 where estimation is discussed it is assumed that the functions relating θ and Π^* are based on the sample moments.

From a practical point of view the REID specification may be motivated for an ID system which is based on a well-established theory whereas the GEID specification should possibly be applicable when the model is of a more tentative character. This viewpoint suggests that one allows some relations of the model to be REID-specified, whereas the other relations are GEID-specified. The disturbance term in a REID relation catches up purely random effects which can be regarded as uncorrelated (or independent) with all the predetermined variables but in a GEID relation the disturbance consists of purely random effects together with the effects of left-out variables which motivates the correlations with variables in the other relations. The left-out variables may or may not be included in the ID system as a whole.

Another interpretation of GEID and REID systems is made by Wold (see Chapter 1) by means of the concepts of open and closed systems.

According to this interpretation the correlations between disturbances and the predetermined variables are caused by variables which have not been included in the system as a whole, i.e., a system which is open to effects not taken care of inside the system. A REID system is closed, i.e., not affected by external variables.

2.3. *Autocorrelation in GEID Systems*

It has been shown by Bodin (1974) that the occurrence of lagged endogenous variables or autocorrelated exogenous variables among the predetermined variables in GEID systems usually introduces autocorrelation in ε_t. For use in the next section where the estimation of GEID systems is considered we introduce the following distinction:

Definition: With reference to the decomposition of ε_t in (2.5b), $\varepsilon_t = \Lambda Z_t + u_t$, autocorrelation in ε_t is said to be of *closed-system type* if u_t is autocorrelated and *open-system type* otherwise.

3. The GEID Estimator

3.1. *Definition of the GEID Estimator*

Since the disturbances in a GEID-specified system may be correlated with the predetermined variables or with certain linear expressions in the predetermined variables all the usually employed estimators yield inconsistent parameter estimates on such systems. (One exception is the maximum likelihood method; see later in this section.) This feature was stressed by Wold when introducing the Fix-Point method, an iterative method which in the case of convergence yields consistent estimates; Wold (1965). However, there is no guarantee for convergence and due to the nonlinearity in a GEID system different start values may lead to different estimates. This makes it inconvenient to define an estimator as the operative result of this iterative procedure, and motivated the suggestion of the GEID estimator; Ågren (1972a).

Again with reference to the introductory chapter the GEID estimator is given by the following definition.

Definition: The *GEID estimator* is defined as the real solutions (if any) of the following set of equations:

$$y_i y^{*\prime}_{(i)} = b_{(i)} y^*_{(i)} y^{*\prime}_{(i)} + g_{(i)} z_{(i)} y^{*\prime}_{(i)},$$
$$y_i z'_{(i)} = b_{(i)} y^*_{(i)} z'_{(i)} + g_{(i)} z_{(i)} z'_{(i)}, \qquad i = 1, \cdots, n, \tag{3.1}$$
$$y^*_i = b_{(i)} y^*_{(i)} + g_{(i)} z_{(i)},$$

such that $I - B$ is non-singular.

The extension of this definition to the case with models including identities is straight forward and has been given by Bodin (1974). The extension to nonlinear ID systems has been performed by Edgerton (1973c, and Chapter 9).

3.2. On the Properties of the GEID Estimator

The asymptotic properties of the GEID estimator have been studied by Ågren (1972a, 1975) and Edgerton (1973c, and Chapter 9). Ågren has shown that the GEID estimator is consistent and asymptotically normally distributed. Edgerton has generalized these results to nonlinear ID systems for which he has suggested a modified version of the GEID estimator.

The GEID estimator is applicable both to REID and GEID systems. For GEID systems we show that this estimator is the same as the maximum likelihood estimator under the appropriate normality assumptions. We have shown in Section 2 that the SF parameters can be expressed as nonlinear functions of the URF parameters.

We shall now show that the same functions relate the GEID estimator of the SF parameters to the OLS estimator of the URF parameters. The OLS estimator, $\hat{\Pi}_i$, of the ith row of Π is given by

$$\hat{\Pi}_i = y_i z'(zz')^{-1}, \qquad i = 1, \cdots, n. \tag{3.2}$$

Let us next consider the estimator of the SF parameters obtained by multiplying each term in (2.8) by z'_t and adding over t,

$$\sum_{t=1}^{T} y_{it} z'_t = b_{(i)} \sum_{t=1}^{T} y^*_{(i)t} z'_t + g_{(i)} \sum_{t=1}^{T} z_{(i)t} z'_t + a_i \sum_{t=1}^{T} \hat{\varphi}_{it} z'_t, \qquad i = 1, \cdots, n, \tag{3.3}$$

where we have put $u_{it} z'_t = 0$. By using (2.9) an equivalent form of the above equation is given by

$$\sum_{t=1}^{T} y_{it} z'_t = \sum_{j=1}^{m} \Pi_{ij}(B, G, a_i) \sum_{t=1}^{T} z_{jt} z'_t, \qquad i = 1, \cdots, n. \tag{3.4}$$

According to (3.3) and (3.4) the SF estimator given by the former equation, i.e., $\hat{\theta}$ is related to the OLS estimator of Π, i.e., $\hat{\Pi}$ exactly as the relation between the corresponding population parameters, i.e., as [cf. (2.10)]

$$\hat{\theta} = f(\hat{\Pi}^*). \tag{3.5}$$

Since $\hat{\varphi}_{it}$ is constructed to be uncorrelated with $y_{(i)t}$ and $z_{(i)t}$ it follows from (3.3) that any solution $\hat{\theta}$ also satisfies (3.1), which is the definition of the GEID estimator. Hence $\hat{\theta}$ is the GEID estimator. An immediate implication of this result is formulated in the following theorem, where we also have used a result by Zellner (1962) which states that under normality assumptions the maximum likelihood estimator of the URF coefficients equals the OLS estimator of these coefficients:

Theorem 1: If u_t is multivariate normal with expectation zero and with a non-singular covariance matrix Σ_u which is independent of t and if u_t is serially independent and independent of the predetermined variables, then for GEID systems the GEID estimator and the maximum likelihood estimator are both given by (3.5).

Comment 1: Theorem 1 is not valid in the case of a REID system. For such systems $\alpha_i = 0$ [see (2.8)] and the relation between θ and Π^* in (2.10) is not fulfilled. The GEID estimator is still given by (3.5) but not the maximum likelihood estimator.

Comment 2: A result similar to Theorem 1 has been given by Lyttkens (1970d) but under more restrictive assumptions.

Provided the functions relating the GEID estimator to the OLS estimator of the URF parameters fulfil general regularity conditions [see Wilks (1962, p. 103)] the consistency of the GEID estimator is an immediate consequence of Theorem 1 and the consistency of the OLS estimator of the URF parameters. Sufficient conditions for the consistency of the OLS estimator are given by Wold (1963a), the fundamental assumption being the asymptotic zero correlation between the disturbances u_i and the predetermined variables and that the sample moments tend in probability to the corresponding population moments; see also Christ (1966).

Remembering that $\varepsilon_t = \Lambda z_t + u_t$, we may have autocorrelation in ε_t of closed-system type and some components of z_t may be lagged endogenous variables and still the GEID estimator is consistent. This suggests that for GEID systems, tests for autocorrelation should be performed on the residuals obtained in the URF and not on those obtained from the structural form since in the latter case a significant value of the test statistic can be caused by autocorrelation of the closed-system type, i.e., due to Λz_t.

Provided the functions relating the GEID estimator to the OLS estimator of the URF parameters fulfil general regularity conditions, asymptotic normality of the GEID estimator can be established from the asymptotic normality of the OLS estimator. Sufficient conditions for this are given by Durbin (1960). Durbin's model allows for lagged endogenous variables among the predetermined variables and does not assume that u_t is normally distributed. If u_t is normally distributed and if the system is GEID-specified then the GEID estimator is asymptotically efficient.

3.3. *On the Computation of the GEID Estimator*

The GEID estimator is defined by a system of equations which is nonlinear in the unknown parameters. This system usually can not be solved algebraically. Exceptions occur for very special cases, e.g. when the model is small and many relations are just-identified; see Lyttkens (1970a, b) and Bodin (1974), and also Chapter 4 in this volume. The basic numerical method that has been used to find the GEID estimator is Wold's (1965) iterative Fix-Point method. In principle this approach works with two phases in each iteration step: a least-squares step and a step including the calculation of new proxies of y^*. This approach is computationally much simpler than more common methods to solve nonlinear algebraic equations such as those based on Newton's method. A comparison between such methods and the FP methods has not been performed. In a large Monte Carlo study by Mosbaek and Wold et al. (1970) of the properties of this method it was found that convergence was difficult to obtain for certain models. This gave rise to several modifications of the FP method, e.g. the Fractional FP method by Ågren (1972a) and the Recursive FP method by Bodin (1974).

4. On the Choice of GEID Structure

In the final stage of the process of model construction we often have definite sets of endogenous variables y_t and predetermined variables z_t but the particular model relating these has not been chosen. Let us assume that the following two models (M_1 and M_2) are given:

$$y_t = \beta_i \eta_t^{*(i)} + \Gamma_i z_t + \varepsilon_t^{(i)}, \qquad i = 1, 2, \tag{4.1}$$

with

$$\varepsilon_t^{(i)} = \Lambda_i z_t + u_t^{(i)}. \tag{4.2}$$

It is further assumed that the coefficient matrices are of the same orders in M_1 and M_2, but they differ in the positions (and possibly the number) of the non-zero elements. Furthermore the conditional distributions of $\varepsilon_t^{(1)}$ and $\varepsilon_t^{(2)}$ given z_t are different but the URF disturbances $u_t^{(1)}$ and $u_t^{(2)}$ are identically distributed.

We consider two approaches to the selection of model in this situation. Since the GEID estimator is based on the least-squares criterion a natural approach is to use the sum of squares of the estimated residuals as a basis for the choice of model, the *R^2-Criterion.* Under the assumption of normality of the URF disturbances another approach can be based on the *Likelihood Criterion.*

4.1. The R^2-Criterion

The R^2-criterion is based on the total sum of the R_i^2-values calculated for all the behavioural relations in the model. It has been suggested by Edgerton (1973c) as a criterion to be used in the case of multiple solutions to select that solution which corresponds to a REID system. The extension of this criterion to the case of multiple structures is immediate although it means that one is especially interested in structures which are close to REID structures.

4.2. The Likelihood Criterion

Let us assume that the URF disturbances are normally distributed. Since the URF disturbances of both models are identical it follows [cf. (2.9)] that both models give rise to the same likelihood in the maximum likelihood solution. Thus this criterion cannot be used as a basis for the choice of model. We obtain the following theorem:

Theorem 2: Different GEID structures estimated by the maximum likelihood method yield the same likelihood as long as the same set of endogenous and predetermined variables enter both structures.

Comment 1: This theorem is a generalization of a result by Lyttkens (1970d) that multiple solutions for the same structure have the same likelihood.

Comment 2: The result may seem surprising but can be easily realized since if we start by a given structure and put one extra restriction on one parameter, say $\beta_{ij} = 0$, then one extra element is added to the vector α_i, i.e., for each extra restriction which is put on any element in β_i or Γ_i, one extra free parameter is added to Λ_i. With our interpretation all GEID systems can be considered as just-identified systems, or possibly underidentified remembering that the nonlinearity of f in (3.5) sometimes gives rise to multiple solutions.

4.3. *Tests for REID versus GEID Systems*

Let us consider structure M_1 again and ask whether it is possible to test if it should be REID- or GEID-specified. Our null hypothesis (H_0) is that it is REID-specified, i.e., that $\Lambda_1 = 0$ and the alternative hypothesis (H_A) is that it is GEID-specified, i.e., that $\Lambda_1 \neq 0$. We can use a likelihood-ratio test in this situation. There is however a special difficulty with this test, since it is sensitive not only to a non-zero Λ_1 but also to alternative structures of β and Γ, e.g. if M_2 were in fact the correct structure with $\Lambda_2 = 0$ we could still obtain a significant value. Then we would accept M_1 as a GEID system when instead M_2 as a REID system would be the true model.

In summary, in practice it seems to be impossible to test whether a system should be specified according to the REID or GEID specification by using the likelihood-ratio criterion since the true structure of β and Γ can never be assumed to be known. In conclusion the choice must be based on other considerations.

4.4. *An Illustration*

Consider the following two models.

Model M_1:

$$\begin{aligned} y_{1t} &= \beta_{12}\eta^*_{2t} + \gamma_{11}z_{1t} + \gamma_{12}z_{2t} + \varepsilon_{1t}, \\ y_{2t} &= \gamma_{23}z_{3t} + \gamma_{24}z_{4t} + \varepsilon_{2t}; \end{aligned} \tag{4.3}$$

Model M_2:

$$\begin{aligned} y_{1t} &= \qquad \gamma_{11}z_{1t} + \gamma_{12}z_{2t} + \varepsilon_{1t}, \\ y_{2t} &= \qquad \gamma_{23}z_{3t} + \gamma_{24}z_{4t} + \varepsilon_{2t}. \end{aligned} \tag{4.4}$$

According to (2.8) the above models may both be rewritten and we obtain

Model M_1:

$$\begin{aligned} y_{1t} &= \beta_{12}\eta^*_{2t} + \gamma_{11}z_{1t} + \gamma_{12}z_{2t} + \alpha_{11}\varphi_{11,t} + u_{1t}, \\ y_{2t} &= \qquad \gamma_{23}z_{3t} + \gamma_{24}z_{4t} + \alpha_{21}\varphi_{21,t} + \alpha_{22}\varphi_{22t} + u_{2t}; \end{aligned} \tag{4.5}$$

Model M_2:

$$\begin{aligned} y_{1t} &= \qquad \gamma_{11}z_{1t} + \gamma_{12}z_{2t} + \alpha_{11}\varphi_{11,t} + \alpha_{12}\varphi_{12,t} + u_{1t}, \\ y_{2t} &= \qquad \gamma_{23}z_{3t} + \gamma_{24}z_{4t} + \alpha_{21}\varphi_{21,t} + \alpha_{22}\varphi_{22,t} + u_{2t}. \end{aligned} \tag{4.6}$$

Both models have the same URF, namely

$$\begin{aligned} y_{1t} &= \Pi_{11}z_{1t} + \Pi_{12}z_{2t} + \Pi_{13}z_{3t} + \Pi_{14}z_{4t} + u_{1t}, \\ y_{2t} &= \Pi_{21}z_{1t} + \Pi_{22}z_{2t} + \Pi_{23}z_{3t} + \Pi_{24}z_{4t} + u_{2t}, \end{aligned} \tag{4.7}$$

and according to (2.9) this can be regarded as a reformulation of (4.5) as well as of (4.6). This implies that the likelihood function for model M_1 will have the same maximum value as for model M_2. What happens is that the removal of one parameter β_{12} from the first equation in model M_1 adds a new parameter $\alpha_{12}\varphi_{12,t}$ to the first equation of model M_2. Hence the choice of model can not be based on the likelihood function in this case.

Note: Theorem 1 on the equivalence of the GEID and ML estimators assumes that all GEID correlations are free, i.e., none is prescribed to be zero. Using the FP method one can estimate all GEID correlations. By putting zero restrictions on the "small" GEID correlations one could, in a second step, possibly gain in efficiency by using the ML method on the system.

Chapter 4

THE PARAMETRIC FIX-POINT (PFP) AND THE ALGEBRAIC FIX-POINT (AFP) METHODS

EJNAR LYTTKENS

1. The Parametric Fix-Point (PFP) Method as Applied to Systems without Identities

1.1. The Explicit Use of the Reduced Form Parameters

1.1.1. The initial approximation. The systematic part η_{it}^*, which enters the reformulated or respecified structural form (I.1.17b),[1] is a linear combination of $z_{1t}, \cdots, z_{mt}$ as seen from formula (I.1.18b). This property persists for the estimate y_{it}^*. Here this condition will be imposed already on the starting value, so that $y_{it}^{(0)} = w_i^{(0)} z_t$, where $w_i^{(0)}$ is a row vector. This condition on the starting values, which was prescribed by Wold (1965, 1966) in his pioneering papers on the Fix-Point method, restricts the choice of starting values only in cases where the sample size T exceeds the number of predetermined variables m. In this chapter it will be assumed that $T > m$. Thus the starting value (I.2.2a) $y_{it}^{(0)} = y_{it}$ is not allowed in the present context, while the starts (I.2.2b–d) fulfill the condition imposed here. Note that the starting value (I.2.2b) $y_{it}^{(0)} = 0$ also in the present context needs the additional condition that $b_{ij}^{(1)} = 0$. Furthermore the starting value (I.2.2c) $y_{it}^{(0)} =$ any z_{jt} requires such a choice that no predetermined variable occurs more than once in any vector $[y_{(i)t}^{(0)\prime}, z_{(i)t}']'$. In the sequel the starting approximation will be written in the following form:

$$y_t^{(0)} = W^{(0)} z_t. \tag{1.1}$$

1.1.2. The step from s to s + 1. Let the sth approximation of y_t^* be written as

$$y_t^{(s)} = W^{(s)} z_t. \tag{1.2}$$

Introducing this expression into relation (I.2.3), we get

[1] Formulae of other chapters will be indicated by Roman numerals; i.e. (I.1.17b) refers to (1.17b) of Chapter 1.

$$y_t = B^{(s+1)}W^{(s)}z_t + G^{(s+1)}z_t + e_t^{(s+1)}. \tag{1.3}$$

With $W^{(s)}$ kept constant, the elements of $B^{(s+1)}$ and $G^{(s+1)}$ which are not prescribed zeros are obtained by applying the least squares method to each of the reformulated or respecified equations in approximation (1.3). By introducing expression (1.2) for $y_t^{(s)}$ and the corresponding expression for $y_t^{(s+1)}$ into formula (I.2.4a) we obtain by the method of equating coefficients,

$$W^{(s+1)} = B^{(s+1)}W^{(s)} + G^{(s+1)}. \tag{1.4}$$

The step from s to $s+1$ involves two semi-steps, namely (i) the least squares method applied to each component of (1.3), and (ii) the calculation of $W^{(s+1)}$ from (1.4). The latter formula is the specific one of the method; Lyttkens (1969a). In order to change as little as possible in the ordinary FP procedure, we can alternatively replace the semi-step (i) by the calculation of $y_t^{(s)}$ from (1.2) and then apply the least squares method to each component of (I.2.3), while the semi-step (ii), the calculation of $W^{(s+1)}$ from (1.4), is left unchanged.

1.1.3. Rounding errors. Apart from the effect of rounding errors the original Fix-Point (FP) method and the Parametric Fix-Point (PFP) method follow each other step by step. More precisely, when the start $y_t^{(0)} = W^{(0)}z_t$ is given, the difference between $y_t^{(s)}$ as obtained by the FP method and $W^{(s)}z_t$ as obtained by the PFP method is due to rounding errors only; Lyttkens (1973b). However, it may happen that the FP method at first approximately follows the PFP method step by step and seems to converge, but finally diverges. This case is investigated by Bodin (1970, 1973b, 1974) who refers to it as apparent convergence.

1.1.4. The Parametric Solved system Fix-Point (PSFP) method. The parametric approach can also be applied to the Solved system Fix-Point (SFP) method. By introducing formula (1.2) as applied to approximation number $s+1$ into formula (I.2.4b), the method of equating coefficients gives the formula

$$W^{(s+1)} = [I - B^{(s+1)}]^{-1}G^{(s+1)}. \tag{1.5}$$

In this case, however, the original formula (I.2.4b) implies that $y_{it}^{(s+1)}$ is a linear combination of $z_{1t}, \cdots, z_{mt}$, irrespective of the starting approximation; hence the start (I.2.2a) $y_{it}^{(0)} = y_{it}$ is also allowed in this case. This method has been investigated thoroughly by Bergström (1974). The parametric version and the original version of the solved system Fix-Point method follow each other step by step, they converge or diverge together. These methods will not be dealt with in the sequel.

1.2. *The Elimination of the Structural Coefficients of the Predetermined Variables*

Let the sth approximation of the estimate of the systematic part of the vector $y_{(i)t}$ be written as

$$y_{(i)t}^{(s)} = W_{(i)}^{(s)} z_t, \tag{1.6}$$

where $W_{(i)}^{(s)}$ is the matrix of those rows of $W^{(s)}$ which pertain to $y_{(i)t}$. Then equation (I.2.3b) can be written in the following way:

$$y_{it} = b_{(i)}^{(s+1)} W_{(i)}^{(s)} z_t + g_{(i)}^{(s+1)} z_{(i)t} + e_{it}^{(s+1)}, \tag{1.7}$$

where the elements of $b_{(i)}^{(s+1)}$ and $g_{(i)}^{(s+1)}$ are obtained by the method of least squares with the elements of $W_{(i)}^{(s)}$ considered as given quantities. Let $z_{(i)t}^{**}$ denote the vector of those predetermined variables, which occur in the interdependent system, but are absent from the ith structural equation. The sth approximation of the matrices of the coefficients of the components of $z_{(i)t}$ and $z_{(i)t}^{**}$ in the reduced form expression for the vector $y_{(i)t}$ will be denoted $W_{(i)}^{*(s)}$ and $W_{(i)}^{**(s)}$, respectively. Then the reformulated or respecified structural equation (1.7) can be rewritten as

$$y_{it} = b_{(i)}^{(s+1)} W^{**(s)} z_{(i)t}^{**} + [b_{(i)}^{(s+1)} W^{*(s)} + g_{(i)}^{(s+1)}] z_{(i)t} + e_t^{(s+1)}. \tag{1.8}$$

Let $w_i^{(s+1)}$ be the row vector of the coefficients in the reduced form expression for y_{it} in approximation number $s+1$, and let $w_i^{*(s+1)}$ and $w_i^{**(s+1)}$ be the vectors of the elements of $w_i^{(s+1)}$, which pertain to $z_{(i)t}$ and $z_{(i)t}^{**}$, respectively. Then we have from formula (1.4)

$$w_i^{*(s+1)} = b_{(i)}^{(s+1)} W_{(i)}^{*(s)} + g_{(i)}^{(s+1)}, \tag{1.9}$$

$$w_i^{**(s+1)} = b_{(i)}^{(s+1)} W_{(i)}^{**(s)}. \tag{1.10}$$

Hitherto we have displayed the step from s to $s+1$ according to Section 1.1.2 for the ith structural equation. In order to get a procedure where the structural coefficients of the predetermined variables are eliminated, formulae (1.8) and (1.9) will be combined to give

$$y_{it} = b_{(i)}^{(s+1)} W_{(i)}^{**(s)} z_{(i)t}^{**} + w_i^{*(s+1)} z_{(i)t} + e_{it}^{(s+1)}. \tag{1.11}$$

From this equation the elements of $b_{(i)}^{(s+1)}$ and $w_i^{*(s+1)}$ are obtained by means of the method of least squares with the elements of $W_{(i)}^{**(s)}$ considered as given quantities. Let $y_{i.} = [y_{i1}, \cdots, y_{iT}]$ denote the row vector of the observed values of the ith endogenous variable, while $Z_{(i)} = [z_{(i)1}, \cdots, z_{(i)T}]$ denotes the matrix of the observed values of the predetermined variables in the original form of the ith structural equation and $Z_{(i)}^{**} = [z_{(i)1}^{**}, \cdots, z_{(i)T}^{**}]$ denotes the matrix of the observed values of the remaining predetermined variables of the system. The normal equations can be comprised into two matrix equations in the following way:

$$y_{i.} Z_{(i)}^{**\prime} W_i^{**(s)\prime} = b_{(i)}^{(s+1)} W_{(i)}^{**(s)} Z_{(i)}^{**} Z_{(i)}^{**\prime} W_{(i)}^{**(s)\prime} + w_i^{*(s+1)} Z_{(i)} Z_{(i)}^{**\prime} W_{(i)}^{**(s)\prime}, \tag{1.12a}$$

$$y_{i.} Z'_{(i)} = b_{(i)}^{(s+1)} W_{(i)}^{**(s)} Z_{(i)}^{**} Z'_{(i)} + w_i^{*(s+1)} Z_{(i)} Z'_{(i)}. \tag{1.12b}$$

From the matrix equation (1.12b), postmultiplied by $[Z_{(i)} Z'_{(i)}]^{-1}$, we get

$$w_i^{*(s+1)} = y_{i.} Z'_{(i)} [Z_{(i)} Z'_{(i)}]^{-1} - b_i^{(s+1)} W_{(i)}^{**(s)} Z_{(i)}^{**} Z'_{(i)} [Z_{(i)} Z'_{(i)}]^{-1}. \tag{1.13}$$

By introducing this expression for $w_i^{*(s+1)}$ into relation (1.12a), and solving the relation thus obtained for $b_{(i)}^{(s+1)}$, the following formula is obtained:

$$b_{(i)}^{(s+1)} = h_{(i)} W_{(i)}^{**(s)\prime} [W_{(i)}^{**(s)} L_{(i)} W_{(i)}^{**(s)\prime}]^{-1}, \tag{1.14}$$

where

$$h_{(i)} = y_{i.} Z_{(i)}^{**\prime} - y_{i.} Z'_{(i)} [Z_{(i)} Z'_{(i)}]^{-1} Z_{(i)} Z_{(i)}^{**\prime}, \tag{1.15a}$$

$$L_{(i)} = Z_{(i)}^{**} Z_{(i)}^{**\prime} - Z_{(i)}^{**} Z'_{(i)} [Z_{(i)} Z'_{(i)}]^{-1} Z_{(i)} Z_{(i)}^{**\prime}. \tag{1.15b}$$

Thereafter the row vectors $w_i^{*(s+1)}$ and the $w_i^{**(s+1)}$ are obtained from formulae (1.13) and (1.10).

Although the explicit calculation of $g_{(i)}^{(s+1)}$ in each iteration step is not necessary for the procedure just described, we write down the following expression, obtained from relation (1.9),

$$g_{(i)}^{(s+1)} = w_i^{*(s+1)} - b_{(i)}^{(s+1)} W_{(i)}^{*(s)}. \tag{1.16}$$

1.3. *The Iteration in Terms of the Reduced Form Parameters Only*

For the investigation of the properties of the iterative procedure to be performed later it is convenient to consider the iteration in terms of the reduced form coefficients only. By introducing expression (1.14) for $b_{(i)}^{(s+1)}$ into relation (1.10) the following formula is obtained:

$$w_i^{**(s+1)} = h_{(i)} W_{(i)}^{**(s)\prime} (W_{(i)}^{**(s)} L_{(i)}^{**(s)} W_{(i)}^{**(s)\prime})^{-1} W_{(i)}^{**(s)} , \tag{1.17}$$

where the row vector $h_{(i)}$ and the matrix $L_{(i)}$ are defined by formulae (1.15a–b). With due regard to expression (1.10), formula (1.13) can be written in the following way:

$$w_i^{*(s+1)} = y_{i.} Z'_{(i)} [Z_{(i)} Z'_{(i)}]^{-1} - w_i^{**(s+1)} Z_{(i)}^{**} Z'_{(i)} [Z_{(i)} Z'_{(i)}]^{-1}. \tag{1.18}$$

From formulae (1.17) and (1.18) it is seen that the elements of $w_i^{(s+1)}$ are homogeneous rational functions with the homogeneity degree zero of the elements of $W_{(i)}^{**(s)}$. With respect to the elements of one row of $W_{j(i)}^{**(s)}$, considered separately, the elements of $w_i^{(s+1)}$ can be written as the ratio between two homogeneous polynomials of the second degree. When all elements of $W_{(i)}^{**(s)}$ are considered simultaneously, the elements of $w_i^{(s+1)}$ can be written as ratios between two homogeneous polynomials of the degree twice the number of rows in $W_{(i)}^{**(s)}$. From these homogeneity properties it follows that the elements of $w_i^{(s+1)}$ as functions of $W_{(i)}^{**(s)}$ only depend on the ratios between the elements of each row of $W_{(i)}^{**(s)}$. Especially it should be noted that $w_i^{(s+1)}$ does not depend on $w_i^{(s)}$.

1.4. *Special Cases where the Estimation can Partially be Performed in Advance of the Iterative Procedure*

1.4.1. A pure regression equation. If the ith structural equation is a pure regression equation in the sense that no endogenous variables occur on the right-hand side, the vector $g_{(i)}$ is obtained directly with the aid of the least squares method, so that

$$g_{(i)} = y_{i.} Z'_{(i)} (Z_{(i)} Z'_{(i)})^{-1}, \tag{1.19}$$

where $w_i^* = g_{(i)}$ and $w_i^{**} = 0$, the ith row or W is kept constant during the iterative procedure and it is of course unnecessary to repeat the calculation (1.19) each iteration step.

1.4.2. A just identified equation. The number of endogenous variables on the right-hand side of a just identified equation equals the number of those predetermined variables in the system, which are absent from the equation. This implies that $W_{(i)}^{**(s)}$ is a square matrix, so that formula (1.14) is reduced to

$$b_{(i)}^{(s+1)} = h_{(i)}L_{(i)}^{-1}[W_{(i)}^{**(s)}]^{-1}. \tag{1.20}$$

When this expression is introduced into formula (1.10) or if use is made of formula (1.17), the following formula is obtained:

$$w_i^{**(s+1)} = h_{(i)}L_{(i)}^{-1}. \tag{1.21}$$

Thus $w_i^{**(s+1)}$ does not depend on s and so is the case with $w_i^{*(s+1)}$ according to formula (1.18). It follows that w_i can be calculated in advance of the iterative procedure by means of the formula

$$w_i = y_{i.}Z'(ZZ')^{-1}, \tag{1.22}$$

that is, w_i is obtained from the unrestricted reduced form, when the ith structural equation is just identified. The just identified equation is in this sense equivalent to a pure regression equation with all predetermined variables of the system present. The value of w_i obtained in this way is introduced into each approximation of W and the iterative procedure is then applied to the other equations only. The calculation of $b_{(i)}$ and $g_{(i)}$ can be made after the completion of this iterative procedure.

If the system contains both pure regression equations and just identified equations, the rows of W corresponding to these equations are introduced into all approximations of W occurring during the iterative procedure, which is then conveniently applied to the other structural equations only.

1.4.3. An equation, where the estimated structural coefficients coincide with those of the Two-Stage Least Squares (TSLS) method. As stated in the preceding subsection the rows of W, pertaining to endogenous variables on the left-hand side of just identified equations can be obtained from the Unrestricted Reduced Form, that is the first stage of the TSLS method. According to the suggestion of the preceding paragraph, these rows of W, determined in this way, are introduced into each approximation of W. Let us now consider an equation, where all endogenous variables on the right-hand side occur on the left-hand side of as many just identified equations. If the ith equation is of this type, we have

$$W_{(i)} = Y_{(i)}Z'(ZZ')^{-1}, \tag{1.23}$$

where $Y_{(i)}$ is the matrix of the observed values of the endogenous variables, which occur on the right-hand side of the ith equation in its original structural form. Since (1.23) is valid for all approximations of $W_{(i)}$, the vectors $b_{(i)}^{(s+1)}$ and $g_{(i)}^{(s+1)}$ obtained by applying the least squares method to relation (1.7) are TSLS estimates for all iterations. Also $w_i^{*(s+1)}$ and $w_i^{**(s+1)}$, obtained from relations (1.9) and (1.10) are the same during the whole iterative procedure. Thus the vector w_i can be obtained without iteration also in this case. It should be noted that the vector w_i in this case pertains to the GEID estimate of the restricted reduced form. Since also in this case the iteration is unnecessary, we can again introduce the elements of the vector w_i in all approximations and exclude the ith equation from the iterative procedure.

As a further extension, which combines Sections 1.4.1 and 1.4.2, let us consider a structural equation, where the endogenous variables on the right-hand side occur as left-hand variables of pure regression equations or just identified equations. Such an equation can be dealt with in essentially the same way. Thus, when the rows of W, pertaining to endogenous variables on the left-hand side of pure regression equations, just identified equations and equations where the endogenous variables on the right-hand side occur on the left-hand side of pure regression equations or just identified equation, are introduced into each approximation $W^{(s)}$, then the iterative procedure can be restricted to the other equations only. This device can sometimes be extended further in a way to be indicated in Section 7.1.

2. The Parametric Fix-Point (PFP) Method in the Presence of Identities

2.1. Method I: The Direct Application of the Iterative Procedure

The structural coefficients of an identity are known in advance and therefore the first semi-step in the step from s to $s+1$ in the iterative procedure is omitted for the identities. Thus let the prescribed values of the structural coefficients be introduced into each approximation of B and G. According to Method I, suggested by Ågren (1972a), the second semi-step is performed in the same way for all structural relations. For the parametric approach considered here this means that relation (1.4) is used. Otherwise stated, formulae (1.9) and (1.10) are still valid for behavioural relations, but for identities they are replaced by

$$w_i^{*(s+1)} = \beta_{(i)} W_{(i)}^{*(s)} + \gamma_{(i)}, \tag{2.1a}$$

$$w_i^{**(s+1)} = \beta_{(i)} W_{(i)}^{**(s)}. \tag{2.1b}$$

The further results of Sections 1.2 and 1.3 are valid for behavioural relations only. Thus, for each row of $W^{(s+1)}$ pertaining to endogenous variables on the left-hand side of behavioural relations, the elements are homogeneous rational functions of the elements of $W^{(s)}$ with homogeneity degree zero. The rows of $W^{(s+1)}$ corresponding to variables on the left-hand side of identities are, according to (2.1a–b), linear functions of the elements of $W^{(s)}$.

2.2. *Method II: An Alternative Treatment of the Identities*

The following device draws from Lyttkens (1973a): The typical feature of Method II is that ${}_2y_t^{(s)}$ is calculated from ${}_1y_t^{(s)}$ by means of the identities, so that

$${}_2y_t^{(s)} = \beta_{21}\,{}_1y_t^{(s)} + \beta_{22}\,{}_2y_t^{(s)} + \Gamma_2 z_t, \tag{2.2}$$

whence

$${}_2y_t^{(s)} = \beta_{21}^*\,{}_1y_t^{(s)} + \Gamma_2^* z_t, \tag{2.3}$$

where

$$\beta_{21}^* = [I - \beta_{22}]^{-1}\beta_{21}, \tag{2.4a}$$

$$\Gamma_2^* = [I - \beta_{22}]^{-1}\Gamma_2. \tag{2.4b}$$

When use is made of the parametric device,

$${}_1y_t^{(s)} = W_1^{(s)} z_t, \tag{2.5a}$$

$${}_2y_t^{(s)} = W_2^{(s)} z_t, \tag{2.5b}$$

the following relation is obtained from (2.3) by equating coefficients

$$W_2^{(s)} = \beta_{21}^* W_1^{(s)} + \Gamma_2^*, \tag{2.6}$$

and the sth approximation of W is defined as the combined matrix

$$W^{(s)} = \begin{bmatrix} W_1^{(s)} \\ \\ W_2^{(s)} \end{bmatrix}. \tag{2.7}$$

Then, for each behavioural equation, $b_{(i)}^{(s+1)}$ and $g_{(i)}^{(s+1)}$ are obtained by applying the least squares method to (1.7), and the elements of $w_i^{(s+1)}$ are obtained with the aid of relations (1.9) and (1.10), or alternatively with the aid of formulae (1.17) and (1.18).

With the aid of the results in Section 1.3 and condition (2.3), it is found that the elements of $W^{(s+1)}$ also for this method are homogeneous rational functions of the elements of $W^{(s)}$ with homogeneity degree zero. When expression (2.6) for $W_2^{(s)}$ is introduced, we can conclude that the elements of $W^{(s+1)}$ can be written as rational functions of the elements of $W_1^{(s)}$ only. In this way of writing the elements of $w_i^{**(s)}$ are not excluded from the rational functions, which give the elements of $w_i^{(s+1)}$.

Method II is described by Ågren (1972a) as an elimination of identities. By introducing expression (2.3) for ${}_2y_t^{(s)}$ in the behavioural relation, a system is obtained where ${}_2y_t^{(s)}$ does not occur explicitly. With the aid of (2.5a–b) we obtain, for the corresponding parametric approach,

$${}_1y_t = B_{11}^{(s+1)}W_1^{(s)}z_t + B_{12}^{(s+1)}[\beta_{21}^*W_1^{(s)}z_t + \Gamma_2^*z_t] + G_1^{(s+1)}z_t + {}_1e_t^{(s+1)}. \qquad (2.8)$$

Then $B_{11}^{(s+1)}$, $B_{12}^{(s+1)}$, and $G_1^{(s+1)}$ are obtained by applying the least squares method to each equation of this system. Thereafter we have in equivalence with the device (2.2)–(2.7) and (1.9)–(1.10),

$$W_1^{(s+1)} = [B_{11}^{(s+1)} + B_{12}^{(s+1)}\beta_{21}^*]W_1^{(s)} + B_{12}^{(s+1)}\Gamma_2^* + G_1^{(s+1)}. \qquad (2.9)$$

An alternative explanation of Method II which avoids the respecification of the identities is given by Lyttkens (1970c, 1973b).

2.3. *Method III: Eliminating Identities and Solving the ith Structural Equation for y_{it}*

When the expression for ${}_2y_t$ according to the identities is substituted into the original behavioural relations, a system is obtained where y_{it} can occur on the right-hand side of the ith equation as well. If this ith equation is solved for y_{it} and the ensuing equation is reformulated or respecified, the resulting equation can be written as

$$y_{it} = \beta_{0.i}\begin{bmatrix} {}_1\eta_t^* \\ \beta_{21(i)}^*\,{}_1\eta_t^* + \Gamma_2^*z_t \end{bmatrix} + \gamma_{0.i}z_t + \varepsilon_{it}, \qquad (2.10)$$

where $\beta_{21(i)}^*$ is the matrix obtained if the ith column of β_{21}^* is replaced by zeros, and the row vector $[\beta_{0.i}, \gamma_{0.i}]$ is proportional to the row vector $[\beta_i, \gamma_i]$. Accordingly

$$\beta_{0.ij} = \beta_{ij} \Big/ \left(1 - \sum_{k=p+1}^{n} \beta_{ik}\beta^*_{ki}\right), \tag{2.11a}$$

$$\gamma_{0.ij} = \gamma_{ij} \Big/ \left(1 - \sum_{k=p+1}^{n} \beta_{ik}\beta^*_{ki}\right), \tag{2.11b}$$

where β^*_{ki} is the elements of $\boldsymbol{\beta}^*_{21}$ pertaining to y_{kt} and y_{it}.

Method III, suggested by Ågren (1972a) under the name Method IIb, is the Fix-Point method applied to the behavioural relations in the form (2.10).

The step from s to $s+1$ in the parametric version of Method III can be described as follows: Let the vector $W^{(s)}_{\{i\}}$ be defined as

$$W^{(s)}_{\{i\}} = \begin{bmatrix} W^{(s)}_1 \\ \\ W^{(s)}_{2\{i\}} \end{bmatrix}, \tag{2.12}$$

where

$$W^{(s)}_{2\{i\}} = \boldsymbol{\beta}^*_{21\{i\}} W^{(s)}_1 + \Gamma_2. \tag{2.13}$$

Furthermore let $W_{(\{i\})}$ be the matrix of those rows of $W_{\{i\}}$ which pertain to the vector variable $y_{(i)t}$. Then the approximation now considered of the estimated version of (2.10) can be written as

$$y_{it} = b^{(s+1)'}_{0(i)} W^{(s)}_{(\{i\})} z_t + g^{(s+1)'}_{0(i)} z_{(i)t} + e^{(s+1)}_{it}. \tag{2.14}$$

The least squares method, applied to this equation, gives $b^{(s+1)'}_{0(i)}$ and $g^{(s+1)'}_{0(i)}$, and the new approximation of the estimated reduced form coefficients of the ith endogenous variable are obtained from the formula

$$w^{*(s+1)}_i = b^{(s+1)'}_{0(i)} W^{*(s)}_{(\{i\})} + g^{(s+1)'}_{0(i)}, \tag{2.15a}$$

$$w^{**(s+1)}_i = b^{(s+1)'}_{0(i)} W^{**(s)}_{(\{i\})}, \tag{2.15b}$$

where $W^{*(s)}_{(\{i\})}$ and $W^{**(s)}_{(\{i\})}$ are the matrices of those columns of $W^{(s)}_{(\{i\})}$ which pertain to $z_{(i)t}$ and $z^{**}_{(i)t}$, respectively. In the step from s to $s+1$ this procedure is performed for every behavioural equation.

After the fulfilment of the iterative procedure the estimates of the original structural coefficients appearing in the behavioural equations are obtained from

$$b_{ij} = b_{0.ij} \Big/ \left(1 + \sum_{k=p+1}^{n} b_{0.ik}\beta^*_{ki}\right), \tag{2.16a}$$

$$g_{ij} = g_{0.ij} \Big/ \left(1 + \sum_{k=p+1}^{n} b_{0.ik}\beta^*_{ki}\right) . \tag{2.16b}$$

Following the procedure of Sections 1.2 and 1.3, we have

$$w_i^{**(s+1)} = h_{(i)} W_{(i)}^{**(s)\prime} [W_{(\{i\})}^{**(s)} L_{(i)} W_{(\{i\})}^{**(s)\prime}]^{-1} W_{(\{i\})}^{**(s)}, \tag{2.17}$$

where $h_{(i)}$ and $L_{(i)}$ are defined by (1.15a–b) and then $w_i^{*(s+1)}$ is obtained from (1.18).

As to the expressions of the elements of $W_1^{(s+1)}$ in terms of the elements of $W_1^{(s)}$ the essential difference from Method II is that the elements of $w_i^{(s)}$ do not occur in the rational functions which give the elements of $w_i^{(s+1)}$.

3. Convergence Properties of the Parametric Fix-Point (PFP) Method

As pointed out in Section 1.3, the reduced form coefficients in one approximation are rational functions of the reduced form coefficients in the preceding approximation. This leads to the matrix-valued function

$$W^{(s+1)} = F(W^{(s)}). \tag{3.1}$$

With the elements of W and $F(W)$ arranged as vectors, let $\partial F(W)/\partial W$ denote the Jacobian matrix of the partial derivatives of the elements of $F(W)$ with respect to the elements of W. A criterion for the convergence to a Fix-Point from a start in the neighbourhood of it, so called local convergence, is that all eigenvalues of $\partial F(W)/\partial W$, evaluated in the Fix-Point itself, lie inside the unit circle; Lyttkens (1973a, b). For the local convergence of the original Fix-Point method where the reduced form coefficients are not explicitly used, we have to add Ågren's criterion [Ågren and Wold (1969), Ågren (1972a)], that the eigenvalues of B lie inside the unit circle. The local convergence criterion of the original Fix-Point method is thus split up into one part within the z-space and one-part orthogonal to this space; Bodin (1974). The instances of apparent convergence [Bodin (1970, 1973b, 1974)], mentioned in the introduction, occur in cases where Ågren's condition is not fulfilled.

When identities are present the methods dealt with in this paper can also be brought in the form (3.1). For Method II, however, it follows from the last paragraph of Section 2.2 that it is possible to consider the elements of W_1 only so that

$$W_1^{(s+1)} = F^*(W_1^{(s)}), \tag{3.2}$$

where the elements of $F^*(W_1)$ are rational functions of the elements of W_1. From the Jacobian matrix of $F^*(W_1)$ a local convergence criterion is obtained in the same way as before. Also the iteration procedure III admits an iteration function of the form (3.2) and the corresponding local convergence criterion. Method III is constructed in such a way, that the rational functions occuring in the ith row of $F^*(W_1)$ do not involve the elements of w_i.

4. The Parametric Fractional Fix-Point (PFFP) Method

The idea of the Fractional Fix-Point (FFP) method [Ågren (1969, 1970, 1972a, 1973a)] is to apply a relaxation factor α, say, to formula (I.2.4a) for the Fix-Point iterations. When $y_t^{(s)} = W^{(s)}z_t$, the relaxation factor can equivalently be applied to formula (1.4) for the parametric Fix-Point iteration [Lyttkens 1969a, 1973b)] so that

$$W^{(s+1)} = (1-\alpha)W^{(s)} + \alpha[B^{(s+1)}W^{(s)} + G^{(s+1)}], \tag{4.1}$$

where $B^{(s+1)}$ and $G^{(s+1)}$ as before are obtained by applying squares method to each component of (1.3). For the ith structural equation we have then, by applying the relaxation factor to relations (1.9) and (1.10),

$$w_i^{*(s+1)} = (1-\alpha)w_i^{*(s)} + \alpha[b_{(i)}^{(s+1)}W_{(i)}^{*(s)} + g_{(i)}^{(s+1)}], \tag{4.2a}$$

$$w_i^{**(s+1)} = (1-\alpha)w_i^{**(s)} + \alpha b_{(i)}^{(s+1)}W_{(i)}^{**(s)}. \tag{4.2b}$$

When identities are present and Method I is used, formulae (2.1a–b) are treated in the same way. For Method II, however, relation (2.6) is left unchanged. This method can also be described as an application of the relaxation factor to formula (2.9) so that

$$W_1^{(s+1)} = (1-\alpha)W^{(s)} + \alpha\{[B_{11}^{(s+1)} + B_{12}^{(s+1)}B_{21}^*]W_1^{(s)} + B_{12}^{(s+1)}\Gamma_2^* + G_1^{(s+1)}\}. \tag{4.3}$$

As to Method III, formulae (2.12) and (2.13) are not changed, but the relaxation factor is applied to formula (2.15a–b), so that

$$w_i^{*(s+1)} = (1-\alpha)w_i^{*(s)} + \alpha[b_{0(i)}^{(s+1)}W_{(\{i\})}^{*(s)} + g_{0(i)}^{(s+1)}], \tag{4.4a}$$

$$w_i^{**(s+1)} = (1-\alpha)w_i^{**(s)} + \alpha b_{0(i)}^{(s+1)}W_{(\{i\})}^{**(s)}. \tag{4.4b}$$

It should be pointed out that formula (1.17) in the present case, even for Methods I and II, is modified to

$$w_i^{**(s+1)} = (1-\alpha)w_i^{**(s)} + \alpha h_{(i)} W_{(i)}^{**(s)\prime}[W_{(i)}^{**(s)} L_{(i)} W_{(i)}^{**(s)\prime}]^{-1} W_{(i)}^{**(s)}, \tag{4.5}$$

while formula (1.18) is unchanged since the effect of α on this linear relation is already taken care of by $w_i^{**(s+1)}$. An analogous result holds for Method III inasmuch as $W_{(i)}^{(s)}$ is replaced by $W_{(\{i\})}^{(s)}$ in formula (4.5). It follows that the relaxation factor can also be applied to the iteration function (3.1), so that

$$W^{(s+1)} = (1-\alpha)W^{(s)} + \alpha F(W^{(s)}). \tag{4.6}$$

The Jacobian matrix of $(1-\alpha)W + \alpha F(w)$ is $(1-\alpha)I + \alpha(\partial F(W)/\partial W)$. The criterion for local convergence is that the eigenvalues of $(1-\alpha)I + \alpha(\partial F(W)/\partial W)$ lie inside the unit circle. An extensive investigation of this condition for local convergence is performed by Bodin (1974).

As to Methods II and III the iteration can be expressed in terms of $W_1^{(s+1)}$ simply by applying the relaxation factor to formula (3.2), which gives

$$W_1^{(s+1)} = (1-\alpha)I + \alpha F^*(W_1^{(s)}), \tag{4.7}$$

and the criterion for local covergence is analogous to the one just considered.

5. The Parametric Recursive Fix-Point (PRFP) Method

5.1. The Recursive Procedure Applied to all Equations of the System

The recursive Fix-Point method [Bodin (1969, 1970, 1973b, 1974)] takes account of the knowledge of $y_{1t}^{(s+1)}, \cdots, y_{i-1,t}^{(s+1)}$, $t = 1, \cdots, T$, when the coefficients of the ith structural equation are estimated in approximation $s+1$. The Parametric Recursive Fix-Point method (PRFP) takes account of the knowledge of the $i-1$ first rows of W in approximation $s+1$, when the coefficients of the ith structural equation is estimated in approximation $s+1$.

Let $W^{(s,s+1;i)}$ be the approximation of W obtained if the $i-1$ first rows are used in approximation $s+1$ and the remaining rows in approximation s. If use is made of this matrix we obtain instead of (1.7) the following relation:

$$y_{it} = b_{(i)}^{(s+1)} W_{(i)}^{(s+1,s;i)} z_t + g_{(i)}^{(s+1)} z_{(i)t} + e_{it}^{(s+1)}, \tag{5.1}$$

where $W_{(i)}^{(s,s+1;i)}$ is the matrix of those rows of $W^{(s,s+1;i)}$ which pertain to the vector variable $y_{(i)t}$. The elements of $b_{(i)}^{(s+1)}$ and $g_{(i)}^{(s+1)}$ are obtained by means of the method of least squares with $W_{(i)}^{(s,s+1;i)}$ considered as known. With the relaxation factor α we have

$$w_i^{*(s+1)} = (1-\alpha)w_i^{*(s)} + \alpha[b_{(i)}^{(s+1)}W_{(i)}^{*(s,s+1;i)} + g_{(i)}^{(s+1)}] \tag{5.2a}$$

$$w_i^{**(s+1)} = (1-\alpha)w_i^{**(s)} + \alpha b_{(i)}^{(s+1)}W_{(i)}^{**(s,s+1;i)} \tag{5.2b}$$

where $W_{(i)}^{*(s,s+1;i)}$ and $W_{(i)}^{**(s,s+1;i)}$ are the matrices of those columns of $W_{(i)}^{(s,s+1;i)}$ which pertain to $z_{(i)t}$ and $z_{(i)t}^{**}$, respectively. The procedure can immediately be extended to Method I for systems including identities with due regard to the fact that the structural coefficients involved in relation (5.2a–b) are given constants, when identities are concerned.

It should be pointed out that formulae (4.5) and (1.18) for $w_i^{**(s+1)}$ and $w_i^{*(s+1)}$ are valid in the case now considered if the approximation $W_{(i)}^{(s)}$ is replaced by the approximation $W_{(i)}^{(s,s+1;i)}$. Since the $i-1$ first rows of $W^{(s,s+1;i)}$ are in approximation number $s+1$, the investigation of the local convergence properties is more complicated in this case. A close study of these local convergence properties is undertaken by Bodin (1974).

5.2. *The Recursive Procedure Applied to the Behavioural Equations Only, in the Presence of Identities*

Let $W_1^{(s,s+1;i)}$ be the approximation of W_1 obtained by combining the $i-1$ first rows in approximation $s+1$ and the remaining rows in approximation s. The matrix $W^{(s,s+1;i)}$ is defined as a combined matrix in the following way:

$$W^{(s,s+1;i)} = \begin{bmatrix} W_1^{(s,s+1;i)} \\ \\ W_2^{(s,s+1;i)} \end{bmatrix}, \tag{5.3}$$

with

$$W_2^{(s,s+1;i)} = B_{21}^* W_1^{(s,s+1;i)} + \Gamma_2^*. \tag{5.4}$$

This definition of $W^{(s,s+1;i)}$ is used in (5.1), and after application of the least squares method, in relations (5.2a–b). This is the recursive version of Method II described in Section 2.2.

For a recursive version of Method III use will be made of a combined matrix $W_{(i)}^{(s,s+1;i)}$ defined as follows:

$$W_{\{i\}}^{(s,s+1;i)} = \begin{bmatrix} W_1^{(s,s+1;i)} \\ \\ W_{2\{i\}}^{(s,s+1;i)} \end{bmatrix}, \tag{5.5}$$

with

$$W_{2(i)}^{(s,s+1;i)} = B_{21\{i\}}^{*} W_1^{(s,s+1;i)} + \Gamma_2^{*}. \tag{5.6}$$

Let $W_{(\{i\})}^{(s,s+1;i)}$ be the matrix of those rows of $W_{\{i\}}^{(s,s+1;i)}$ which pertain to the vector variable $y_{(i)t}$. In analogy to (2.14) the following equation is obtained:

$$y_{it} = b_{0(i)}^{(s)} W_{(\{i\})}^{(s,s+1;i)} z_t + g_{(0)i}^{(s+1)} z_{(i)t} + e_{it}^{(s+1)}. \tag{5.7}$$

After having applied the least squares method to this equation, we have

$$w_i^{*(s+1)} = (1-\alpha) w_i^{*(s)} + \alpha [b_{0(i)}^{(s+1)} W_{(\{i\})}^{*(s,s+1;i)} + g_{(i)}^{(s+1)}], \tag{5.8a}$$

$$w_i^{**(s+1)} = (1-\alpha) w_i^{**(s)} + \alpha b_{0(i)}^{(s+1)} W_{(\{i\})}^{**(s,s+1;i)}, \tag{5.8b}$$

where $W_{(\{i\})}^{*(s,s+1;i)}$ and $W_{(\{i\})}^{**(s,s+1;i)}$ denote the columns of $W_{(\{i\})}^{(s,s+1;i)}$ which pertain to $z_{(i)t}$ and $z_{(i)t}^{**}$, respectively.

6. The Fix-Point Method with Pseudovariables

The PFP method dealt with hithero has the drawback that the original programs for the Fix-Point method cannot be used as they stand. If the hitherto size T equals the number m of predetermined variables, the endogenous variables can be expressed as linear combinations of the predetermined variables, provided that no exact linear combination persists between the predetermined variables themselves. When the sample size exceeds the number of predetermined variables, a number of pseudovariables will be constructed which give rise to row vectors with q elements.

Remembering that the Fix-Point estimates depend on the matrices ZZ' and YZ' we shall construct two matrices of pseudovariables, namely an $m \times m$ matrix $\tilde{Z}$ and an $n \times m$ matrix $\tilde{Y}$, such that [Lyttkens (1969a, 1973b)]

$$\tilde{Z}\tilde{Z}' = ZZ', \tag{6.1a}$$

$$\tilde{Y}\tilde{Z}' = YZ'. \tag{6.1b}$$

The choice of the pseudovariables is arbitrary to some extent. The matrix $\tilde{Z}$

will be chosen as a triangular matrix, and the matrix $\tilde{Y}$ will be chosen so that the combined matrix $\begin{bmatrix} \tilde{Z} \\ \tilde{Y} \end{bmatrix}$ consists of the first m columns of a triangular matrix. For abbreviation the following notations will be introduced:

$$A = [a_{jk}] = ZZ', \qquad i = 1, \cdots, n, \quad j, k = 1, \cdots, m. \tag{6.2a}$$

$$C = [c_{ik}] = YZ', \tag{6.2b}$$

Then the elements of $\tilde{Z}$ and $\tilde{Y}$ will be chosen in the following way:

$$\tilde{z}_{11} = \sqrt{a_{11}}, \tag{6.3a}$$

$$\tilde{z}_{j1} = a_{j1}/\tilde{z}_{11}, \qquad j = 2, \cdots, m, \tag{6.3b}$$

$$\tilde{z}_{12} = 0, \tag{6.3c}$$

$$\tilde{z}_{22} = \sqrt{a_{22} - \tilde{z}_{21}^2}, \tag{6.3d}$$

$$\tilde{z}_{j2} = (a_{j2} - \tilde{z}_{j1}\tilde{z}_{21}), \qquad j = 3, \cdots, m, \tag{6.3e}$$

$$\tilde{z}_{13} = \tilde{z}_{23} = 0, \tag{6.3f}$$

$$\tilde{z}_{33} = \sqrt{a_{33} - \tilde{z}_{31}^2 - \tilde{z}_{32}^2}, \tag{6.3g}$$

$$\tilde{z}_{j3} = (a_{j3} - \tilde{z}_{j1}\tilde{z}_{31} - \tilde{z}_{j2}\tilde{z}_{32})/\tilde{z}_{33}, \qquad j = 4, \cdots, m, \tag{6.3h}$$

$$\cdots\cdots\cdots\cdots\cdots\cdots\cdots\cdots$$

$$\tilde{z}_{jm} = 0, \qquad j = 1, \cdots, m-1, \tag{6.3i}$$

$$\tilde{z}_{mm} = \sqrt{a_{mm} - \tilde{z}_{1m}^2 - \tilde{z}_{2m}^2 - \cdots - \tilde{z}_{m-1,m}^2}, \tag{6.3j}$$

and

$$\tilde{y}_{i1} = c_{i1}/\tilde{z}_{11}, \tag{6.4a}$$

$$\tilde{y}_{i2} = (c_{i2} - \tilde{y}_{i1}\tilde{z}_{21})/\tilde{z}_{22}, \tag{6.4b}$$

$$\tilde{y}_{i3} = (c_{i3} - \tilde{y}_{i1}\tilde{z}_{31} - \tilde{y}_{i2}\tilde{z}_{32})/\tilde{z}_{33}, \tag{6.4c}$$

$$\cdots\cdots\cdots\cdots\cdots\cdots\cdots\cdots$$

$$\tilde{y}_{im} = (c_{im} - \tilde{y}_{i1}\tilde{z}_{m1} - \tilde{y}_{i2}\tilde{z}_{m2} - \cdots - \tilde{y}_{i,m-1}\tilde{z}_{m,m-1})/\tilde{z}_{mm}, \tag{6.4d}$$

with $i = 1, \cdots, n$.

Let $\tilde{z}_\tau$ and $\tilde{y}_\tau$ be the vectors of the elements in the τth column of $\tilde{Z}$ and $\tilde{Y}$. In terms of the pseudovariables the estimated multirelation system can be written as

$$\tilde{y}_\tau = B\tilde{y}_\tau + G\tilde{z}_\tau + \tilde{d}_\tau, \tag{6.5}$$

where $\tilde{d}_\tau$ is the estimated residual vector. The corresponding reformulated or respecified version of the system is

$$\tilde{y}_t = B\tilde{y}^*_\tau + G\tilde{z}_\tau + \tilde{e}_\tau, \tag{6.6}$$

with

$$\tilde{y}^*_\tau = B\tilde{y}^*_\tau + G\tilde{z}_\tau, \tag{6.7}$$

where $\tilde{e}_\tau$ is the estimated residual vector.

Every approximation of $y^*_{i\tau}$, with $\tau = 1, \cdots, m$, can be written as a linear combination of the elements of $\tilde{z}_\tau$. In other words there are no random disturbances orthogonal to the z-space, which can disturb the application of the Fix-Point method to (6.6) and (6.7). In this sense the application of the Fix-Point method to (6.6) and (6.7) is equivalent to the PFP method dealt with in the previous sections. This holds true also for the methods relating to the case where identities occur. The equivalence holds for the SFP, PFP, and RPF method as well. The condition for local convergence is therefore the same as that of the corresponding parametric method. A direct convergence analysis of the pseudovariables approach is performed by Ågren (1972b). It should further be mentioned that the OLS and TSLS starts coincide when the pseudovariables are used. In fact the application of the OLS method to each relation of (6.5) gives the TSLS estimates of B and Γ.

At last it should be pointed out that the method of this section as well as the methods dealt with in the preceding sections are of interest only when the sample size exceeds the number of predetermined variables, or more precisely when the rank of the matrix Z is smaller than the sample size T.

7. The Algebraic Fix-Point (AFP) Method

7.1. The Finite Consecutive Case

As stated in Section 1.4 there are three types of structural equations, for which the corresponding relations of $y^*_t = Wz_t$ can be directly obtained without iteration, namely:

(i) pure regression equations, i.e., equations without endogenous variables on the right-hand side;

(ii) just identified equations;

(iii) equations where the endogenous variables on the right-hand side occur on the left-hand side of equations belonging to (i) and (ii).

Obvious extensions of the cases under (iii) are

(iv) equations, where the endogenous variables on the right-hand side occur on the left-hand side of equations belonging to (i), (ii), and (iii);

(v) equations where the endogenous variable on the right-hand side occur on the left-hand side of equations belonging to (i), (ii), (iii) or (iv). etc.

When the ith equation is just identified, $y_{it}^* = w_i z_t$ is obtained from the unrestricted reduced form, as shown in Section 1.4.2 while the estimation of the structural coefficients is postponed until all components of y_t^* relating to the variables on the right-hand side of the equation have been obtained. For identities which may occur in categories (iii), (iv), etc., the least squares estimation of the structural coefficients is of course omitted. The procedure is related to the Recursive Fix-Point (RFP) method in the following way:

When the ith structural equation is just identified it is convenient to replace this equation by $y_{it} = w_i z_t + e_t$ where w_i is obtained from formula (1.22). After this replacement, we try to reorder the system [Bodin (1974) and Chapter 2] so that the β-matrix becomes subdiagonal. Such a system can be estimated by just one iteration of the RFP method with the relaxation factor $\alpha = 1$. Thereafter the structural coefficients of the just identified equations are estimated in the way described before.

This consecutive procedure has been applied by Lyttkens (1967, 1970b) to one version of the Girshick–Haavelmo (1947) model, and by Bodin (1974) to this version as well as another one.

7.2. *The Use of Already Estimated Components of y_t in Other Equations*

For systems where not all equations can be estimated by the method set forth in the preceding section, we estimate as many equations as possible.

In the remaining part of the system we regard as predetermined variables the already known components of y_t^* which occur in this part of the system, together with the components of z_t which occur there. If the number of linearly independent predetermined variables, obtained in this way is smaller than the number of predetermined variables in the whole system, it is worthwhile to look for equations, which are just identified with respect to the new set of predetermined variables. For these equations we consider again the empirical least squares regression of the left-hand variable on the new set of predetermined variables, and in this way new components of y_t^* are obtained, and the scheme of the preceding section can be tried again. This procedure is used for the first version of the Girshick–Haavelmo model by Lyttkens (1967, 1970b), and for Basmann's (1963, 1965) model by Ågren (1972a).

7.3. *Elimination of Identities*

Hitherto the identities have been dealt with in the same way as the behavioural relation, except for the omission of the least squares estimation of the structural coefficients. This corresponds to Method I dealt with in Section 2.1. Sometimes it may be worthwhile to start from Method III dealt with in Section 2.3. This way of proceeding has been applied to Johnston's (1972) model, which consists of two behavioural equations and one identity. One of the behavioural equations is just identified, so that one component of y_t^* is directly obtained. Then with the aid of the second relation according to Method III, the other component of y_t^* is obtained. The procedure used by Lyttkens (1967, 1973a) can be interpreted in this way. Another way of dealing with this system is presented by Bodin (1974).

7.4. *The Original Summers Model*

The equilibrium condition of equality between demand and supply has induced Summers (1965) to consider a two-relation model, where the same endogenous variable occurs on the left-hand side of both equations. In the respecified or reformulated form [Lyttkens and Wold (1970)] the system can be written as

$$y_{1t} = \beta_{12}\eta_{2t}^* + \gamma_{11}z_{1t} + \gamma_{12}z_{2t} + \varepsilon_{1t}, \tag{7.1a}$$

$$y_{1t} = \beta_{22}\eta_{2t}^* + \gamma_{23}z_{3t} + \gamma_{24}z_{4t} + \varepsilon_{1t}. \tag{7.1b}$$

The two equations have the same residual ε_{1t} which equals the residual in the reduced form expression for y_{1t}. On the additional assumption that $E(y_t \mid \eta_t^*) = \eta_t^*$ the AFP estimation is performed by Lyttkens (1973b). The essential steps of this estimation are:

(i) The row vector $w_1 = (w_{11}, w_{12}, w_{13}, w_{14})$ is obtained from formula (1.22), i.e., from the unrestricted reduced form.

(ii) The inverse values $1/b_{22}$ and $1/b_{12}$ are calculated as the least squares regression coefficients of y_{2t} on the two variables $w_{11}z_{1t} + w_{12}z_{2t}$ and $w_{13}z_{3t} + w_{14}z_{4t}$.

8. Application to a Model with Two Overidentified Behaviour Relations and One Identity

8.1. The Model and its Transformation

In all models treated hitherto in this section at least one of the rows of W is obtained from the empirical regression of the pertaining endogenous variable on some or all predetermined variables of the system. When no such estimation is admitted, the AFP estimation is rather complicated even for simple models. For Summers' model with different variables on the left-hand side of the two equations, the AFP estimation requires the solution of a quintic [Lyttkens (1967, 1970a, 1973b), Bodin (1968, 1974)], and for a simple three-equation loop model, the AFP estimation leads to a nonic [Lyttkens (1973b), Bodin [(1974)]. The model to be dealt with in this section has two behavioural relations and one identity. In contrast to Johnston's model treated in Section 7.3, both the behavioural relations are overidentified. The structural form of the model to be considered is

$$y_{1t} = \beta_{13}y_{3t} + \gamma_{11}z_{1t} + \delta_{1t}, \tag{8.1a}$$

$$y_{2t} = \beta_{23}y_{3t} + \gamma_{22}z_{2t} + \delta_{2t}, \tag{8.1b}$$

$$y_{3t} = y_{1t} + y_{2t} + z_{3}, \tag{8.1c}$$

or in reformulated or respecified form,

$$y_{1t} = \beta_{13}\eta^*_{3t} + \gamma_{11}z_{1t} + \varepsilon_{1t}, \tag{8.2a}$$

$$y_{2t} = \beta_{23}\eta^*_{3t} + \gamma_{22}z_{1t} + \varepsilon_{2t}, \tag{8.2b}$$

$$y_{3t} = \eta^*_{1t} + \eta^*_{2t} + z_{3t} + \varepsilon_{3t}. \tag{8.2c}$$

Another form of the model is obtained by introducing expression (8.1c) for y_{3t} into (8.1a–b). If each of the resulting equations is solved for the left-hand variable before reformulation or respecification, they give

$$y_{1t} = \beta_{0.13}(\eta^*_{2t} + z_{3t}) + \gamma_{0.11}z_{1t} + \varepsilon_{1t}, \tag{8.3a}$$

$$y_{2t} = \beta_{0.23}(\eta^*_{1t} + z_{3t}) + \gamma_{0.22}z_{2t} + \varepsilon_{2t}, \tag{8.3b}$$

where

$$\beta_{0.13} = \beta_{13}/(1 - \beta_{13}), \tag{8.4a}$$

$$\gamma_{0.11} = \gamma_{11}/(1 - \beta_{13}), \tag{8.4b}$$

$$\beta_{0.23} = \beta_{23}/(1 - \beta_{23}), \tag{8.5a}$$

$$\gamma_{0.22} = \gamma_{22}/(1 - \beta_{23}). \tag{8.5b}$$

These are simple special cases of formulae (2.11a–b).

8.2. PFP Estimation According to Method III with the Use of Ratios

When the reduced form coefficients are known in approximation number s, the next approximation of the estimated version of (8.3a–b) can be written, according to Section 2.3, as

$$y_{1t} = b_{0.13}^{(s+1)}\{w_{21}^{(s)}z_{1t} + w_{22}^{(s)}z_{2t} + (w_{23}^{(s)} + 1)z_{3t}\} + g_{0.11}^{(s+1)}z_{1t} + e_{1t}^{(s+1)}, \tag{8.6a}$$

$$y_{2t} = b_{0.23}^{(s+1)}\{w_{11}^{(s)}z_{1t} + w_{12}^{(s)}z_{2t} + (w_{13}^{(s)} + 1)z_{3t}\} + g_{0.22}^{(s+1)}z_{2t} + e_{2t}^{(s+1)}, \tag{8.6b}$$

where $b_{0.13}^{(s+1)}$ and $g_{0.11}^{(s+1)}$, $b_{0.23}^{(s+1)}$ and $g_{0.22}^{(s+1)}$ can be obtained by means of the least squares method applied to (8.6a) and (8.6b). Then the reduced form coefficients in this approximation are obtained from the relations

$$w_{11}^{(s+1)} = b_{0.13}^{(s+1)}w_{21}^{(s)} + g_{0.11}^{(s+1)}, \tag{8.7a}$$

$$w_{12}^{(s+1)} = b_{0.13}^{(s+1)}w_{22}^{(s)}, \tag{8.7b}$$

$$w_{13}^{(s+1)} = b_{0.13}^{(s+1)}(w_{23}^{(s)} + 1), \tag{8.7c}$$

$$w_{21}^{(s+1)} = b_{0.23}^{(s+1)}w_{11}^{(s)}, \tag{8.7d}$$

$$w_{22}^{(s+1)} = b_{0.23}^{(s+1)}w_{12}^{(s)} + g_{0.22}^{(s+1)}, \tag{8.7e}$$

$$w_{23}^{(s+1)} = b_{0.23}^{(s+1)}(w_{13}^{(13)} + 1). \tag{8.7f}$$

With due regard to expressions (8.7a) and (8.7e), (8.6a) and (8.6b) can be written as

$$y_{1t} = b_{0.13}^{(s+1)}\{w_{22}^{(s)}z_{2t} + (w_{23}^{(s)} + 1)z_{3t}\} + w_{11}^{(s+1)}z_{1t} + e_{1t}^{(s+1)}, \tag{8.8a}$$

$$y_{2t} = b_{0.23}^{(s+1)}\{w_{11}^{(s)}z_{1t} + (w_{13}^{(s)} + 1)z_{3t}\} + w_{22}^{(s+1)}z_{2t} + e_{2t}^{(s+2)}, \tag{8.8b}$$

and from these equations $b_{0.13}^{(s+1)}$, $w_{11}^{(s+1)}$, $b_{0.23}^{(s+1)}$ and $w_{22}^{(s+1)}$ can be obtained by means of the least squares method as applied to (8.8a) and (8.8b). We shall now spell out the use of ratios.

With the aid of (8.7c) and (8.7f) the system (8.8a--b) can be written in the form

$$y_{1t} = w_{13}^{(s+1)}(q_2^{(s)}z_{2t} + z_{3t}) + w_{11}^{(s+1)} + e_{1t}^{(s+1)}, \tag{8.9a}$$

$$y_{2t} = w_{23}^{(s+1)}(q_1^{(s)}z_{1t} + z_{3t}) + w_{22}^{(s+1)}z_{2t} + e_{2t}^{(s+1)}, \tag{8.9b}$$

where

$$q_1^{(s)} = w_{11}^{(s)}/(w_{13}^{(s)} + 1), \tag{8.10a}$$

$$q_2^{(s)} = w_{22}^{(s)}/(w_{23}^{(s)} + 1). \tag{8.10b}$$

Let D be the determinant of the product sums $\sum_t z_{it}z_{jt}$, $i, j = 1, 2, 3$, and let furthermore E and H be the determinants obtained from D by replacing the elements in the first or third column, respectively, by $\sum z_{1t}y_{1t}$, $\sum z_{2t}y_{1t}$, and $\sum z_{3t}y_{1t}$. The minors obtained by deleting the ith row and jth column of the determinants D, E, and H will be denoted by D_{ij}, E_{ij} and H_{ij}. Then the application of the least squares method to relation (8.9a) gives

$$w_{11}^{(s+1)} = f_{11}(q_2^{(s)}), \tag{8.11a}$$

$$w_{13}^{(s+1)} = f_{13}(q_2^{(s)}), \tag{8.11b}$$

where

$$f_{11}(q_2) = \frac{E_{22} + (E_{23} + E_{32})q_2 + E_{33}q_2^2}{D_{22} + 2D_{23}q_2 + D_{33}q_2^2}, \tag{8.12a}$$

$$f_{13}(q_2) = \frac{H_{22} + H_{32}q_2}{D_{22} + 2D_{23}q_2 + D_{33}q_2^2}. \tag{8.12b}$$

For the ratio $q_1^{(s+1)} = w_{11}^{(s+1)}/(w_{13}^{(s+1)} + 1)$ we write

$$q_1^{(s+1)} = U_1(q_2^{(s)}), \tag{8.13}$$

where

$$U_1(q_2) = \frac{E_{22} + (E_{23} + E_{32})q_2 + E_{33}q_2^2}{D_{22} + H_{22} + (2D_{23} + H_{32})q_2 + D_{33}q_2^2}. \tag{8.14}$$

With the notations J and K for the determinants obtained from D, when the elements of the second and third column respectively are replaced by the product sums $\sum z_{1t}y_{2t}$, $\sum z_{2t}y_{2t}$, and $\sum z_{3t}y_{3t}$ with the minors indicated in the same way as before, the application of the least squares method to relation (8.9b) gives

$$w_{22}^{(s+1)} = f_{22}(q_1^{(s)}), \tag{8.15a}$$

$$w_{23}^{(s+1)} = f_{23}(q_1^{(s)}), \tag{8.15b}$$

where

$$f_{22}(q_1) = \frac{J_{11} - (J_{13} + J_{31})q_1 + J_{33}q_1^2}{D_{11} + 2D_{13} + D_{33}q_1^2}, \tag{8.16a}$$

$$f_{23}(q_1) = \frac{K_{11} - K_{31}q_1}{D_{11} + 2D_{13}q_1 + D_{33}q_1^2}. \tag{8.16b}$$

For the ratio $q_2^{(s+1)} = w_{22}^{(s+1)}/(w_{23}^{(s+1)} + 1)$ we write

$$q_2^{(s+1)} = U_2(q_1^{(s)}), \tag{8.17}$$

where

$$U_2(q_1) = \frac{J_{11} - (J_{13} + J_{31})q_1 + J_{33}q_1^2}{D_{11} + K_{11} + (2D_{13} - K_{31})q_1 + D_{33}q_1^2}. \tag{8.18}$$

Combining two steps of iteration, we have

$$q_1^{(s+2)} = U(q_1^{(s)}), \tag{8.19}$$

where the function

$$U(q_1) = U_1\{U_2(q_1)\} \tag{8.20}$$

can be written as a quotient between two polynomials of the fourth degree. The condition for the local convergence of the iterative procedure is that the absolute value of the derivative $U'(q_1)$ as evaluated in the Fix-Point has its absolute value smaller than one. Remembering that U is a compound function we have at the Fix-Point that $U'(q_1) = U_1'(q_2)U_2'(q_1)$.

8.3. *AFP Estimation*

If use is made of formula (8.19) in a Fix-Point, the AFP estimation of q_1 is obtained from the equation

$$q_1 = U(q_1), \tag{8.21}$$

which can be transformed to a quintic. After having obtained q_1 from this equation, q_2 is calculated from the formula

$$q_2 = U_2(q_1), \tag{8.22}$$

with definition (8.18) for $U_2(q_1)$. The estimated reduced form coefficients are then obtained with the aid of the functions (8.12a–b) and (8.15a–b), so that

$$w_{11} = f_{11}(q_2), \tag{8.23a}$$

$$w_{12} = q_2 f_{13}(q_2), \tag{8.23b}$$

$$w_{13} = f_{13}(q_2), \tag{8.23c}$$

$$w_{21} = q_1 f_{23}(q_1), \tag{8.23d}$$

$$w_{22} = f_{22}(q_1), \tag{8.23e}$$

$$w_{23} = f_{23}(q_2). \tag{8.23f}$$

The estimated coefficients of (8.3a–b) are calculated from

$$b_{0.13} = w_{12}/w_{22} = w_{13}/(w_{23} + 1), \tag{8.24a}$$

$$g_{0.11} = w_{11} - b_{0.13} w_{21}, \tag{8.24b}$$

$$b_{0.23} = w_{21}/w_{11} = w_{23}/(w_{13} + 1), \tag{8.24c}$$

$$g_{0.22} = w_{22} - b_{0.23} w_{12}. \tag{8.24d}$$

The estimates of the orginal structural coefficient, appearing in (8.1a–b) and (8.2a–b), are obtained by introducing estimated quantities in (8.4a–b) and (8.5a–b) and solving for the original coefficients. This gives

$$b_{13} = b_{0.13}/(1 + b_{0.13}), \tag{8.25a}$$

$$g_{11} = g_{0.11}/(1 + b_{0.13}), \tag{8.25b}$$

$$b_{23} = b_{0.23}/(1 + b_{0.23}), \tag{8.25c}$$

$$g_{22} = g_{0.22}/(1 + b_{0.23}). \tag{8.25d}$$

Instead of utilizing the estimates of the coefficients in (8.3a–b), we can use the following relations obtained from the identity (8.1c):

$$w_{31} = w_{11} + w_{21}, \tag{8.26a}$$

$$w_{32} = w_{12} + w_{22}, \tag{8.26b}$$

$$w_{33} = w_{13} + w_{23} + 1, \tag{8.26c}$$

and then calculate the estimates of the original structural coefficients from

$$b_{13} = w_{12}/w_{32} = w_{13}/w_{33}, \tag{8.27a}$$

$$g_{11} = w_{11} - b_{13}w_{31}, \tag{8.27b}$$

$$b_{23} = w_{21}/w_{31} = w_{23}/w_{33}, \tag{8.27c}$$

$$g_{22} = w_{22} - b_{23}w_{32}. \tag{8.27d}$$

8.4. A Numerical Example

Table 1 gives a numerical example of the rare case where more than one AFP solution is found. The calculation of the functions $U_1(q_2)$ and $U_2(q_1)$ gives

$$U_1(q_2) = \frac{2(1+q_2^2)}{1+5q_2-4q_2^2}, \tag{8.28a}$$

$$U_2(q_1) = \frac{1+q_1^2}{1+4q_1-q_1^2}. \tag{8.28b}$$

The quintic for q_1 has in this case four different real roots, one of which is double. It should be noted that this numerical example is constructed so that $\sum_t z_{it}z_{jt} = 0$ for $i \neq j$. In contrast to the AFP estimation of Summers' model [Lyttkens 1970a], this feature does not prevent the occurrence of plural solutions. The values of the ratios q_1 and q_2 and the pertaining values of the reduced form coefficients are given in Table 2. The numerical example is constructed so that the first set of coefficients in Table 2 is identical with those obtained from the unrestricted reduced form. The fourth value of q_1 is the double root of the quintic.

TABLE 1
Numerical example of model (8.1a–c) with four different sets of AFP estimates of the parameters.

t	y_{1t}	y_{2t}	y_{3t}	z_{1t}	z_{2t}	z_{3t}
1	−1	−3	−5	1	1	−1
2	−1	−5	−5	1	−1	1
3	−2	−3	−4	0	1	1
4	3	3	5	0	−1	−1
5	0	5	5	−1	0	0
6	0	3	3	−1	0	0
7	1	1	2	0	0	0
8	0	−1	−1	0	0	0

TABLE 2
The four sets of AFP estimates of the ratios q_1 and q_2 and the reduced form coefficients of the numerical example.

Set no.	q_1	q_2	w_{11}	w_{12}	w_{13}	w_{21}	w_{22}	w_{23}	w_{31}	w_{32}	w_{33}
1	2.0	1.0	−0.5	−1.25	−1.25	−4	−1	−2	−4.5	−2.25	−2.25
2	1.0	0.5	−0.5	−0.75	−1.50	−3	−1	−3	−3.5	−1.75	−3.50
3	−1.0	−0.5	−0.5	0.25	−0.50	−1	−1	1	−1.5	−0.75	1.50
4	−0.5	−1.0	−0.5	0.00	0.00	0	−1	0	−0.5	−1.00	1.00

TABLE 3
Modified structural coefficients, the derivatives $U_1'(q_2)$, $U_2'(q_1)$, $U'(q_1) = U_1'(q_2)U_2'(q_1)$, and the product $b_{0.13}b_{0.23}$.

Set no.	q_1	q_2	$b_{0.13}$	$g_{0.11}$	$b_{0.23}$	$g_{0.23}$	$U_1'(q_2)$	$U_2'(q_1)$	$U'(q_1)$	$b_{0.13}b_{0.23}$
1	22.0	1.0	1.25	4.50	8	9.0	5.00	0.80	4.0	10.0
2	1.0	0.5	0.75	1.75	6	3.5	0.40	0.25	0.1	4.5
3	−1.0	−0.5	−0.25	−0.75	2	−1.5	2.80	0.25	0.7	−0.5
4	−0.5	−1.0	0.00	−0.50	0	−1.0	−0.31	3.20	1.0	0.0

Table 3 gives the modified structural coefficients, typical of Method III, together with the quantities needed for judging the local convergence of the iterative procedure. Thus the condition of local convergence of the iterative procedure $|U'(q_1)| < 1$ holds for the second and third sets only. Especially it should be noted that the criterion for local convergence is violated for the first set, where the estimated reduced form coefficients coincide with those of the unrestricted reduced form. It is conjectured that this is an exceptional case.

The local convergence condition $|U'(q_1)| < 1$ applies to the parametric version of Method III, dealt with in Section 2.3. For the original version of Method III [Ågren 1972a] we have to add Ågren's criterion which for the estimated version of (8.3a–b) is reduced to the condition $|b_{0.13}b_{0.23}| < 1$. This condition is fulfilled for the third and fourth set. Thus the third set is the only one which fulfills both the conditions, that is the only set for which the original version of Method III has local convergence.

Table 4 gives the AFP estimates of the structural coefficients, obtained from formulae (8.25a–d) or (8.27a–d). It should be noted that the first set of estimated structural coefficients coincide with those of the TSLS method.

It should be recalled that the residuals of the restricted reduced form are the same as the residuals of the respecified structural form (8.2a–c) or,

TABLE 4
The four sets of AFP estimates of the structural coefficients for the numerical example.

Set no.	q_1	q_2	b_{13}	g_{11}	b_{23}	g_{22}
1	2.0	1.0	0.556	2.0	0.889	1.0
2	1.0	0.5	0.429	1.0	0.857	0.5
3	−1.0	−0.5	−0.333	−1.0	0.667	−0.5
4	−0.5	−1.0	0.000	−0.5	0.000	−1.0

TABLE 5
Residual sums of squares for the numerical example.

Set no.	q_1	q_2	Σe_{1t}^2	Σe_{2t}^2	Σe_{3t}^2
1	2	1	2.5	4	8.5
2	1	0.5	3.75	12	19.75
3	−1	−0.5	13.75	76	109.75
4	−0.5	−1	15	84	121

concerning the first two residuals, the modification (8.3a–b). For comparison Table 5 gives the four different sets of residual sums of squares according to the AFP estimation. The residual sums of squares of the first set are the smallest ones in accordance with the fact that the reduced form of the first set coincides with the unrestricted reduced form. By the least squares criterion the first set of estimated coefficients is the best one. If we restrict our attention to sets for which the criterion of local convergence of the iterative process is fulfilled, the second set of estimated coefficients is the best one. As to the original FP method, however, the condition for local convergence is fulfilled for the third set of estimated coefficients only.

8.5. *The Use of Ratios in Connection with Method II*

All work hitherto in this section leans on Method III. The basic device is to express the iteration in one dimension by means of the iteration function (8.19), which leads to the AFP estimation by solving (8.21). Alternative expressions for q_1 and q_2 are obtained from (8.23b–d, f), and in combination with the original expression and (8.26a–c) a further expansion can be made in the following way:

$$q_1 = w_{11}/(w_{13}+1) = w_{21}/w_{23} = (w_{11}+w_{21})/(w_{13}+w_{23}+1) = w_{31}/w_{13}, \quad (8.29a)$$

$$q_2 = w_{22}/(w_{23}+1) = w_{12}/w_{13} = (w_{12}+w_{22})/(w_{13}+w_{23}+1) = w_{32}/w_{33}. \quad (8.29b)$$

Then we see that (8.9a–b) can be used in connection with Method II, if we calculate the ratios

$$q_1^{(s)} = (w_{11}^{(s)} + w_{21}^{(s)})/(w_{13}^{(s)} + w_{23}^{(s)} + 1), \tag{8.30a}$$

$$q_2^{(s)} = (w_{12}^{(s)} + w_{22}^{(s)})/(w_{23}^{(s)} + w_{23}^{(s)} + 1), \tag{8.30b}$$

and then use is made of (8.11a–b) and (8.15a–b). In terms of the ratios we obtain

$$q_1^{(s+1)} = V_1(q_1^{(s)}, q_2^{(s)}), \tag{8.31a}$$

$$q_2^{(s+1)} = V_2(q_1^{(s)}, q_2^{(s)}), \tag{8.31b}$$

where with the aid of the functions (8.12a–b) and (8.16a–b),

$$V_1(q_1, q_2) = \frac{f_{11}(q_2) + q_1 f_{23}(q_1)}{f_{13}(q_2) + f_{23}(q_1) + 1}, \tag{8.32a}$$

$$V_2(q_1, q_2) = \frac{q_2 f_{13}(q_2) + f_{22}(q_1)}{f_{13}(q_2) + f_{23}(q_1) + 1}. \tag{8.32b}$$

Obviously this framework is not convenient for obtaining the AFP estimates of q_1 and q_2. The condition for local convergence of the PFP Method II is that the Jacobian matrix of $V_1(q_1, q_2)$ and $V_2(q_1, q_2)$ as evaluated in the Fix-Point has both its eigenvalues inside the unit circle. For the original FP Method II, we have to add Ågren's criterion, which in this case reduces to $|b_{13} + b_{23}| < 1$. The results of the calculations are given in Table 6. Also for Method II the second and third sets fulfil the local convergence criterion for the parametric version, while the original version, which also requires Ågren's criterion to be fulfilled, has local convergence only for the third set of estimated coefficients.

TABLE 6

The partial derivatives of the functions $V_1(q_1, q_2)$ and $V_2(q_1, q_2)$, the largest absolute eigenvalue, say $|\lambda|$, of the Jacobian matrix, and the sum $b_{13} + b_{23}$.

Set no.	q_1	q_2	$\frac{\partial V_1}{\partial q_1}$	$\frac{\partial V_1}{\partial q_2}$	$\frac{\partial V_2}{\partial q_1}$	$\frac{\partial V_2}{\partial q_2}$	$\lvert\lambda\rvert$	$b_{13} + b_{23}$
1	2.0	11.0	8/9	15/9	16/45	5/9	1.570	1.444
2	1.0	0.5	6/7	2/35	1/7	3/7	0.796	1.286
3	−1.0	−0.5	2/3	−14/15	1/3	−1/3	0.911	0.333
4	−0.5	−1.0	4/5	−5/16	8/5	0	1.212	0.000

If Method I is applied with a start, for which $y_{3t}^{(0)} = y_{1t}^{(0)} + y_{2t}^{(0)} + z_{3t}$, the first and second approximations of the structural coefficients coincide, and so do the third and fourth approximations, and so on. In fact, approximation numbers $2s - 1$ and $2s$ according to Method I coincide with approximation number s according to Method II. Therefore, in model (8.1a–c) the convergence analysis performed for Method II holds for Method I as well.

8.6. The Case where More than One Predetermined Variable Occurs in One of the Behavioural Relations

The model

$$y_{1t} = \beta_{12}y_{2t} + \gamma_{11}z_{1t} + \delta_{1t}, \tag{8.33a}$$

$$y_{2t} = \beta_{21}y_{1t} + \gamma_{22}z_{2t} + \gamma_{24}z_{4t} + \delta_{2t}, \tag{8.33b}$$

$$y_{3t} = y_{1t} + y_{2t} + z_{3t}, \tag{8.33c}$$

can, in an approximation corresponding to (8.9a–b), be written as

$$y_{1t} = w_{13}^{(s+1)}(q_2^{(s)}z_{2t} + z_{3t} + q_4^{(s)}z_{4t}) + w_{11}^{(s+1)}z_{1t} + e_{1t}^{(s+1)}, \tag{8.34a}$$

$$y_{2t} = w_{23}^{(s+1)}(q_1^{(s)}z_{1t} + z_{3t}) + w_{22}^{(s+1)}z_{2t} + w_{24}^{(s+1)}z_{4t} + e_{2t}^{(s+1)}, \tag{8.34b}$$

where $q_1^{(s)}$ and $q_2^{(s)}$ are defined by (8.10a–b) and $q_4^{(s)} = w_{24}^{(s)}/(w_{23}^{(s)} + 1)$. The procedure used in Section 8.2 leads to iteration functions of the form

$$q_1^{(s+1)} = U_1(q_2^{(s)}, q_4^{(s)}), \tag{8.35a}$$

$$q_2^{(s+1)} = U_2(q_1^{(s)}), \tag{8.35b}$$

$$q_4^{(s+1)} = U_4(q_1^{(s)}), \tag{8.35c}$$

where $U_2(q_1)$ and $U_4(q_1)$ are quotients between two second-degree polynomials in q_1 with the same polynomial in the denominator, while $U_1(q_2, q_4)$ is a ratio between two second-degree polynomials in q_2 and q_4. Again by combining two iteration steps, we have

$$q_1^{(s+2)} = U(q_1^{(s)}), \tag{8.36a}$$

where

$$U(q_1) = U_1\{U_2(q_1), U_4(q_1)\}, \tag{8.36b}$$

and the equation $q_1 = U(q_1)$ can again be transformed to a quintic. A quintic is also obtained in the case of any number of additional predetermined variables in (8.33b).

8.7. *The Case where the Same Additional Variable Occurs in Both Behavioural Equations*

If the additional predetermined variable occurs in both behavioural relations, say

$$y_{1t} = \beta_{12}y_{2t} + \gamma_{11}z_{1t} + \gamma_{14}z_{4t} + \delta_{1t}, \tag{8.37a}$$

$$y_{2t} = \beta_{21}y_{1t} + \gamma_{22}z_{2t} + \gamma_{24}z_{4t} + \delta_{2t}, \tag{8.37b}$$

$$y_{3t} = y_{1t} + y_{2t} + z_{3t}, \tag{8.37c}$$

the approximation corresponding to (8.9a–b) is

$$y_{1t} = w_{13}^{(s+1)}(q_2^{(s)}z_{2t} + z_{3t}) + w_{11}^{(s+1)}z_{1t} + w_{14}^{(s+1)}z_{4t} + e_{1t}^{(s+1)}, \tag{8.38a}$$

$$y_{2t} = w_{23}^{(s+1)}(q_1^{(s)}z_{1t} + z_{3t}) + w_{22}^{(s+1)}z_{2t} + w_{24}^{(s+1)}z_{4t} + e_{2t}^{(s+1)}, \tag{8.38b}$$

where $q_1^{(s)}$ and $q_2^{(s)}$ are defined by (8.10a–b). Let D be the determinant of the product sums $\sum z_{it}z_{jt}$, $i, j = 1, 2, 3, 4$, E and H the determinants obtained from D replacing the elements of the first or third column, respectively, by $\sum y_{1t}z_{1t}$, $\sum y_{1t}z_{2t}$, $\sum y_{1t}z_{3t}$, $\sum y_{1t}z_{4t}$, while J and K are the determinants obtained from D replacing the second or third columns, respectively, by $\sum y_{2t}z_{1t}$, $\sum y_{2t}z_{2t}$, $\sum y_{2t}z_{3t}$, $\sum y_{2t}z_{4t}$. With these determinants, (8.11)–(8.27) can be applied to the estimation of the present model.

Another way of describing the extension is to consider the determinants D, E, H, J, K as third-order determinants with the elements $\sum y_{it}z_{jt}$ and $\sum z_{it}z_{jt}$ replaced by $\sum y_{it}z_{jt} - (\sum y_{it}z_{4t} \sum z_{jt}z_{4t}/\sum z_{4t}^2)$ and $\sum z_{it}z_{jt} - (\sum z_{it}z_{4t} \sum z_{jt}z_{4t}/\sum z_{4t}^2)$ when (8.11)–(8.27) are used.

Since the condition $\sum z_{4t}e_{1t} = \sum z_{4t}e_{2t} = 0$ implies that $\sum z_{4t}d_{1t} = \sum z_{4t}d_{2t} = 0$, the estimates of γ_{14} and γ_{24} are obtained from

$$g_{14} = (\textstyle\sum y_{1t}z_{4t} - b_{13}\sum y_{3t}z_{4t} - g_{11}\sum z_{1t}z_{4t})/\sum z_{4t}^2, \tag{8.39a}$$

$$g_{24} = (\textstyle\sum y_{2t}z_{4t} - b_{23}\sum y_{3t}z_{4t} - g_{22}\sum z_{2t}z_{4t})/\sum z_{4t}^2. \tag{8.39b}$$

The procedure used here can in an obvious way be extended to the case where more than one additional predetermined variable occurs in both the behavioural relations simultaneously.

9. Alternative Procedures when Subsystems Occur

When n^* structural equations form a subsystem involving only n^* current endogenous variables and m^* predetermined variables, any estimation method belonging to the Fix-Point family of methods can be applied to the subsystem separately; Lyttkens (1973b). For instance, even if the model considered in Section 8 were a subsystem, the AFP method could be applied just in the way described. In a case, where a structural equation of the subsystem has m^*+1 variables, the equation is just identified with respect to the subsystem, and it can be replaced by a regression equation on the m^* predetermined variables of the subsystem in the way described in Sections 1.4.2 and 7.1.

The n^* components of y_t^*, which are obtained from the separate estimation of the subsystem, can be treated as predetermined variables, when the rest of the system is estimated. This is the way of proceeding used in Section 7.2 in connection with the AFP estimation. In the special case where the residuals of the structural equations of the subsystem are independent of the residuals of the structural equations outside the subsystem, a consistent estimate is also obtained if the endogenous variables of the subsystem themselves are treated as predetermined variables when the rest of the system is estimated; see Lyttkens (1973b).

Finally it should be noted that if the n^* equations of the subsystem belong to a larger subsystem containing n^*+n^{**} equations, then the separate estimation of the inner subsystem containing n^* equations is followed by a separate application of the procedures of the preceding paragraph to the remaining n^{**} equations of the larger subsystem. The larger subsystem is considered as one subsystem, when the rest of the system is estimated. This procedure can be extended to subsystems of any order.

Chapter 5

ESTIMATION OF REAL-WORLD MODELS BY FIX-POINT AND OTHER METHODS

REINHOLD BERGSTRÖM

1. Introduction

Ever since the pioneering work of Haavelmo, it has been known that the Ordinary Least Squares (OLS) method is inconsistent for models that are interdependent. Many of the methods that have been developed for interdependent systems and which give consistent estimates have one serious drawback. They cannot be used for models with undersized samples, i.e., in cases where the number of predetermined variables is smaller than the number of observations. For modern econometric models this is rather the rule than the exception.

By suitable modifications some of the more common methods can be applied to models with undersized samples. The best-known example is the Two-Stage Least Squares (TSLS) method. However, there are methods that can be used in the case of undersized samples without modifications. One such method is the Fix-Point (FP) method, another the Iterative Instrumental Variables (IIV) method. One further method that is applicable to undersized samples is the Full Information Maximum Likelihood method with Diagonal covariance matrix (FIMD). In contrast to FP and IIV this method is consistent only if the covariance matrix of the structural residuals is diagonal.

In this chapter two moderately large econometric models are estimated by means of FP and other methods. The models are a linear version of the well-known Klein–Goldberger model and a recent model of the Czechoslovak economy. The models have been more fully analyzed in Bergström (1974 and 1976). Comparisons will also be made with the performance of FP in the case of other real-world econometric models.

2. The IIV Method

In order to describe the IIV method we use the basic specification of the system given in Chapter 1.

The IIV estimator is defined as a solution to the nonlinear system

$$y_i Y^{*\prime}_{(i)} = b_{(i)} Y_{(i)} Y^{*\prime}_{(i)} + g_{(i)} Z_{(i)} Y^{*\prime}_{(i)}, \tag{2.1a}$$

$$y_i Z'_{(i)} = b_{(i)} Y_{(i)} Z'_{(i)} + g_{(i)} Z_{(i)} Z'_{(i)}. \tag{2.1b}$$

The estimator can be obtained by various methods. The Iterative Instrumental Variables (IIV) method, introduced in Lyttkens (1966), consists of two stages in each iteration. In the first stage, we use proxies of $Y^*_{(i)}$ denoted by $Y^{(s)}_{(i)}$, and obtain proxies of $b_{(i)}$ and $g_{(i)}$ by using $Y^{(s)}_{(i)}$ and $Z_{(i)}$,

$$y_i Y^{(s)\prime}_{(i)} = b^{(s)}_{(i)} Y_{(i)} Y^{(s)\prime}_{(i)} + g^{(s)}_{(i)} Z_{(i)} Y^{(s)\prime}_{(i)}, \tag{2.2a}$$

$$y_i Z'_{(i)} = b^{(s)}_{(i)} Y_{(i)} Z'_{(i)} + g^{(s)}_{(i)} Z_{(i)} Z'_{(i)}. \tag{2.2b}$$

In the second stage, new proxies of $Y^*_{(i)}$ are obtained from

$$y^{(s+1)}_t = (I - B^{(s)})^{-1} G^{(s)} z_t, \qquad t = 1, T. \tag{2.3}$$

In Bergström (1974) two alternative methods are proposed. The first stage of these is identical to the one above, while the second for the SIIV method is

$$y^{(s+1)}_i = b^{(s)}_{(i)} Y^{(s)}_{(i)} + g^{(s)}_{(i)} Z_{(i)}. \tag{2.4}$$

By performing stage 2 of a relation directly after stage 1 and always using the most recent proxies of $Y^*_{(i)}$, a method is obtained that normally is faster than SIIV, the RSIIV method. The two stages can be written as

$$y_i Y^{(s,s+1)\prime}_{(i)} = b^{(s)}_{(i)} Y_{(i)} Y^{(s,s+1)\prime}_{(i)} + g^{(s)}_{(i)} Z_{(i)} Y^{(s,s+1)\prime}_{(i)}, \tag{2.5a}$$

$$y_i Z'_{(i)} = b^{(s)}_{(i)} Y_{(i)} Z'_{(i)} + g^{(s)}_{(i)} Z_{(i)} Z'_{(i)}, \tag{2.5b}$$

and

$$y^{(s+1)}_i = b^{(s)}_{(i)} Y^{(s,s+1)}_{(i)} + g_{(i)} Z_{(i)}. \tag{2.6}$$

Here $Y^{(s,s+1)}_{(i)}$ always includes the most recent proxies that are available. In many cases the speed of convergence of the methods can be improved by the introduction of a relaxation factor; see Bergström (1974).

In order to compare IIV with FP it will be remembered that the GEID estimator (see Chapter 3) is defined as a real solution to

$$y_i Y^{*\prime}_{(i)} = b_{(i)} Y^*_{(i)} Y^{*\prime}_{(i)} + g_{(i)} Z_{(i)} Y^{*\prime}_{(i)}, \tag{2.7a}$$

$$y_i Z'_{(i)} = b_{(i)} Y^*_{(i)} Z'_{(i)} + g_{(i)} Z_{(i)} Z'_{(i)}. \tag{2.7b}$$

This estimator can be obtained by several methods. The original method was the Fix-Point (FP) method introduced by Wold (1965).[1] Each iteration consists of two stages. The first stage is a regression of y_i on $Y^{(s)}_{(i)}$ and $Z_{(i)}$, i.e.,

$$y_i Y^{(s)\prime}_{(i)} = b^{(s)}_{(i)} Y^{(s)}_{(i)} Y^{(s)\prime}_{(i)} + g^{(s)}_{(i)} Z_{(i)} Y^{(s)\prime}_{(i)}, \tag{2.8a}$$

$$y_i Z'_{(i)} = b^{(s)}_{(i)} Y^{(s)}_{(i)} Z'_{(i)} + g^{(s)}_{(i)} Z_{(i)} Z'_{(i)}. \tag{2.8b}$$

The second stage is the same as for SIIV, i.e.,

$$y^{(s+1)}_i = b^{(s)}_{(i)} Y^{(s)}_{(i)} + g^{(s)}_{(i)} Z_{(i)}. \tag{2.9}$$

The convergence properties of FP are improved by RFP [Bodin (1974)] which is a similar modification of FP as RSIIV of SIIV.

SFP finally [Bergström (1974)] is the method of FP type that corresponds to IIV, i.e., has the same second stage while the first stage is given by (2.8).

When using the IIV and SFP methods it is necessary to invert $I - B^{(s)}$, which is time-consuming for large systems. Thus these methods are slower than the others per iteration for such models. A reordering of the system can improve the convergence properties of RSIIV and RFP. The other methods are not affected by this.

As the methods used to obtain the estimators described above are iterative, the convergence properties are very important. Exact conditions for convergence have been derived in Bergström (1974), Bodin (1974) and Ågren (1972a). These involve matrices of order $nT \times nT$ or $nm \times nm$ which means that they are difficult to use for large models.

However, approximate criteria have also been obtained. With a relaxation factor, α, the approximate condition for convergence of SIIV and FFP[2] is that

$$\rho[(1-\alpha)I + \alpha B] < 1, \tag{2.10}$$

where ρ denotes the spectral radius. If we write B as the sum of a strictly lower triangular matrix, L, and a strictly upper triangular matrix, U, i.e.,

$$B = L + U, \tag{2.11}$$

[1] In the following we are going to talk of FP estimates although formally GEID estimates would be more correct.

[2] FFP is FP with a relaxation factor. For the other methods no special name accompanies the introduction of this device.

the approximate condition for RSIIV and RFP is

$$\rho[(I-\alpha L)^{-1}((1-\alpha)I+\alpha U)]<1. \tag{2.12}$$

The approximate condition for RF-FP is

$$\rho[(1-\alpha)I-\alpha(I-B)^{-1}B_0]<1, \tag{2.13}$$

where B_0 is obtained by setting all elements in B that belong to identities as 0. There is no easy approximate condition for IIV.

For a detailed discussion of the convergence properties of the various IIV and FP methods we refer to Bergström (1974) and Chapter 2.

3. Estimation of the Klein–Goldberger Model

3.1. The Model

The Klein–Goldberger model in its original form was presented in Klein and Goldberger (1955). In this form it consists of 15 behavioural relations and 5 identities. A further study of some properties of the model was given by Goldberger (1959). Klein (1966a, 1966b and 1969) has presented a number of modifications of the original model. The one described in Klein (1966b, pp. 77–81) will mainly be used in this chapter. The specification of the model can be found in Table A.1 in Appendix A. Table A.2 in this appendix lists the variables included.

Besides the 11 behavioural relations included in Table A.1, the model consists of four further relations in which only predetermined variables are included among the explanatory variables. If we assume that the residuals of these four relations are uncorrelated with the residuals of all other relations, these endogenous variables can be regarded as predetermined in the estimation of the remaining 11 behavioural relations. In this way the estimates of FIML, IIV, FIMD and FP are not changed, compared with the case when the whole system is estimated. TSLS and LIML will, however, be slightly affected by the change of some endogenous variables into predetermined variables. As the variables that are changed in this way are very few, the changes in the estimates should be limited.

It should be noted that in the computation of the systematic parts of the endogenous variables (y_t^*) the treatment of some endogenous variables as predetermined ones will improve the y_t^* values. For example, when ex post forecasts of GNP are computed we use the correct value of private investment in plant and equipment (I_p) instead of the y_t^* value of this variable computed from the ordinary regression. What is important is that the change is the same for all methods, so that comparisons can still be made.

In Klein's original version of the model there are four identities. Of these three are retained, while the identity

$$whN_W = p(W_1 + W_2) \tag{3.1}$$

is dropped.

In this way we avoid nonlinearity. The price we have to pay for this is to treat the price variable, p, as exogenous. Economically this is, of course, not very satisfactory.

In the present version of the model a large number of identites are introduced in order to avoid composite variables.

The estimated version of the model consists of 23 endogenous variables in all. The number of predetermined variables is 24. Klein (1966b) gives estimates for the time period 1929–41, 1946–62. However, he does not include the data. Therefore, it has been necessary to use the data included in Klein (1969). As these do not cover the year 1946, which is of doubtful value anyhow, the time period used is 1929–41, 1947–62; 29 observations in all. It is possible to test the forecasting ability of the different methods as we also have data for 1963–65.

The model is built around the seven basic equations of a Keynesian system. The model is completed by a disaggregation of some of the variables and an explanation of factor shares.

Usually consumption is disaggregated into at least two parts. Although this is done in some versions of the model, it is not done in this case. The reason is a desire to make the system more manageable.

Investment, on the other hand, is separated into three parts, namely:

1. residential construction (equation 2),
2. inventory investment (equation 3),
3. private investment in plant and equipment.

The last component is entirely explained by predetermined variables, and if we make the assumptions about non-correlation of residuals that was mentioned earlier this equation does not have to be included.

In a Keynesian system the production function really determines the demand for labour, given the total demand and the capital stock. In Klein's version of the model the dependent variable of equation 6 is the total product of the non-government sector. To avoid getting the same left-hand variable in two equations, which cannot be allowed when FP is used, a shift had to be made. The left-hand variable chosen is, instead, the demand for labour. In view of what we said above about the meaning of the equation, this does not seem to be very unreasonable. (It should be noticed that for the symmetric methods the estimates are not influenced by which variable is regarded as dependent.)

Equation 8 is another of the fundamental Keynesian equations explaining changes in the nominal wages by means of unemployment and lagged changes in prices. The total private wage bill is explained by the total non-government product and the lagged private wage bill.

Of the remaining equations one explains hours-worked as a function of the change in nominal wages and unemployment. One further demand component is also considered, the imports. Here we have a traditional equation with GNP and relative import prices as explanatory factors.

The three remaining relations explain various factor shares necessary to link disposable income with GNP.

3.2. The TSLS and LIML Estimation

As earlier mentioned we have 29 observations and 24 predetermined variables. This fact causes some problems when we use TSLS and LIML. The small number of degrees of freedom makes TSLS practically identical to OLS in this case, if we use the original version of the method.

These estimates are not included here. Instead estimates have been obtained by the procedure that is normally used for undersized samples. This procedure was in principle proposed by Kloek and Mennes (1960). However, a minor modification of their approach has been employed.

In the first stage of the ordinary TSLS method each endogenous variable is regressed on all predetermined variables. When this is impossible Kloek and Mennes suggested that a certain number of principal components should be used instead. Their original suggestion was that in the estimation of the ith relation each endogenous variable on the right-hand side of this relation in the first stage should be regressed on the predetermined variables included in the relation and a certain number of principal components extracted from the covariance matrix of those predetermined variables not included in the relation.

Principal components can be used in several other ways. In the present study each endogenous variable has been regressed on a number of principal components in the first stage. Principal components corresponding to the largest eigenvalues have been used. This method has the advantage compared with the original Kloek and Mennes approach that the same set of regressors is used throughout the first stage. Some eigenvalues of the covariance matrix of the predetermined variables are given in Table 1.

The first component thus explains 98.7% of the variance, and the first 5 components 99.8%. It is, of course, not unexpected to obtain these results, because of the very dominant trend present in almost all variables. This also means that not too many principal components should be needed in the TSLS estimation. There are no clearcut criteria that can be used to determine the appropriate number; see Mitchell (1970) and Bergström (1970). In Table 2 some characteristics are tabulated. It can be seen that the average Q^2 value[3] for less than 6 principal components is markedly lower

TABLE 1
Eigenvalues of the covariance matrix of the predetermined variables, M_{zz}.

Principal components	Eigenvalues λ_i	$\lambda_i/\Sigma\lambda_i$	Cumulative sum $\lambda_i/\Sigma\lambda_i$
1	19078.92	0.9867	0.9867
2	102.25	0.0053	0.9920
3	65.40	0.0034	0.9954
4	46.64	0.0024	0.9978
5	10.82	0.0006	0.9984

TABLE 2
Some characteristics of different TSLS and LIML estimates.

Principal components	TSLS			LIML		
	Average Q^2	Estimates of equation 1		Average Q^2	Estimates of equation 1	
4	0.6121	0.2700	0.7551	−0.1912	0.0554	0.9857
5	0.8669	0.5205	0.4852	0.8203	0.3567	0.6615
6	0.8863	0.5081	0.4986	0.8902	0.2818	0.7421
7	0.8861	0.4881	0.5201	0.8905	0.2889	0.7345
8	0.8872	0.4847	0.5238	0.8893	0.2463	0.7803
9	0.8877	0.4944	0.5134	0.8906	0.2838	0.7398
10	0.8868	0.5326	0.4723	0.8854	0.1724	0.8597
11	0.8831	0.5335	0.4714	0.8939	0.3164	0.7049
12	0.8827	0.5335	0.4713	0.8931	0.3220	0.6989
13	0.8824	0.5313	0.4737	0.8922	0.3135	0.7080
14	0.8797	0.5464	0.4574	0.8519	0.3885	0.6273
15	0.8803	0.5436	0.4605	0.8635	0.3254	0.6952
16	0.8793	0.5436	0.4604	0.8204	0.3181	0.7031
17	0.8794	0.5455	0.4584	0.8108	0.3158	0.7055

[3] Q^2 is the reduced form equivalent to R^2 and is defined as $Q_i^2 = 1 - \Sigma(y_{it} - y_{it}^*)^2/\Sigma(y_{it} - \bar{y}_{it})^2$, where y_{it}^* is a forecast of y_{it}.

than in the other cases. 6–10 principal components yield more or less equivalent results. Estimates based on 9 principal components which give the highest average Q^2 value have been selected for TSLS, but it is possible that a more detailed analysis could reveal another version as slightly better.

It is possible to extract principal components from the correlation matrix, too. For a discussion see Bergström (1970, 1971).

It is a well-known fact that LIML is more sensitive to multicollinearity than TSLS and OLS; see e.g. Klein (1966b). This is confirmed by the estimation of this model. For the consumption function LIML estimates are not even obtained. The reason for this is that non-real eigenvalues occur. In principle all eigenvalues are of course real and the presence of non-real values is an indication of the extremely severe numerical problems caused by the multicollinearity, which causes M_{zz} to be almost singular. It is possible to get by this difficulty by rescaling the variables and/or using deviations from the means. In these cases we obtain estimates but they are very unsatisfactory.

However, in view of the difficulties mentioned above a method based on principal components has been used in this case, too. The ordinary LIML method can be described as follows. The estimates of the ith relation are those that minimize the ratio[4]

$$\lambda = (b_{[i]} W^* b'_{[i]})/(b_{[i]} W b_{[i]}), \tag{3.2}$$

where

$$W^* = Y_{[i]} Y'_{[i]} - Y_{[i]} Z'_{(i)} \{Z_{(i)} Z'_{(i)}\}^{-1} Z'_{(i)} Y_{[i]}, \tag{3.3}$$

$$W = Y_{[i]} Y'_{[i]} - Y_{[i]} Z' \{ZZ'\}^{-1} Z' Y'_{[i]}, \tag{3.4}$$

and $g_{(i)}$ is given by

$$g_{(i)} = b_{[i]} Y_{[i]} Z'_{(i)} \{Z_{(i)} Z'_{(i)}\}^{-1}, \tag{3.5}$$

and λ is in practice obtained as the smallest eigenvalue of

$$|W^* - \lambda W| = 0. \tag{3.6}$$

When $m \geq T$ the matrix W will be singular and the procedure breaks down. But instead of using all predetermined variables we can extract

[4] $b_{[i]}$ is a vector of order $1 \times (n_i + 1)$ consisting of the non-zero elements of the ith row of B when the system is symmetrically specified. $Y_{[i]}$ is similarly defined. Notice the difference between $Y_{(i)}$ and $Y_{[i]}$.

principal components and use a suitable number of these in the computation of the matrix W. An added advantage is that the problem of multicollinearity, which is often very sever, is reduced. The procedure above is outlined in Klein (1966b) and an application of the method can be found in Bergström (1971).

As can be seen from Table 2 any number of principal components between 6 and 13 seems to be acceptable. The differences in average Q^2 value are very small. The estimates of the first equation, included because they are generally most volatile, are less stable than those of TSLS. (We also notice that they indicate a lower short-run propensity to consume than the estimates of TSLS, 0.3 instead of 0.5.) Starting with 14 principal components unreasonable values are obtained in equation 6, which explains the less good Q^2 values from then onwards. In this case, too, the version with the highest average Q^2 value has been selected. This means that 11 principal components have been used.

3.3. *A Comparison of the Parameter Estimates*

Both IIV and FP estimates have been obtained without difficulty. For an analysis of the speed of convergence of different procedures we refer to Bergström (1974).

Already a quick glance at the parameter estimates (Appendix A) shows that FIML in many cases gives values that deviate from those obtained by other methods. In order to verify this, the number of extreme estimates of each parameter value has been counted. As extreme values the largest and the smallest of the seven estimates have been defined. In all 24 parameters have been included, the constant terms not being considered.

From Table 3 we see that for only 4 of the 24 parameters FIML did not give an extreme value. Another method that is somewhat more liable to give deviating estimates than the others, is FP.

TABLE 3
Number of extreme values.

OLS	6
TSLS	0
LIML	4
IIV	4
FIML	20
FIMD	5
FP	9

The consumption function shows large differences. This is often the case, as the correlation between the included explanatory variables is very high, which tends to give a mix-up of the effects. The short-run marginal propensity to consume (*mpc*) varies between 0.56 and 0.17 according to our estimates. The lower value is given by FIML. In the same way the coefficient of lagged consumption varies considerably. However, the sums of the absolute value of the coefficients is almost equal for all the methods. It varies between 1.0024 for OLS and 1.0334 for FIML. This means that they all give a long-run *mpc* that is about 1.

The equation, explaining investment in residential construction, shows small differences. In the equation explaining inventory investments we find further differences. The method deviating is again FIML. It gives a higher value to the sales variable and also a larger negative influence of the stock variable. The equation can be written as

$$\Delta H = 0.2028(X - I_H) - 37.27 - 0.8828H_{-1}. \tag{3.7}$$

The differences in the import equation are, on the whole, small. In the hours-worked equation we again encounter large differences. The extremes are FIML and FP, the former method indicating an effect on h of an increase in $w - w_{-1}$, almost three times that indicated by FP.

As mentioned earlier the left-hand variable has been changed in equation 6. This does not affect the symmetric methods LIML, IIV, FIML and FIMD, but the other methods are influenced. This should be borne in mind when the estimates are studied. To facilitate this, the alternative specification is also given. The differences are large. This is the only case when the methods disagree as to the sign of a parameter. FIML gives an unsatisfactory negative relationship between capital stock and production. This means that it indicates very large effects of changes in the labour inputs. The other extreme is FP with small values for the labour inputs.

In the wage-share equation we find FIML and FP once again as extremes. FP allocates about 12% more of a production increase to labour in the short run. However, the long-run figures are very similar, 0.58 and 0.57. Most of the other methods are fairly close together, around a short-run value of 0.40.

In equation 8, explaining wages, we find FIML deviating from the other methods considerably, giving very small weight to lagged changes in prices. The other methods, with FP at the other extreme, attach less importance to the number of persons out of work.

FIML and FP fail to agree with the other methods in the corporative savings equations, too. Here, however, the deviations are in the same direction. They indicate a much smaller negative influence on corporate savings of earlier dividends than the other methods do.

The differences in equations 10 and 11 are small, FIML showing estimates some distance away from those of the other methods.

3.4. *Ex post Forecasts in the Sampling Period*

In Table 4 the Q^2 values and the reduced form residuals based on the ex post forecasts with true predetermined variables in the estimation period are given. There is of course a close connection between the two measures, but is should be noticed that relatively large differences between different methods as measured by the mean square error can look very small when related to the total variance of an endogenous variable which happens when Q^2 is used.

A ranking between OLS, IIV, FIMD, FIML and FP has been made. LIML and TSLS are not included as their results depend on which version is selected. In the ranking only the first 14 endogenous variables are included. The reason for this is that the others, with two exceptions, are

TABLE 4

Ex post forecasts based on true predetermined variables, Q_i^2 and mean square error (*MSE*).

Endogenous variable	*MSE*					Q_i^2
	OLS	IIV	FIML	FIMD	FP	FP
1	35.85	28.78	28.35	29.86	26.56	0.9945
2	1.79	1.86	1.95	1.83	1.80	0.9471
3	5.72	5.68	6.42	5.72	5.54	0.9911
4	0.9748	0.9690	0.9732	0.9930	0.9563	0.9693
5	8.87	7.02	8.37	7.48	7.66	0.6445
6	1.29	1.08	1.55	1.19	0.74	0.7828
7	17.45	14.89	14.87	15.21	13.34	0.9959
8	0.0048	0.0047	0.0056	0.0047	0.0044	0.5484
9	9.20	9.76	8.73	9.65	10.33	0.8052
10	7.6974	7.80	7.85	7.79	7.7016	0.9354
11	0.5096	0.5108	0.6673	0.5105	0.5115	0.9766
12	52.78	45.09	39.49	46.49	40.36	0.9968
13	13.72	12.14	9.39	12.74	13.49	0.9804
14	39.54	35.92	31.12	36.68	30.21	0.9941
15	38.76	32.25	32.22	33.27	29.81	0.9976
16	1.29	1.08	1.54	1.19	0.74	0.9937
17	52.78	45.09	39.49	46.49	40.36	0.9960
18	52.78	45.09	39.49	46.49	40.36	0.8322
19	8.87	7.02	8.37	7.48	7.66	0.4907
20	0.0048	0.0047	0.0056	0.0047	0.0044	0.9978
21	1.29	1.08	1.55	1.19	0.74	0.9369
22	11.52	8.15	11.62	8.47	8.75	0.8572
23	1.79	1.86	1.95	1.83	1.80	0.9940

TABLE 5
Summary statistics based on Q^2 for variables y_1–y_{14} together with GNP forecasts.

Method	Q^2			*GNP*	
	Rank	Best result	Average	Average absolute percentage error	Q^2
OLS	50.0	3	0.8776	2.56	0.9958
IIV	38.5	1	0.8942	2.51	0.9964
FIML	46.0	3	0.8750	—[a]	0.9969
FIMD	46.5	0	0.8897	2.53	0.9963
FP	29.0	7	0.8982	2.24	0.9968

[a] Unavailable.

linear combinations of the 14 variables mentioned above, and predetermined variables. This is illustrated by the fact that their residual variances have already appeared among the first 14 variables. Thus the reduced form residuals of relations 6 and 16 are the same, just to give one example.

We find that FP performs very well. IIV is the second best method, while OLS is worse than FIML and FIMD. A closer study reveals a few notable features.

(1) Employment (equation 6) is very well explained by FP, compared with the other methods. The *MSE* of FP is 30–50% lower than the *MSE* of the other methods, an unusually large difference.

(2) The change in wages is not so well explained by FIML as by the other methods.

(3) For some variables all methods give unsatisfactory results (Q^2 lower than 0.9). They are hours worked, the employment variable, y_6, and the wage change.

(4) FIML is substantially better than the other methods for the variable *P*.

A special study of the ability to forecast GNP has been made. All methods are about equally good, although FIML and FP are slightly better than the others.

3.5. *Forecasts after the Estimation Period*

As mentioned earlier it has been possible to make forecasts for 1963–65. The results are summarized in Table 6. In making the forecasts the true values of the predetermined variables have been used.

TABLE 6
Average absolute percentage error, 1963–65.

Variable	OLS	IIV	FIML	FIMD	FP	LIML	TSLS
y_1	1.91	1.65	1.44	1.79	1.76	1.64	1.83
y_2	8.31	7.85	8.00	7.96	7.73	7.80	8.08
y_3	1.06	0.90	1.53	0.90	0.94	1.02	1.02
y_4	4.42	4.49	3.50	4.32	4.31	4.38	4.40
y_5	0.77	0.18	0.70	0.44	0.47	0.40	0.64
y_6	7.06	10.13	11.47	7.23	12.36	11.20	8.16
y_7	0.59	0.39	0.22	0.47	0.48	0.37	0.51
y_8	23.41	23.30	20.67	23.33	24.13	22.96	23.32
y_9	41.05	29.41	8.08	33.44	26.45	26.19	37.63
y_{10}	5.29	4.38	5.92	4.77	4.80	4.17	5.20
y_{11}	1.05	1.06	1.14	1.05	1.06	1.06	1.05
y_{12}	0.73	0.53	0.26	0.66	0.67	0.53	0.67
y_{13}	3.24	2.53	1.77	2.99	2.88	2.58	3.05
y_{14}	0.47	0.23	0.50	0.30	0.48	0.29	0.36
y_{15}	0.73	0.56	0.45	0.67	0.67	0.57	0.68
y_{16}	0.44	0.64	0.69	0.46	0.78	0.70	0.51
y_{17}	0.81	0.60	0.29	0.73	0.75	0.59	0.75
y_{18}	9.77	7.03	3.40	8.70	8.82	6.98	8.95
y_{19}	13.70	3.17	12.32	7.78	8.47	7.02	11.44
y_{20}	0.75	0.74	0.62	0.75	0.77	0.71	0.73
y_{21}	7.77	11.55	12.02	8.35	14.40	12.57	9.37
y_{22}	21.00	16.71	16.59	19.08	18.65	16.52	20.12
y_{23}	2.49	2.35	2.39	2.38	2.32	2.34	2.42
Average	6.82	5.67	4.95	6.02	6.27	5.77	6.56

We can see that none of the methods give satisfactory results for some of the variables. These are y_2, y_6, y_8 and y_9, all of which have a larger average absolute percentage error than 5. (We limit the discussion to the first 14 variables.) This result is in excellent agreement with the behaviour during the estimation period. These variables all have Q^2 values less than 0.95, while, with one exception, none of the others have. This means that a good performance in the estimation period is an indication of good forecasts. The single exception is the variable $y_5 = h$, for which a Q^2 value of about 0.60 is followed by extremely small forecast errors (less than 1%).

When the different methods are compared OLS is clearly worse than the others. Of these IIV has the lowest rank, while FIML performs best for the largest number of variables, and also has the lowest average error. On the other hand FIML is also the worst method for quite a number of variables.

It is interesting to notice that FIML achieved the best result in the estimation period for three variables, S_c, X and P, and that this performance is repeated in the forecast period. For these variables FIML is very much superior to the other methods. The average absolute percentage

TABLE 7
A ranking of different methods based on the average absolute percentage error for variables y_1–y_{14}, 1963–65.

Method	Rank	Best result	Worst result	Average absolute percentage error[a]
OLS	56.5	1.5	7	6.82
IIV	31	3.5	1	5.67
FIML	39	7	4	4.95
FIMD	38	1	0	6.02
FP	45.5	1	2	6.27

[a] All 23 variables.

TABLE 8
Forecasts of the GNP, 1963–65.

Method	Level			Percentage increase		
	1963	1964	1965	1963	1964	1965
Actual	492.6	516.0	539.2	3.40	4.75	4.50
OLS	485.6	513.9	537.3	1.98	4.33	4.15
IIV	488.5	513.6	537.5	2.58	4.29	4.18
FIML	490.4	514.4	539.1	2.96	4.44	4.48
FIMD	487.3	513.4	537.1	2.33	4.24	4.10
FP	487.7	512.9	537.0	2.40	4.15	4.09

error is only 31, 49 and 70% of that of the second best method. In the same way the variables where FIML performs badly are also those where the performance was less satisfactory in the estimation period.

For GNP all methods give good results (0.26–0.73% average error). This is not too surprising as the three years under study show a smooth increase in the GNP. The detailed results are given in Table 8.

The methods all slightly underestimate the increase in the GNP during all three years. Except for FIML the error is about 1% the first year and only 0.5% the other two. The FIML error is very small.

3.6. Impact Multipliers

In Table 9 some of the impact multipliers (restricted reduced form coefficients) are presented.

In all there are 552 multipliers, most of which are different from zero, so a heavy restriction is necessary in the presentation. The best-known multiplier is that associated with the effect of government spending on the

GNP. It is clear that different methods give very different results. At one extreme we find OLS with 1.79 and at the other FIML with 1.39. IIV is the

TABLE 9
Impact multipliers.

(a) Change in X generated by a unit change in

	$p_m - p$	W_2	I_p	T_c/p	T/p	$G + F_e$	$G + T/P$
OLS	14.239	0.555	1.834	−0.194	−1.157	1.787	0.630
TSLS	12.611	0.476	1.688	−0.142	−0.950	1.650	0.700
LIML	10.716	0.293	1.473	−0.061	−0.575	1.449	0.874
IIV	9.310	0.315	1.473	−0.088	−0.613	1.448	0.835
FIML	9.482	0.173	1.401	−0.090	−0.358	1.392	1.034
FIMD	13.021	0.405	1.562	−0.096	−0.785	1.529	0.744
FP	10.612	0.248	1.555	−0.131	−0.603	1.532	0.929

(b) Change in C generated by a unit change in

	$p_m - p$	W_2	I_p	T_c/p	T/p	$G + F_e$
OLS	4.358	0.203	0.584	−0.155	−0.921	0.547
TSLS	3.243	0.371	0.454	−0.110	−0.740	0.424
LIML	1.731	0.209	0.251	−0.044	−0.410	0.234
IIV	1.609	0.231	0.268	−0.065	−0.449	0.250
FIML	0.896	0.101	0.137	−0.053	−0.210	0.132
FIMD	2.846	0.311	0.360	−0.074	−0.605	0.334
FP	2.021	0.177	0.308	−0.093	−0.429	0.292

(c) Change in H generated by a unit change in

	$p_m - p$	W_2	I_p	T_c/p	T/p	$G + F_e$
OLS	1.689	0.066	0.218	−0.023	−0.137	0.212
TSLS	1.536	0.058	0.206	−0.017	−0.116	0.201
LIML	1.436	0.039	0.197	−0.008	−0.077	0.194
IIV	1.117	0.038	0.177	−0.011	−0.073	0.174
FIML	1.599	0.029	0.236	−0.015	−0.060	0.235
FIMD	1.509	0.047	0.181	−0.011	−0.091	0.177
FP	1.408	0.033	0.206	−0.017	−0.080	0.203

(d) Effects on the components of the GNP of a unit change in G

	C	I_R	H	F_i	$G + F_c$	X
OLS	0.547	0.077	0.212	0.049	1.000	1.787
TSLS	0.424	0.068	0.201	0.044	1.000	1.650
LIML	0.234	0.059	0.194	0.038	1.000	1.449
IIV	0.250	0.058	0.174	0.034	1.000	1.448
FIML	0.132	0.061	0.235	0.035	1.000	1.302
FIMD	0.334	0.062	0.177	0.044	1.000	1.529
FP	0.292	0.074	0.203	0.037	1.000	1.532

method with the second lowest value. We find the same relationship when studying the effect on the GNP of a rise (cut) in personal taxes. According to OLS the decrease is 1.16 while FIML gives as low a figure as 0.36. The so-called balanced budget multiplier, defined as $dX/dG + dX/d(T/P)$, is of considerable interest. The values given by different methods are included in Table 9.

While OLS gives a very low value, FIML comes close to the value 1, which is the value obtained in a simple Keynesian model. FP, too, comes fairly close to 1.

The reason for the different government spending multipliers can be studied in the table. Almost all the difference lies in the effect on personal consumption. This is 4.2 times as high for OLS as it is for FIML. This depends on the different short-run propensities to consume (high according to OLS, low according to FIML). A study of the multipliers over a longer range would probably show diminishing differences between the methods, as effects of lagged consumption begin to be noticeable. The effect of changes in G on other variables differs little between the methods.

4. Estimation of a Model of the Czechoslovak Economy

4.1. The Model

The model is presented in great detail in Sujan et al. (1972) and a shorter presentation is given in English in Sujan and Tkáč (1973). In the following the specification given in the latter paper will mainly be used.

There are 17 behavioural relations and 10 identities in this specification of the model. In order to avoid composite variables, which lead to constraints between the parameters, a number of new variables and identities have been introduced in the present version of the model. The number of endogenous variables thus obtained is 40. This is of course also the number of relations in the model. As mentioned before 17 of these are behavioural. The number of predetermined variables is 43. Of these 22 are exogenous and 21 lagged endogenous.

The specification of the model is given in Table 10, while the variables are defined in Appendix B.

Relations 1–3 are production functions. The three sectors of the economy dealt with are manufacturing, construction and agriculture. The functions are linear with capital stocks and labour as the main explanatory factors. In addition to these several other factors are included. In the case of the agricultural product no less than 6 explanatory variables are included in addition to the constant term.

TABLE 10
Specification of the model.

Behavioural relations

	Endogenous variables	Predetermined variables
1	18 19 34	1 2
2	20 35	1 3 4
3	16 36	1 6 7 8 9
4	39	1 10
5	21 22 39	1
6	23 24 25	1
7	24 26	1 5
8	37	1 11
9	27 28 38 40	1 12
10	29	1 13 14 15
11	10	1 16
12	10	1 12 17
13	10	1 18
14	30	1 19
15	31	1 20
16	32	1 21 22
17	33	1 23 24

Identities

18 $y_{18} = y_{14} - z_{19}$
19 $y_{19} = y_5 - 1.25y_{26}$
20 $y_{20} = y_{15} - z_{20}$
21 $y_{21} = y_4 - 0.5z_{30}$
22 $y_{22} = y_8 - z_{31} - z_{32}$
23 $y_{23} = y_{19} + y_{27} + z_{26} + z_{31} + z_{34}$
24 $y_{24} = y_{14} + y_{15} + y_{16} + y_{17} + z_{35}$
25 $y_{25} = y_3 - y_{28} + y_{39} + y_{40} + z_{33} + z_{39}$
26 $y_{26} = y_6 + 0.2z_{36}$
27 $y_{27} = y_3 + y_{39} + y_{40} + z_{33} - z_{34}$
28 $y_{28} = -y_{19} + y_{21} + y_{22} + z_{24} - z_{26} + z_{32} + z_{39}$
29 $y_{29} = y_9 - z_{40}$
30 $y_{30} = y_{39} - z_{41}$
31 $y_{31} = y_{40} - z_{42}$
32 $y_{32} = y_3 - z_6$
33 $y_{33} = y_{17} - y_{24} + z_{43}$
34 $y_{34} = 0.5y_{11} + z_{25}$
35 $y_{35} = 0.5y_{12} + z_{27}$
36 $y_{36} = 0.5y_{13} + 0.5z_{28} - 0.5z_{29}$
37 $y_{37} = (11/12)y_7 + (1/12)z_{37}$
38 $y_{38} = 0.5y_{10} + 0.5z_{13} - 0.5z_{38}$
39 $y_{39} = y_1 - 4.4z_4$
40 $y_{40} = y_2 + 0.2z_5$

Both exports and imports are explained in the model (relations 4 and 5). The production in manufacturing is included in both relations. In the export function the foreign trade turn-over of the COMECON countries is an important variable.

Relations 6 and 7 describe the formation of the most important parts of the personal incomes. In the first of these relations the average monthly real wages and incomes from cooperative farms (M') are explained, while in the second the corresponding annual incomes (R^m) are explained as a linear function of M', total employment (Z) and time. However, it should be borne in mind that by definition

$$R^m = \text{const} \cdot M' \cdot Z.$$

By using relation 7, however, a nonlinearity is avoided.

Relation 8 is the consumption function with 'other real monetary income' as explanatory variable in addition to R^m. The latter variable is lagged one month.

Relations 9 and 10 are investment functions. The development of accumulation into fixed capital and unfinished construction is explained by, among other things, the increase in national income and the increase in fixed capital stock lagged six months. The next relation describes how the accumulation is transformed into an increase in the stock of productive capital.

The increase in the stock of capital is separated into three parts in relations 11–13. The same three sectors of the economy as mentioned before are dealt with and in addition to the increase in the total stock of capital the respective shares in the increase in the productive capital are included among the explanatory factors.[5]

The remaining four behavioural relations explain the number of employees in four different sectors of the economy. For manufacturing, construction and agriculture the most important explanatory variables are the increase in production and lagged production in the sector itself.

As usual during the construction of a model a large number of alternative specifications of each relation were tried. These alternatives were estimated by OLS and the final choice based on these estimates. A special feature of the definite model is the occurrence of several composite variables among the dependent variables. Thus in relation 1 we find $Y^{pr} + 4.4D^{63}$, in relation 2 $Y^{st} - 0.2t$, and so on. The construction of these variables is not based on economic theory. The reason is instead a desire to diminish the effect of multicollinearity. The result is, however, that several relations are specified in a way that is not fully based on economic theory.

The data required to estimate the model are given by Sujan

[5]The specification of these relations is rather doubtful. The ratio between two endogenous variables (e.g. ΔF^{pr} and ΔF in relation 11) is included as an exogenous variable (Q^{pr} in that relation).

et al. (1972) for the years 1955–70. It has also been possible to obtain data for the years 1971–72. At the same time as these were obtained it was found that some of the earlier data had been revised, which is a not uncommon situation.[6] Thus the estimates given in this paper should not necessarily coincide with those given in Sujan and Tkáč (1973) even if the same estimation methods are used.

A special study has been made of the model performance when the specification of some of the relations is varied. Results are reported in Bergström (1976).

4.2. A Comparison Between the Model and Models Based on the Keynesian Theory

In the construction of the model the specificaton of each relation is based on the 'Marxian economic theory, on actual conditions of the Czechoslovak economy and on previous experience with the construction of econometric models in CSSR and abroad, especially in socialist countries' [Sujan and Tkáč (1973)]. Macroeconomic models exist for many Western countries, too. These are in general based on the theories presented by Keynes. A comparison with such models is instructive.

To start with it can be noticed that the model has no monetary sector. Most Keynesian models have at least a small monetary sector, although it is usually not developed in much detail in smaller models.

When we compare the real sectors a good starting point is the basic national income identity, which in this model is written as follows:

$$Y = S^{OS} + S^{SP} + V - D + A + S^{t}. \tag{4.1}$$

This identity can basically be found in most econometric models. A difference in the meaning of one of the variables between socialist and Western economies should be noticed. In the former a difference is made between accumulation (A) and the actual transformation of this into increased fixed capital. In Western economies on the other hand, the variable corresponding to A is normally denoted as the sum of fixed capital formation and increase in stocks.[7]

S^{t} is an exogenous variable, which is the difference between the national income produced and the national income measured from the demand

[6] The requisite data were obtained by direct communication with the model constructors.

[7] In the National Account Statistic published by the UN, A is in fact defined as net fixed capital formation + increase in stocks, for Czechoslovakia, too.

side.[8] Otherwise all the variables in (4.1) except public consumption are endogenous in this model, while in Keynesian models the exports (V) often are exogenous. In Keynesian models private consumption is usually disaggregated into at least two parts, non-durables and durables. A more fundamental difference is that only part of A is explained by a separate equation in this model. This is the accumulation into fixed capital, while the remaining part, accumulation into stocks is explained through an identity. In Keynesian models this variable has a separate relation, which means that the total income (or production) is decided from the demand side.

In a Keynesian model the production function in reality explains the level of employment. In the present model on the other hand, separate equations are needed to explain employment, as the production functions 1–3 decide the national income.

4.3. The TSLS Estimation

As mentioned before we have $m = 43$ predetermined variables, but only observations at $T = 16$ points of time. Thus we have an undersized sample. This means that the original form of TSLS is impossible to use. However, by modifying the method estimates can be obtained. The same principle as for the Klein–Goldberger model will be used. As mentioned in connection with this model, the principal components that are used can be extracted not only from the covariance matrix of the predetermined variables but also from the correlation matrix of these variables. If we use the covariance matrix the first component explains 97.08% of the total variance and the first five 99.93%. With the correlation matrix on the other hand a much larger number of principal components is needed to explain the same part of the total variance. This result is normally obtained. In Bergström (1970, 1971, 1974) results for a number of other models are given.

The reason why we get the results just mentioned when we use the covariance matrix is the strong common trend in almost all the variables with large variances. This is illustrated in Table 11 where the correlations between the various predetermined variables and the time trend (z_5) and the lagged national income (z_{34}) are given.

We find values larger than 0.90 except for a very small number of variables. Obviously the dummy variables are among these. Other such variables are some agricultural variables, the change in unfinished construction and the shares of various sectors in the increase in the productive fixed capital.

[8] In the UN National Account Statistics it is denoted as a statistical discrepancy. It should be noted that it is always positive and varies little.

TABLE 11
Correlation between the predetermined variables (2–43) and z_5 and z_{34}.

	z_5	z_{34}		z_5	z_{34}		z_5	z_{34}		z_5	z_{34}
2	0.98	0.99	13	1.00	0.97	24	0.98	0.97	35	0.96	0.96
3	0.91	0.93	14	0.32	0.46	25	1.00	0.97	36	0.99	0.99
4	0.03	0.07	15	0.20	0.09	26	0.99	0.98	37	0.99	0.99
5	1.00	0.98	16	−0.16	−0.20	27	0.99	0.98	38	1.00	0.97
6	−0.31	−0.20	17	0.28	0.30	28	0.99	0.94	39	−0.85	−0.86
7	0.32	0.26	18	−0.33	−0.26	29	0.98	0.94	40	0.61	0.68
8	−0.18	−0.19	19	0.99	0.97	30	1.00	0.97	41	0.99	0.99
9	0.09	0.09	20	0.96	0.98	31	1.00	0.98	42	0.94	0.97
10	0.99	0.97	21	−0.95	−0.93	32	0.98	0.99	43	0.99	0.96
11	0.93	0.92	22	−0.14	−0.11	33	0.93	0.98			
12	−0.42	−0.44	23	0.99	0.96	34	0.98	1.00			

At least if we use principal components from the covariance matrix we could expect a relatively small number of components to be sufficient in view of the large part of the variance that is explained by the first components. As mentioned in Section 3.2 there are no clear-cut criteria that can be used to determine the optimal number of components, which means that some arbitrariness cannot be avoided.

The TSLS estimates have been obtained, not by the original Kloek and Mennes method, but by the modification described in connection with the Klein–Goldberger model. This means that a regressor (instrument) $\hat{y}_i$ is the same irrespective of in which relation it is used. This is not the case when the Kloek–Mennes approach is strictly adhered to.

Here we use the forecast properties as the criterion when the best TSLS version is selected. In Table 13 the average Q^2 value and the root mean square error (*RMSE*) of the ex post forecasts of the national income (obtainable from y_{27}) are given.

When we use the covariance matrix we find an improvement as we increase the number of principal components. 10 principal components yield the best results for both our criteria. In the following we denote these estimates by TSPC1. It should be stressed that, starting with 6 principal components there is little gain in increasing the number of components. As the number of components becomes large the estimates approach the OLS estimates.

If the correlation matrix is used the two best versions are those with 9 and 10 principal components. We select the latter and denote it by TSPC2. The average Q^2 value is in general slightly lower than when the covariance matrix is used. With less than 6 components the result is very unsatisfactory.

TABLE 12
Eigenvalues of the covariance and correlation matrices of the predetermined variables.

Number of principal components	Eigenvalue λ_i of covariance matrix	$\lambda_i / \Sigma \lambda_i$	Cumulative sum $\lambda_i / \Sigma \lambda_i$	Eigenvalue λ_i of correlation matrix	Cumulative sum $\lambda_i / \Sigma \lambda_i$
1	373936.2	0.9708	0.9708	29.00	0.6904
2	8279.7	0.0215	0.9923	3.66	0.7776
3	2089.3	0.0054	0.9977	2.32	0.8329
4	395.1	0.0010	0.9987	1.90	0.8782
5	199.8	0.0006	0.9993	1.32	0.9097
6	152.3	0.0004	0.9997	1.19	0.9380
7	62.1	0.0001	0.9998	0.99	0.9616
8	22.3			0.52	0.9740
9	16.4			0.47	0.9852
10	10.8			0.28	0.9918
11	8.4			0.18	0.9961
12	4.6			0.08	0.9979
13	2.9			0.06	0.9993
14	1.5			0.02	0.9997

TABLE 13
Average Q^2 value (taken over all the endogenous variables) and root mean square error (*RMSE*) for the national product; different TSLS versions; ex post forecasts in the estimation period.

Number of principal components	Covariance matrix		Correlation matrix	
	Average Q_i^2	*RMSE* Y	Average Q_i^2	*RMSE* Y
4	0.8485	2.14	0.7340	5.55
5	0.8863	2.45	0.7017	6.14
6	0.8977	2.28	0.8909	2.27
7	0.8996	2.25	0.8974	2.21
8	0.9027	2.17	0.8995	2.10
9	0.9049	2.13	0.9022	2.10
10	0.9056	2.08	0.9019	2.06
11	0.9024	2.10	0.9010	2.10
12	0.8968	2.35	0.8982	2.24
13	0.9002	2.17	0.9008	2.16
14	0.9004	2.14	0.9007	2.16
15	0.9005	2.14	0.9005	2.14

4.4. The FP and IIV Estimation

As pointed out before, the number of iterations (*NOIT*) that are needed to reach convergence depends on which iterative method that is used to obtain the estimates. As convergence criterion we have used a relative accuracy of 10^{-6} in the structural parameter estimates. For the system in its original form some results are given in Table 14.

The table shows that RFP should converge faster than FFP. *NOIT* is well in accordance with the spectral radius criterion when we use RFP. FFP has not been tried. It is interesting to notice that SFP will not converge for larger values of α than 0.8 and that the optimal value is as small as 0.6. In this case we obtain convergence in a small number of iterations. However, because of the shorter time needed for each iteration RFP is faster if we look at the time needed.

RSIIV is slower than RFP and considerably slower than IIV which converges for $\alpha = 1.0$ in contrast to SFP. Both these observations are well in line with the results given in Bergström (1974).

As mentioned before, the convergence properties of RFP and RSIIV can be improved if the system is reordered. In Bodin (1974) several algorithms are proposed that lead to reorderings of the system with faster convergence when RFP and RSIIV are used. In Figures 1–3 the B matrix for the original system and two reordered versions are shown. In general we aim at orderings with few B parameters above the main diagonal. The figures clearly show that this object is reached. In the original ordering of the system we have 34 parameters above the main diagonal, while this is

TABLE 14

Spectral radii (ρ) obtained from the approximate criteria and number of iterations (*NOIT*) for different relaxation factors α.

	ρ				
α	FFP	RFP	SFP	SIIV	RSIIV
0.5			0.6863		
0.6			0.6235		
0.7			0.7193		
0.8		0.7750	0.9616	0.8899	0.8205
0.9	0.8282	0.7288		0.8715	0.7785
1.0	0.8214	0.6739		0.8883	0.8352
1.1	1.0036	0.9589		1.0165	1.2104

	NOIT			
α	RFP	SFP	IIV	RSIIV
0.6		25		
0.7		32		
0.9	53			
1.0	45		19	>75

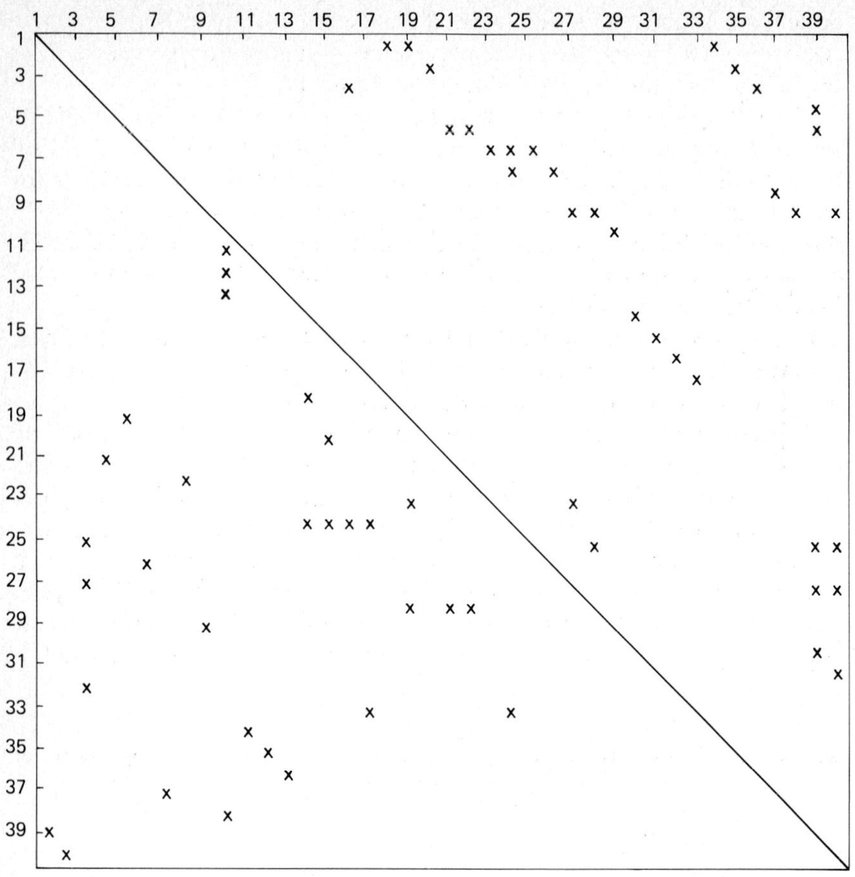

FIGURE 1. The β matrix of the original system; $\times$ denotes a non-zero element.

reduced to 8 in both the reordered cases. Table 15 shows how much the convergence properties of RSIIV and RFP are improved. By using the reordering we now find that RSIIV is superior to IIV.

4.5. The Parameter Estimates of Different Methods

The parameter estimates are shown in Appendix B. On the whole the estimates are stable and the differences between the different methods fairly small. We find cases of different signs in three relations, viz. 1, 5 and 7. In relation 7, IIV indicates a negative but non-significant effect on the

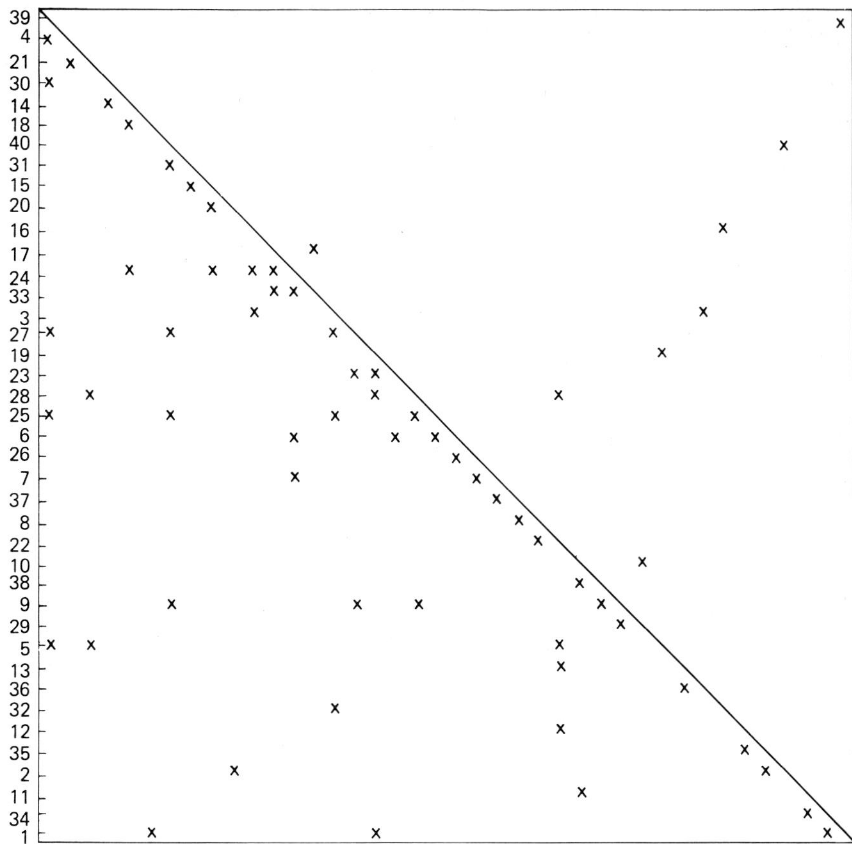

FIGURE 2. The β matrix after reordering, Version A.

manufacturing product of an increase in imports. OLS seems to exaggerate the effect of this variable. The effect of the machinery fixed capital is greater than the effect of the increase in the number of employees. In relation 5, FP deviates clearly, showing a negative effect of an increase in the personal consumption on the imports. This is unsatisfactory. In relation 7, finally, FP and TSPC1 indicate a small positive effect of the time trend on the total annual real wage incomes. All the other methods indicate substantial negative effects. It is interesting to notice that FP and TSPC1 for this relation produce structural residuals that display a clear positive auto-correlation. A similar tendency towards non-random residuals is shown by FP in relation 11. Here we find indicators of negative autocorre-

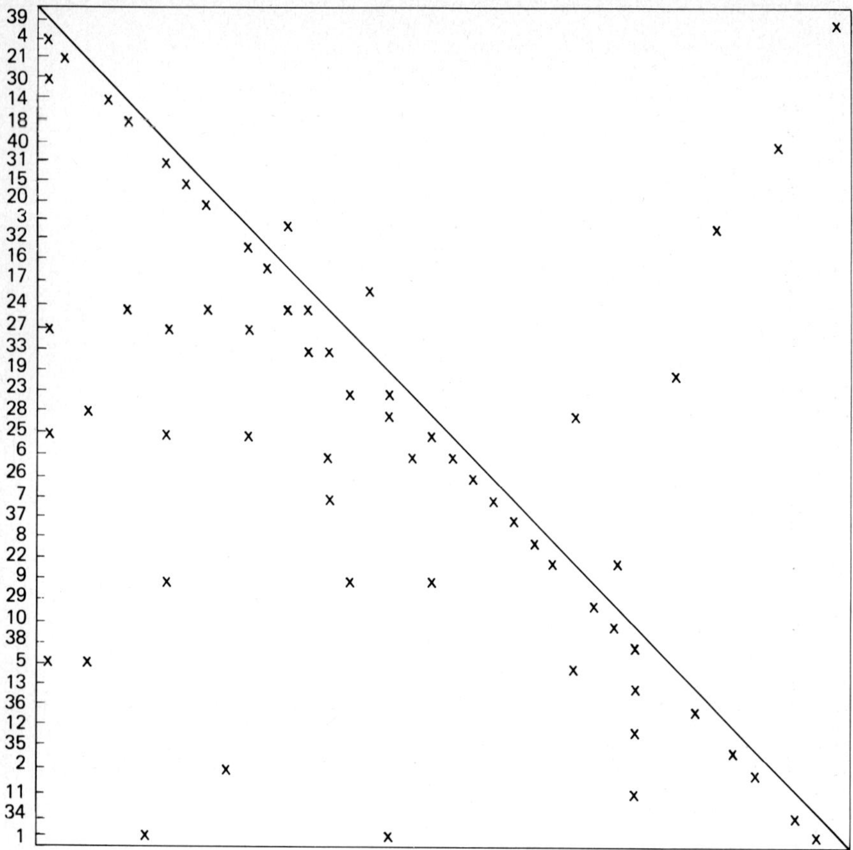

FIGURE 3. The β matrix after reordering, Version B.

lation. The parameter estimates also deviate although less dramatically than in relation 7. In the remaining relations no clear cases of autocorrelation in the structural residuals can be found. Clearly discernible differences between the parameter estimates of the different methods can be noticed for several of the other relations. These will not be commented on in detail.

In Table 16 the structural form R^2, not corrected for degrees of freedom, is given. By definition the value of OLS must be the highest. In most cases the R^2 values given by the other methods are very close the value given by OLS. Several exceptions are to be found, notably when we look at FP, but also in some cases for IIV. The most important of these are listed below. The results in Table 16 should be borne in mind when we discuss the forecasts obtained by the different methods.

TABLE 15
Spectral radii (ρ) obtained from the approximate criteria and *NOIT* for different α; two reordered versions.

	Version A				Version B			
	RFP		RSIIV		RFP		RSIIV	
α	ρ	*NOIT*	ρ	*NOIT*	ρ	*NOIT*	ρ	*NOIT*
0.8	0.6593		0.7105		0.6551		0.7123	
0.9	0.5363		0.5768		0.5282		0.5835	
1.0	0.3769	16	0.3130	20	0.3615	16	0.2892	19
1.1	0.4614		0.5318		0.4652		0.5308	
1.2	0.9281		1.0406		0.9326		1.0384	

TABLE 16
$1-R^2$ for FP and IIV with $1-R^2$ for OLS as unit; relations with an FP or IIV value ≥ 1.25 included.

Relation	FP	IIV
1	1.83	1.81
2	1.25	1.72
5	1.80	1.07
7	4.56	1.05
9	1.44	1.15
11	8.13	1.00
12	1.43	1.00

4.6. Forecasts

In Sujan and Tkáč (1973) forecasts for 1971 are given on the basis of three assumptions as to the development of the exogenous variables. This is the only investigation of the forecast properties of the model that has been performed. We have data for two years after the estimation period. Thus the forecast properties can be studied for these years in addition to the estimation period.

For the estimation period ex post forecasts have been computed on the basis of true values for the predetermined variables. In Table 17 the root mean square errors of these forecasts are given for six methods. In addition we give Q^2 for the best method FP.

The value of Q^2 shows how well the model is able to reproduce the endogenous variables in the sample period. There are only 6 endogenous variable with a Q^2 value that is lower than 0.90. All of these are defined as

TABLE 17

RMSE and Q_i^2 based on the ex post forecasts in the estimation period.

Variable	Q_i^2	*RMSE*					
	FP	OLS	TSPC1	TSPC2	IIV	FIMD	FP
1	0.9969	1.8861	1.8570	1.8289	1.9035	1.8544	1.6468
2	0.9771	0.7539	0.7355	0.7398	0.9616	0.7378	0.7139
3	0.9632	0.5688	0.5686	0.5663	0.5671	0.5677	0.5631
4	0.9865	1.0528	1.0619	1.0587	1.0202	1.0341	1.0593
5	0.9941	1.5709	1.5326	1.5105	1.5127	1.5251	1.3914
6	0.9858	30.067	28.408	30.389	29.060	27.509	26.469
7	0.9959	2.0310	1.8641	1.9953	2.1225	2.0087	1.7114
8	0.9950	2.3713	2.2861	2.3791	2.4361	2.3099	2.0585
9	0.9384	2.6543	2.5753	2.6801	2.9608	2.6066	2.4932
10	0.9240	2.3184	2.1113	2.3589	2.3314	2.2202	2.0795
11	0.9346	0.7190	0.6297	0.7314	0.7292	0.6929	0.6100
12	0.9508	0.0643	0.0581	0.0649	0.0643	0.0617	0.0560
13	0.9864	0.8830	0.8123	0.8870	0.8965	0.8583	0.8372
14	0.9894	23.675	24.090	24.584	24.813	24.203	23.589
15	0.9655	10.722	10.345	10.437	11.354	10.408	10.224
16	0.9872	29.596	29.396	29.488	29.518	29.649	29.354
17	0.9974	11.036	11.110	11.029	11.293	11.139	10.889
18	0.2678	23.675	24.090	24.584	24.813	24.203	23.589
19	0.6886	1.5709	1.5326	1.5105	1.5127	1.5251	1.3914
20	0.2530	10.722	10.345	10.437	11.354	10.408	10.224
21	0.9963	1.0528	1.0619	1.0587	1.0202	1.0341	1.0593
22	0.6248	2.3714	2.2862	2.3792	2.4362	2.3100	2.0586
23	0.9977	3.3939	3.3260	3.2707	3.5348	3.3277	2.9685
24	0.9929	27.526	28.199	27.058	29.559	28.542	28.098
25	0.9417	2.9443	2.6390	2.6638	3.1851	3.0912	2.4209
26	0.9908	30.067	28.408	30.389	29.060	27.509	26.469
27	0.9051	2.1415	2.0824	2.0562	2.4170	2.0977	1.8659
28	0.9964	2.2238	2.1311	2.1846	2.2982	2.2910	1.9705
29	0.9050	2.6543	2.5753	2.6801	2.9608	2.6066	2.4932
30	0.7852	1.8861	1.8570	1.8289	1.9035	1.8544	1.6468
31	0.7925	0.7536	0.7353	0.7396	0.9612	0.7376	0.7134
32	0.9551	0.5688	0.5686	0.5663	0.5671	0.5677	0.5631
33	0.9638	29.330	30.262	28.800	32.247	30.722	29.244
34	0.9999	0.3595	0.3148	0.3657	0.3646	0.3464	0.3050
35	0.9999	0.0321	0.0291	0.0325	0.0322	0.0309	0.0280
36	0.9954	0.4415	0.4062	0.4435	0.4483	0.4292	0.4186
37	0.9965	1.8616	1.7086	1.8289	1.9456	1.8412	1.5686
38	0.9757	1.1590	1.0555	1.1792	1.1656	1.1100	1.0397
39	0.9969	1.8861	1.8570	1.8289	1.9035	1.8544	1.6468
40	0.9836	0.7539	0.7355	0.7398	0.9616	0.7378	0.7139

first differences. For the levels of these variables we obtain higher Q^2 values, of course. The variables where the model is least successful are y_{18} and y_{20} which denote the change in the number of employees in manufacturing and construction. The Q^2 values here are as low as 0.27 and 0.25. Looking at levels (y_{14} and y_{15}) we obtain as high values as 0.9894 and

0.9655. For the other variables given as first differences, the model performs better. For the change in personal consumption the Q^2 value is 0.62, while for the change in imports it is 0.69.

The most important single variable of the model is the total national income. As a measure of this variable we have y_{27} which shows the change in the national income. Here the model is very successful, giving a Q^2 value of 0.9051.

When we compare the different methods it is immediately clear that FP performs better than the others. To facilitate a comparison a ranking has been made on the basis of variables $y_1 - y_{17}$, $y_{23} - y_{28}$ and y_{33}. The remaining endogenous variables are all linear combinations of one of the above-mentioned variables and predetermined variables. Thus the *RMSE*'s for these variables merely repeat information already included in the *RMSE*'s of the 24 variables mentioned above. Results are shown in Table 18. FP is completely superior to the other methods. Of these IIV fails rather badly which is unusual; compare e.g. Bergström (1974). TSPC1, TSPC2 and FIMD are slightly better than OLS.

Table 19 shows the average absolute percentage errors for the years 1971 and 1972. Only OLS and FP are included as there is little point in comparing the methods on the basis of such scant data. However, we notice that out of the 24 variables considered earlier, FP performs better than OLS for 19 items.

Table 19 also shows that the ex ante forecast errors are of the same magnitude as the ex post errors. The only variable given as a level for which the model can be said to fail is $y_9(A^I)$ where the average absolute percentage error is 16.33. However, it was unusually large (6.90) already in the estimation period. For the variables given as differences the percentage errors are in many cases large. For ΔY we notice an improvement from the estimation period (from 21.08 to 14.37).

Table 20 shows the forecasts for some variables in more detail. It is notable that the model overestimates several of the variables.

TABLE 18
Important characteristics of the ex post forecasts in the sample period.

Method	Rank	Best result	*RMSE* $y_{27} = Y - Y_{-1}$
OLS	103.5	0	2.14
TSPC1	71.0	1	2.08
TSPC2	87.0	2	2.06
FP	32.0	20	1.87
IIV	123.5	1	2.42
FIMD	87.0	0	2.10

TABLE 19
Average absolute percentage errors of the ex ante forecasts for the years 1971 and 1972, compared with the average absolute percentage errors in the estimation period.

Variable	FP Estimation period	FP Forecast period	OLS Forecast period	Variable	FP Estimation period	FP Forecast period	OLS Forecast period
1	1.17	2.32	2.38	21	2.54	0.55	0.58
2	2.94	4.57	4.30	22	43.43	81.53	127.66
3	1.77	2.54	2.42	23	0.99	0.41	1.16
4	4.64	1.02	1.07	24	0.37	1.00	1.10
5	2.33	0.48	2.48	25	4.61	6.41	7.21
6	1.79	6.49	7.80	26	1.44	5.24	6.30
7	1.19	3.22	6.11	27	21.08	14.37	15.67
8	1.17	3.22	5.03	28	1.08	2.72	3.04
9	6.90	16.33	16.47	29	7.71	19.01	19.17
10	6.35	21.88	23.61	30	23.10	50.84	52.16
11	5.98	22.42	21.43	31	49.65	41.75	39.13
12	7.25	11.83	12.48	32	98.94	84.43	80.35
13	13.95	19.35	22.43	33	0.95	0.89	1.06
14	0.85	0.92	0.88	34	0.18	0.72	0.69
15	1.73	0.36	0.30	35	0.30	0.57	0.60
16	1.58	2.27	2.29	36	4.43	10.30	11.98
17	0.82	3.03	3.16	37	1.10	2.97	5.63
18	78.90	81.03	82.24	38	3.27	10.91	11.78
19	69.47	8.38	44.30	39	1.18	2.32	2.38
20	142.90	12.62	11.29	40	2.72	4.12	3.87

TABLE 20
Actual and forecast values of selected endogenous variables for FP.

Variable	1971		1972	
	Actual	Forecast	Actual	Forecast
Y^{pr}	181.43	187.09	190.05	192.93
Y^{st}	30.09	28.89	33.70	31.96
Y^{p0}	27.68	26.95	28.49	27.80
R^{m}	159.34	164.15	168.25	174.01
S	192.44	197.85	201.79	209.11
ΔF	44.77	59.18	46.46	51.84
ΔD	5.30	4.52	5.38	5.27
V	80.40	79.70	87.13	87.33
ΔS^{os}	7.77	13.18	7.83	15.15
Z	7110	7165	7182	7270
M^{r}	1866	1955	1953	2064
ΔY	14.25	17.99	17.51	17.96

5. The Performance of FP Compared with other Methods for Some Other Real-World Models

In addition to the models discussed above the Fix-Point method has been applied to a number of real-world models together with other estimation methods. Detailed results are given in Bergström (1970, 1971, and 1974) both as regards the convergence properties of FP and IIV and the quality of the parameter estimates and forecasts of a large number of methods.

Three small models of 5–8 relations (Girshick–Haavelmo, Klein I and Christ) and three larger models of 17–36 relations (Pavlopoulos, Dutta–Su, and Yu) have been analyzed. For the small models all the usual estimation methods (OLS, TSLS, LIML, 3SLS, IIV, FP, FIML, FIMD) can be and have been used without difficulty. However, as soon as the number of observations is smaller than the number of predetermined variables only some of the methods can be used, viz. OLS, FP, IIV and FIMD. Modifications of TSLS and LIML are also possible in this case and have been included.

The forecasting properties have been investigated by means of the ex post forecasts in the sampling period with true predetermined variables. As a measure of the quality of these forecasts we have used the Q^2 criterion. Results obtained by a ranking on the basis of this criterion are given in Tables 21 and 22. For each model the methods have been ranked for each endogenous variable. The values given in the tables are the rank-sums over all the variables. Thus, for example, for Klein's model I with 8 endogenous variables, the best possible rank-sum is 8 and the worst possible one is 64.

For the smaller models, FP in particular, but also IIV are superior to all the other methods considered. For the larger models FP is, with one exception, the best method, but the superiority is less marked than for the small models. A comparison between e.g. OLS and FP usually reveals systematic but rather small differences in favour of FP. No explanation for the less good behaviour of FP in the case of Dutta–Su's model has been found.

It is important to stress that the relationships observed in the sampling period need not necessarily hold when forecasts are made. What evidence we have from Monte Carlo studies, Bergström (1974), and limited predictive tests, indicates that larger differences are repeated in the quality of the forecasts, while the importance of smaller differences should not be overstressed.

A special study has been made of Christ's model, consisting of four behavioural relations and three identities; see Christ (1966) and Bergström (1974). 24 different versions of this model are obtained by considering the 24 different investment functions proposed by Christ. All these versions of the model have been estimated by the methods mentioned above.

TABLE 21
Rankings for three small models based on the value of Q^2.

Method	Girshick–Haavelmo	Klein I	Christ	Σ
OLS	32 (8)	62 (8)	30 (4)	20
TSLS	21 (6)	34 (5)	37 (5)	16
3SLS	23 (7)	28 (3)	54 (8)	18
LIML	17 (5)	36 (6)	45 (7)	18
FIML	16 (4)	58 (7)	44 (6)	17
FIMD	15 (3)	31 (4)	18.5 (3)	10
IIV	13 (2)	27 (2)	15 (2)	6
FP	7 (1)	12 (1)	8.5 (1)	3

TABLE 22
Rankings based on the Q^2 criterion for three large models.

Method	Pavlopoulos	Dutta–Su	Yu
OLS	47 (4)	105.0 (3)	66.5 (3)
FIMD	36 (2)	58.0 (1)	50.5 (2)
IIV	37 (3)	66.5 (2)	75.0 (4)
FP	20 (1)	118.5 (4)	48.0 (1)

It might be expected that the methods show different sensitivity to changes in the specification of the model. As a measure of this we take the change in the short-run marginal propensity to consume (*mpc*) in the consumption function as the specification of the investment function is changed.

IIV and FP are full-information methods, in the sense that the specification of the whole model influences the estimates of a certain relation. As expected we find these methods to be very sensitive to changes in the specification of the model. Overall they also give lower values of *mpc* than the other methods.

For the larger models that have been investigated, the large differences between the estimates of different methods indicated in Table 23 have only seldom been encountered.

Usually econometric models are used for forecasting purposes. As we have data for three years after the sample period in Christ's model, a predictive testing is possible. Table 24 gives a summary of some results. The superiority of FP but also FIMD and IIV over TSLS is striking. While FP manages an average absolute error of less than 5 in 12 cases out of 24, the figure for TSLS is only 3. Many of the versions where the iterative methods are superior are undoubtedly bad models from an econometric point of view. It is therefore interesting to study the 4 versions selected by Christ as being best (his final choice is version 17). These, by the way, from a forecasting point of view, are not the best ones.

TSLS is inferior to the iterative methods even for these versions. A conclusion from this study is, that if we manage to select the best version of the model it does not matter much which method we use, but if we select an alternative that is not quite optimal the iterative methods still give good results, while use of e.g. TSLS can be quite disastrous. A study of Q^2 shows that the inferiority of the non-iterative methods could have been discovered in the sampling period already.

TABLE 23

Range of *mpc* for different methods in the 24 different versions of Christ's model.

	OLS	TSLS	3SLS	LIML	IIV	FP	FIMD
Min.	0.6612	0.6576	0.6811	0.6503	0.3804	−4.2124	0.3355
Max.	0.6612	0.6983	0.7518	0.7634	3.5512	0.4771	1.0968

TABLE 24

Average absolute error over all the 7 endogenous variables and the 3 forecast years (1960–62) in billions of 1954 dollars.

	Number of version with average error		
Method	0–5	5–10	> 10
OLS	2	5	17
TSLS	3	4	17
3SLS	2	4	18
LIML	4	11	9
IIV[a]	6	6	5
FIMD	9	14	1
FP	12	11	1

[a] Only versions 1–17 included because of convergence difficulties.

TABLE 25

Average absolute error for some versions.

Version	TSLS	LIML	IIV	FIMD	FP
8	20.12	5.20	4.89	4.81	5.00
15	11.18	13.29	12.45	7.12	9.24
17	4.67	3.77	2.56	2.55	3.49
20	22.72	67.78	—	5.99	5.65

For Christ's model above we have noticed two properties of the FP and IIV methods (most pronounced for FP) compared with OLS, TSLS and 3SLS, viz.

(1) They often give unreasonable values to the structural parameters in view of economic theory.

(2) They give high Q^2 values and good forecasts, seldom giving the useless results that OLS, TSLS and 3SLS often display.

A further study shows that for those model versions where the prediction properties of OLS and TSLS are unacceptable, FP and the other iterative methods often give reasonable results. These are obtained by means of a distortion of the structural form parameter estimates. Thus, FP, IIV and FIMD are more prediction oriented and should be more reliable when forecasts are to be made from the model. Another way of interpreting these results is that when the different methods show large differences in the structural parameter estimates, it is an indication that the model is a less good one.

Appendix A: The Klein–Goldberger Model

TABLE A.1
The specification of the model.

Behavioural relations

	Endogenous variables	Predetermined variables
1	1 14	1 2
2	2 14	1
3	3 15	1 3
4	4 12	1 4 5
5	5 8 21	1
6	6 18 19 23	1
7	7 17	1 8
8	8 21	1 9
9	9 22	1 10
10	10 12	1 11
11	11 23	1 6 12

Identities

12	$-y_1-y_2-y_3+y_4+y_{12}=-z_3+z_{14}+z_{21}$
13	$y_7+y_{11}-y_{12}+y_{13}=-z_7-z_{18}-z_{24}$
14	$y_9-y_{12}+y_{14}=-z_{18}-z_{19}-z_{20}-z_{24}$
15	$y_3-y_{12}+y_{15}=z_3$
16	$-y_6+y_{16}=0.95z_{15}-z_{16}$
17	$-y_{12}+y_{17}=-z_7$
18	$-y_{17}+y_{18}=-0.95z_{13}$
19	$-y_5+y_{19}=-0.95z_{17}$
20	$-y_8+y_{20}=z_{22}$
21	$y_{16}+y_{21}=z_{23}$
22	$-y_{13}+y_{10}+y_{22}=-z_{19}$
23	$-y_2+y_{23}=z_{14}$

TABLE A.2
List of variables.

Endogenous	Exogenous
$y_1=C=C_D+C_N$	$z_1=1$
$y_2=I_R$	$z_2=C_{-1}$
$y_3=H$	$z_3=H_{-1}$
$y_4=F_i$	$z_4=(F_i)_{-1}$
$y_5=h$	$z_5=p_m-p$
$y_6=N_w-N_G+N_e$ $-0.95(N_w-N_G+N_e)_{-1}$	$z_6=r-r_{-1}$
$y_7=W_1$	$z_7=W_2$
$y_8=w-w_{-1}$	$z_8=(W_1)_{-1}$
$y_9=S_c$	$z_9=p_{-1}-p_{-2}$
$y_{10}=P-P_c$	$z_{10}=(P_c-T_c/p-S_c)_{-1}$

$y_{11} = Q$
$y_{12} = X$
$y_{13} = P$
$y_{14} = Y$
$y_{15} = X - (H - H_{-1})$
$y_{16} = N_w$
$y_{17} = X - W_2$
$y_{18} = X - W_2 - 0.95(X - W_2)_{-1}$
$y_{19} = h - 0.95h_{-1}$
$y_{20} = w$
$y_{21} = N - N_e - N_w$
$y_{22} = P_c - T_c/p$
$y_{23} = I_R + I_P$

$z_{11} = (P - P_c)_{-1}$
$z_{12} = Q_{-1}$
$z_{13} = (X - W_2)_{-1}$
$z_{14} = I_p$
$z_{15} = (N_w - N_G + N_e)_{-1}$
$z_{16} = N_e - N_G$
$z_{17} = h_{-1}$
$z_{18} = T_i/p$
$z_{19} = T_c/p$
$z_{20} = T/p$
$z_{21} = G + P_e$
$z_{22} = w_{-1}$
$z_{23} = N - N_e$
$z_{24} = D_A/p$

TABLE A.3
Definitions of variables.

C_D = Consumer expenditures on durable goods in billions of 1954 dollars.
C_N = Consumer expenditures on non-durable goods and services in billions of 1954 dollars.
I_p = Expenditures for private producers' plant and equipment in billions of 1954 dollars.
I_R = Expenditures for non-farm residential construction in billions of 1954 dollars.
I_H = Inventory investment in billions of 1954 dollars.
H = End-of-year stock of inventories in billions of 1954 dollars.
F_i = Imports of goods and services in billions of 1954 dollars.
F_e = Exports of goods and services in billions of 1954 dollars.
G = Government expenditures on goods and services in billions of 1954 dollars.
X = Gross national product in billions of 1954 dollars.
W_1 = Private employee compensation in billions of 1954 dollars.
W_2 = Public employee compensation in billions of 1954 dollars.
P = Corporate and noncorporate profit in billions of 1954 dollars.
Q = Rent and interest income in billions of 1954 dollars.
Y = Disposable personal income in billions of 1954 dollars.
S_c = Corporate retained earnings in billions of 1954 dollars.
N_w = Number of employees in millions of persons.
N_G = Number of government employees in millions of persons.
N_e = Number of self-employed in millions of persons.
h = Index of hours worked per week, 1954:1.00.
w = Average annual wage earnings in thousands of dollars.
N = Total labor force in millions of persons.
p = Index of the general price level, 1954:1.00.
P_c = Net corporate profits before tax and after inventory valuation adjustment in billions of 1954 dollars.
D_A = Capital consumption at accounting cost in billions of current dollars.
r = Corporate bond yield in percent.
r_s = Yield on prime commercial paper, 4–6 months, in percent.
T = Reconciling account (partial) between net national income and disposable income in billions of current dollars.
T_c = Corporate income tax liability in billions of current dollars.
T_i = Reconciling account between net national product and net national income in billions of current dollars.
p_m = Implicit deflator of imports, 1954:1.00.

TABLE A.4
Structural parameter estimates for seven methods.[a]

Relation 1

C	Y	Const.	C_{-1}
OLS	0.5652 (0.0771)	−4.8429 (1.9529)	0.4372 (0.0835)
TSLS	0.4944 (0.0889)	−4.6174 (1.9889)	0.5134 (0.0962)
LIML	0.3164	−4.0519	0.7049
IIV	0.3420 (0.1261) (0.1070)	−4.1333 (2.2642) (2.2503)	0.6773 (0.1361) (0.1158)
FIML	0.1757	−3.8843	0.8577
FIMD	0.4322	−4.4200	0.5803
FP	0.3134	−3.8084	0.7068

Relation 2

I_R	Y	Const.
OLS	0.0800 (0.0031)	−5.8866 (0.6729)
TSLS	0.0797 (0.0031)	−5.8261 (0.6739)
LIML	0.0795	−5.7786
IIV	0.0796 (0.0031) (0.0031)	−5.8058 (0.6752) (0.6736)
FIML	0.0809	−6.0636
FIMD	0.0798	−5.8425
FP	0.0792	−5.7149

[a]Standard errors in parentheses. For IIV the first standard error is computed assuming a symmetric GEID system, the second one on the assumption of a CLID system [for an explanation, see Bergström (1974)].

Relation 3

H	$X - I_H$	Const.	H_{-1}
OLS	0.1346	−24.1934	0.4194
	(0.0208)	(3.9622)	(0.0968)
TSLS	0.1387	−24.9708	0.4008
	(0.0212)	(4.0403)	(0.0987)
LIML	0.1547	−27.9905	0.3274
IIV	0.1363	−24.5195	0.4115
	(0.0213)	(4.0643)	(0.0993)
	(0.0246)	(4.6704)	(0.1147)
FIML	0.2028	−37.2692	0.1172
FIMD	0.1311	−23.5359	0.4354
FP	0.1530	−27.6207	0.3327

Relation 4

F_i	X	Const.	$(F_i)_{-1}$	$P_m - P$
OLS	0.0275	−0.7558	0.4780	−7.9667
	(0.0061)	(0.5502)	(0.1318)	(3.7051)
TSLS	0.0265	−0.7280	0.5001	−7.6427
	(0.0063)	(0.5522)	(0.1356)	(3.7650)
LIML	0.0261	−0.7151	0.5091	−7.3935
IIV	0.0235	−0.6466	0.5614	−6.4293
	(0.0064)	(0.5564)	(0.1365)	(3.7794)
	(0.0065)	(0.5588)	(0.1387)	(3.8455)
FIML	0.0248	−0.9372	0.5546	−6.8097
FIMD	0.0290	−0.7949	0.4480	−8.5176
FP	0.0239	−0.6947	0.5551	−6.9259

Relation 5

h	$w - w_{-1}$	$N - N_w - N_e$	Const.
OLS	− 34.6666	− 1.7645	113.1345
	(5.3147)	(0.1534)	(1.3485)
TSLS	− 42.8527	− 1.9593	115.0475
	(7.2964)	(0.1973)	(1.7977)
LIML	− 46.5043	− 2.0344	115.8342
IIV	− 52.9063	− 2.1699	117.2353
	(16.953)	(0.3688)	(3.7290)
	(15.904)	(0.3305)	(3.4079)
FIML	− 72.6499	− 2.6335	121.8124
FIMD	− 35.1611	− 1.8078	113.4272
FP	− 28.8286	− 1.5656	111.4364

Relation 6

$N_W - N_G + N_e -$ $0.95(N_W - N_G + N_e)_{-1}$	$X - W_2 -$ $0.95(X - W_2)_{-1}$	$h - 0.95h_{-1}$	$I_P + I_R$	Const.
OLS	0.1099	− 0.0070	− 0.0087	0.7890
	(0.0196)	(0.0631)	(0.0141)	(0.4611)
TSLS	0.1313	− 0.1017	− 0.0150	0.9977
	(0.0246)	(0.0909)	(0.0153)	(0.5081)
LIML	0.1534	− 0.1470	− 0.0232	1.0438
IIV	0.1711	− 0.2394	− 0.0289	1.2976
	(0.0370)	(0.1347)	(0.0200)	(0.6340)
	(0.0405)	(0.0887)	(0.0217)	(0.5554)
FIML	0.0791	− 0.1103	0.0107	1.1562
FIMD	0.1344	− 0.1329	− 0.0157	1.0972
FP	0.2138	− 0.1584	− 0.0491	0.8069

Relation 6′

$X_2 - W_2 -$ $0.95(X - W_2)_{-1}$	$N_w - N_G + N_e -$ $0.95(N_w - N_G + N_e)_{-1}$	$h - 0.95h_{-1}$	$I_P + I_R$	Const.
OLS	9.10	0.6370	0.7916	− 7.18
TSLS	7.62	0.7746	0.1142	− 7.59
LIML	6.52	0.9583	0.1512	− 6.80
IIV	5.84	1.3992	0.1689	− 7.58
FIML	12.64	1.3944	− 0.1353	− 14.62
FIMD	7.44	0.9888	0.1168	− 8.16
FP	4.68	0.7409	0.2297	− 3.77

Relation 7

W_1	$X - W_2$	Const.	$(W_1)_{-1}$
OLS	0.4233	−10.9838	0.2653
	(0.0236)	(1.0954)	(0.0434)
TSLS	0.4110	−10.6783	0.2877
	(0.0249)	(1.1191)	(0.0456)
LIML	0.4305	−11.1747	0.2522
IIV	0.3996	−10.3572	0.3083
	(0.0263)	(1.1504)	(0.0482)
	(0.0335)	(1.2586)	(0.0614)
FIML	0.3550	−9.4558	0.3914
FIMD	0.4132	−10.7171	0.2836
FP	0.4748	−12.1098	0.1698

Relation 8

$w - w_{-1}$	$N - N_e - N_w$	Const.	$p_{-1} - p_{-2}$
OLS	−0.0169	0.1843	0.5902
	(0.0042)	(0.0296)	(0.3070)
TSLS	−0.0185	0.1929	0.5827
	(0.0042)	(0.0294)	(0.3024)
LIML	−0.0178	0.1900	0.5568
IIV	−0.0155	0.1755	0.6417
	(0.0044)	(0.0310)	(0.3121)
	(0.0040)	(0.0281)	(0.2928)
FIML	−0.0213	0.2170	0.1363
FIMD	−0.0151	0.1727	0.6579
FP	−0.0145	0.1679	0.7439

Relation 9

S_G	$P_C - T_c/p$	Const.	$(P_C - T_c/p)_{-1}$
OLS	0.8319	−1.1889	−0.6237
	(0.0628)	(1.4540)	(0.1326)
TSLS	0.8510	−1.4439	−0.6235
	(0.0648)	(1.4699)	(0.1328)
LIML	0.8935	−1.9716	−0.6280
IIV	0.8560	−1.4954	−0.6254
	(0.0671)	(1.4876)	(0.1330)
	(0.0619)	(1.5060)	(0.1331)

FIML	0.7495	−4.1431	−0.1406
FIMD	0.8779	−1.7727	−0.6269
FP	0.7836	−2.0616	−0.4461

Relation 10

$P - P_G$	X	Const.	$(P - P_C)_{-1}$
OLS	0.0235 (0.0096)	2.4205 (1.6293)	0.7245 (0.0953)
TSLS	0.0232 (0.0096)	2.4167 (1.6294)	0.7274 (0.0954)
LIML	0.0200	2.4242	0.7552
IIV	0.0206 (0.0097) (0.0099)	2.4235 (1.6322) (1.6323)	0.7498 (0.0959) (0.0987)
FIML	0.0269	3.2841	0.6688
FIMD	0.0219	2.4222	0.7387
FP	0.0221	2.4837	0.7347

Relation 11

Q	$I_P + I_R$	Const.	$r - r_{-1}$	Q_{-1}
OLS	0.0485 (0.0096)	−0.4532 (0.6196)	0.3788 (0.3387)	0.9513 (0.0380)
TSLS	0.0474 (0.0097)	−0.4644 (0.6199)	0.3680 (0.3400)	0.9548 (0.0380)
LIML	0.0464	−0.4475	0.3958	0.9552
IIV	0.0473 (0.0096) (0.0097)	−0.4497 (0.6198) (0.6198)	0.3891 (0.3389) (0.3395)	0.9537 (0.0380) (0.0382)
FIML	0.0332	−0.6875	1.2242	0.9953
FIMD	0.0483	−0.4526	0.3806	0.9517
FP	0.0475	−0.4644	0.3828	0.9540

Appendix B: The Model of the Czechoslovak Economy

TABLE B.1
Endogenous variables of the model.

$y_1 = Y^{pr} + 4.4D^{63}$	$y_{21} = V$
$y_2 = Y^{st} - 0.2t$	$y_{22} = S^{os} - S^{os}_{-1}$
$y_3 = Y^{po}$	$y_{23} = Y + S^s + D$
$y_4 = V - 0.5V_{-1}$	$y_{24} = Z$
$y_5 = D + 0.25D_{-1}$	$y_{25} = A + S^t$
$y_6 = M^r - 0.2M^r_{-1}$	$y_{26} = M^r$
$y_7 = R^m$	$y_{27} = Y - Y_{-1}$
$y_8 = S$	$y_{28} = S^{os} + S^{sp} + S^t + V - D$
$y_9 = A^I$	$y_{29} = A^{ZF}$
$y_{10} = F - F_{-1}$	$y_{30} = Y^{pr} - Y^{pr}_{-1}$
$y_{11} = F^{pr} - F^{pr}_{-1}$	$y_{31} = Y^{st} - Y^{st}_{-1}$
$y_{12} = F^{st} - F^{st}_{-1}$	$y_{32} = Y^{po} - Y^{po}_{-1}$
$y_{13} = J - J_{-1}$	$y_{33} = O^p - Z^{vo}$
$y_{14} = Z^{pr}$	$y_{34} = 0.5(F^{pr} + F^{pr}_{-1})$
$y_{15} = Z^{st}$	$y_{35} = 0.5(F^{st} + F^{st}_{-1})$
$y_{16} = Z^{po}$	$y_{36} = 1/2(J - J_{-2})$
$y_{17} = Z^{no}$	$y_{37} = 1/12\{11R_m + R_{m-1}\}$
$y_{18} = Z^{pr} - Z^{pr}_{-1}$	$y_{38} = 1/2\{F - F_{-2}\}$
$y_{19} = D - D_{-1}$	$y_{39} = Y^{pr}$
$y_{20} = Z^{st} - Z^{st}_{-1}$	$y_{40} = Y^{st}$

TABLE B.2
Predetermined variables of the model.

$z_1 = 1$	$z_{23} = Z^{uo}_{-1}$
$z_2 = Y^{pr}_{-1} - 0.4Y^{pr}$	$z_{24} = S^{sp}$
$z_3 = Y^{st}_{-1} - 0.35Y^{st}_{-2}$	$z_{25} = F^{pr}_{-1}$
$z_4 = D^{63}$	$z_{26} = D_{-1}$
$z_5 = t$	$z_{27} = F^{st}_{-1}$
$z_6 = Y^{po}_{-1}$	$z_{28} = J_{-1}$
$z_7 = K^r$	$z_{29} = J_{-2}$
$z_8 = M^e$	$z_{30} = V_{-1}$
$z_9 = D^{po}$	$z_{31} = S^s$
$z_{10} = K - 0.5K_{-1}$	$z_{32} = S^{os}_{-1}$
$z_{11} = R^o$	$z_{33} = Y^{ov}$
$z_{12} = D^{55}$	$z_{34} = Y_{-1}$
$z_{13} = F_{-1}$	$z_{35} = Z^{ov}$
$z_{14} = Z^{NV}_{-2}$	$z_{36} = M^r_{-1}$
$z_{15} = D^{66}$	$z_{37} = R_{m-1}$
$z_{16} = Q^{pr}$	$z_{38} = F_{-2}$
$z_{17} = Q^{st}$	$z_{39} = S^t$
$z_{18} = Q^{po}$	$z_{40} = A^{NV}$
$z_{19} = Z^{pr}_{-1}$	$z_{41} = Y^{pr}_{-1}$
$z_{20} = Z^{st}_{-1}$	$z_{42} = Y^{st}_{-1}$
$z_{21} = Z^{po}_{-1}$	$z_{43} = O^p$
$z_{22} = D^{60}$	

TABLE B.3
Definition of variables.

Y^{pr} =	National income produced in manufacturing.
Y^{st} =	National income produced in construction.
Y^{po} =	National income produced in agriculture.
V =	Total volume of exports.
D =	Total volume of imports.
M^{r} =	Average monthly real wages and incomes from cooperative farms in Kčs.
R^{m} =	Total annual real wage incomes of the poopulation and incomes from cooperative farms in Kčs.
S =	Personal consumption of the population and expenditures on services.
A^{I} =	Accumulation into fixed capital and unfinished construction.
ΔF =	Increase in productive fixed capital in the national economy.
ΔF^{pr} =	Increase in machinery fixed capital in manufacturing.
ΔF^{st} =	Increase in machinery fixed capital in construction.
ΔJ =	Increase in the number of tractor units in agriculture (15 HP) in thousands.
Z^{pr} =	Average number of employees in manufacturing.
Z^{st} =	Average number of employees in construction.
Z^{po} =	Average number of employees in agriculture.
Z^{no} =	Average number of employees in non-productive sectors.
Z^{vo} =	Average number of employees in productive sectors.
Z =	Average number of employees in the national economy.
Y =	Total national income produced.
S^{os} =	Personal consumption of the popoulation.
A =	Accumulation.
A^{ZF} =	Accumulation into fixed capital.
F =	Productive fixed capital in the national economy, stocks at the end of the year.
F^{pr} =	Machinery fixed capital in manufacturing, stocks at the end of the year.
F^{st} =	Machinery fixed capital in construction, stocks at the end of the year.
J =	Tractor units in agriculture (15 HP) in thousands, stocks at the end of the year.
Y^{ov} =	National income produced in other productive industries.
R^{o} =	Other real monetary income of the population.
S^{sp} =	Material public consumption.
S^{s} =	Expenditures of the population on services.
A^{NV} =	Change in the unfinished construction.
A^{NV}_{-2} =	Change in the unfinished construction with a two-year lag.
Z^{ov} =	Average number of employees in other productive industries.
K^{r} =	Fodder consumption in agriculture in millions of tons.
Q^{pr} =	Share of machinery and equipment in manufacturing in the total increase in productive fixed capital, measured in percentages.
Q^{st} =	Share of machinery and equipment in construction in the total increase in productive fixed capital, measured in percentages.
Q^{po} =	Share of tractors in agriculture in the total increase in productive fixed capital, measured in percentages.
K =	Foreign trade turnover of COMECON countries, converted into milliards of Kčs in constant prices (the model uses transformation of this variable in the form $K-0.5K_{-1}$).
S^{t} =	Losses in the balance of national income utilization.
O^{p} =	Population in productive age.
M^{e} =	Meteorological variable expressing the impact of weather on agricultural production (Iowa index in %).

D^{po} =	Dummy variable — exceptional influences on the national income creation in agriculture (1959, 1961 and 1963 = −1, 1958 and 1969 = 1, for the remaining years = 0).
D^{55} =	Dummy variable — exceptional influences on the accumulation into unfinished construction and on the increase in machinery fixed capital in construction in 1955 (1955 = 1, in the other years = 0).
D^{60} =	Dummy variable — exceptional infiuence on employment in agriculture in 1960 (1960 = 1, in the other years = 0).
D^{63} =	Dummy variable — exceptional influences on the national income creation in manufacturing and construction in 1963 (1963 = 1, in the other years = 0).
D^{66} =	Dummy variable — exceptional influence on the total increase in productive fixed capital in 1966 (1966 = 1, in the other years = 0).
t =	Linear time trend (1955 = 1, ..., 1970 = 16).
l =	Constant terms of regression equations.

TABLE B.4
Structural parameter estimates.[a]

Relation 1	y_{18}	y_{19}	y_{34}	z_2	R^2	d
OLS	0.0323	0.3578	0.1890	1.2770	0.9979	1.93
	(0.0168)	(0.1897)	(0.0591)	(0.1226)		
FIMD	0.0261	0.2306	0.1951	1.2663	0.9977	1.58
IIV	0.0752	−0.0703	0.2641	1.1518	0.9961	1.96
	(0.0556)	(0.3267)	(0.0709)	(0.1420)		
FP	0.0775	0.1817	0.1708	1.3427	0.9961	2.09
TSPC1	0.0482	0.3080	0.2054	1.2504	0.9977	2.05
	(0.0216)	(0.2999)	(0.0665)	(0.1341)		
TSPC2	0.0533	0.2220	0.2212	1.2222	0.9975	1.95
	(0.0229)	(0.3683)	(0.0681)	(0.1358)		

Relation 2	y_{20}	y_{35}	z_3	z_4	R^2	d
OLS	0.0436	0.5840	0.8031	−2.7878	0.9837	2.03
	(0.0191)	(0.1684)	(0.1223)	(0.9175)		
FIMD	0.0244	0.5557	0.8283	−3.3041	0.9822	2.12
IIV	0.0974	0.6494	0.7416	−1.3305	0.9719	2.00
	(0.1222)	(0.2254)	(0.2306)	(1.4018)		
FP	0.0610	0.4289	0.9269	−2.6982	0.9796	2.03
TSPC1	0.0233	0.5604	0.8247	−3.5128	0.9819	2.17
	(0.0237)	(0.1610)	(0.1318)	(0.9256)		
TSPC2	0.0297	0.5695	0.8163	−3.2700	0.9828	2.11
	(0.0237)	(0.1761)	(0.1296)	(0.9553)		

[a] Standard errors in parentheses.

Relation 3

	y_{16}	y_{36}	z_6	z_7	z_8	z_9	R^2	d
OLS	0.0026	0.1019	0.3868	0.7185	0.1546	2.0297	0.9618	2.37
	(0.0010)	(0.0518)	(0.0862)	(0.2416)	(0.0435)	(0.4228)		
FIMD	0.0026	0.1010	0.3878	0.7122	0.1557	2.0273	0.9617	2.37
IIV	0.0027	0.0996	0.3819	0.7173	0.1525	2.0364	0.9617	2.35
	(0.0009)	(0.0539)	(0.0884)	(0.2438)	(0.0434)	(0.4240)		
FP	0.0026	0.0958	0.3780	0.7056	0.1584	1.9852	0.9616	2.31
TSPC1	0.0026	0.0859	0.3692	0.6848	0.1573	1.9272	0.9610	2.23
	(0.0010)	(0.0553)	(0.0880)	(0.2551)	(0.0440)	(0.4367)		
TSPC2	0.0026	0.0930	0.3785	0.6942	0.1542	2.0189	0.9616	2.32
	(0.0010)	(0.0534)	(0.0873)	(0.2464)	(0.0435)	(0.4249)		

Relation 4

	y_{39}	z_{10}	R^2	d
OLS	0.1085	0.0372	0.9872	1.94
	(0.0491)	(0.0091)		
FIMD	0.1019	0.0384	0.9871	1.96
IIV	0.1189	0.0353	0.9871	1.90
	(0.0565)	(0.0105)		
FP	0.1064	0.0375	0.9872	1.95
TSPC1	0.1090	0.0371	0.9872	1.94
	(0.0498)	(0.0092)		
TSPC2	0.1092	0.0370	0.9872	1.94
	(0.0496)	(0.0092)		

Relation 5

	y_{21}	y_{22}	y_{39}	R^2	d
OLS	0.6660	0.2243	0.2173	0.9959	2.17
	(0.1191)	(0.1011)	(0.0696)		
FIMD	0.6971	0.1802	0.1996	0.9959	2.19
IIV	0.7736	0.2278	0.1538	0.9956	2.20
	(0.2102)	(0.1514)	(0.1220)		
FP	0.9181	−0.0351	0.0745	0.9927	1.98
TSCP1	0.6704	0.2204	0.2150	0.9959	2.18
	(0.1230)	(0.1167)	(0.0717)		
TSCP2	0.7089	0.2225	0.1924	0.9959	2.21
	(0.1222)	(0.1313)	(0.0714)		

Relation 6

	y_{23}	y_{24}	y_{25}	R^2	d
OLS	6.2180	−0.3951	−5.0870	0.9929	1.64
	(0.5639)	(0.0825)	(1.3126)		
FIMD	5.4470	−0.2987	−3.0070	0.9914	1.44
IIV	5.7572	−0.3333	−3.9982	0.9924	1.55
	(0.6444)	(0.0883)	(1.8612)		
FP	5.6274	−0.3267	−3.2166	0.9916	1.45
TSPC1	6.0678	−0.3706	−4.9605	0.9928	1.63
	(0.5744)	(0.0842)	(1.3385)		
TSCP2	6.2931	−0.4013	−5.4458	0.9928	1.45
	(0.6221)	(0.0891)	(1.5037)		

Relation 7

	y_{24}	y_{26}	z_5	R^2	d
OLS	0.0267	0.0826	−1.0252	0.9998	1.41
	(0.0012)	(0.0028)	(0.2119)		
FIMD	0.0266	0.0821	−0.9968	0.9998	1.38
IIV	0.0273	0.0846	−1.1894	0.998	1.54
	(0.0012)	(0.0028)	(0.1971)		
FP	0.0199	0.0685	0.2986	0.9991	0.41
TSPC1	0.0238	0.0722	0.1997	0.995	0.66
	(0.0018)	(0.0046)	(0.3307)		
TSPC2	0.0258	0.0787	−0.7285	0.9998	1.07
	(0.0013)	(0.0032)	(0.2331)		

Relation 8

	y_{37}	z_{11}	R^2	d
OLS	0.9707	0.3436	0.9982	2.25
	(0.0425)	(0.1109)		
FIMD	0.9620	0.3652	0.9982	2.22
IIV	0.9631	0.3624	0.9982	2.22
	(0.0453)	(0.1177)		
FP	0.9320	0.4480	0.9981	2.02
TSPC1	0.9551	0.3855	0.9982	2.18
	(0.0430)	(0.1120)		
TSPC2	0.9591	0.3754	0.9982	2.20
	(0.0425)	(0.1106)		

Relation 9

	y_{27}	y_{28}	y_{38}	y_{40}	z_{12}	R^2	d
OLS	0.1723	−0.1347	1.0637	1.2639	−3.7735	0.9932	2.57
	(0.0806)	(0.0349)	(0.0854)	(0.2403)	(1.3383)		
FIMD	0.1603	0.1325	1.0367	1.2836	−3.7726	0.9931	2.56
IIV	0.1253	−0.1153	0.9757	1.2531	−3.8131	0.9922	2.40
	(0.1124)	(0.0513)	(0.1409)	(0.3388)	(1.6132)		
FP	0.2932	−0.0981	1.0680	0.9497	−6.3313	0.9903	2.59
TSPC1	0.1221	−0.1433	0.9994	1.3731	−5.6494	0.9906	2.62
	(0.1153)	(0.0427)	(0.1157)	(0.3052)	(1.4722)		
TSPC2	0.0945	−0.1508	1.0078	1.4574	−3.5683	0.9985	2.50
	(0.0925)	(0.0400)	(0.0965)	(0.2793)	(1.3886)		

Relation 10

	y_{29}	z_{13}	z_{14}	z_{15}	R^2	d
OLS	0.5625	0.0126	1.2935	−4.1858	0.9782	2.05
	(0.0764)	(0.0051)	(0.1919)	(1.5924)		
FIMD	0.5131	0.0152	1.3144	−4.1657	0.9774	2.02
IIV	0.4259	0.0199	1.3514	−4.1303	0.0719	1.80
	(0.1080)	(0.0068)	(0.2184)	(1.8196)		
FP	0.4686	0.0169	1.3985	−3.2695	0.9746	1.70
TSPC1	0.5292	0.0148	1.2407	−3.9570	0.9774	1.91
	(0.0855)	(0.0055)	(0.1985)	(1.6228)		
TSPC2	0.5802	0.0123	1.2362	−4.8007	0.9778	2.25
	(0.0849)	(0.0054)	(0.1958)	(1.6120)		

Relation 11

	y_{10}	z_{16}	R^2	d
OLS	0.3138	0.2535	0.9984	1.78
	(0.0030)	(0.0102)		
FIMD	0.3138	0.2535	0.9984	1.78
IIV	0.3142	0.2537	0.9983	1.76
	(0.0039)	(0.0105)		
FP	0.3219	0.3513		
TSPC1	0.3155	0.2892	0.9968	2.65
	(0.0051)	(0.0143)		
TSPC2	0.3134	0.2565	0.9983	1.85
	(0.0036)	(0.0103)		

Relation 12

	y_{10}	z_{12}	z_{17}	R^2	d
OLS	0.0253	0.2093	0.2966	0.9898	2.39
	(0.0011)	(0.0468)	(0.0142)		
FIMD	0.0253	0.2093	0.2966	0.9898	2.39
IIV	0.0253	0.2093	0.2966	0.9898	2.39
	(0.0011)	(0.0474)	(0.0142)		
FP	0.0243	0.1187	0.2933	0.9840	2.33
TSPC1	0.0254	0.2035	0.3075	0.9889	2.38
	(0.0011)	(0.0396)	(0.0148)		
TSPC2	0.0254	0.2045	0.2945	0.9897	2.46
	(0.0011)	(0.0381)	(0.0142)		

Relation 13

	y_{10}	z_{18}	R^2	d
OLS	0.2700	12.9215	0.9950	2.00
	(0.0190)	(0.2551)		
FIMD	0.2699	12.9214	0.9950	2.00
IIV	0.2643	12.9064	0.9950	2.00
	(0.0199)	(0.2542)		
FP	0.2630	12.7496	0.9948	1.82
TSPC1	0.2688	12.7800	0.9949	1.84
	(0.0194)	(0.2564)		
TSPC2	0.2708	12.9560	0.9950	2.03
	(0.0193)	(0.2559)		

Relation 14

	y_{30}	z_{19}	R^2	d
OLS	3.9600	0.9563	0.9908	1.80
	(1.7255)	(0.0259)		
FIMD	2.7190	0.9581	0.9905	1.88
IIV	2.6881	0.9582	0.9904	1.88
	(2.0414)	(0.0265)		
FP	3.5291	0.9566	0.9908	1.83
TSPC1	4.2326	0.9559	0.9908	1.77
	(1.8692)	(0.0259)		
TSPC2	4.4495	0.9559	0.9908	1.75
	(1.7889)	(0.0259)		

Relation 15

	y_{31}	z_{20}	R^2	d
OLS	4.8622 (1.6175)	1.0035 (0.0465)	0.9729	1.62
FIMD	3.9121	1.0003	0.9721	1.61
IIV	2.6537 (2.2403)	0.9960 (0.0508)	0.9690	1.58
FP	4.2794	1.0024	0.9726	1.62
TSPC1	4.0240 (1.8416)	1.0001 (0.0470)	0.9723	1.61
TSPC2	4.1117 (1.7402)	1.0002 (0.0469)	0.9724	1.61

Relation 16

	y_{32}	z_{21}	z_{22}	R^2	d
OLS	7.4611 (3.3334)	0.9579 (0.0327)	− 120.4686 (36.3597)	0.9862	1.45
FIMD	7.1119	0.9577	− 120.0344	0.9862	1.43
IIV	8.1836 (3.3985)	0.9583 (0.0327)	− 121.3670 (36.7055)	0.9862	1.50
FP	8.2199	0.9581	− 112.8184	0.9861	1.39
TSPC1	8.2386 (3.5148)	0.9587 (0.0328)	− 124.5974 (37.1630)	0.9862	1.55
TSPC2	7.4898 (3.3641)	0.9576 (0.0327)	− 118.6263 (36.7819)	0.9862	1.43

Relation 17

	y_{23}	z_{23}	z_{24}	R^2	d
OLS	0.1228 (0.0371)	0.7449 (0.1159)	5.4779 (2.7847)	0.9977	2.16
FIMD	0.1228	0.7449	5.4779	0.9977	2.16
IIV	0.1193 (0.0361)	0.7485 (0.1129)	5.4425 (2.7628)	0.9977	2.17
FP	0.1107	0.7827	4.7121	0.9976	2.22
TSPC1	0.1246 (0.0373)	0.7452 (0.1158)	5.4409 (2.7830)	0.9977	2.16
TSPC2	0.1229 (0.0381)	0.7371 (0.1171)	5.6702 (2.7952)	0.9977	2.15

Chapter 6

A SEARCH FOR ASYMPTOTICALLY EFFICIENT ESTIMATORS

Especially Estimators of the GEID (FP) Type in the Case of Autoregressive Errors

JAN SELÉN

1. Introduction

The theme of this contribution is a search for more efficient estimators, in the asymptotic sense, within the framework of *REID* systems. Following two lines of development, referred to as structural-form oriented methods and reduced-form oriented methods respectively, we will obtain the GEID (FP) estimator, with the GEID-EF estimator as an extension and also two estimators equivalent to TSLS and 3SLS.

Continuing these two lines of development when the system has autoregressive errors, we will obtain estimators with desirable properties. The limiting distributions of full and limited information members of the two classes are given. Computational methods are presented, and the results of some simulation experiments discussed. Finally the methods are applied to Klein's model I.

The structural-form oriented methods can be regarded as possibilities in the case of undersized samples. A systematic development of structural-form and reduced-form oriented methods was introduced in my dissertation [Selén (1975)] from which the larger part of the material in this contribution stems. The GEID-EF estimator, which under the classic assumptions is asymptotically efficient, is presented here for the first time as is the extension to the case of autoregressive errors.

In our presentation we follow the often used principle of separating the estimating equations defining the estimators from the numerical methods. This approach was introduced for the FP-method by Ågren (1972a). The numerical methods we suggest can in principle be regarded as a combination of Cochrane–Orcutt iterations [see Cochrane and Orcutt (1950)] and FP-iterations [see Chapters 1 and 2 of this volume]. Cochrane and Orcutt introduced an estimator for a simple case of autoregressive errors.

Estimators designed for the case of autoregressive errors and analogous to those to be discussed here are the limited information methods considered by Theil (1958), Sargan (1964), Amemiya (1966), Fair (1972),[1] Lyttkens (1975), and Hatanaka (1976). See also Chapter 7 of this volume.

Corresponding full information methods have been considered by Fair (1972), Dhrymes et al. (1974), Dhrymes and Erlat (1974), Dhrymes and Taylor (1976), and Hatanaka (1976).

Maximum likelihood methods in the case of autoregressive errors are discussed by Sargan (1961), Hendry (1971, 1974), Goldfeld and Quandt (1972), Chow and Fair (1973), and Selén (1975).

2. Serially Uncorrelated Errors

2.1. Specification and Basic Concepts

2.1.1. The Classic ID system. The *basic system* considered in this contribution is the linear interdependent system generally referred to as the *Classic ID system* throughout the volume. The system is assumed to consist of p behavioral relations and q identities. The formal specification is given in the section of abbreviations and notations and in the first two chapters.

2.1.2. The REID system. Our developments will be based on the results of the application of a reformulation principle due to Wold. The *Reformulated Interdependent* (REID) system is the ID system obtained when using this principle. The SF of the REID system is obtained when the endogenous explanatory variables of the Classic ID system are replaced by their systematic parts, and the error terms are modified accordingly. See the formulas named 'REID and GEID, in SF' in the section of abbreviations.

When the systematic parts of the endogenous variables are obtained by conditioning on all the predetermined variables, we have the *REID specification.* Implications of the REID specification are that the expected values of the REID disturbances ε_t are zero, and that these disturbances are uncorrelated with all the predetermined variables.

More general than the REID specification, in the sense that the number of zero correlations between the disturbances ε_t and the predetermined variables are fewer, is the *GEID specification.* Background and details concerning these two specifications are found in Chapters 1 and 2.

[1]See also Fair's paper: The estimation of simultaneous equation models with lagged endogenous variables and first order serially correlated errors, *Econometrica* 38 (1970) 507–516.

2.1.3. Basic assumptions. Let us first introduce the notations for the observation matrices. It is assumed that all variables are observed for T periods ($t = 1, T$). The observation matrices Y and Z are of orders $n \times T$ and $m \times T$, respectively.[2]

The $1 \times T$ vector y_i denotes $(y_{i1}, y_{i2}, \cdots, y_{iT})$. The contents of the $nT \times 1$ column vector vec y is $[y_1, \cdots, y_n]'$ and vec $_1y = [y_1, \cdots, y_p]'$, i.e. only the observations of the left-hand variables of the behavioral relations are included.

For our deductions concerning the limiting distributions of the estimators to apply, a set of basic assumptions is required. These assumptions are that: [1] The system is linear in the parameters and the variables. [2] The matrix $[I - \beta]$ is non-singular. [3] The predetermined variables are not linearly dependent. [4] The system is identified. [5] The pre-sample values of the lagged endogenous variables are known. [6] The moment matrix of the predetermined variables is well-behaved in the limit. [7] The exogenous variables z_t^e are bounded and conceptually held fixed in repeated samples. The limiting matrix $\lim_{T\to\infty} M^\nu$ is assumed to exist for $\nu = 1, 2, \cdots$ where

$$M^\nu = (T - \nu)^{-1} \sum_{t=1}^{T-\nu} z_t^e z_{t+\nu}^{e\prime}.$$

[8] The parameters of the components of z that are lagged endogenous are such that the system is stable. [9] The random variables $_1\delta_t$ are stochastically independent vectors that are identically distributed with expectation zero and moment matrix Φ ($t = 1, T$). The matrix Φ is non-stochastic, has finite elements and is positive definite. [10] The expectation of $_1\delta_t$ is identical to the zero vector at time points $1, 2, \cdots, t$ when conditioned on the exogenous variables and the lagged endogenous variables. [11] The disturbances have finite moments up to the fourth order. Other assumptions are usual regularity conditions, such as the existence of inverse matrices, and more specific assumptions. The latter are given in the theorems.

The assumptions concerning the disturbance terms have here been placed on the SF disturbances of the classic ID system, δ_t. In all essential aspects, however, they carry over to the RF disturbances ε_t.

Finally we note that assumption 10 is modified for the GEID specification and that assumption 11 is needed only for the establishment of asymptotic normality.

[2] To conform with the notational system of the volume the vectors and matrices of the observations consist of T columns instead of T rows which was the case in Selén (1975).

2.2. Structural-Form and Reduced-Form Oriented Estimators

2.2.1. Introduction. Starting from the REID system we will define two classes of estimators in this section. In subsequent sections members of the two classes will be given.

Let us first consider the ith behavioral relation of the REID system. This can be written, for all observations simultaneously, as

$$y_i = \beta_{(i)}\eta^*_{(i)} + \gamma_{(i)}Z_{(i)} + \varepsilon_i, \tag{2.1}$$

where the notations are the same as throughout the volume.

The relation (2.1) is compactly written as

$$y_i = \alpha_i\chi_i + \varepsilon_i, \tag{2.2}$$

where y_i and ε_i are $1 \times T$ vectors, $\alpha_i = (\beta_{(i)}\gamma_{(i)})$ of order $1 \times (n_i + m_i)$ contains the unknown structural parameters and χ_i of order $(n_i + m_i) \times T$ contains the corresponding explanatory variables.

The difficulty of using OLS estimation on equations (2.1) or (2.2) is that $\eta^*_{(i)}$ is unobservable. To estimate this quantity let us consider two different representations of the reduced form. The first, the *Restricted Reduced Form* (RRF), is the reduced form as generated from the structural form, i.e.,

$$y_t = [I - \beta]^{-1}\Gamma z_t + \varepsilon_t = \eta^*_t + \varepsilon_t. \tag{2.3}$$

The second, the *Unrestricted Reduced Form* (URF), is defined as the unrestricted projection of y_t on z_t or

$$y_t = E(y_t \mid z_t) + \varepsilon_t = \eta^*_t + \varepsilon_t. \tag{2.4}$$

where η^*_t and ε_t in general are not the same as in (2.3).

The different alternatives open the possibility of two different approaches for defining estimators. We will call the approach based on the RRF (2.3) *structural-form oriented.* The second approach is based on the URF (2.4) and will be called *reduced-form oriented.*

To separate between the data matrices for the regressors of the two approaches the symbols X^S_i and X^R_i are introduced for the estimates of χ_i in (2.2). The superscript S in X^S_i indicates that $\eta^*_{(i)}$ is estimated from the structural parameters through the RRF. The superscript R in X^R_i in the same way indicates that the URF is utilized. The contents of the $(n_i + m_i) \times T$ matrices X^S_i and X^R_i is written $[Y^{*\prime}_{(i)}Z'_{(i)}]'$ although $Y^*_{(i)}$ is different in the two cases. In the following it should be obvious from the context which approach $Y^*_{(i)}$ refers to, whenever the symbol is used.

Comparing (2.3) and (2.4) we see that the estimates of the reduced-form oriented methods in principle can be obtained in two steps whereas the structural-form oriented methods require the solution of nonlinear systems of equations.

An important advantage of the structural-form oriented methods is that they are more modest as regards the number of observations required for their application. These methods can be used when the reduced form oriented methods break down in the unrestricted reduced form. Even for medium-size models the URF contains a large number of predetermined variables as regressors.

A second important advantage of some of the structural-form oriented methods is that they are consistent under more general specifications of the GEID type.

In the following sections members of the two classes are defined. Since our interest is directed towards a study of efficiency we will start with the limited-information methods, proceed to the full-information methods and later end with the estimators for the case of autoregressive disturbances. To enable a ready comparison of the methods the treatment will be rather detailed.

2.2.2. Two limited-information methods. We will in this section consider two limited-information methods, both of which thus ignore the correlations between the errors of different relations. First, the structural-form oriented GEID estimator is obtained through the RRF. The origin and history of this method is given in Chapters 1 and 2. Second, a reduced-form oriented estimator equivalent to the *Two Stage Least Squares* (TSLS) method of Basmann (1957) and Theil (1953, 1958) is defined.

In the following the estimated parameters of a single relation i are denoted a_i, where a is the $\Sigma(n_i + m_i)$ row vector $(a_1, \cdots, a_p)$.

Definition 1: A structural-form oriented estimator, the *GEID* estimator, is defined as the real solutions a_i $(i = 1, p)$, if any, of the system

$$X_i^S y_i' = X_i^S X_i^{S\prime} a_i', \qquad i = 1, p, \tag{2.5}$$

$$Y^* = [I_n - B]^{-1} GZ. \tag{2.6}$$

Definition 2: A reduced-form oriented estimator, the *TSLS* estimator, is defined as the solution a_i $(i = 1, p)$, if any, of the system

$$X_i^R y_i' = X_i^R X_i^{R\prime} a_i', \qquad i = 1, p, \tag{2.7}$$

$$y_i^* = y_i Z'[ZZ']^{-1} Z, \qquad i = 1, n. \tag{2.8}$$

Comments: (1) Eliminating Y^* in (2.5) using (2.6) we get a nonlinear system in the unknown parameters. This opens the possibility of several real solutions. The real solutions belonging to a sequence of solutions that converge in probability to the true parameter values will be called estimators in the *strict sense* if any such exist; cf. Ågren (1972a).

(2) The number of observations required for estimation is different for the two estimators. The reduced-form oriented method requires that this number is at least as large as m, the number of predetermined variables, whereas this is not required for the structural-form oriented estimator.

We will now give the asymptotic distributions of the estimators. The results can be derived through the procedures of Section 2.2.3 below. For more details concerning the deductions under our set of basic assumptions, see Selén (1975).

Theorem 1: Under the basic assumptions in Section 2.1.3 a GEID estimator in the strict sense exists for the REID-specified system. The normal limiting distribution is[3]

$$T^{1/2}(a-\alpha)\sim N(0, \operatorname{plim} T[\chi([I_n-\beta]^{-1}\otimes I_T)\chi']^{-1}$$
$$\times \operatorname{plim} T^{-1}\chi[\Xi\otimes I_T]\chi' \operatorname{plim} T[\chi([I_n-\beta]^{-1}\otimes I_T)\chi']^{-1\prime}),$$

where $\chi=\operatorname{diag}(\chi_1,\cdots,\chi_p)$ and Ξ is a $p\times p$ covariance matrix with (ij)th element $E(\varepsilon_{it}\varepsilon_{jt})=\xi_{ij}$. In the case of identities the last $n-p$ rows and columns in $[I_n-\beta]^{-1}$ are deleted.

Theorem 2: Under the basic assumptions in Section 2.1.3 the TSLS method is a consistent estimator of a REID-specified system. The limiting distribution is

$$T^{1/2}(a-\alpha)\sim N(0, \operatorname{plim} T[\chi\chi']^{-1} \operatorname{plim} T^{-1}\chi[\Phi\otimes I_T]\chi' \operatorname{plim} T[\chi\chi']^{-1}),$$

where the (ij)th element of the $p\times p$ matrix Φ is $E(\delta_{it}\delta'_{it})=\varphi_{ij}$.

Comments: (3) Although interpreted as a limited-information method the GEID estimator has full-information features which are reflected in the asymptotic covariance matrix. Neither the TSLS, nor the GEID estimator is asymptotically more efficient in general than the other method.

(4) The GEID estimator is consistent under the more general GEID specification; see Chapters 1 and 2.

[3] Parentheses ( ) and brackets [ ] are in the following expressions used to simplify the readability only. Parentheses do not generally denote row vectors.

2.2.3. Two full-information methods. In this subsection we will give a structural-form oriented estimator and a reduced-form oriented estimator. The latter is equivalent to the *Three Stage Least Squares* (3SLS) method of Zellner and Theil (1962).

To prepare for the definitions we write the structural form of the respecified system for all behavioral relations and all observations simultaneously as

$$\begin{bmatrix} y_1' \\ \vdots \\ y_p' \end{bmatrix} = \begin{bmatrix} \chi_1' & \cdot & \cdot & 0 & \cdot & 0 \\ \vdots & \vdots & \vdots & \vdots & \vdots & \vdots \\ 0 & 0 & \cdot & \cdot & \cdot & \chi_p' \end{bmatrix} \begin{bmatrix} \alpha_1' \\ \vdots \\ \alpha_p' \end{bmatrix} + \begin{bmatrix} \varepsilon_1' \\ \vdots \\ \varepsilon_p' \end{bmatrix}, \tag{2.9}$$

or more compactly as

$$\text{vec}\,_1 y = \chi'\alpha' + \text{vec}\,_1\varepsilon. \tag{2.10}$$

The notations in (2.9) were given in connection with (2.2). In the following we will assume that the covariance matrix of the disturbances, vec $_1\varepsilon$ is

$$\Xi \otimes I_T. \tag{2.11a}$$

This implies that the covariance matrix of vec $_1\delta$ can be written as

$$\Phi \otimes I_T. \tag{2.11b}$$

The estimators we will give could all be replaced by the generalized least squares method estimating seemingly unrelated regressions suggested by Zellner (1962), if η^* and thus χ were observable. Notations in the definitions that follow are $X^S = \text{diag}(X_1^S, \cdots, X_p^S)$ and $X^R = \text{diag}(X_1^R, \cdots, X_p^R)$. X^S and X^R are χ estimated utilizing the restricted and unrestricted reduced forms, respectively.

Definition 3: A structural-form oriented estimator, the *GEID Efficient* (GEID-EF) method, is defined as the real solutions a, if any, of the system

$$X^S[\theta \otimes I_T]\text{vec}\,_1 y = X^S[\theta \otimes I_T]X^{S\prime}a', \tag{2.12}$$

$$Y^* = [I_n - B]^{-1}GZ, \tag{2.13}$$

where

$$\theta = \Phi^{-1}[(I_p - \beta_{11}) - \beta_{12}(I_{n-p} - \beta_{22})^{-1}\beta_{21}]. \tag{2.14}$$

In the case of no identities $\theta = \Phi^{-1}[I_n - \beta]$. The partitioning of β is given in the section of abbreviations.

Definition 4: A reduced-form oriented estimator, the *3SLS* method, is defined as the solution a, if any, of the system

$$X^{R}[\Phi^{-1} \otimes I_T] \operatorname{vec}_1 y = X^{R}[\Phi^{-1} \otimes I_T] X^{R\prime} a', \tag{2.15}$$

$$y_i^* = y_i Z'[ZZ']^{-1} Z, \qquad i = 1, n. \tag{2.16}$$

Comments: (5) The matrices θ and Φ^{-1} [see (2.14) and (2.11b)], the weighting matrices of the estimators, are specified as known. We will later indicate that the asymptotic properties are unaffected when replacing these matrices with consistent estimates.

(6) Neither of these estimators are in general consistent for the GEID specification. The name of the GEID-EF method is chosen to stress the similarity to the definition of the GEID estimator.

(7) The system of equations in Definition 3 is nonlinear in the unknown elements of β and Γ since Y^* is a function of these elements and a is a vector of them. The real solutions belonging to a sequence of solutions that converge in probability to the true parameter values are called estimators in the strict sense, if any such exist.

(8) The sample sizes required for estimation differ between the structural-form oriented estimator and the reduced-form oriented estimator: the latter is more demanding.

(9) The one-to-one correspondence between REID and Classic ID systems implies that the estimators although defined for REID systems share the same properties for Classic ID systems, as do the limited information methods given in Definitions 1 and 2.

To deduce the asymptotic properties of the GEID-EF estimator we start by inserting the system (2.13) of the definition into (2.12). The estimator can then be written as

$$F(a, M) = 0, \tag{2.17}$$

where F is a vector of n_p functions. The vector a is a vector of the n_p unknown parameters and M a vector of all moments $T^{-1} y_i z_j'$, $T^{-1} z_i z_j'$ that occur. The weighting matrix θ is assumed known and its elements do not enter as arguments. The only functions of y and z involved are second-order sample moments which, according to the basic assumptions, converge in probability to the corresponding population moments. Under certain regularity conditions the implicit function theorem will lead to the existence of a sequence of GEID-EF estimates in the strict sense for the REID-specified system; cf. Ågren (1972a) who established consistency of the GEID estimator for the GEID specified system.

We proceed to derive the asymptotic distribution of the GEID-EF estimator for the REID specified system. The result is given in Theorem 3 below.

The first step in the derivation is to obtain an expression for $a - \alpha$. To this end we will follow the approach used by Lyttkens (1970d) in deducing the asymptotic covariance matrix of the GEID estimator. The ith relation of the REID system (2.1) is written as

$$y'_i = [\eta^{*\prime}_{(i)} Z'_{(i)}](\beta_{(i)} \gamma_{(i)})' + \varepsilon'_i, \tag{2.18}$$

and the corresponding estimated relation as

$$y'_i = [Y^{*\prime}_{(i)} Z'_{(i)}](b_{(i)} g_{(i)})' + e'_i. \tag{2.19}$$

Subtracting (2.19) from (2.18) we get, for all relations,

$$\begin{bmatrix} \varepsilon'_1 - e'_1 \\ \cdot \quad \cdot \\ \\ \cdot \quad \cdot \\ \varepsilon'_p - e'_p \end{bmatrix} = \begin{bmatrix} Y^{*\prime}_{(1)} Z'_{(1)} \cdot 0\,0 \cdot 0 \\ \cdot \qquad\qquad \cdot \\ \\ \cdot \qquad\qquad \cdot \\ 0 \cdot\cdot \qquad Y^{*\prime}_{(p)} Z'_{(p)} \end{bmatrix} \begin{bmatrix} b'_{(1)} - \beta'_{(1)} \\ \cdot \quad \cdot \\ \\ \cdot \quad \cdot \\ g'_{(p)} - \gamma'_{(p)} \end{bmatrix}$$
$$+ \begin{bmatrix} Y^{*\prime}_{(1)} - \eta^{*\prime}_{(1)} \\ \cdot \\ \\ \cdot \\ 0 \cdot\cdot\, Y^{*\prime}_{(p)} - \eta^{*\prime}_{(p)} \end{bmatrix} \begin{bmatrix} \beta'_{(1)} \\ \cdot \\ \\ \cdot \\ \beta'_{(p)} \end{bmatrix}, \tag{2.20}$$

which can be written compactly as

$$\operatorname{vec}({}_1\varepsilon - {}_1e) = X^{S\prime}(a - \alpha)' + [\beta \otimes I_T] X_1^{S\prime}. \tag{2.21}$$

According to the definition of a REID system and (2.18) and (2.19) we have

$$\operatorname{vec}\, {}_1y = \operatorname{vec}\, {}_1\eta^* + \operatorname{vec}\, {}_1\varepsilon = \operatorname{vec}\, {}_1y^* + \operatorname{vec}\, {}_1e. \tag{2.22}$$

This implies that (2.21) can be rewritten as

$$\operatorname{vec}({}_1\varepsilon - {}_1e) = ([I - \beta]^{-1} \otimes I_T) X^{S\prime}(a - \alpha)'. \tag{2.23}$$

Let us premultiply this equation by $T^{-1/2} X^S [\theta \otimes I_T]$. Rearranging and using the fact that $X^S[\theta \otimes I_T] \operatorname{vec}\, {}_1e = 0$, which holds according to the definition of the estimator, we obtain[4]

$$T^{1/2}(a - \alpha)' = [T^{-1} X^S(\theta[I - \beta]^{-1} \otimes I_T) X^{S\prime}]^{-1} T^{-1/2} X^S(\theta \otimes I_T) \operatorname{vec}\, {}_1\varepsilon. \tag{2.24}$$

[4] The deduction applies to models without identities. In the case of identities the result can be written as (2.24) also. The dimensions of a, χ, ε and X^S remain the same but in $[I - \beta]^{-1}$ the last $n - p$ rows and columns are deleted.

This expression is similar to a usual expression in the derivation of the limiting distribution of the 3SLS estimator, cf. Dhrymes (1970), and indicates the second step in our derivation for the GEID-EF estimator. The crucial difference vis-à-vis the corresponding expression for the 3SLS method is that the y_i^*'s in X^S depend on the estimates of the structural parameters, see (2.13). We have however already established the consistency of the estimator. It is therefore possible to proceed as follows to obtain the asymptotic distribution for (2.24) using the fact that a is a root belonging to a sequence of solutions that converges to the true parameter values. The distribution is essentially determined by the asymptotic distribution of $T^{-1/2}X^S[\theta \otimes I_T] \text{ vec }_1\varepsilon$ provided the probability limit of the remaining term on the right side exists and is non-stochastic. For the latter we obtain

$$\text{plim } T^{-1}X^S(\theta[I-\beta]^{-1} \otimes I_T)X^{S\prime} = \text{plim } T^{-1}\chi(\theta[I-\beta]^{-1} \otimes I_T)\chi', \tag{2.25}$$

since the remainder is of smaller order in probability. The (ij)th submatrix of the right-hand side is $\mu_{ij}\chi_i\chi_j'$ where μ_{ij} is a scalar constant. χ_i represents the 'true' regressors of the ith relation, and can be written

$$\chi_i' = Z'J_i, \tag{2.26}$$

where J_i is a $m \times (n_i + m_i)$ matrix containing the restricted reduced form parameters defining the n_i η^*'s of relation i, and constants or selection elements that assure that the predetermined variables of relation i are included.

We conclude that the existence of the non-stochastic probability limit of $T^{-1}ZZ'$, which is assumed non-singular, implies that the same holds for

$$\text{plim}[T^{-1}\chi(\theta[I-\beta]^{-1} \otimes I_T)\chi']^{-1}, \tag{2.27}$$

assuming that the inverse exists.

The derivation of the asymptotic distribution of $T^{-1/2}X^S[\theta \otimes I_T] \text{ vec }_1\varepsilon$ is as follows. We know that

$$T^{-1/2}X^S[\theta \otimes I_T] \text{ vec }_1\varepsilon = T^{-1/2}\begin{bmatrix} \sum_t x_{pt}^s \nu_{1.\,1}\varepsilon_t \\ \vdots \\ \sum_t x_{pt}^s \nu_{p.\,1}\varepsilon_t \end{bmatrix}, \tag{2.28}$$

where ${}_1\varepsilon_t$ is the $p \times 1$ vector containing the disturbances at time-point t, while $\nu_{i.}$ denotes the ith row of θ and x_{it}^s the tth column of X_i^S. The right-hand side is expanded to become

$$T^{-1/2}\begin{bmatrix} \hat{J}_1' \ldots 0 \ldots 0 \\ 0 \\ \cdot \\ \cdot \\ 0 \quad \ldots \quad \hat{J}_p' \end{bmatrix}\begin{bmatrix} \sum_t z_t \nu_{1.1}\varepsilon_t \\ \cdot \\ \cdot \\ \cdot \\ \sum_t z_t \nu_{p.1}\varepsilon_t \end{bmatrix} = T^{-1/2}\hat{J}\sum v_t, \tag{2.29}$$

where $\hat{J}_i$ contains estimated RRF parameters and constants, cf. (2.26), and z_t is the $m \times 1$ vector of the predetermined variables. Consistency implies that plim $\hat{J}$ exists and is non-stochastic. The limiting distribution is therefore essentially determined by $T^{-1/2}\sum v_t$. The basic assumptions made for the disturbances imply that the vectors $(\nu_{1.1}\varepsilon_t, \cdots, \nu_{p.1}\varepsilon_t)$, $(t = 1,2,\cdots)$, are stochastically independent for different t's, have a covariance matrix with desirable properties, expectation zero and finite moments up to the fourth order. Together with the regularity assumptions made concerning the behavior of the exogenous variables and the dynamic properties of the system this implies that the central limit theorem of Schönfeld (1971, p. 125) is applicable.[5] We now have a vector $T^{-1/2}\sum v_t$ that converges in distribution to a random variable and a matrix, essentially (2.27), that converges in probability to a constant. We thus conclude from a convergence theorem of Cramér (1946, p. 254) that the limiting distribution $T^{-1/2}(a-\alpha)'$ is normal with covariance matrix

$$\text{plim}\,\Lambda^{-1}\text{plim}\,T^{-1}[\chi(\theta\Xi\theta'\otimes I_T)\chi']\,\text{plim}\,\Lambda'^{-1}, \tag{2.30}$$

where plim Λ^{-1} is (2.25). The matrix θ was in the definition of the estimator given as $\Phi^{-1}(I-\beta)$ for the case of no identities. The inner product in the specification of Λ, i.e. $\theta[I-\beta]^{-1}$, then becomes Φ^{-1}, which is equivalent to $\theta\Xi\theta'$, and (2.30) is simplified.

The results are summarized:

Theorem 3: Under the basic assumptions in Section 2.1.3 a GEID-EF estimator in the strict sense exists for the REID-specified system. This estimator is asymptotically efficient under general conditions. Its limiting distribution is written as

$$T^{1/2}(a-\alpha) \sim N(0, \text{plim}\,T[\chi(\Phi^{-1}\otimes I_T)\chi']^{-1}).$$

The asymptotic results for the 3SLS method can be obtained in a similar way. The expression corresponding to (2.24) is

$$T^{1/2}(a-\alpha)' = (T^{-1}X^R[\Phi^{-1}\otimes I_T]X^{R\prime})^{-1}T^{-1/2}X^R[\Phi^{-1}\otimes I_T]\,\text{vec}\,{}_1\delta, \tag{2.31}$$

[5] The theorem of Schönfeld is somewhat stronger than necessary referring to convergence in quadratic mean rather than in probability.

and a development corresponding to the above yields the following results; cf. Selén (1975):

Theorem 4: Under the basic assumptions in Section 2.1.3 the 3SLS method is a consistent estimator of the REID specified system. The limiting distribution is identical to the one given in Theorem 3. The 3SLS method is known to be asymptotically efficient under general conditions.

2.2.4. The consequences of unknown weighting matrices. We have hitherto assumed that the weighting matrices of the full-information methods are known. In practice this assumption is unrealistic. The standard approach to extend the applicability of similar estimators is to replace the unknown weighting matrices by consistent estimates. To show that the limiting distributions remain the same is fairly simple, at least in the absence of lagged endogenous variables. We could e.g. utilize a convergence theorem saying that convergence in probability to a random variable implies convergence in distribution to the distribution of that variable; cf. Dhrymes (1970, p. 93). Provided

$$\operatorname{plim} T^{1/2}(a^* - \alpha) = \operatorname{plim} T^{1/2}(a - \alpha), \tag{2.32}$$

where α is the true parameter vector and a the estimated vector when the weighting matrix is known and a^* the estimated vector when the weighting matrix is estimated, then the desired result is obtained.

The use of the TSLS residuals gives the usual 3SLS results. Likewise the use of the TSLS residuals and β estimates give asymptotically efficient GEID-EF estimates. To avoid the URF with its requirements concerning sample size, the GEID residuals and β estimates could be used for GEID-EF. Alternatively the definition of GEID-EF could be modified by adding estimating equations for Φ in terms of the GEID-EF parameter estimates and the observations. The weighting matrix θ is then estimated by replacing the unknown elements of Φ and β with their corresponding estimates. The resulting highly nonlinear estimator can be written as $F(a, M) = 0$, i.e., a vector of functions with vector arguments a (the unknown parameters) and M (the second-order moments). The implicit function theorem is used to establish consistency. The covariance matrix is obtained as

$$D^2(a) = D\Sigma_{MM}D', \tag{2.33}$$

where Σ_{MM} is the covariance matrix of sample moments and D contains the first-order partial derivatives of f with respect to the components of M, cf. the deduction for the GEID estimator by Ågren (1972a); $a = f(M)$ denotes a GEID-EF estimator in the strict sense.

3. Autoregressive Errors

3.1. The Transformed System

3.1.1. The basic transformed system. In this section we will consider the situation where the vector of structural disturbances is adequately represented by a first-order vector autoregressive (AR) process. To simplify the argument assume that the basic system consists merely of behavioral relations.[6] The AR process can thus be written as

$$\delta_t = R\delta_{t-1} + \delta_t^+, \tag{3.1}$$

where $R = [\rho_{ij}]$ is a $p \times p$ matrix of parameters.

Arbitrary elements in R may a priori be zero, the case where R is diagonal is important and will be given special attention. δ_t^+ is a $p \times 1$ vector of disturbances.

Inserting the basic system,

$$y_t = \beta y_t + \Gamma z_t + \delta_t, \tag{3.2}$$

in (3.1) we obtain the *transformed system*

$$y_t = \beta y_t + R[I - \beta]y_{t-1} + \Gamma z_t - R\Gamma z_{t-1} + \delta_t^+, \tag{3.3}$$

which is a base for our developments. To simplify the notation it is assumed that the y's and z's are observable for $(T+1)$ periods $(t = 0, T)$ when discussing the transformed system, which then is valid for $(t = 1, T)$. The point with the transformed system is that all assumptions involving δ_t earlier now can be transferred to δ_t^+. The price that is paid is the more complicated parameter structure and the presence of lagged endogenous variables even if z_t is purely exogenous. The assumption of a linear system is violated and some mild regularity conditions are required; cf. Malinvaud (1964, ch. 9.5). The rest of the basic assumptions are retained, bearing in mind that the group of predetermined variables is now extended. The covariance matrix $E(\delta_t^+\delta_t^{+\prime})$ is denoted by Ψ.

3.1.2. The reformulated transformed system. Following the reformulation principle indicated in Section 2.1.2 we will respecify the transformed system (3.3) to admit a predictor specification of the structural form. Define the $p \times 1$ vector η_t^{**} as the systematic part of the restricted reduced form of (3.3),

[6] Identities are accomodated at the cost of notational complications mainly. The required modifications will be taken up in connection with the definitions and the theorems.

$$\eta_t^{**} = [I-\beta]^{-1}\Gamma z_t + [I-\beta]^{-1}R[I-\beta]y_{t-1} - [I-\beta]^{-1}R\Gamma z_{t-1}. \quad (3.4)$$

The system (3.3) can now be respecified as

$$y_t = \beta\eta_t^{**} + R[I-\beta]y_{t-1} + \Gamma z_t - R\Gamma z_{t-1} + \varepsilon_t^{+}. \quad (3.5)$$

We have thus obtained the structural form of the *Reformulated Interdependent Autoregressive Disturbances* (REID-AR) system.[7] The reduced form of the REID-AR system is identical to the reduced form of the transformed system, namely

$$y_t = \Omega z_t + [I-\beta]^{-1}R[I-\beta]y_{t-1} - [I-\beta]^{-1}R\Gamma z_{t-1} + \varepsilon_t^{+}. \quad (3.6)$$

The definition of η_t^{**} in (3.4) and the REID-AR specification

$$\eta_{it}^{**} = E(y_{it} \mid z_t, y_{t-1}, z_{t-1}), \qquad i = 1, p, \quad (3.7)$$

implies that

$$E(y_{it} \mid \eta_{(i)t}^{**}, z_{(i)t}, y_{(i)t-1}, z_{(i)t-1}) = \beta_{(i)}\eta_{(i)t}^{**} + [R(I-\beta)]_{(i)}y_{(i)t-1} + \gamma_{(i)}z_{(i)t} - [R\Gamma]_{(i)}z_{(i)t-1}, \quad (3.8)$$

(i.e., the expectation of the left-hand side variable of relation i $(i = 1, p)$ given the components of η_t^{**}, z_t, y_{t-1} and z_{t-1} occurring on the right-hand side) is an unbiased predictor.

In accordance with the GEID specification we can decrease the number of variables upon which the y_t's are conditioned and still obtain unbiased predictors. Details of this are discussed in Selén (1973) where the implications of (3.6) and (3.7), which are similar to the implications discussed in Section 2.1.2, are also explained. In a similar manner it can be shown that the GEID-A estimator discussed below is consistent under more general conditions than its reduced-form oriented counterpart.

A second approach to the reformulation of an ID system with correlated disturbances is to start from the REID system,

$$y_t = \beta\eta_t^{*} + \Gamma z_t + \varepsilon_t, \quad (3.9)$$

where the disturbances are assumed to be generated according to

$$\varepsilon_t = R_\varepsilon \varepsilon_{t-1} + \varepsilon_t^{+}. \quad (3.10)$$

Rewriting (3.10) utilizing (3.9) we get

$$y_t = \beta\eta_t^{*} + R_\varepsilon y_{t-1} - R_\varepsilon\beta\eta_{t-1}^{*} + \Gamma z_t - R_\varepsilon\Gamma z_{t-1} + \varepsilon_t^{+}. \quad (3.11)$$

To limit the discussion in the following we will make a choice between the two alternatives; the REID-AR system as written in (3.5) and the

[7] Earlier called REIDA.

REID-system in (3.11). Our choice is (3.5). One reason for this are the possibilities of comparisons to other developments, where generally the autoregressive process is specified for δ_t and not ε_t, the base for (3.11). It is also simple to work with the system (3.5) interpreting ε_t^+ as the disturbance of a 'new' system, differing from the original mainly through restrictions placed on the structural parameters. A similar interpretation of the disturbance ε_t^+ is not feasible for the alternative (3.11). The implications of the REID specification concern ε_t and not ε_t^+; it is in fact easy to show that in general the disturbances ε_t^+ and the predetermined variables that are lagged endogenous are not uncorrelated. For the second approach this means difficulties obtaining consistent estimators in the presence of lagged endogenous variables. The small sample properties of one estimator based on (3.9) in the absence of lagged endogenous variables is studied in Selén (1973).

3.2. Extensions of Structural-Form and Reduced-Form Oriented Estimators

3.2.1. Two principles. In this section two principles for extending the structural-form and reduced-form oriented estimators are suggested. The first approach will not give estimators as efficient as the second. On the other hand, the estimates are easier to calculate for the first approach as will be indicated later. The alternatives are introduced through the following simple one-relational model:

$$y_t = \gamma z_t + \delta_t, \tag{3.12}$$

$$\delta_t = \rho\delta_{t-1} + \delta_t^+, \tag{3.13}$$

where γ and ρ are scalar parameters and y_t, z_t, δ_t and δ_t^+ denote scalar variables. The notations in (3.12) and (3.13) apply to the rest of this subsection only.

Equation (3.13), where the δ_t^+'s are serially uncorrelated, specifies a covariance pattern for the disturbances δ. Given that ρ is known we can form the Generalized Least Squares (GLS) estimator of γ,

$$c = (zQ^{-1}z')^{-1}zQ^{-1}y', \tag{3.14}$$

which is a minimum variance linear estimator. Q is the covariance matrix of the error vector δ; z and y denote observation vectors. Typically ρ is unknown, but this parameter can be consistently estimated by applying ordinary least squares to (3.12) calculating the corresponding residuals, and applying ordinary least squares to (3.13). Q can now be consistently estimated, and through a GLS-step a consistent estimate of γ is obtained.

One can show that the asymptotic distribution of the estimator so defined is identical to the distribution of the original GLS estimator (3.14). The procedure where the autoregressive process is used to consistently estimate a covariance matrix which is used in the generalized least squares step will be referred to as the *GLS approach*.

The transformed system,

$$y_t = \gamma z_t + \rho y_{t-1} - \rho\gamma z_{t-1} + \delta_t^+, \tag{3.15}$$

as obtained from (3.12) and (3.13), is the base presenting the *calculated residuals as regressors* (CRR) approach which is the second principle. Rewriting (3.15) as

$$y_t = \gamma z_t + \rho\delta_{t-1} + \delta_t^+, \tag{3.16}$$

we have notationally eliminated the nonlinear parameter structure. The new difficulty is that δ_{t-1} is unknown and unobservable. It is, however, possible to estimate the variable through a least squares step applied to (3.12). Inserting the estimates d_{t-1} in (3.16), the parameters are estimated regressing y_t on z_t and d_{t-1}. In this way we have defined a two-step estimator.

A modification of the procedure is to define an estimator using the following set of equations:

$$\begin{aligned} yz' &= czz' + rd_\ell z' \\ yd'_\ell &= czd'_\ell + rd_\ell d'_\ell, \qquad d = y - cz, \end{aligned} \tag{3.17}$$

where d_ℓ is d lagged one period. The difference is that the estimates of the disturbances and of γ and ρ should simultaneously satisfy a set of equations. The method may be interpreted as an iterated two-step procedure. In other words, the estimate of γ obtained in the second step above is used to calculate new estimates of the disturbances, which as inserted in (3.16) are used in a least squares step producing estimates of γ and ρ, of which the former is used to re-estimate the disturbances and so forth until convergence is attained.

The three estimation methods presented for the case where the parameter ρ is unknown — GLS, two-step and (3.17) — are discussed in Selén (1974) where z_t is assumed stochastic and generated by a process $z_t = \theta z_{t-1} + w_t$. The results of Grether and Maddala (1972) are utilized to show that the two CRR methods are inferior to the GLS approach method, and that (3.17) is superior to the two-step procedure as regards asymptotic efficiency. Even the small sample properties are examined in Selén (1974). Using Monte Carlo experiments it is indicated that the ranking based on the asymptotic results essentially holds even for finite samples. One interesting finding is that a modification of the method used to introduce the GLS approach above seems to have a better performance for finite samples, although the asymptotic properties are identical. The modification is similar to the modification of the two-step method to (3.17) earlier, i.e., it is required that the estimates of the disturbances used to estimate Q should be obtained by utilizing the estimate of γ given by that method. In the following a similar estimation principle is utilized.

We have now introduced the two principles and indicated that one is superior. As regards simultaneous equations one would expect this difference to carry over. Discussing the estimation of simultaneous equations we have to take other factors into account, for example computational problems. The GLS approach implies, in its general form, an estimation of the whole system simultaneously and is more complicated. In the CRR approach it is in principle sufficient to work with one relation at a time.

3.2.2. The CRR approach. The reformulated transformed interdependent system consisting of p behavioral relations was written in (3.5). Simplifying the expression by introducing δ_{t-1} as defined from the Classic ID system, we obtain

$$y_t = \beta\eta_t^{**} + \Gamma z_t + R\delta_{t-1} + \varepsilon_t^+, \tag{3.18}$$

which is the basic relation used for defining the estimators. With (3.18) it is possible to allow for a non-diagonal autoregressive structure matrix and still obtain estimates through rather simple procedures, as will be indicated in Section 4.1. The ith relation of the estimated version of (3.18) can be written for all observations as

$$y_i' = [Y_{(i)}^{**\prime} Z_{(i)}' d_{(i)\ell}'](b_{(i)} c_{(i)} r_{(i)})' + e_i^{+\prime}, \tag{3.19a}$$

$$y_i' = X_i^{\mathrm{ST}\prime} d_{(i)\ell}'](a_i r_{(i)})' + e_i^{+\prime}, \tag{3.19b}$$

where $Y_{(i)}^{**}, Z_{(i)}$ and $d_{(i)\ell}$ are the data matrices of the ith relation. The subscript ℓ in general indicates observation matrices for lagged variables, $r_{(i)}$ denotes the ith row of R with prescribed zero elements deleted and the symbol X_i^{ST} indicates that y_i^{**} is estimated from the structural parameters, through the restricted reduced form. We are now prepared to define a structural form oriented estimator which is an extension of the GEID estimator.[8]

Definition 1: The *GEID-A* estimator is defined as the real solutions $(a_i r_{(i)})$, $i = 1, p$, if any, of the system

$$[X_i^{\mathrm{ST}\prime} d_{(i)\ell}']' y_i' = [X_i^{\mathrm{ST}\prime} d_{(i)\ell}']'[X_i^{\mathrm{ST}\prime} d_{(i)\ell}'](a_i r_{(i)})', \tag{3.20}$$

[8] The extension was introduced in Selén (1973).

$$Y^{**} = [I_n - B]^{-1}GZ + [I_n - B]^{-1}RD_\ell, \tag{3.21}$$

$$d_j = y_j - b_{(j)}Y_{(j)} - g_{(j)}Z_{(j)}, \qquad j = 1, p, \tag{3.22}$$

where the ith row of the $p \times T$ matrix D_ℓ is $d_{i\ell}$.

Comments: (1) It is easily shown that the GEID-A estimator reduces to the GEID estimator if all elements of R are zero *a priori* and if the first observation is included.

(2) Being a highly nonlinear estimator the GEID-A method may give rise to several solutions. By use of the implicit function theorem the existence of an estimator in the strict sense is established; cf. Section 2.2.3.

(3) The complications in the case of identities are minor. Still the p behavioral relations can be written as in (3.19a, b), which leaves (3.20) unchanged, as is (3.22). The y_i^{**}'s in (3.21) are obtained for all the $p+q$ endogenous variables by changing B and C (cf. the section of abbreviations) and replacing RD_ℓ by $(D'_\ell R' : 0]'$, where 0 is the zero matrix of order $T \times q$.

The corresponding extension of the TSLS estimator results in the following reduced form oriented method.

Definition 2: A TSLS type estimator is defined as the real solutions $(a_i r_{(i)})$, $i = 1, p$, if any, of

$$[X_i^{RT\prime} d'_{(i)\ell}]' y'_i = [X_i^{RT\prime} d'_{(i)\ell}]'[X_i^{RT\prime} d'_{(i)\ell}](a_i r_{(i)})', \tag{3.23}$$

$$y_i^{**} = y_i Z^{Tr\prime}[Z^{Tr} Z^{Tr\prime}]^{-1} Z^{Tr}, \tag{3.24}$$

$$d_j = y_j - b_{(j)}Y_{(j)} - g_{(j)}Z_{(j)}, \qquad j = 1, p, \tag{3.25}$$

where $Z^{Tr} = [Z' Y'_\ell Z'_\ell]'$ is the matrix of observations of the predetermined variables of the transformed system. There are T columns and at most $m + n + m$ rows since superfluous rows are deleted in the case of lagged variables in the basic system (2.1). The superscript RT is used to emphasize that the y_i^{**}'s are obtained from the unrestricted Reduced form corresponding to the Transformed system.

As is seen this nonlinear estimator is demanding as regards the sample size required. In (3.24) the endogenous variables are regressed on all predetermined variables and all lagged endogenous and predetermined variables. We expect that the properties of this estimator are inferior to those of the corresponding methods obtained through the GLS-approach. Since the computational properties are not considerably better the method will not be considered further.

A derivation of the asymptotic distribution of the GEID-A estimator is given under simplifying assumptions in Selén (1975). The result is reproduced in the following theorem:

Theorem 1: Under the basic assumptions in Section 2.1.3, as modified in Section 3.1.1, and assuming that all predetermined variables are purely exogenous, the asymptotic marginal distribution of the strict GEID-A estimator, if any, is

$$T^{1/2}(a-\alpha) \sim N(0, \mathrm{A}_1 \operatorname{plim}[T^{-1}\chi^{\mathrm{Tr}}(\Sigma \otimes I_T)\chi^{\mathrm{Tr}\prime}]\mathrm{A}_1'),$$

where Σ denotes the covariance matrix of the disturbances of the reduced form of the transformed system and χ^{Tr} is $X^{\mathrm{ST}} = \operatorname{diag}[X_1^{\mathrm{ST}}, \cdots, X_p^{\mathrm{ST}}]$ with y_i^{**} replaced by η_i^{**}. The superscript Tr indicates that the systematic part of the endogenous variables of the transformed system is used in χ^{Tr}. Furthermore, $\mathrm{A}_1 = [I + \mathrm{A}_2^{-1}\mathrm{F}R_p]^{-1}\mathrm{A}_2$, where $\mathrm{A}_2 = \chi^{\mathrm{Tr}}([I-\beta]^{-1} \otimes I_T)\chi^{\mathrm{Tr}\prime}$ and $\mathrm{F} = \operatorname{plim} X^{\mathrm{ST}}([I-\beta]^{-1} \otimes I_T)X_{a\ell}'$, where $X_{a\ell}$ is the blockdiagonal matrix $I_p \otimes [Y_{(1)\ell}Z_{(1)\ell}, \cdots, Y_{(p)\ell}Z_{(p)\ell}]$. Finally, R_p is the $p\Sigma(n_i + m_i) \times \Sigma(n_i + m_i)$ matrix where the first $\Sigma(n_i + m_i)$ rows contain a blockdiagonal submatrix with $\rho_{1j}I_{n_j+m_j}$ as its jth block. If ρ_{1j} is zero this block is the zero matrix. In the following $\Sigma(n_i + m_i)$ rows $\rho_{2j}I_{n_j+m_j}$ forms the jth block and so forth.

3.2.3. The GLS approach. (I) Limited-Information methods. In this section we will consider modifications of the TSLS and GEID estimators which allow for serial correlations of the disturbances. The starting point is the structural form of the reformulated transformed system (3.5) which can be written as

$$\begin{bmatrix} y_1' - \sum_k \rho_{1k} y_{k\ell}' \\ \vdots \\ y_p' - \sum_k \rho_{pk} y_{k\ell}' \end{bmatrix} = \begin{bmatrix} \chi_1^{\mathrm{Tr}\prime} - \rho_{11}X_{1\ell}', & -\rho_{12}X_{2\ell}' & \cdots & -\rho_{1p}X_{p\ell}' \\ \vdots & & & \\ -\rho_{p1}X_{1\ell}' & & \cdots & \chi_p^{\mathrm{Tr}\prime} - \rho_{pp}X_{p\ell}' \end{bmatrix}$$

$$\times \begin{bmatrix} \alpha_1' \\ \vdots \\ \alpha_p' \end{bmatrix} + \begin{bmatrix} \varepsilon_1^{+\prime} \\ \vdots \\ \varepsilon_p^{+\prime} \end{bmatrix}, \tag{3.26}$$

where the y_i's are $1 \times T$ vectors; $y_{i\ell}$ is y_i lagged one period, $\chi_i = [\eta_{(i)}^{**\prime} Z_{(i)}']'$ and $X_{i\ell}$ is $X_i = [Y_{(i)}' Z_{(i)}']'$ lagged one period. The summation index k ranges from 1 to p. As before y_i contains the observed values of the explained variable of the ith relation and X_i the observed values of the corresponding explanatory variables. The system (3.26) is complicated, with every parameter in β and Γ appearing in every relation, a condition which in principle calls for full-information estimation. To simplify and retain the limited-information feature of the estimators to be considered, we assume that R is diagonal. The ith relation can now be written

$$y'_i - \rho_{ii} y'_{i\ell} = [\chi_i^{\mathrm{Tr}\prime} - \rho_{ii} X'_{i\ell}]\alpha'_i + \varepsilon_i^{+\prime}. \tag{3.27}$$

The restricted reduced form of the system (3.26) is

$$y_t = (I - \beta)^{-1}[\Gamma z_t + R([I - \beta]y_{t-1} - \Gamma z_{t-1})] + \varepsilon_t^+, \tag{3.28}$$

written at time point t.

We are now ready to define the estimators,[9] and we start with the reduced-form oriented method.

Estimates of $\eta_{(i)}^{**}$ are obtained from the unrestricted reduced form of the transformed system, where z_t, y_{t-1} and z_{t-1} are the regressors and Z^{Tr} is the corresponding data matrix as given in Definition 2. Estimates of ρ_{ii}, denoted r_{ii} $(i = 1, p)$, are obtained from the structural disturbances δ_i ; cf. (3.1). X_i^{RT} and d_i denote the estimates of χ_i^{Tr} and δ_i, respectively, and the subscript ℓ indicates that the corresponding matrix contains observations on variables lagged one period.

Definition 3: A reduced-form oriented estimator, the *2SLS-ARD* estimator, is defined as the real solutions a_i and r_{ii} $(i = 1, p)$, if any, of the system

$$[X_i^{\mathrm{RT}\prime} - r_{ii} X'_{i\ell}]'[y'_i - r_{ii} y'_{i\ell}] = [X_i^{\mathrm{RT}\prime} - r_{ii} X'_{i\ell}]'[X_i^{\mathrm{RT}\prime} - r_{ii} X'_{i\ell}]a'_i, \tag{3.29}$$

$$y_i^{**} = y_i Z^{\mathrm{Tr}\prime}[Z^{\mathrm{Tr}} Z^{\mathrm{Tr}\prime}]^{-1} Z^{\mathrm{Tr}}, \tag{3.30}$$

$$d_{i\ell} d'_i = d_{i\ell} d'_{i\ell} r_{ii}. \tag{3.31}$$

Comments: (4) In the case of identities (3.30) applies to all the endogenous variables.

(5) This estimator is in principle that suggested by Fair (see footnote 1) and by Dhrymes et al. (1974). Hatanaka (1976) considers similar estimators which are computationally simple. In all three papers asymptotic covariance matrices are given.

The limiting distribution is here given in the following theorem.

Theorem 2: Under the basic assumptions in Section 2.1.3, as modified in Section 3.1.1, and the assumption that R is diagonal, the asymptotic distribution of the strict 2SLS-ARD estimator is obtained as

[9] The estimators of Definitions 2 and 3 were in Selén (1975) called A2SLS and AGEID, respectively.

$$T^{1/2}(a-\alpha, r-\rho) \sim N(0, \operatorname{plim} TA_{\mathrm{RL}}^{-1} \operatorname{plim} T^{-1}B_{\mathrm{RL}} \operatorname{plim} TA_{\mathrm{RL}}^{-1}),$$

where

$$A_{\mathrm{RL}} = \begin{bmatrix} Q\,Q' & Q\,\Delta_\ell' \\ \Delta_\ell Q' & \Delta_\ell\Delta_\ell' \end{bmatrix},$$

$$B_{\mathrm{RL}} = \begin{bmatrix} Q(\Psi\otimes I_T)Q' & Q(\Psi\otimes I_T)\Delta_\ell' \\ \Delta_\ell(\Psi\otimes I_T)Q' & \Delta_\ell(\Psi\otimes I_T)\Delta_\ell' \end{bmatrix},$$

$a=(a_1,\cdots,a_p)$, $r=(r_{11}, r_{22},\cdots, r_{pp})$ and $Q'=[\chi^{\mathrm{Tr}\prime}-(R\otimes I_T)X_\ell']$. The latter is the $pT\times\Sigma(n_i+m_i)$ data matrix on the right-hand side of (3.26). Δ_ℓ is the $p\times pT$ blockdiagonal matrix with $\delta_{i\ell}$ as its ith block and Ψ denotes the covariance matrix of δ_t^+.

For the structural-form oriented counterpart we give the following definition. The difference vis-à-vis the 2SLS-ARD estimator lies in (3.33) below, where the restricted reduced form of the transformed system is utilized.

Definition 4: A structural-form oriented estimator, the *GEID-ARD* estimator is defined as the real solutions $a_i=(b_{(i)}c_{(i)})$ and r_{ii}, $i=1,p$, if any, of the system

$$[X_i^{\mathrm{ST}\prime}-r_{ii}X_{i\ell}']'[y_i'-r_{ii}y_{i\ell}'] = [X_i^{\mathrm{ST}\prime}-r_{ii}X_{i\ell}']'[X_i^{\mathrm{ST}\prime}-r_{ii}X_{i\ell}']a_i', \tag{3.32}$$

$$Y^{**} = [I_n-B]^{-1}GZ+[I_n-B]^{-1}\mathrm{R}D_\ell, \tag{3.33}$$

$$d_{i\ell}d_i' = d_{i\ell}d_{i\ell}'r_{ii}, \tag{3.34}$$

where $i=1,p$. The ith row of D_ℓ is $d_{i\ell}=y_{i\ell}-b_{(i)}Y_{(i)\ell}-g_{(i)}Z_{(i)\ell}\cdot X_i^{\mathrm{ST}\prime}=(Y_{(i)}^{**\prime}Z_{(i)}')$.

Comments: (6) For the modification in case of identities see the modification of GEID-AREF in Section 3.2.4 below.

Theorem 3: Under the basic assumptions in Section 2.1.3, as modified in Section 3.1.1, and the assumption that R is diagonal, the asymptotic distribution of the strict GEID-ARD estimator is obtained as

$$T^{1/2}(a-\alpha, r-\rho) \sim N(0, \operatorname{plim} TA_{\mathrm{SL}}^{-1} \operatorname{plim} T^{-1}B_{\mathrm{SL}} \operatorname{plim} TA_{\mathrm{SL}}^{\prime-1}),$$

where

$$A_{\mathrm{SL}} = \begin{bmatrix} Q([I-\beta]^{-1}\otimes I_T)Q' & Q\Delta_\ell' \\ \Delta_\ell Q' & \Delta_\ell\Delta_\ell' \end{bmatrix}, \qquad \Sigma = E(\varepsilon_t^+\ \ \varepsilon_t^{+\prime}),$$

and

$$B_{SL} = \begin{bmatrix} Q(\Sigma \otimes I_T)Q' & Q(\Sigma[I-\beta]^{-1'} \otimes I_T)\Delta_\ell' \\ \Delta_\ell([I-\beta]^{-1'}\Sigma \otimes I_T)Q' & \Delta_\ell([I-\beta]^{-1'}\Sigma[I-\beta]^{-1} \otimes I_T)\Delta_\ell' \end{bmatrix}.$$

The matrices Q and Δ_ℓ were given in Theorem 2. In the case of identities the last $n-p$ rows and columns in $[I-\beta]^{-1}$ are deleted.

Comments: (7) The given distributions in Theorems 2 and 3 are obtained through the procedures outlined in the following section.

(8) If all elements of R are prescribed zeroes we see that the expressions are reduced to those of the TSLS and GEID estimators.

3.2.4. The GLS approach. (II) Full-information methods. The extension of the full-information methods to the case where R is diagonal is immediate. Developing the 3SLS estimator, say, in the same way as TSLS in the previous subsection, we get a three-stage least squares estimator for the autocorrelated case. For all the full-information methods the asymptotic normal distributions are obtained through the technique outlined in the following pages.

The system of equations in the general case where R is non-diagonal was written in (3.26), which can be rewritten compactly as

$$\text{vec}\, y - (R \otimes I_T)\,\text{vec}\, y_\ell = [\chi' - (R \otimes I_T)X_\ell']\alpha' + \text{vec}\,\varepsilon^+. \tag{3.35}$$

The notation vec y in place of vec $_I y$ is due to the fact that the system is assumed to merely contain behavioral relations. The main difference when R is not diagonal is that the matrix of observations on the regressors is not diagonal either, which means that structural parameters of relation i say, are included in other relations. Assuming that the covariance matrix of vec ε^+ is $\Sigma \otimes I_T$ where Σ is a $p \times p$-matrix, it is easily realized that the covariance matrix of vec δ^+ is of the same form, that is $\Psi \otimes I_T$. We are now prepared to extend the GEID-EF and 3SLS estimators.

Definition 5: A reduced form oriented estimator, the *3SLS-AR* method, is defined as the real solutions a and r, if any, of the system

$$[X^{RT'} - (R \otimes I_T)X_\ell']'[\Psi^{-1} \otimes I_T][\text{vec}\, y - (R \otimes I_T)\,\text{vec}\, y_\ell]$$
$$= [X^{RT'} - (R \otimes I_T)X_\ell']'[\Psi^{-1} \otimes I_T][X^{RT'} - (R \otimes I_T)X_\ell']a', \tag{3.36}$$

$$y_i^{**} = y_i Z^{Tr'}[Z^{Tr} Z^{Tr'}]^{-1} Z^{Tr}, \qquad i = 1, p, \tag{3.37}$$

$$D_{de}[\Psi^{-1} \otimes I_T]\text{vec } d = D_{de}[\Psi^{-1} \otimes I_T]D'_{de}r', \tag{3.38}$$

where D_{de} is a blockdiagonal matrix containing in the ith block the d_j-vectors corresponding to the unknown elements in the jth row of R. The row vector r contains the estimated counterparts of the R elements row by row; vec d is the vector $(d_1, \cdots, d_p)'$. The superscript RT indicates that y_i^{**} is obtained from the URF.

Definition 6: A structural-form oriented estimator, the *GEID-AREF* method, is defined as the real solutions a and r, if any, of the system

$$[X^{ST\prime} - (R \otimes I_T)X'_e]'[P \otimes I_T][\text{vec } y - (R \otimes I_T)\text{vec } y_e]$$

$$= [X^{ST\prime} - (R \otimes I_T)X'_e]'[P \otimes I_T][X^{ST\prime} - (R \otimes I_T)X'_e]a', \tag{3.39}$$

$$Y^{**} = [I_n - B]^{-1}GZ + [I_n - B]^{-1}RD_e, \tag{3.40}$$

$$D_{de}[\tilde{\Psi}^{-1} \otimes I_T]\text{vec } d = D_{de}[\tilde{\Psi}^{-1} \otimes I_T]D'_{de}r', \tag{3.41}$$

where

$$\tilde{\Psi}^{-1} = [I_n - B]^{-1\prime}P \quad \text{and} \quad P = \Psi^{-1}[I_n - \beta].$$

The superscript ST indicates that y^{**} is obtained from the RRF. Other notations are explained in the previous definitions.

Comments: (9) The 3SLS-AR estimator for the case where R is a full matrix was in principle suggested by Dhrymes, who calls the method CIFIDA; Dhrymes–Erlat (1974). The case where R may contain zero-elements was considered by Selén (1975) and Hatanaka (1976).

(10) In the case of identities the behavioral relations are still written as in (3.35), which leaves (3.36) and (3.39) unchanged. The y_i^{**}'s are obtained for all n endogenous variables as follows: In (3.37) $i = 1, n$, and in (3.40) RD_e is replaced $[D'_eR' : 0]'$ where 0 is the zero matrix of order $T \times q$. In $[I_n - \beta]$ and its inverse, which are used to define P, and in Ψ the last $n - p$ rows and columns are deleted.

(11) The modifications in case of unknown weighting matrices Ψ^{-1} and P are discussed in Section 3.2.5. In that section the alternatives to the 3SLS-AR method of Hatanaka (1976) and Dhrymes–Taylor (1976) are also presented.

Let us now proceed to the question of the asymptotic distributions of the estimators given in Definitions 5 and 6.

The limiting distribution of the 3SLS-AR method is deduced in Selén (1975). The result can be summarized as:

Theorem 4: Under the basic assumptions in Section 2.1.3, as modified in Section 3.1.1, the asymptotic distribution of the strict 3SLS-AR estimator can be written as

$$T^{1/2}(a-\alpha, r-\rho) \sim N\left(0, \operatorname{plim} T\begin{bmatrix} A_1 & Q \\ Q' & U \end{bmatrix}^{-1}\right),$$

where

$$A_1 = [\chi^{\mathrm{Tr}\prime} - (R \otimes I_T)X_\ell']'[\Psi^{-1} \otimes I_T][\chi^{\mathrm{Tr}\prime} - (R \otimes I_T)X_\ell'],$$

$$Q = [\chi^{\mathrm{Tr}\prime} - (R \otimes I_T)X_\ell']'[\Psi^{-1} \otimes I_T]\Delta_{d\ell}',$$

$$U = \Delta_{d\ell}[\Psi^{-1} \otimes I_T]\Delta_{d\ell}'.$$

$\Delta_{d\ell}$ is the blockdiagonal matrix with the $\delta_{j\ell}$'s that are regressors in the ith equation of $\delta_t = R\delta_{t-1} + \delta_t^+$ as its ith block. χ^{Tr} is X^{RT} with y_i^{**} replaced by the corresponding η_i^{**}.

That the 3SLS-AR estimator is as efficient as the full-information maximum likelihood method applied to the transformed system, is verified by the results of Selén (1975) and Hatanaka (1976). The well known result that 3SLS as applied to the basic system is asymptotically efficient when there are no restrictions in the covariance matrix of the disturbances, therefore carries over.

The limiting distribution of the GEID-AREF estimator can be deduced through a procedure given for a related method in Selén (1975, pp. 93–94). Since space is limited, and the method is not used in later applications, we only give some comments and not a formal proof.

The GEID-AREF estimator can be written

$$F(a, r, M) = 0, \tag{3.42}$$

where F is a vector of functions and M a vector of second-order moments of elements of y_t, z_t, y_{t-1} and z_{t-1}. This is very similar to results obtained for other structural-form oriented estimators earlier; cf. the GEID-EF estimator (2.17). Since the sample moments converge to the corresponding population moments, the consistency can be established by imposing some regularity conditions on F, and using the implicit function theorem; see Section 2.2.3.

The deduction of the limiting distribution is based on the system of equations obtained by subtracting the estimated reformulated system from the corresponding true system. This gives an expression for $a - \alpha$ in terms of $\mathrm{R} - R$. An expression for $r - \rho$ or $\mathrm{R} - R$ in $a - \alpha$ is obtained from (3.41). Solving the resulting system of equations and applying arguments similar to those for the GEID-EF method earlier the desired result is obtained.

Theorem 5: Under the basic assumptions in Section 2.1.3, as modified in Section 3.1.1, the strict GEID-AREF estimator is asymptotically equivalent to the strict 3SLS-AR estimator.

3.2.5. Modifications of the full-information methods in the case of unknown weighting matrices. The weighting matrices Ψ^{-1} and P were specified as known in Definitions 5 and 6, respectively. A natural extension is to replace them by consistent estimates. As is the case with the usual 3SLS method we cannot in general utilize the residuals obtained from a TSLS type method in the 'third step' of e.g. 3SLS-AR, when R contains non-diagonal elements. An estimate of the required covariance matrix utilizing the 2SLS-ARD residuals is in general not consistent. A better approach is to use the second-order moments of the residuals d_t^+ as obtained from the Classic ID counterpart to (3.35), or

$$\operatorname{vec} y - [\mathrm{R} \otimes I_T] \operatorname{vec} y_\ell = (X' - [\mathrm{R} \otimes I_T] X_\ell')a' + \operatorname{vec} d^+, \tag{3.43}$$

where a and R or r are the 3SLS-AR estimates given in (3.36)–(3.38) and X is the blockdiagonal matrix with $[Y'_{(i)} Z'_{(i)}]'$ as typical element. An estimator for the general case is defined by adding

$$\hat{\Psi} = T^{-1} \sum_t d_t^+ d_t^{+\prime} \tag{3.44}$$

to (3.36)–(3.38) above. This is a first alternative for 3SLS-AR.

A second alternative, which is computationally simpler, starts with the calculation of initial β and γ estimates ignoring the serial correlation of the disturbances. Using functions of the exogenous and lagged exogenous variables as instrumental variables, consistent estimates are obtained through the basic, untransformed system. The estimates are consistent also in the presence of lagged endogenous variables.

The residuals d_t are calculated and regressed on the lagged residuals to obtain $\tilde{R}$, a consistent R-estimate. The second-order moments of the residuals $d_t^+ = d_t - \tilde{R} d_{t-1}$ now resulting, consistently estimate Ψ. Estimates of the β's and γ's and the unknown elements of R are then obtained according to Definition 5 with Ψ replaced by its estimate.

The instrumental variables in the initial step may be chosen differently. The lack of a routine rule for their selection is a weakness of the approach.

The conjecture that the limiting distribution of 3SLS-AR is unaffected by replacing the weighting matrix with an initial consistent estimate, as in the second alternative, is supported by the results of Dhrymes–Erlat (1974) and Hatanaka (1976). A derivation for the first alternative, where the weighting matrix is defined in the 3SLS-AR estimates, uses the implicit function theorem, according to the lines outlined in the last part of Section 2.2.4.

The modifications of the GEID-AREF method when the weighting matrix P is unknown are similar. The first alternative is to define an estimate of P in terms of the moments of the CLID residuals using the estimates of the GEID-AREF method, which gives rise to a highly nonlinear method; see the suggestion for GEID-EF in Section 2.2.4. The second alternative is to estimate P initially and separately through instrumental variables as indicated above. Estimators similar to the here modified 3SLS-AR method which are computationally simple have been suggested by Hatanaka (1976) and Dhrymes–Taylor (1976).

4. Computational Methods and Applications

4.1. Fix-Point and Related Methods

4.1.1. Introduction. Whilst the calculation of estimates of the reduced-form oriented methods starts with the estimation of the URF and, at least for the case of serially uncorrelated errors, proceeds with the calculation of final estimates in one or two steps, the application of the structural-form oriented methods is based on iterative processes. It is not necessary to use iterative least squares procedures for solving the nonlinear normal equations as we suggest, but it is rather simple to write satisfactory computer programs in this case.

It is not possible here to give details concerning the numerical methods for all of the estimators introduced. It is hoped that an outline of the general principles, together with the definitions given earlier and a thorough discussion of an illustration will give sufficient information. Further details can be found in Selén (1975).

The main feature of the numerical methods here is that the parameters are divided into sets. In an iterative process each set is estimated separately in each iteration step whilst holding the rest of the parameters constant.

Our methods can be regarded as generalizations of the *Fix-Point* (FP) method introduced by Wold. The FP method works by using as its phases of estimation the SF parameters and the conditional expectations of y, and is given in Chapter 1 of this volume. Improvements of the method are discussed in Chapter 2. Our methods take account of the principles that can be extracted from that chapter.

4.1.2. The calculation of GEID-EF estimates. Let us as an illustration consider the calculation of GEID-EF estimates. Iterative least squares methods for the other estimators are obtained analogously. The calculation of GEID-A estimates is for example based on phases giving proxies of the conditional expectations η_t^{**}, cf. (3.21), proxies of the structural parameters β, Γ and R, cf. (3.20), and proxies of the structural disturbances δ_t, cf. (3.22), respectively. The phases correspond to the enumerated parts of the defining equations. The phases of the other methods are similarly defined.

The GEID-EF estimator was given in Section 2.2.3. A characteristic feature of the method is that the weighting matrix $\Phi^{-1}[(I-\beta_{11})-\beta_{12}(I-\beta_{22})^{-1}\beta_{21}]$, where Φ is the covariance matrix of the SF disturbances of the classic ID system, is utilized. If this weighting matrix is unknown different procedures are possible. One alternative is to base the calculations on the results of some consistent estimator and iterate phases 1 and 2 below. We could e.g. utilize the results of TSLS or GEID to estimate the weighting matrix which then is kept constant throughout the iterations. Let $\hat{\theta}^{(s)}$ denote this estimate. Then the following phases form an iteration step:

Phase 1: y_t is regressed on $y_t^{(s)}$ and z_t through GLS,

$$X^{S(s)}[\hat{\theta}^{(s)} \otimes I_T]\operatorname{vec}{}_1 y = X^{S(s)}[\hat{\theta}^{(s)} \otimes I_T]X^{S(s)\prime}a^{(s+1)\prime}, \tag{4.1}$$

giving the proxy $a^{(s+1)}$; the column vector that contains the non-zero elements of $B^{(s+1)}$ and $C^{(s+1)}$. In terms of the columns of those matrices we obtain

$$y_{it} = b_{(i)}^{(s+1)\prime} y_{(i)t}^{(s)} + g_{(i)}^{(s+1)\prime} z_{(i)t} + e_{it}^{(s+1)}, \qquad t = 1,T, \quad i = 1,p. \tag{4.2}$$

For the notations in (4.1) see equation (2.12) in the definition of the method.

Phase 2: Proxies of $\eta_t^*, y_t^{(s+1)}$ are calculated as

$$y_{it}^{(s+1)} = \mu\,[b_{(i)}^{(s+1)\prime} y_{(i)t}^{(s)} + g_{(i)}^{(s+1)\prime} z_{(i)t}] + (1-\mu) y_{it}^{(s)}, \qquad t = 1,T, \quad i = 1,p, \tag{4.3}$$

where μ is a relaxation factor.

A second alternative, which does not rely on the results of other consistent methods, is obtained by adding a third phase:

Phase 3: Proxies of δ_t, $d_t^{(s+1)}$, are calculated as

$$d_{it}^{(s+1)} = b_{(i)}^{(s+1)\prime} y_{(i)t} + g_{(i)}^{(s+1)\prime} z_{(i)t}, \qquad t = 1,T, \quad i = 1,p, \tag{4.4}$$

and Φ is estimated by

$$\hat{\varphi}_{ij}^{(s+1)} = T^{-1} \sum_t d_{it}^{(s+1)} d_{jt}^{(s+1)}, \qquad i,j = 1,p. \tag{4.5}$$

Proxies $\hat{\theta}^{(s+1)}$ are obtained,

$$\hat{\theta}^{(s+1)} = \kappa[\hat{\Phi}^{(s+1)}[(I - B_{11}^{(s+1)}) - B_{12}^{(s+1)}(I - \beta_{22})^{-1}\beta_{21}]] + (1 - \kappa)\hat{\theta}^{(s)}, \quad (4.6)$$

where the scalar constant κ is a relaxation factor.

It seems advisable to carry out this scheme as a double iteration procedure. This means that we start from an initial $\hat{\theta}^{(0)}$ estimate obtained according to phase 3 utilizing for example the results of an OLS step. Phases 1 and 2 are then iterated with for example $y_t^{(0)} = y_t$ as the start, until convergence is attained. These final estimates and residuals are utilized in phase 3 to calculate $\hat{\theta}^{(1)}$, which is used when iterating phases 1 and 2 anew. After convergence, phase 3 is again applied, and phases 1 and 2 are iterated again. The process is terminated when the application of phase 2 does not change the estimates. The relaxation factors μ and κ may be used to improve the convergence properties.

Note finally that phase 2 is extended in the case of identities, new η_t^* proxies are then also calculated for the identities using

$$y_{it}^{(s+1)} = \mu[\beta_{(i)}y_{(i)t}^{(s)} + \gamma_{(i)}z_{(i)t}] + (1 - \mu)y_{it}^{(s)}. \quad (4.7)$$

4.2. Some Simulation Experiments

4.2.1. Framework. In order to shed some light on the small sample properties of the estimators we have considered, a modest simulation experiment has been carried out. There is no possibility here of giving the detailed results. They have also for the most part already been reported in Selén (1975). We will merely give the main conclusions and some illustrations.

The main aim of the Monte Carlo study was to compare the methods that do not account for serial correlation (the group I methods) with the methods accounting for serial correlation with a diagonal structure matrix R (the group II methods) or a full structure matrix R (the group III methods).

The estimation methods applied were essentially those given earlier. Other estimation methods were OLS, FIML and FIML modified for the case of autoregressive errors. The latter, here referred to as the FIML-AR method, is, together with its asymptotic covariance matrix, given for a general case in Selén (1975), where arbitrary zero restrictions in the structure matrix R are allowed. The method when R is diagonal is here referred to as FIML-ARD. Within the FIML-AR framework restrictions between all the parameters, including those in R, are easily handled. The estimation methods applied here and in Section 4.3, are given in Table 1.

TABLE 1
Estimation methods used in the applications.

Group	Notation[a]	Definition	Comment
I	OLS	—	
	TSLS	2.2	
	GEID	2.1	
	GEID-EF	2.3	Weighting matrix estimated
	3SLS	2.4	utilizing TSLS residuals
	FIML	—	
II	2SLS-ARD	3.3	
	GEID-ARD	3.4	
	3SLS-ARD	3.5	Weighting matrix estimated by the first alternative, (3.43)–(3.44)
	GEID-AD	3.1	
	FIML-AR	—	
III	GEID-A	3.1	
	3SLS-AR	3.5	Weighting matrix estimated by the first alternative, (3.43)–(3.44)
	FIML-AR	—	

[a]The ending 'D' denotes a method where all off-diagonal elements in R are zero.

The model used is the small two-relational model, known as Summers' model, with two different exogenous variables in each relation. The asymmetric model was written with y_1 and y_2 on the left-hand side of the respective relations. The β and γ parameters were constant, 0.5 and 0.4243 respectively, whilst different R structures were tried. The latter varied from an R matrix with zero elements only, to an R matrix with large diagonal elements, and finally to full R matrices with small and large off-diagonal elements, respectively. The exogenous variables were stochastic and uncorrelated. Their variance was 1.0. The covariance between the SF disturbances of the basic system was 0.03215. Their variance was 0.0643. The sample sizes were 60 and 30 observations respectively, and the number of replications for each experiment 50.

4.2.2. Results. Comparing the Mean Square Errors, $MSE = K^{-1}\sum_k (a_{ijk} - \alpha_{ij})^2$ where a_{ijk} is the estimate of the parameter α_{ij} in sample k for the various methods, it turned out that the differences on the whole were as could be expected from the large sample theory. OLS, affected both by simultaneity bias and serial correlation was completely inferior, and is left out from the following discussion.

The methods not accounting for serial correlation were generally inferior except for the structures with weak or no serial correlation. In these cases their behavior was similar to the other methods. The loss in accounting for serial correlation when none existed was minor. This is illustrated in experiment A below.

Applying the CRR method GEID-A, a maximal loss in efficiency, as measured by the *MSE* and somewhat larger than the factor two, appeared. This occurred when R was diagonal with elements 0.9. A large non-diagonal element in R affected the group II methods severely. They were then inferior to GEID-A, and also to the methods not accounting for serial correlation. It was not possible to discriminate between the methods within a certain group, except for the conclusion that GEID-A was slightly inferior to the other group III members.

As an illustration we give in Table 2 the *MSE*'s obtained for two

TABLE 2
Mean square errors multiplied by 10^5.

	β_{12}	β_{21}	γ_{11}	γ_{12}	γ_{23}	γ_{24}	ρ_{11}	ρ_{12}	ρ_{21}	ρ_{22}
(a) *Experiment A*										
OLS	1161	1123	189	225	283	185				
TSLS	141	240	131	148	157	159				
GEID	141	246	182	229	236	213				
GEID-EF	154	242	120	115	122	136				
3SLS	144	237	117	114	121	135				
FIML	160	237	122	109	121	137				
2SLS-ARD	151	282	125	144	168	160	1777			2711
GEID-ARD	172	309	181	224	257	209	1776			2683
3SLS-ARD	150	265	114	121	119	135	1671			2363
FIML-ARD	Not calculated									
GEID-A	161	270	183	226	237	208	1917	2159	2200	2468
3SLS-AR	162	280	120	124	124	137	2168	2121	2676	2854
FIML-AR	182	302	130	123	133	153	2352	2170	2824	2746
(b) *Experiment B*										
OLS	1277	1239	165	145	174	195				
TSLS	147	143	97	91	138	108				
GEID	149	141	127	119	198	166				
GEID-EF	148	143	96	82	112	99				
3SLS	144	145	94	84	111	99				
FIML	Not calculated									
2SLS-ARD	94	187	62	52	123	101	5517			14080
GEID-ARD	88	172	44	34	119	89	5249			14410
3SLS-ARD	85	150	49	38	96	81	18230			2084
FIML-ARD	82	149	47	37	98	75	14132			14640
GEID-A	91	64	64	47	58	56	1348	925	997	949
3SLS-AR	52	55	30	29	48	53	1300	879	1058	997
FIML-AR	55	59	29	29	51	55	4723	1474	1381	1092

models; one with an empty R matrix (experiment A) and one with the full matrix where $\rho_{11}=0.5$, $\rho_{12}=0.4$, $\rho_{21}=0.7$, $\rho_{22}=0.2$ (experiment B). As indicated in the headings of the table the MSE's are multiplied by 10^5. The number of observations was 60. Neither model is of the more general type allowing for correlations between some of the predetermined variables and some of the disturbances; cf. Chapter 1. For such models some methods of the GEID-type should be superior as they are consistent, although not always simultaneously, while the other methods are not.

Concerning the results[10] for the whole set of experiments, we can further report that the comparison between the results applying the asymptotic covariance expressions and the variances obtained empirically showed relatively good agreement, especially for the larger sample size.

The structural-form oriented methods were often good as regards the fit for the RRF in the sample period as indicated by Q_i^2.

The behavior of the numerical methods was good in all the experiments. In no sample were difficulties with convergence observed. The convergence of the iterative least squares methods was rapid; the maximum number of iterations required for the 2SLS-ARD, GEID-A and 3SLS-AR methods was for example 17 in experiment B. The total CPU time required to generate data, calculate OLS, TSLS, 2SLS-ARD, GEID-A and 3SLS-AR estimates and associated statistics was about 6 minutes and 30 seconds on the IBM 360/155 in that experiment. The calculation of maximum likelihood estimates by a slightly modified Davidon–Fletcher-Powell algorithm was slower and a CPU time of 3 minutes and 30 seconds was required for FIML-AR and FIML-ARD together. It should however be emphasized that the time comparisons are, at best, only approximative since the convergence criteria used in the two cases were not equivalent.

4.3. *Estimation of Klein's Model I*

4.3.1. The model. This small model was given by Klein (1950). It consists of three behavioral relations, and in all seven endogenous variables. The behavioral relations explain consumption, investment and wages. They are specified as follows:

$$C_t = \alpha_{10} + \alpha_{11} P_t + \alpha_{12} W_t + \alpha_{13} P_{t-1} + \delta_{1t}, \tag{4.8}$$

$$I_t = \alpha_{20} + \alpha_{21} P_t + \alpha_{22} P_{t-1} + \alpha_{23} K_{t-1} + \delta_{2t}, \tag{4.9}$$

[10] The second-order moments of the estimators do not always exist. It was therefore checked whether the comparisons were distorted by extreme results for any method and sample. This was not the case.

$$W_t^0 = \alpha_{30} + \alpha_{31}F_t + \alpha_{32}F_{t-1} + \alpha_{33}(t-1931) + \delta_{3t}, \tag{4.10}$$

where the α's denote the parameters. The variables are C_t aggregate consumption, I_t net investment, W_t^0 private wage bill, P_t profits, W_t total wage bill, K_t capital stock, F_t private product, and t time trend. The subscript $t-1$ signifies lagged variables.

The remaining five endogenous variables Y_t (national income), P_t, K_t, W_t and F_t are defined through five identities. The details can be found in Selén (1975); see also Chapter 7 in this volume.

4.3.2. The results. The methods, given in Table 1 (with some modifications specified below), were applied to the system using the 21 observations given by Klein. The resulting parameter estimates, with the associated standard deviations as calculated from the asymptotic formulae, are given in Table 3. The residual characteristics are shown in Tables 4 and 5. As regards the group II and III methods, the characteristics were calculated for the residuals of the transformed system, using the 20 observations then available.

The values of the Durbin–Watson 'd'-statistic for the group I methods indicate that the more sophisticated methods should perhaps be applied with only one non-zero element ρ_{11} — or no non-zero element — in R. The 'd'-values of the first relation are contained in the inconclusive region of the test, while the others are contained in the region of non-rejection. But the purpose here is to examine the applicability of the estimation methods, and the main alternatives are therefore a diagonal and a full autoregressive structure matrix R.

As is seen in the tables, two sets of FIML-AR estimates were obtained. Both correspond to local maxima and are earlier given by Hendry (1971, 1974). The likelihood of the second is the highest. This solution was only attained when the starting values of the iterative procedure were chosen in a very close neighbourhood. The first solution—denoted FIML-AR$_1$—was obtained when starting with all parameters zero, from the FIML estimates or from the FIML-ARD estimates.

A systematic search for several extrema was not performed.[11] Generally we were satisfied with finding one solution. For some estimators even this

[11] According to our experience the problem of multiple solutions is of minor importance in practice as no such solutions have been observed for the least squares type methods presented here. This is in accordance with the findings for the GEID estimator reported in Chapter 2. In the case of several solutions, Edgerton (1973c) has suggested for the GEID estimator that the solution maximizing the sum of the multiple correlation coefficients of the RF should be chosen. An analogous procedure seems possible for our methods.

limited aim was hard to attain. The iterative methods used to calculate GEID-ARD and 3SLS-AR estimates turned out to be very sensitive to the choice of starting values. GEID-ARD and 3SLS-AR belong to the GLS-approach methods.

GEID-A the 'calculated residuals as regressors' approach method, worked — as expected — better in this respect. The GEID-ARD estimates had to be calculated in three steps. The starting point for an initial GEID-ARD estimation, with ρ_{22} and ρ_{33} *a priori* equal to zero, was the y_i^{**} obtained from the restricted reduced form as derived from the corresponding set of 2SLS-ARD estimates. The solution thus obtained was the starting point in a second estimation round with ρ_{33} *a priori* equal to zero. The final GEID-ARD estimates are shown in the tables. They were found with the estimates of the second round as starting values. The number of iterations and the CPU-time given in Table 6 refer to this third round only. With other starting procedures the method did not converge.

It was still harder to find 3SLS-AR estimates. For the case with R full some different starting values — i.e., different initial disturbance covariance matrices — were tried, but within the iteration limit of 200 iterations no convergence was reached. Not even with a fixed 'known' covariance matrix did the method work; e.g. when the disturbance covariance matrix of the FIML-AR$_1$ solution was tried. The case with a diagonal R matrix worked better. With a known 'fixed' covariance matrix, estimates were obtained rather easily. When the 3SLS-ARD estimator was extended by adding equations for the estimation of the covariance matrix, according to the first alternative of Section 3.2.5, no final estimates were reached unless ρ_{33} (or ρ_{22} and ρ_{33}) were *a priori* zero. The 3SLS-ARD results for the case with ρ_{33} restricted are given in the tables.

Let us discuss the estimates somewhat. The signs of the coefficients in Table 3 are not always expected. The coefficient for P_t in the consumption function should, according to economic theory, have positive sign. FIML, GEID-ARD and GEID-A give negative values, but the associated standard deviations are on the other hand rather large. The behavior for the investment function is similar. We expect positive signs for P_t here too, but negative values are obtained for several estimators.

A general impression is that the methods accounting for serial correlation do not give estimates more unrealistic than the standard methods. The increase in fit, going from the methods of group I with four parameters per relation to those of group II and III with five and seven parameters per relation respectively, is demonstrated in Tables 4 and 5. When interpreting the figures it should be kept in mind that the values are not corrected for degrees of freedom.

TABLE 3

Klein's model I. Estimated structural parameters and associated standard deviations (within parentheses).

(a) *Consumption Function*

	P_t	W_t	P_{t-1}	δ_{1t-1}	δ_{2t-1}	δ_{3t-1}	Const.
OLS	0.193 (0.082)	0.796 (0.036)	0.090 (0.082)				16.24
TSLS	0.017 (0.118)	0.810 (0.040)	0.216 (0.107)				16.55
GEID	0.022 (0.111)	0.794 (0.041)	0.256 (0.109)				16.50
GEID-EF	0.037 (0.099)	0.802 (0.035)	0.225 (0.099)				16.45
3SLS	0.125 (0.108)	0.790 (0.038)	0.163 (0.100)				16.44
FIML	0.232 (0.312)	0.802 (0.036)	0.386 (0.217)				18.34
GEID-AD	0.016	0.705	0.154	0.694			22.39
2SLS-ARD	0.040 (0.159)	0.770 (0.068)	0.157 (0.119)	0.419 (0.028)			18.88
GEID-ARD	0.028	0.804	0.265	0.210			16.81
3SLS-ARD[a]	0.128 (0.095)	0.789 (0.050)	0.155 (0.083)	0.290 (0.155)			16.55
FIML-ARD	0.204 (0.056)	0.632 (0.063)	0.114 (0.057)	0.73 (0.13)			23.05
GEID-A	0.054	0.765	0.262	0.536	−0.212	−0.143	18.96
$\text{FIML-AR}_{\text{I}}$[b]	0.089 (0.070)	0.730 (0.056)	0.224 (0.099)	0.72 (0.33)	−0.23 (0.17)	−0.33 (0.42)	18.70
$\text{FIML-AR}_{\text{II}}$	0.152 (0.060)	0.547 (0.087)	0.014 (0.068)	0.90 (0.12)	0.11 (0.24)	−0.22 (0.37)	29.56

(b) *Investment Function*

	P_t	P_{t-1}	K_{t-1}	δ_{1t-1}	δ_{2t-1}	δ_{3t-1}	Const.
OLS	0.480 (0.087)	0.333 (0.091)	−0.112 (0.024)				10.13
TSLS	0.150 (0.173)	0.616 (0.163)	−0.158 (0.036)				20.28
GEID	0.089 (0.167)	0.665 (0.165)	−0.166 (0.038)				22.19
GEID-EF	0.029 (0.153)	0.713 (0.149)	−0.172 (0.031)				23.62
3SLS	0.013 (0.162)	0.756 (0.153)	−0.195 (0.033)				28.18
FIML	−0.801 (0.491)	1.052 (0.352)	−0.148 (0.030)				27.26
GEID-AD	0.055	0.686	−0.189		−0.058		27.18
2SLS-ARD	−0.001 (0.250)	0.730 (0.221)	−0.198 (0.055)		−0.042 (0.218)		29.07
GEID-ARD	0.032	0.698	−0.194		−0.034		28.36
3SLS-ARD[a]	−0.314 (0.311)	0.969 (0.273)	−0.255 (0.068)		−0.584 (0.192)		41.97

FIML-ARD	0.104 (0.096)	0.634 (0.107)	−0.176 (0.033)		−0.03 (0.21)		24.49
GEID-A	−0.108	0.794	−0.158	0.531	−0.267	−1.021	21.60
FIML-AR$_I$[b]	−0.378 (0.158)	1.043 (0.180)	−0.240 (0.048)	0.27 (0.70)	0.10 (0.31)	−1.64 (0.85)	38.63
FIML-AR$_{II}$	0.297 (0.059)	0.583 (0.090)	−0.016 (0.022)	−0.40 (0.21)	−0.39 (0.20)	−1.26 (0.31)	−11.14

(c) *Wage Equation*

	F_t	F_{t-1}	$t-1931$	δ_{1t-1}	δ_{2t-1}	δ_{3t-1}	Const.
OLS	0.440 (0.029)	0.146 (0.034)	0.130 (0.029)				1.50
TSLS	0.439 (0.036)	0.147 (0.039)	0.130 (0.029)				1.50
GEID	0.401 (0.046)	0.171 (0.051)	0.162 (0.038)				2.39
GEID-EF	0.386 (0.032)	0.194 (0.035)	0.155 (0.027)				1.91
3SLS	0.401 (0.032)	0.181 (0.034)	0.150 (0.028)				1.78
FIML	0.234 (0.049)	0.285 (0.045)	0.235 (0.034)				5.79
GEID-AD	0.432	0.136	0.125			−0.581	2.58
2SLS-ARD	0.433 (0.030)	0.145 (0.034)	0.117 (0.025)			−0.134 (0.027)	2.02
GEID-ARD	0.436	0.129	0.122			−0.098	2.80
3SLS-ARD[a]	0.393 (0.027)	0.171 (0.027)	0.132 (0.026)				2.96
FIML-ARD	0.456 (0.025)	0.123 (0.027)	0.134 (0.025)			0.21 (0.13)	1.93
GEID-A	0.460	0.065	0.078	0.435	−0.067	0.351	5.23
FIML-AR$_I$[b]	0.395 (0.021)	0.169 (0.023)	0.134 (0.025)	−0.01 (0.36)	0.12 (0.13)	−0.38 (0.37)	2.90[c]
FIML-AR$_{II}$	0.548 (0.026)	−0.022 (0.044)	0.075 (0.029)	0.23 (0.13)	0.13 (0.17)	0.49 (0.23)	5.33[d]

[a] ρ_{33} is *a priori* zero.
[b] FIML-AR$_{II}$ is the solution with the largest likelihood.
[c] Hendry (1971) obtained 1.42.
[d] Hendry (1971) obtained 4.50.

TABLE 4

Klein's model I. Residual characteristics for the CLID-specified structural form: R^2, the multiple correlation coefficient squared, and 'd', the Durbin–Watson statistic.

	R^2			'd'		
	C_t	I_t	W_t^0	C_t	I_t	W_t^0
OLS	0.981	0.931	0.987	1.37	1.81	1.96
TSLS	0.977	0.885	0.987	1.49	2.09	1.96
GEID	0.976	0.866	0.986	1.51	2.07	2.09
GEID-EF	0.977	0.844	0.986	1.50	2.05	2.17
3SLS	0.980	0.826	0.986	1.42	2.00	2.16
FIML	0.953	−0.063	0.952	1.37	1.24	1.49
GEID-AD	0.973	0.868	0.985	1.92	2.02	1.59
2SLS-ARD	0.975	0.850	0.989	1.78	2.03	2.07
GEID-ARD	0.970	0.861	0.988	1.75	2.03	2.05
3SLS-ARD[a]	0.978	0.706	0.986	1.70	1.86	2.29
FIML-ARD	0.980	0.881	0.987	1.91	2.06	2.18
GEID-A	0.971	0.880	0.989	1.89	2.28	1.95
FIML-AR_I[b]	0.978	0.785	0.989	1.90	2.18	2.23
FIML-AR_{II}	0.972	0.953	0.985	1.84	2.58	1.78

[a, b] See footnotes a and b of Table 3.

TABLE 5

Klein's model I. Residual characteristics for the reduced form: Q^2, the multiple correlation coefficient squared.

	C_t	I_t	W_t^0	Y_t	P_t	K_t	W_t	F_t
OLS	0.825	0.632	0.887	0.790	0.497	0.945	0.921	0.785
TSLS	0.913	0.833	0.928	0.902	0.786	0.975	0.950	0.900
GEID	0.918	0.835	0.930	0.905	0.788	0.976	0.951	0.903
GEID-EF	0.918	0.834	0.928	0.905	0.792	0.975	0.950	0.903
3SLS	0.914	0.831	0.929	0.903	0.785	0.975	0.950	0.901
FIML	0.884	0.684	0.868	0.842	0.724	0.953	0.908	0.839
GEID-AD	0.942	0.851	0.959	0.930	0.806	0.972	0.971	0.932
2SLS-ARD	0.935	0.850	0.949	0.920	0.815	0.972	0.964	0.923
GEID-ARD	0.928	0.850	0.944	0.914	0.806	0.971	0.960	0.917
3SLS-ARD[a]	0.930	0.829	0.934	0.912	0.814	0.967	0.954	0.914
FIML-ARD	0.929	0.853	0.947	0.917	0.804	0.972	0.963	0.920
GEID-A	0.946	0.905	0.963	0.942	0.854	0.982	0.974	0.944
FIML-AR_I[b]	0.946	0.894	0.957	0.939	0.856	0.980	0.970	0.940
FIML-AR_{II}	0.907	0.872	0.953	0.902	0.762	0.976	0.967	0.905

[a, b] See footnotes a and b of Table 3.

TABLE 6

Klein's model I. The behavior of the numerical methods; CPU time and number of iterations required.

	CPU time in seconds	Number of iterations
GEID	5	17
GEID-EF	8	18
GEID-AD	6	28
2SLS-ARD		17
GEID-ARD	16	38
3SLS-ARD[a]	22	50
FIML-ARD[c]	19	
GEID-A	13	59
FIML-AR_1[b,c]	21	

[a,b] See footnotes a and b of Table 3.

[c] The convergence criterion for the FIML methods is different from that of the other methods.

5. Summary and Discussion

Our studies have resulted in several estimation methods, with different properties for the case of autoregressive errors. The asymptotic properties of the methods are given mainly by their place in our development scheme and not by their membership in either of the two classes: structural-form or reduced-form oriented methods.

We have indicated that many of the methods suggested by the authors mentioned in the introduction are, in principle, members of our class of reduced-form oriented methods. The reduced-form oriented methods suffer, broadly speaking, from a weakness which is not shared by their structural-form oriented counterparts — namely that they require a large number of observations for their application. The structural-form oriented methods are, however, not the only alternatives for this situation of undersized samples. A different approach is to base the developments on instrumental variables. Hatanaka (1976) and Dhrymes–Taylor (1976) have made such suggestions. Their approach has computational advantage since the estimates are obtained non-iteratively, but suffers from certain arbitrariness in the choice of instrumental variables, and no routine method for their selection is given. This weakness is not shared by our structural-form oriented methods, but on the other hand the calculation of the estimates here is somewhat more complicated. Our results from the applications indicate that these computational complications are of minor importance. The estimates were generally obtained easily.

Our studies have been motivated by efficiency considerations. Emphasis can however also be laid on criteria other than those concerning the quality of the parameter estimates. A different criterion is the prediction error within the observation period as measured by $1-Q^2$. Our results from the applications indicate that methods of the GEID type work well here. This is not surprising since, for example, the GEID method minimizes a quantity very similar to the total prediction error of the basic system given the restrictions imposed by the model. Also the CRR approach method for the case of autoregressive errors, GEID-A, scores well on Q^2, although the method is not fully efficient. Together with the applicability of the method for undersized samples, its robustness concerning some correlations between the disturbances and the predetermined variables, and the simple computations based on OLS regressions, this merits consideration of the method.

Chapter 7

EXTENSIONS OF THE GEID AND IIV ESTIMATORS

The Case of Serially Correlated Residuals and Lagged Endogenous Variables

REINHOLD BERGSTRÖM

1. Introduction

In the estimation of simultaneous equation systems, interest has for a long time focussed on the problems caused by the correlation between the residuals and some of the explanatory variables. The problem has been dealt with extensively in the literature and a number of consistent methods proposed. Most of the earlier chapters of this volume contain further contributions in this area of research.

Another important problem has only recently started to be discussed in more detail. This is the occurrence of serially correlated errors. In general serially correlated errors mean that ordinary standard methods are inefficient and in the case of lagged endogenous variables even inconsistent.

This chapter contains a discussion of methods that give consistent estimates in the case of serially correlated errors and lagged endogenous variables. The methods are all extensions of the FP and IIV methods. In addition to the most common situation, that of the residuals being formed by an autoregressive process, the case of residuals formed by a process of moving summation is also analyzed.

The properties of the methods are investigated by means of both Monte Carlo experiments and applications to real-world models. Special emphasis is placed on the treatment of a model by Fair, as this model displays serial correlation in the residuals to an unusual degree.

In general the common standard methods are found to be very inferior to the methods discussed in this chapter and it cannot be too strongly emphasized how important it is to consider use of the extensions of the FP and IIV methods considered here.

2. Estimation Methods

2.1. Residuals Formed by a Process of Moving Summation

The system is written in the same basic form and with the same notations as in earlier chapters of this volume. To get a more compact notation we are also going to use the following specification:

$$y_i = \alpha_{(i)} X_{(i)} + \delta_i, \tag{2.1}$$

where $\alpha_{(i)} = (1 \times (n_i + m_i))$, $X_{(i)} = ((n_i + m_i) \times T)$, and y_i and δ_i are defined as before. The notation $X^*_{(i)}$ for the matrix consisting of $Y^*_{(i)}$ and $Z_{(i)}$ will also be used.

We assume that the residuals are formed by a process of moving summation, i.e.,

$$\delta_t = \nu_t + K\nu_{t-1}, \tag{2.2}$$

where $\cdots \nu_{t-1}, \nu_t, \nu_{t+1} \cdots$ is a series of independently distributed residuals. Clearly, δ_t and y_{t-1} are not independent in this case. This means that ordinary estimation methods, such as FP and IIV, are not consistent when the predetermined variables include lagged endogenous variables. In order to obtain consistent modifications of the GEID and IIV estimators we have to eliminate two difficulties, viz.

(1) Components of y_{t-1} that are included among the predetermined variables are correlated with the residuals δ_t and ε_t. As these components are used as regressors in the definition of the GEID estimator and as instrumental variables in the definition of the IIV estimator, both these methods become inconsistent. The problem is solved by using the corresponding components of y^*_{t-1} instead of the components of y_{t-1}, when the regressors and instruments are constructed.

(2) Components of the restricted reduced form y^*_t are also included as regressors and instrumental variables in the definition of the two estimators. As y^*_t is a function of those components of y_{t-1} that are included among the predetermined variables, it will not be independent of δ_t and ε_t. Consequently we have another source of inconsistency for the IIV and GEID estimators. The solution of the problem is again a substitution of the relevant components of y_{t-1} by components of y^*_{t-1}, this time in the formation of y^*_t.

The estimators thus obtained can be written as

$$\hat{\alpha}_{(i)} = y_i X^{*\prime}_{(i)} \{X_{(i)} X^{*\prime}_{(i)}\}^{-1}, \tag{2.3}$$

and

$$\hat{\alpha}_{(i)} = y_i X^{*\prime}_{(i)} \{X^*_{(i)} X^{*\prime}_{(i)}\}^{-1}. \tag{2.4}$$

The estimators will be noted IIV-ACMS2 and GEID-ACMS2. It should be noted that definitions (2.3) and (2.4) are formally the same as the definitions of the IIV and GEID estimators. The important difference lies in the modified definition of some of the components of $X^*_{(i)}$.

The two estimators are not consistent as soon as more than two terms ν_t are included in δ_t. Depending on the number of terms in δ_t, consistent modifications of IIV and GEID can easily be obtained.

In the case when an infinite number of terms are included in δ_t the following modification can be used. If we write out the lagged endogenous variables explicitly, we obtain

$$y_t = \beta y_t + \Gamma_1 y_{t-1} + \cdots + \Gamma_q y_{t-q} + \Gamma^I z^I_t + \delta_t. \tag{2.5}$$

In this expression q is the maximum lag in the model. The restricted reduced form is obtained as

$$\eta^*_t = \Pi_1 y_{t-1} + \cdots + \Pi_q y_{t-q} + \Pi^I z^I_t, \tag{2.6}$$

where $\Pi_1, \cdots, \Pi_q, \Pi^I$ can be expressed in terms of $\beta, \Gamma_1, \cdots, \Gamma_q$ and Γ^I. By computing y^*_t by the following recursive formula:

$$y^*_t = P_1 y^*_{t-1} + \cdots + P_q y^*_{t-q} + P^I z^I_t, \tag{2.7}$$

and then using formulae (2.3) and (2.4), we obtain two new estimators IIV-ACMS and GEID-ACMS. When $t \leqq q$ the procedure cannot be used as given in (2.7). In practice we use y_{t-d} instead of y^*_{t-d} when $t \leqq d$. This will not impair the asymptotic properties of the methods.

The basic idea behind IIV-ACMS and IIV-ACMS2 is presented in Lyttkens (1974), where the methods are presented as iterative procedures and not as estimators. In the case of IIV-ACMS the original idea was given by Klein.

The equations defining the estimators are non-linear and iterative procedures are required to obtain values of the estimators. For IIV-ACMS2 and IIV-ACMS modifications of the IIV method have been used; for GEID-ACMS2 and GEID-ACMS modifications of the SFP method. The modifications are fairly obvious and are not presented here.

2.2. *Residuals Formed by an Autoregressive Process*

When the residuals are assumed to be formed by an autoregressive process of the first order they can be written as

$$\delta_t = R\delta_{t-1} + \delta_t^+, \tag{2.8}$$

where $\cdots \delta_{t-1}^+, \delta_t^+, \delta_{t+1}^+ \cdots$ are independently distributed and R is a matrix of order $n \times n$. It is common that some elements in R are a priori specified to be zero. The most important of these special cases is the one in which R is diagonal.

Including the systematic part of the system we now have

$$y_t = \beta y_t + \Gamma z_t + R\delta_{t-1} + \delta_t^+. \tag{2.9}$$

In this case, too, a respecified system is possible. Introduced by Selén (1975, see also Chapter 6 of this volume), we can write

$$y_t = \beta\eta_t^{**} + \Gamma z_t + R\delta_{t-1} + \varepsilon_t^+, \tag{2.10}$$

where

$$\eta_t^{**} = (I - \beta)^{-1}\{\Gamma z_t + R\delta_{t-1}\}, \tag{2.11}$$

and

$$\varepsilon_t^+ = (I - \beta)^{-1}\delta_t^+.$$

In this case, too, it is obvious that y_{t-1} and δ_t are not independent. Thus both FP and IIV as well as other standard methods will give inconsistent estimates. Of the methods considered in Section 2.1, IIV-ACMS and GEID-ACMS are consistent in this situation, too. However, more efficient methods can be obtained by using the fact that the residuals are formed by an autoregressive process. The IIV-AC estimator introduced in Bergström (1975c) is defined as the solutions to the equations

$$y_i Y_{(i)}^{**\prime} = b_{(i)} Y_{(i)} Y_{(i)}^{**\prime} + g_{(i)} Z_{(i)} Y_{(i)}^{**\prime} + r_i D_L Y_{(i)}^{**\prime}, \tag{2.12}$$

$$y_i Z_{(i)}' = b_{(i)} Y_{(i)} Z_{(i)}' + g_{(i)} Z_{(i)} Z_{(i)}' + r_i D_L Z_{(i)}', \tag{2.13}$$

$$y_i D_L' = b_{(i)} Y_{(i)} D_L' + g_{(i)} Z_{(i)} D_L' + r_i D_L D_L',$$

$$Y^{**} = (I - B)^{-1} GZ + (I - B)^{-1} RD_L, \tag{2.14}$$

$$D = Y - BY - GZ. \tag{2.15}$$

Of the new notations r_i denotes the estimate of the ith row of R. D_L is a matrix of order $n \times T$ consisting of the estimates of the lagged residuals. In the definition of the estimator all parameters in R have been considered unknown. If some of the values of R are a priori known to be zero, the estimation is modified. In the special case when R is assumed to be diagonal we denote the estimator IIV-ACD.

The estimator of GEID-type that corresponds to IIV-AC is described in Selén (1975, see also Chapter 6) and denoted GEID-A. Instead of using $Y_{(i)}^{**}$ and D_L as instrumental variables as in (2.13) they are used as regressors to obtain GEID-A. The special case when R is diagonal will be denoted GEID-AD.

When the autoregressive case is discussed for unirelation models, the equation is usually transformed to facilitate the estimation. In the special case when R is assumed to be diagonal this approach is fruitful for multi-relation systems, too. The ith relation of the model can now be written as

$$y_i = \alpha_{(i)}X_{(i)} + \rho_{ii}\delta_{iL} + \delta_i^+. \tag{2.16}$$

It is easily seen that this expression can be transformed to the following:

$$y_i - \rho_{ii}y_{iL} = \alpha_{(i)}(X_{(i)} - \rho_{ii}X_{(i)L}) + \delta_i^+. \tag{2.17}$$

The following estimator can now be defined:

$$[y_i - r_{ii}y_{iL} - a_{(i)}(X_{(i)} - r_{ii}X_{(i)L})]X_{(i)}^{**\prime} = 0, \tag{2.18}$$

$$r_{ii} = (d_i d_{iL}')(d_{iL}d_{iL}')^{-1}, \tag{2.19}$$

$$Y^{**} = (I - B)^{-1}GZ + (I - B)^{-1}Rd_L, \tag{2.20}$$

$$D = Y - BY - GZ. \tag{2.21}$$

This estimator will be denoted IIV-ACT1. By using $Y_{(i)}^{**} - r_{ii}Y_{(i)L}$ as instrumental variable instead of $Y_{(i)}^{**}$ yet another estimator is obtained. We will denote this estimator IIV-ACT2. IIV-ACT1 and IIV-ACT2 were introduced in Lyttkens (1974) in the form of iterative procedures. In Bergström (1975c) it is pointed out that IIV-ACT1 gives identical estimates to IIV-ACD.

A transformation of the type discussed above is possible for a REID system. As shown in Bergström (1975c) the estimator of GEID type that can be defined in this case is in general not consistent when lagged endogenous variables are present. Thus this case will not be dealt with further. This case is also discussed in Selén (1973). By taking (2.10) as the starting point, another GEID estimator can be obtained which does not have this drawback. For a discussion we refer to Selén (1975).

The estimators discussed in this section are all defined as solutions to highly non-linear systems. In practice the estimators can be obtained by modifications of the corresponding procedures that lead to the IIV and

GEID estimators. For larger models modifications of RSIIV and RFP can be expected to give the fastest convergence. It should be pointed out, however, that because of the number of parameters involved, IIV-AC and GEID-A can only be used for relatively small models. Thus modifications of IIV and SFP should also be considered in such cases.

Modifications of other standard methods for the autoregressive case have also been developed; see e.g. Fair (1973).

3. Monte Carlo Studies

3.1. General Design

The basic structure used in the Monte Carlo experiments will be the one usually called Summers' model. Thus we have

$$y_t = \beta y_t + \Gamma z_t + \delta_t \tag{3.1}$$

$$\beta = \begin{bmatrix} 0 & \beta_{12} \\ \beta_{21} & 0 \end{bmatrix}, \qquad \Gamma = \begin{bmatrix} \gamma_{11} & \gamma_{12} & 0 & 0 \\ 0 & 0 & \gamma_{23} & \gamma_{24} \end{bmatrix}, \tag{3.2}$$

and z_1, z_2 and z_3 are assumed to be exogenous variables with

$$\sigma^2_{z_i} = 1, \quad i = 1, 3, \qquad \rho_{z_i z_j} = 0, \quad i \neq j. \tag{3.3}$$

The endogenous variables are stochastic and consequently vary from sample to sample; z_4 is assumed to be the value of y_1 lagged one period.

The values of the structural parameters are specified as follows:

$$\begin{aligned} &\beta_{12} = -\beta_{21} = 0.5, \\ &\gamma_{11} = \gamma_{12} = \gamma_{23} = \gamma_{24} = 1.0. \end{aligned} \tag{3.4}$$

The residuals are assumed to be formed by an autoregressive process of the first order, i.e.,

$$\delta_t = R\delta_{t-1} + \delta_t^+. \tag{3.5}$$

Two different R matrices will be considered, viz.

$$R = \begin{bmatrix} 0.9 & 0 \\ 0 & 0.9 \end{bmatrix}, \tag{3.6a}$$

$$R = \begin{bmatrix} 0.6 & 0.3 \\ 0.3 & 0.6 \end{bmatrix}. \tag{3.6b}$$

The variance of δ_t^+ equals 0.25. The residuals δ_t^+ are assumed to be normally distributed. The number of samples for each model and sample size is 50. Due to limitations of space a fairly brief presentation of results will be given. For a more detailed report reference is made to Bergström (1975c), where a Monte Carlo study of models with residuals formed by a process of moving summation can also be found.

3.2. Results for the Model with a Diagonal R Matrix

The results of the sampling experiments are given in Table 1. The table confirms that the inconsistent methods IIV and FP perform very badly for models of this type. They both show a large bias for all parameters of the first relation and γ_{24}. In addition FP is also clearly biased for γ_{23}. The results are well in line with the analytical asymptotic results derived for IIV in Bergström (1975c). In general the standard deviations of IIV and FP are also large.

A comparison between the two consistent methods of IIV type, IIV-ACD and IIC-ACT2, shows that the methods are practically equal for the second relation. For the first relation, IIV-ACT2 gives appreciably better results for all parameters, including ρ_{11}. The difference is especially marked for β_{12} and ρ_{11}.

GEID-AD also performs less well than IIV-ACT2. The difference is most pronounced for the first relation and especially for β_{12} and ρ_{11}. Compared with IIV-ACD differences are noticable for ρ_{11} and in favour of IIV-ACD.

It is quite clear that all the three methods that account for the autocorrelation give seriously biased estimates of ρ_{11} and ρ_{22} in small samples. The values of the parameters are underestimated by as much as 10–20% even for the best method when $T = 20$.

IIV-ACMS2 is inconsistent for this type of model which is confirmed by the table. For the consistent method IIV-ACMS, on the other hand, we find practically no bias for $T = 100$. The standard deviation, however, is considerably larger than for those methods that explicitly account for the autoregressive structure of the residuals. Compared with IIV and FP, the consistent method IIV-ACMS is clearly superior for $T = 100$ and in general also better for $T = 40$.

TABLE 1
Means and standard deviations of the estimates of 50 samples; R matrix (3.6a).

Method	β_{12}	γ_{11}	γ_{12}	β_{21}	γ_{23}	γ_{24}	ρ_{11}	ρ_{22}
				$T = 100$ – Mean				
IIV-ACD	0.4925	0.9892	0.9987	−0.5049	1.0056	1.0168	0.8813	0.8673
IIV-ACT2	0.4932	0.9894	0.9946	−0.5064	1.0066	1.0165	0.8917	0.8670
GEID-AD	0.4715	0.9766	0.9941	−0.5033	0.9987	1.0185	0.8884	0.8647
IIV-ACMS	0.5041	0.9943	1.0090	−0.5205	0.9912	0.9912		
IIV-ACMS2	0.7167	1.0862	1.0968	−0.5117	0.9831	1.1271		
IIV	0.8392	1.1362	1.1462	−0.5109	0.9812	1.1828		
FP	0.8060	1.1159	1.1343	−0.5110	1.1057	1.1338		
				$T = 100$ – Standard deviation				
IIV-ACD	0.0996	0.0599	0.0780	0.0492	0.0537	0.0711	0.0425	0.0624
IIV-ACT2	0.0491	0.0566	0.0652	0.0478	0.0542	0.0712	0.0364	0.0639
GEID-AD	0.0798	0.0577	0.0733	0.0509	0.0591	0.0685	0.0416	0.0640
IIV-ACMS	0.1088	0.1382	0.1222	0.1134	0.1300	0.0871		
IIV-ACMS2	0.1241	0.1315	0.1140	0.0946	0.1166	0.1245		
IIV	0.1264	0.1354	0.1193	0.0921	0.1132	0.1410		
FP	0.1323	0.1412	0.1243	0.1059	0.1154	0.1275		
				$T = 40$ – Mean				
IIV-ACD	0.5447	0.9931	1.0147	−0.4961	1.0096	1.0003	0.8053	0.8366
IIV-ACT2	0.5151	0.9775	1.0010	−0.5008	1.0109	0.9988	0.8465	0.8360
GEID-AD	0.5378	0.9846	1.0114	−0.4892	1.0222	1.0268	0.7772	0.8209
IIV-ACMS	0.5862	1.0272	1.0683	−0.5200	1.0423	1.0493		
IIV-ACMS2	0.7029	1.0634	1.1273	−0.5221	1.0277	1.1131		
IIV	0.8074	1.0976	1.1813	−0.5193	1.0294	1.1730		
FP	0.7789	1.1193	1.1208	−0.5064	1.1303	1.1136		
				$T = 40$ – Standard deviation				
IIV-ACD	0.1433	0.1091	0.1175	0.0923	0.0986	0.1393	0.1334	0.1075
IIV-ACT2	0.0645	0.0965	0.0834	0.0978	0.0977	0.1422	0.0955	0.1083
GEID-AD	0.1307	0.1179	0.1183	0.0969	0.1181	0.1188	0.1554	0.1064
IIV-ACMS	0.2277	0.2054	0.2033	0.1760	0.1977	0.3116		
IIV-ACMS2	0.1993	0.1999	0.1974	0.1650	0.1618	0.1600		
IIV	0.1841	0.1990	0.2030	0.1604	0.1601	0.1865		
FP	0.1929	0.2022	0.2170	0.1605	0.2477	0.1924		
				$T = 20$ – Mean				
IIV-ACD	0.5644	1.0238	1.0283	−0.4999	1.0052	0.9997	0.7454	0.7432
IIV-ACT2	0.5395	1.0180	1.0288	−0.5007	1.0057	0.9981	0.8156	0.7428
GEID-AD	0.5543	1.0424	0.9947	−0.4880	1.0252	1.0106	0.6738	0.7248
				$T = 20$ – Standard deviation				
IIV-ACD	0.2209	0.2034	0.1984	0.1223	0.1554	0.1896	0.2511	0.1832
IIV-ACT2	0.1752	0.1970	0.1925	0.1264	0.1556	0.1899	0.2284	0.1828
GEID-AD	0.2256	0.2280	0.2054	0.1302	0.1920	0.2284	0.2847	0.2270

3.3. *Results for the Model with a Non-diagonal R Matrix*

For the model with a non-diagonal R matrix we have only two consistent methods that explicitly use the autoregressive structure of the residuals, viz. GEID-A and IIV-AC. Numerically the parameters of the R matrix are smaller than in the diagonal R case, but IIV and FP are still markedly biased and very much inferior to IIV-AC and GEID-A as shown in Table 2. A comparison between these two methods on the whole shows small differences with the possible exception for the smallest sample size $T = 20$. In this case IIV-AC seems to be preferable.

The small-sample properties of the estimates of R are still bad. All parameters are clearly underestimated. This is especially marked for the elements in the main diagonal of R.

TABLE 2
Means and standard deviations of the estimates of 50 samples; R matrix (3.6b).

Method	β_{12}	γ_{11}	γ_{12}	β_{21}	γ_{23}	γ_{24}	ρ_{11}	ρ_{12}	ρ_{21}	ρ_{22}
					$T = 100$ – Mean					
IIV-AC	0.4855	0.9851	0.9925	−0.5134	1.0106	0.9959	0.5731	0.3016	0.3300	0.5600
GEID-A	0.4834	0.9807	0.9945	−0.5139	1.0073	0.9989	0.5708	0.3051	0.3215	0.5644
IIV	0.7357	1.0933	1.1026	−0.5151	1.0086	1.2679				
					$T = 100$ – Standard Deviation					
IIV-AC	0.0568	0.0501	0.0616	0.0512	0.0538	0.0641	0.0976	0.0808	0.0999	0.0859
GEID-A	0.0573	0.0500	0.0666	0.0509	0.0570	0.0546	0.1004	0.0807	0.0958	0.0859
IIV	0.0771	0.0642	0.0808	0.0660	0.0674	0.0824				
					$T = 40$ – Mean					
IIV-AC	0.5389	0.9864	1.0115	−0.4846	0.9967	1.0037	0.5209	0.2889	0.3019	0.5503
GEID-A	0.5324	0.9805	1.0041	−0.4815	1.0041	1.0030	0.5166	0.2968	0.2923	0.5482
IIV	0.6765	1.0458	1.0905	−0.5078	0.9752	1.2162				
FP	0.7237	1.0674	1.0897	−0.5007	1.0867	1.2138				
					$T = 40$ – Standard deviation					
IIV-AC	0.0976	0.0941	0.1014	0.0889	0.0874	0.1052	0.1437	0.1426	0.1613	0.1461
GEID-A	0.0939	0.1045	0.1035	0.0923	0.0960	0.0962	0.1481	0.1510	0.1638	0.1447
IIV	0.2926	0.1440	0.1205	0.1263	0.2696	0.1263				
FP	0.1012	0.1409	0.1306	0.1047	0.1173	0.1364				
					$T = 20$ – Mean					
IIV-AC	0.5325	1.0093	1.0126	−0.5002	0.9909	1.0043	0.4796	0.2666	0.2437	0.4380
GEID-A	0.5416	1.0248	0.9972	−0.4960	0.9885	1.0029	0.4186	0.2978	0.2425	0.4395
					$T = 20$ – Standard deviation					
IIV-AC	0.2031	0.1861	0.1822	0.1082	0.1452	0.1301	0.2783	0.2517	0.2261	0.2398
GEID-A	0.2110	0.2051	0.1868	0.1105	0.1600	0.1286	0.2909	0.2697	0.2356	0.2434

4. Estimation of Fair's Model of the U.S. Economy

4.1. The Model

In Fair (1970) a model of the U.S. economy is presented. The model, which was designed primarily for short-run forecasting purposes, is fairly small. The forececasting properties of the model are investigated in Fair (1974), where structural parameter estimates are given. These are based on an estimation technique that accounts for both first-order serial correlation and simultaneous bias.

The model consists of four parts. In the first part, housing starts are determined from demand and supply equations. On the basis of values obtained by means of these equations current dollar GNP and a number of its major components are determined in the second part of the model. The third part of the model determines the price level, and consequently also real GNP. The final part of the model determines employment and the labour force. For a more detailed description, reference is made to Fair (1970) and (1974).

The second part of the model is a linear, simultaneous block. The only endogenous variable in this block that is decided in the remainder of the model is housing starts. Thus a complete model can be obtained from this part of the model if housing starts are treated exogenously. This has been done in Fair (1973), where the forecasting performance of several different estimators is compared. No parameter estimates are given in this case. In the following we are going to talk about this part of the original model as 'the model'.

The model is presented in Table 3. The most striking feature is that all variables except *MOOD*, *PE2* and *HSQ* are in current prices. This is highly unusual. The most important explanatory variable is *GNP.* All the consumption functions also include the Michigan Survey Research Index lagged one or two quarters among the explanatory variables. Investments in plant and equipment are similarly explained by an expectations variable in addition to *GNP.* The key variable in the explanation of housing investment is housing starts. In the inventories equation *GNP* is substituted by durable and non-durable consumption expenditures. Imports, finally, are explained by *GNP* only.

The special features of the model in addition to the use of current dollar variables is the important part played by variables of the type *MOOD* and *PE2.* The explicit use of housing starts is also unusual. Finally, *GNP* is used to explain most variables instead of such variables as disposable income, business product etc. This undoubtedly leads to a simpler model, possibly at the expense of some economic reality.

TABLE 3
Fair's model.

	Explanatory variables						
Relation	Endogenous	Exogenous					
1	y_8	z_1	z_2	z_3	z_{13}	z_{14}	
2	y_8	z_3	z_4				
3	y_8	z_3	z_5				
4	y_8	z_1	z_6				
5	y_8	z_1	z_7	z_8	z_9		
6	y_9	z_1	z_{10}	z_{11}	z_{13}	z_{14}	
7	y_8	z_1	z_{13}	z_{14}	z_{15}	z_{16}	z_{17}

Identities

$y_8 = y_1 + y_2 + y_3 + y_4 + y_5 + y_6 - y_7 + z_{12}$
$y_9 = y_1 + y_2$
$y_{10} = y_6 + z_{11}$

Variables

$y_1 = CD$ = Durable consumption expenditures
$y_2 = CN$ = Non-durable consumption expenditures
$y_3 = CS$ = Service consumption expenditures
$y_4 = IP$ = Plant and equipment investment
$y_5 = IH$ = Non-farm housing investment
$y_6 = V - V_{-1}$ = Change in total business inventories
$y_7 = IMP$ = Imports
$y_8 = GNP$ = Gross national product
$y_9 = CD + CN$
$y_{10} = V$ = Stock of total business inventories[a]
$z_{13} = D644$[b]
$z_{14} = D651$
$z_{15} = D684$
$z_{16} = D691$
$z_{17} = D692$

$z_1 = 1$
$z_2 = MOOD_{-1}$ = Michigan Survey Research Center index of consumer sentiment lagged one quarter
$z_3 = MOOD_{-2}$
$z_4 = CN_{-1}$
$z_5 = CS_{-1}$
$z_6 = PE2$ = Two-quarter-ahead expectation of plant and equipment investment
$z_7 = HSQ$ = Quarterly non-farm housing starts
$z_8 = HSQ_{-1}$
$z_9 = HSQ_{-2}$
$z_{10} = (CD + CN)_{-1}$
$z_{11} = V_{-1}$
$z_{12} = EX + G$ = Exports plus government expenditures plus farm housing investment

[a] Arbitrary base-period value 0 in 1953.IV.
[b] The variable takes the value 1 in the fourth quarter of 1964, 0 otherwise.

Dummy variables are introduced into some equations; z_{13} and z_{14} are due to an automobile strike, while the remaining dummy variables are included because of a dock strike.

When the model was estimated the estimates showed a considerable stability in all relations except one. This relation was the one explaining the change in total business inventories. Here large differences and a complete lack of significant parameter estimates were found. Several methods gave a negative sign to the coefficient of $CD + CN$, just to give an example of the unsatisfactory results for this relation. A major cause of this seemed to be a mix-up of the effects of $CD + CN$ and the lagged value of this variable. In order to improve the model $(CD + CN)_{-1}$ was dropped from the relation, while the remainder of the model remained unchanged. It is this version of the model we are going to discuss from now on.

The data are quarterly. In Fair (1974) the estimates of the different equations are not based on the same observation period in all cases. The same is true for different methods in Fair (1973), where FIML estimates are obtained on the basis of data for the period 1960.II–1970.III. These 42 observations have been used for all methods in the present study. In addition to this period, forecasts have been made after the estimation period for the quarters 1970.IV–1973.IV, 13 observations.

Thus, because of differences in sample period and also data revisions, the estimates given by Fair and those in the present study should not coincide even if the same methods were used. Similarly forecast errors are not directly comparable.

4.2. *The Performance of Methods that Disregard Autocorrelated Residuals*

4.2.1. Structural parameters. Estimates are given in Table 4, while some Durbin–Watson statistics can be found in Table 11. To save space standard errors are not included. The estimates of relation 6 are more stable now although they cannot be said to be satisfactory. The estimates are not significantly different from 0, but the signs are at least reasonable. The value of R^2 in this relation is very low (about 0.15), but this is not unusual as the investments in stocks are notoriously difficult to explain.

The most striking results are the values of the Durbin–Watson statistics. 5 of the 7 relations show a very strong positive autocorrelation of the residuals. For relation 7 the value is as small as 0.24. This has considerable impact on the choice of estimator as we shall see later.

It should be pointed out that the Durbin–Watson statistic is not very reliable in the presence of lagged endogenous variables. Results for smaller models indicate that the statistic is biased in such a way that the risk of not discovering a true autocorrelation in the residuals is increased. Thus, although we are going to use the D–W statistic as a rough indicator, the exact values will not be used to any great extent.

TABLE 4
Estimates of Fair's model; 1960.II–1970.III; parameters showing the effect of dummy variables not included.

	Relation 1 (*CD*)				Relation 2 (*CN*)		
	GNP	Const.	$MOOD_{-1}$	$MOOD_{-2}$	*GNP*	$MOOD_{-2}$	CN_{-1}
OLS	0.1100	−32.23	0.1377	0.0803	0.0538	0.0577	0.7898
TSLS	0.1100	−32.22	0.1377	0.0803	0.0509	0.0536	0.8024
IIV	0.1100	−32.22	0.1377	0.0803	0.0567	0.0617	0.7771
FP	0.1115	−42.41	0.1972	0.1182	0.0677	0.0807	0.7280
FIML	0.1122	−46.45	0.2553	0.0978	0.0737	0.0932	0.6998
IIV-ACD	0.1102	−31.03	0.1097	0.0939	0.0466	0.0457	0.8219
GEID-AD	0.1110	−36.45	0.1249	0.1303	0.0498	0.0510	0.8073
IIV-ACT2	0.1101	−31.00	0.1096	0.0938	0.0467	0.0458	0.8215
IIV-ACMS2	0.1100	−32.19	0.1374	0.0803	0.0469	0.0472	0.8203
IIV-ACMS	0.1132	−37.80	0.1818	0.0715	0.0011	−0.0180	1.0192

	Relation 3 (*CS*)			Relation 4 (*IP*)		
	GNP	$MOOD_{-2}$	CS_{-1}	*GNP*	Const.	*PE2*
OLS	0.0314	−0.0236	0.9070	0.0449	−4.18	0.8350
TSLS	0.0303	−0.0234	0.9110	0.0435	−3.96	0.8495
IIV	0.0272	−0.0225	0.9229	0.0317	−2.10	0.9726
FP	0.0349	−0.0231	0.8928	0.0324	−2.22	0.9655
FIML	0.0328	−0.0245	0.9020	0.0359	−2.81	0.9296
IIV-ACD	0.0366	−0.0262	0.8876	0.0902	−9.05	0.3084
GEID-AD	0.0401	−0.0262	0.8740	0.0865	−7.02	0.3202
IIV-ACT2	0.0356	−0.0259	0.8913	0.0812	−7.35	0.3993
IIV-ACMS2	0.0329	−0.0240	0.9011	0.0315	−2.07	0.9744
IIV-ACMS	0.0372	−0.0254	0.8849	0.1459	26.10	2.8303

	Relation 5 (*IH*)				
	GNP	Const.	*HSQ*	HSQ_{-1}	HSQ_{-2}
OLS	0.0158	−3.21	0.0584	0.0873	0.0154
TSLS	0.0158	−3.23	0.0584	0.0873	0.0153
IIV	0.0159	−3.25	0.0584	0.0874	0.0153
FP	0.0158	−3.44	0.0570	0.0882	0.0176
FIML	0.0158	−3.86	0.0613	0.0852	0.0202
IIV-ACD	0.0160	−3.51	0.0592	0.0872	0.0154
GEID-AD	0.0160	−3.45	0.0575	0.0864	0.0176
IIV-ACT2	0.0160	−3.52	0.0592	0.0872	0.0154
IIV-ACMS2	0.0159	−3.25	0.0584	0.0874	0.0153
IIV-ACMS	0.0171	−4.04	0.0579	0.0890	0.0132

	Relation 6 ($V - V_{-1}$)			Relation 7 (*IMP*)	
	CD + *CN*	Const.	V_{-1}	*GNP*	Const.
OLS	0.0771	−8.68	−0.0264	0.0769	−18.30
TSLS	0.1150	−14.91	−0.0466	0.0770	−18.35
IIV	0.1328	−17.83	−0.0560	0.0772	−18.52
FP	0.2112	−30.64	−0.0979	0.0771	−18.42
FIML	0.3324	−50.31	−0.1630	0.0777	−18.83
IIV-ACD	0.8380	−130.03	−0.4534	0.0898	−29.21
GEID-AD	1.1317	−177.86	−0.6123	0.0853	−25.03
IIV-ACT2	0.4393	−66.67	−0.2284	0.0921	−31.67
IIV-ACMS2	0.3018	−45.38	−0.1469	0.0772	−18.52
IIV-ACMS	−0.6735	113.76	0.3770	0.0844	−23.48

The only method of those considered so far that explicitly takes the correlation between the residuals of different relations into account is FIML. Table 5 shows that the covariance matrix of the residuals seems to be far from diagonal. Thus FIML should be considerably more efficient than the other methods and FIMD inconsistent for this model. It is interesting to notice that the residuals of relation 6 are negatively correlated with the residuals of all the other relations except relation 4.

TABLE 5
The correlation between the residuals of the different relations; FIML estimates.

	1	2	3	4	5	6	7
1	1.0000	0.2428	0.1615	0.0240	−0.0854	−0.3083	0.2074
2		1.0000	0.0186	0.0417	−0.0877	−0.3455	0.1425
3			1.0000	0.2586	0.1922	−0.1333	0.0034
4				1.0000	−0.2387	0.4633	−0.5291
5					1.0000	−0.4018	0.5767
6						1.0000	−0.5373
7							1.0000

4.2.2. Ex post forecasts. Table 6 shows the RMSE for all variables except y_9 and y_{10}.[1] Looking at GNP first we find that FIML is the best method followed by FP. The differences are marked, thus the value of FIML is 21% lower than that of TSLS. IIV is also slightly better than OLS and TSLS. For the other variables the differences are much smaller as already pointed out by Fair when comparing FIML with OLS and TSLS. However, a ranking clearly shows the superiority of FIML and FP. Fair (1973) obtains a value of 6.92 for TSLS and 4.97 for FIML in the case of GNP, figures that are slightly larger than those obtained here.

[1] y_9 is the sum of y_1 and y_2 thus repeating the information given by these variables, and the RMSE of y_{10} is identical to that of y_6.

TABLE 6
RMSE of the ex post forecasts.

	y_1	y_2	y_3	y_4	y_5	y_6	y_7	y_8	Rank sum
OLS	1.43	1.51	0.585	1.87	0.549	3.75	1.22	6.18	32.5
TSLS	1.43	1.51	0.587	1.86	0.549	3.74	1.21	6.17	28.5
IIV	1.43	1.50	0.589	1.82	0.550	3.74	1.21	6.04	27.5
FP	1.30	1.49	0.574	1.80	0.549	3.66	1.23	5.26	17.5
FIML	1.29	1.48	0.566	1.78	0.550	3.71	1.28	4.89	17.5
FIMD	1.46	1.53	0.589	1.85	0.552	3.80	1.23	6.30	44.5

The results above can be compared with those given in Chapter 5 for the Klein–Goldberger model. With this model, too, FIML and FP forecast GNP clearly better than other methods. IIV performs relatively better for Klein–Goldberger's model than for Fair's model. Taking all the variables into consideration we find FP as clearly superior while FIML does not perform especially well in the case of the Klein–Goldberger model.

Earlier we noticed a very strong autocorrelation in the residuals of the structural form. As is shown in Table 7 the same is true for the residuals of the reduced form. We still find the strongest autocorrelation in the imports, but GNP, too, shows a very low D–W value. The non-random character of the residuals can clearly be seen in Figure 1. GNP is underestimated in the middle of the period while it is overestimated at the start and also at the end of the period.

TABLE 7
D–W statistic based on the reduced form residuals.

	1	2	3	4	5	6	7	8	9	10
OLS	1.01	2.40	1.36	0.57	1.02	0.83	0.31	0.41	1.68	0.83
FP	1.22	2.37	1.40	0.68	1.01	0.76	0.31	0.50	1.87	0.76

4.2.3. Ex ante forecasts. As mentioned before, forecasts have been produced for 13 quarters after the estimation period. The forecasts were obtained by use of true predetermined variables. Only one-quarter ahead forecasts have been analysed. Table 8 gives the RMSE of the forecasts, and Table 9 the average errors. Thus, the latter table shows whether there is any systematic over- or underestimation. On the basis of a ranking of the methods IIV, FIML and FP come out best. The relative performances observed in the estimation period are consequently to some extent, at least, repeated as judged from these aggregated figures. However, they conceal important differences. FIML fails completely for y_6 and because of this also for y_8. To some extent the same is true for FP. For the other variables

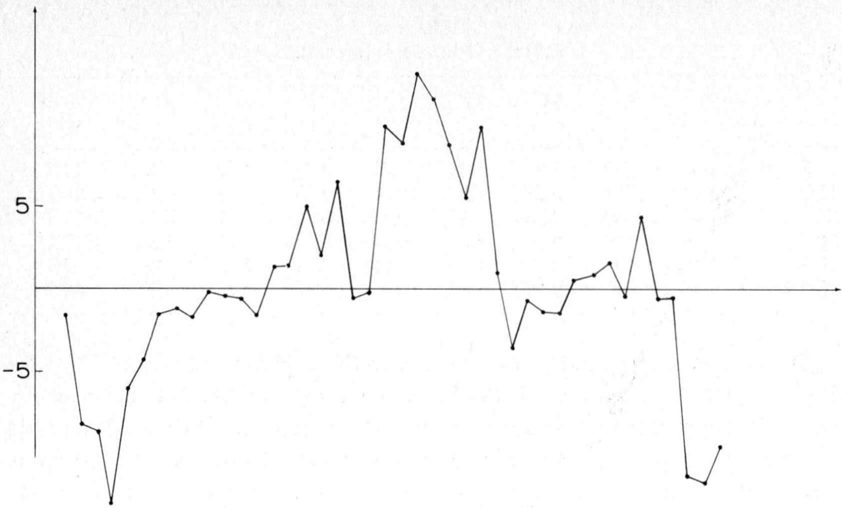

FIGURE 1. Error of the ex post forecasts of *GNP*, IIV.

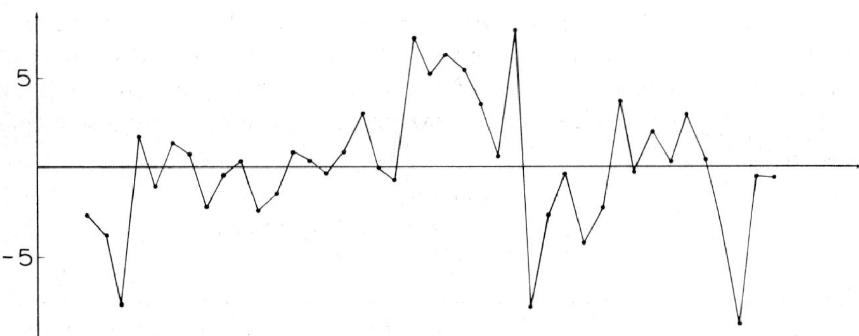

FIGURE 2. Error of the ex post forecasts of *GNP*, IIV-ACT2.

TABLE 8
RMSE of the ex ante forecasts.

	y_1	y_2	y_3	y_4	y_5	y_6	y_7	y_8	Rank sum
OLS	4.95	3.16	1.55	3.74	7.76	5.69	9.81	7.69	32
TSLS	4.87	3.08	1.56	3.71	7.72	6.41	9.63	7.78	29.5
IIV	4.89	3.10	1.54	3.61	7.71	6.86	9.56	7.42	24
FP	4.51	3.08	1.62	3.53	7.54	9.42	9.34	7.58	22.5
FIML	4.10	2.87	1.70	3.49	7.23	14.55	8.48	12.92	23
FIMD	5.26	3.29	1.52	3.66	7.84	5.74	10.10	9.48	38

TABLE 9
Average error of the ex ante forecasts.

	y_1	y_2	y_3	y_4	y_5	y_6	y_7	y_8
OLS	2.25	1.85	−0.01	−1.79	6.74	−3.14	7.88	−2.01
TSLS	2.06	1.73	−0.07	−1.72	6.70	−4.70	7.71	−3.75
IIV	2.14	1.82	−0.08	−0.51	6.69	−5.39	7.65	−3.03
FP	2.27	1.94	0.00	−0.68	6.56	−8.46	7.51	−5.91
FIMD	2.74	1.91	0.09	−1.10	6.81	−0.10	8.14	2.16

except y_3, on the other hand, FIML and FP perform better than the other methods.

A comparison of the size of the errors in the estimation and forecast periods shows that for GNP the errors are about 20% larger for OLS, TSLS and IIV. However, these figures include the quarter 1970.IV when there was an auto strike that influenced GNP, durable consumption and investments in plant and equipment considerably. If we delete this quarter the RMSE for these variables and IIV are diminished to 5.32, 4.59 and 3.09, respectively. Thus GNP is about as well forecast as in the sample period. For FP, FIML and FIMD there are larger differences between the two periods.

When we turn to the other variables we find values of the RMSE in the forecast period that are 2–3 times as large as those in the estimation period for all variables except y_5 and y_7 where the difference is even larger. For these variables we also systematically underestimate the values of the variables. Thus there seems to be a structural change between the estimation and the forecast periods in the case of these variables. This is confirmed by a study of the parameter estimates for all the 55 observations, Table 10. The coefficients of GNP are markedly increased for both these relations. For relation 5 there is a more clear tendency towards autocorrelation in the residuals than for the estimates based on the original estimation peirod.

It might be argued that in practice one-period ahead forecasts are not performed in the way described here. What we have here is more a test of the structure of the model after the estimation period. When the forecasts are computed in reality the model should be re-estimated on the basis of all available information. Thus the forecast for 1973.IV should be based on 54 observations. Use of this principle led to an improvement in the ex ante forecasts of some variables, notably y_5, where for IIV the RMSE was reduced from 7.71 to 3.38. For other variables there was no improvement. For GNP the result was even worse than before with an RMSE of 9.01 for IIV compared with 7.42.

TABLE 10

Estimates of the structural parameters for the period 1960.II–1973.IV (55 observations).

Relation 1 (*CD*)

	GNP	Const.	$MOOD_{-1}$	$MOOD_{-2}$	R^2	*D–W*
OLS	0.1156	−44.79	0.2417	0.0706	0.9926	1.20
IIV	0.1157	−45.04	0.2432	0.0710	0.9926	1.20
FP	0.1171	−52.47	0.2520	0.1309	0.9924	1.13

Relation 2 (*CN*)

	GNP	$MOOD_{-2}$	CN_{-1}	R^2	*D–W*
OLS	0.0604	0.0417	0.7739	0.9990	1.88
IIV8	0.0587	0.0396	0.7811	0.9990	1.89
FP	0.0642	0.0480	0.7571	0.9990	1.85

Relation 3 (*CS*)

	GNP	$MOOD_{-2}$	CS_{-1}	R^2	*D–W*
OLS	0.0161	−0.0173	0.9641	0.9998	2.26
IIV	0.0130	−0.0162	0.9758	0.9998	2.29
FP	0.0157	−0.0168	0.9654	0.9998	2.27

Relation 4 (*IP*)

	GNP	Const.	*PE2*	R^2	*D–W*
OLS	0.0446	−3.74	0.8249	0.9935	0.42
IIV	0.0379	−3.22	0.9056	0.9934	0.45
FP	0.0372	−3.18	0.9152	0.9934	0.45

Relation 5 (*IH*)

	GNP	Const.	*HSQ*	HSQ_{-1}	HSQ_{-2}	R^2	*D–W*
OLS	0.0201	−14.97	0.0585	0.0850	0.0957	0.9827	0.37
IIV	0.0201	−14.97	0.0584	0.0850	0.0955	0.9827	0.37
FP	0.0202	−14.93	0.0555	0.0859	0.0969	0.9826	0.38

Relation 6 ($V - V_{-1}$)

	$CD + CN$	Const.	V_{-1}	R^2	*D–W*
OLS	0.0617	−5.50	−0.0239	0.2303	0.89
IIV	0.0787	−7.98	−0.0350	0.2267	0.89
FP	0.0883	−9.33	−0.0414	0.2215	0.88

Relation 7 (*IMP*)

	GNP	Const.	R^2	*D–W*
OLS	0.0910	−27.68	0.9809	0.33
IIV	0.0911	−27.75	0.9809	0.33
FP	0.0911	−27.74	0.9809	0.33

4.3. *The Performance of Some Methods that Take Autocorrelated Residuals into Account*

4.3.1. Structural parameters. The results obtained so far are not very satisfactory in many respects. One of the main reasons seems to be the strong autocorrelation in the residuals of practically all relations. When lagged endogenous variables are present this means that the methods considered so far are inconsistent. Even if lagged endogenous variables had not been present the methods would not be efficient. The structural parameter estimates of some of the methods discussed in Section 2 are included in Table 4, while estimates of ρ_{ii} are given in Table 11.

The last two methods in Table 14 do not assume an autoregressive residual structure. IIV-ACMS2 gives estimates that do not differ very much from those of IIV. The IIV-ACMS estimates on the other hand deviate substantially from all other estimates for several relations. The estimates of relations 2, 4 and 6 are completely unsatisfactory. GEID-ACMS and GEID-ACMS2 are not included, as the iterative methods failed to converge.

Turning to the methods that assume an autoregressive scheme of the first order, we usually find less startling changes compared with the usual estimates obtained so far. Looking at the estimates of ρ_{ii} we find that these differ considerably from 0 in all cases. The methods do not differ very much. In relations 4 and 7 we find values as high as 0.8–0.9. As to the parameter estimates they are practically unchanged in relations 1 and 5. The changes in relations 2 and 3 are also moderate. However, in relation 4 we find that the parameter of *GNP* is usually doubled while that of *PE2* is halved. In relation 6 we notice large difference between the methods. The parameter of *CD* + *CN* is increased considerably especially for IIV-ACD and GEID-AD. This is accompanied by a much larger negative value of V_{-1}. In the imports relation, finally, the parameter of *GNP* is increased from 0.077 to about 0.085–0.090.

TABLE 11
D–W statistics for IIV and FP, and estimates of ρ_{ii} for other methods.

	Relation						
	1	2	3	4	5	6	7
IIV	1.10	2.36	1.40	0.74	0.90	0.88	0.24
FP	1.02	2.21	1.35	0.73	0.89	0.86	0.25
IIV-ACD	0.4527	−0.2500	0.3161	0.8626	0.5406	0.7852	0.8974
GEID-AD	0.4845	−0.2114	0.2412	0.9138	0.5057	0.7523	0.8360
IIV-ACT2	0.4528	−0.2498	0.3100	0.8510	0.5406	0.6592	0.9107

4.3.2. Ex post forecasts. The ex post forecasts are shown in Table 12. If we compare the three methods in the table, GEID-AD performs slightly better for GNP, the imports and the change in business inventories. Otherwise the differences are small. A comparison with the values given in Fair (1973) for GNP shows that these seem to be slightly lower. Thus for TSLSAUTO1 he obtains the value 3.16 and for FIMLAUTO1 as small a value as 2.48. Compared with the methods used earlier, see Table 6, we obtain considerable improvements for several variables. The most notable cases are the plant and equipment investments and the imports where the RMSE's are diminished by about 30 and 50%, respectively. Considerable improvements are also obtained for the non-farm housing investments, the inventories investments and above all the GNP. We notice that on the whole those variables are improved that correspond to relations with marked changes in the parameter estimates.

TABLE 12
RMSE of the ex post forecasts (comparison of untransformed variables) in the estimation period.

	y_1	y_2	y_3	y_4	y_5	y_6	y_7	y_8
IIV-ACD	1.27	1.47	0.530	1.29	0.483	3.23	0.561	3.97
GEID-AD	1.23	1.45	0.514	1.26	0.476	3.23	0.509	3.48
IIV-ACT2	1.26	1.47	0.528	1.26	0.485	3.06	0.562	3.70

4.3.3. Ex ante forecasts. The RMSE of the ex ante forecasts are given in Table 13. A comparison with Table 8 shows that great improvements are obtained for variables *IP*, *IH* and *IMP*. ΔV and *GNP* are also improved. In spite of the improvements, the results for *IH* and ΔV are still unsatisfactory. There is a systematic overestimation of ΔV and a systematic underestimation of *IH*.

When the ex ante forecasts are analyzed it should be borne in mind that the forecasts are negatively influenced by certain unnormal occurrences during the period, such as the auto strike in 1970.IV, the October war in 1973.IV, and the dock strike in 1971.IV. If these events are taken into consideration the ex ante forecasts are greatly improved as shown in Bergström (1975b).

TABLE 13
RMSE of the ex ante forecasts.

	y_1	y_2	y_3	y_4	y_5	y_6	y_7	y_8
IIV-ACD	4.31	3.48	1.75	1.98	3.91	7.48	3.02	6.50
IIV-ACT2	4.40	3.55	1.75	1.91	3.94	6.26	3.05	6.49

5. Estimation of Other Real-World Models

5.1. Dicks–Miraux's Model

This model explains wages and prices in the U.K. during the period 1948–1959; Dicks–Miraux (1961). It is specified as follows:

$$w_t = \beta_{12}p_t + \gamma_{11} + \gamma_{12}p_{t-1} + \gamma_{13}D_{t-1/4} + \delta_{1t}, \tag{5.1}$$

$$p_t = \beta_{21}w_t + \gamma_{21} + \gamma_{23}I_{t-1/4} + \gamma_{24}X_t + \delta_{2t}. \tag{5.2}$$

p_t denotes prices, w_t wages, D_t the demand for labour, I_t the import prices, and X_t output per man. All variables except D_t are in the form of percentage changes. The observations are yearly. As the model includes one lagged endogenous variable, usual standard methods are inconsistent as soon as the residuals are autocorrelated. It should be noticed that the model is of the type used in the Monte Carlo study in Section 3. In econometric literature this model is usually called Summers' model.

The model is discussed in detail in Bergström (1975a). Table 14 shows the structural parameter estimates. It is immediately clear that the estimates are changed considerably when autoregressive residuals are ac-

TABLE 14
Structural parameter estimates of Dicks–Miraux's model.

	β_{12}	γ_{11}	γ_{12}	γ_{13}	β_{21}	γ_{21}	γ_{24}	γ_{25}	D–W (1)	D–W (2)
OLS	0.3321	3.76	0.1562	2.5629	0.3688	1.91	0.2008	−0.5190	1.29	2.65
	(0.1157)	(0.59)	(0.0983)	(0.7672)	(0.1560)	(1.04)	(0.0307)	(0.1402)		
TSLS	0.3002	3.83	0.1631	2.6912	0.3084	2.28	0.2093	−0.5326	1.37	2.73
	(0.1226)	(0.59)	(0.0991)	(0.7865)	(0.1933)	(1.26)	(0.0348)	(0.1438)		
IIV	0.2977	3.83	0.1637	2.7014	0.3107	2.26	0.2090	−0.5321	1.37	2.73
	(0.1229)	(0.60)	(0.0986)	(0.7906)	(0.2080)	(1.28)	(0.0377)	(0.1387)		
FIML	0.2979	3.83	0.1642	2.6990	0.3124	2.26	0.2086	−0.5345		
FP	0.3009	3.82	0.1660	2.6821	0.3327	2.22	0.2034	−0.5622	1.36	2.68
IIV-AC	0.4195	3.60	0.1236	2.0168	0.3647	2.13	0.1705	−0.5519		
IIV-ACD	0.4155	3.60	0.1294	1.9842	0.1839	3.24	0.2067	−0.6229		
GEID-A	0.4238	3.55	0.1360	1.9057	0.4375	1.80	0.1571	−0.5825		
GEID-AD	0.4027	3.57	0.1479	2.0463	0.1954	3.22	0.2041	−0.6433		
IIV-ACT2	0.4117	3.62	0.1295	2.0065	0.2320	2.91	0.2023	−0.5877		
IIV-ACMS2	0.2997	3.86	0.1557	2.6896	0.3380	2.10	0.2052	−0.5259		
IIV-AMS	0.2995	3.86	0.1565	2.6908	0.3380	2.10	0.2052	−0.5259		
GEID-ACMS2	0.2840	3.88	0.1720	2.5903	0.3649	2.02	0.1990	−0.5533		
GEID-ACMS	0.2823	3.88	0.1725	2.6009	0.3641	2.02	0.1991	−0.5530		

counted for. We also notice that the introduction of a full R matrix has a marked effect on the estimates of the second relation.

In view of the Durbin–Watson values in Table 14 it is not surprising to obtain values of ρ_{11} and ρ_{22} that differ considerably from 0. We also notice that the value of ρ_{21} is numerically very large for both IIV-AC and GEID-A. A study of the forecasts in the sample period shows that the forecasts of the prices are improved if the methods assuming autocorrelation are used. The RMSE is reduced from about 0.79 to 0.65.

TABLE 15
Estimates of the parameters of $R = [\rho_{ij}]$.

	ρ_{11}	ρ_{12}	ρ_{21}	ρ_{22}
IIV-AC	0.3949	0.0662	−0.4882	−0.4989
IIV-ACD	0.3778			−0.5155
GEID-A	0.4029	0.0194	−0.5997	−0.4619
GEID-AD	0.3359			−0.5077
IIV-ACT2	0.3742			−0.5144

TABLE 16
RMSE of the reduced form residuals.

	OLS	IIV	FP	IIV-AC	IIV-ACD
y_1	0.9207	0.9183	0.9126	0.9423	0.8804
y_2	0.7915	0.7901	0.7863	0.6431	0.6634
	GEID-A	GEID-AD	IIV-ACMS	GEID-ACMS	
y_1	0.9236	0.9105	0.9575	0.9393	
y_2	0.6329	0.6508	0.7935	0.7752	

5.2. Klein's Model I

This model, presented in Klein (1950), is well-known. Estimates by nine standard methods are given in Bergström (1974), while FIML estimates in the case of autoregressive residuals can be found in Hendry (1971) and Selén (1975). A detailed discussion of the model is given in Bergström (1975c). Table 17 shows the structural parameter estimates (constants excluded). For this model it is well-known that the estimates of the ordinary standard methods differ considerably. The methods considered here do not differ more dramatically from IIV and FP.

TABLE 17
Structural parameter estimates of Klein's model I.

	β_{15}	β_{17}	γ_{12}	β_{25}	γ_{22}	γ_{23}	β_{38}	γ_{34}	γ_{35}
IIV-ACD	−0.0756	0.7816	0.1975	0.0871	0.6596	−0.1820	0.4427	0.1340	1.1474
GEID-AD	0.0156	0.7047	0.1537	0.0551	0.6861	−0.1894	0.4319	0.1358	1.2462
IIV-ACT2	−0.0889	0.7953	0.1996	0.0827	0.6632	−0.1828	0.4417	0.1349	1.1501
IIV-AC	−0.1179	0.7411	0.2692	−0.2099	0.8370	−0.2040	0.4241	0.1304	1.1575
GEID-A	−0.0546	0.7649	0.2614	−0.1076	0.7938	−0.1584	0.4600	0.0653	0.7835
IIV-ACMS	−0.2995	0.8381	0.4568	−0.0380	0.8528	−0.1568	0.3757	0.2092	1.4396
IIV-ACMS2	−0.1303	0.8252	0.3044	0.1092	0.6204	−0.1613	0.4124	0.1681	1.3910
IIV	−0.1175	0.8215	0.3126	0.1071	0.6530	−0.1638	0.4205	0.1639	1.3484
FP	0.0221	0.7939	0.2561	0.0891	0.6654	−0.1662	0.4006	0.1710	1.6152

For this model the D–W statistic does not indicate serial correlation in the residuals. In spite of this the methods based on a diagonal R matrix give a large value to ρ_{11}. This model is one of the few cases, where methods with a full R matrix can be used. As shown in Table 18, we obtain estimates of ρ_{21} and ρ_{23} that differ very much from 0 in this case.

In Table 19 the quality of the ex post forecasts is shown in the sample period. From Bergström (1974) we already know that FP is clearly better than other standard methods and also that IIV is slightly better than these. In the table we find that the introduction of a diagonal R matrix improves

TABLE 18
Estimates of the parameters of R.

	ρ_{11}	ρ_{12}	ρ_{13}	ρ_{21}	ρ_{22}	ρ_{23}	ρ_{31}	ρ_{32}	ρ_{33}
IIV-AC	0.7226	−0.2910	−0.1111	0.4171	−0.0850	−1.1960	0.1614	0.0131	−0.0688
GEID-A	0.5358	−0.2122	−0.1428	0.5310	−0.2675	−1.0210	0.4349	−0.0669	0.3509
IIV-ACD	0.4551				−0.0500				−0.0838
IIV-ACT2	0.4352				−0.0498				−0.0888
GEID-AD	0.6941				−0.0583				−0.5809

TABLE 19
RMSE of the ex post forecasts in the sample period.

	y_1	y_2	y_3	y_4	y_5
IIV	19.08	13.98	15.51	31.81	18.88
FP	18.46	13.93	15.15	31.30	19.10
IIV-ACD	16.10	13.64	13.16	28.08	17.60
IIV-ACT2	16.19	13.64	13.24	28.19	17.62
GEID-AD	15.13	13.65	11.74	26.65	18.01
IIV-AC	14.54	11.22	11.73	24.24	15.42
GEID-A	14.63	10.89	11.09	23.85	15.67

the ex post forecasts considerably. We also notice that GEID-AD in most cases gives better results than IIV-ACD and IIV-ACT2 which are almost equal. Thus we find the same relationship as between FP and IIV. When a full R matrix is allowed there is a further improvement. GEID-A is better than IIV-AC in 3 cases out of 5. The improvement compared with IIV and FP is considerable (about 25% for the consumption, 20% for the net investment, and 25% for the national income to give a few examples).

5.3. Girshick–Haavelmo's Model

The model is presented in Girshick and Haavelmo (1947) and estimates by 9 methods are given in Bergström (1974).

As shown in Table 20 we have strong indications of positive serial correlation in all the 5 relations. The largest D–W value is in fact 1.28. In consequence with this we obtain large ρ_{ii} values throughout with IIV-ACD and with one exception with IIV-ACT2.

TABLE 20
D–W values of the IIV estimates, and ρ_{ii} values for IIV-ACD and IIV-ACT2.

Relation	D–W	ρ_{ii}	
	IIV	IIV-ACD	IIV-ACT2
1	1.28	0.5945	0.5856
2	1.15	0.5699	−0.0394
3	1.08	0.7173	0.7173
4	0.72	0.6118	0.5669
5	0.87	0.4846	0.4847

In view of the ρ_{ii} estimates, great changes could be expected in the parameter estimates. These are also realized as seen by Table 21. Except for γ_{15} which is close to 0 we obtain much larger numerical values for the parameters in relation 1 than with IIV and other standard methods. By considering the autoregressive structure of the residuals a larger positive effect of the disposable income is indicated as well as a much larger negative effect of prices and the time trend. Similar very considerable changes are observed in many other cases, too. The estimates of the new methods IIV-ACD and IIV-ACT2 cannot be said to be more unreasonable a priori than e.g. the IIV estimates.

TABLE 21
Estimates of Girshick–Haavelmo's model.

	β_{12}	β_{13}	γ_{14}	γ_{15}	β_{22}	β_{24}	γ_{24}
IIV	−0.4863	0.2902	−0.3166	0.0966	0.1889	−0.6211	−0.2242
IIV-ACD	−1.5376	0.6319	−1.2146	−0.0325	0.5252	−0.2977	−0.4401
IIV-ACT2	−1.1867	0.5178	−0.9211	−0.0010	0.1607	−0.6214	−0.3087
	γ_{33}	γ_{35}	β_{45}	γ_{42}	γ_{44}	β_{52}	γ_{54}
IIV	0.2028	0.3673	0.6728	−0.3819	−0.1877	2.7522	0.6053
IIV-ACD	0.1877	0.0424	0.1539	0.1120	0.1993	2.8119	1.0225
IIV-ACT2	0.1877	0.0424	0.2472	0.0756	0.1481	2.7935	1.0138

TABLE 22
Q^2 for the ex post forecasts.

	IIV	IIV-ACD	IIV-ACT2
y_1	0.7341	0.7632	0.7050
y_2	0.5695	0.6615	0.6584
y_3	0.8785	0.9022	0.9022
y_4	0.5607	0.5121	0.5621
y_5	0.5892	0.6437	0.6316

The ex post forecasts differ less than could be expected in view of the parameter estimates given above. However, IIV-ACD performs clearly better for y_1, y_2, y_3 and y_5, worse for y_4.

5.4. Klein–Goldberger's Model

As mentioned before the Klein–Goldberger model exists in many different versions. The one considered here is the linearized version used in Chapter 5. Thus, there are 11 behavioural relations and 12 identities.

In Table 24 the Durbin–Watson statistics are given for IIV and FP. When we use IIV there is very little indication of serial correlation in the residuals. No value is significant, and only in relation 2 do we find a value that is smaller than 1.5. For the FP method on the other hand we find two relations with clear signs of serially correlated errors, viz. relations 5 and 7. There are two further relations with values below 1.5.

Thus we cannot expect that the methods that account for serially correlated errors should produce results that differ very much from those given by e.g. IIV and FP. The difference between IIV-ACD and IIV-ACT2 is very small with one exception. The exception is relation 5 where the estimates of ρ_{ii} are 0.04 and 0.45. The parameter estimates also differ much for this relation. Otherwise the ρ_{ii} estimates are small and not all that strongly correlated with the D–W values of IIV. However, we obtain negative ρ_{ii} values for exactly those relations that have D–W values in excess of 2.

TABLE 23
Parameter estimates of the Klein–Goldberger model.

	Relation 1		Relation 2	Relation 3		Relation 4		
IIV	0.3420	0.6773	0.0796	0.1363	0.4115	0.0235	0.5614	−6.4293
FP	0.3134	0.7068	0.0712	0.1530	0.3327	0.0239	0.5551	−6.9259
IIV-ACT1	0.3389	0.6810	0.0812	0.1660	0.2798	0.0262	0.5145	−8.6061
IIV-ACT2	0.3755	0.6415	0.0812	0.1570	0.3206	0.0265	0.5095	−8.7123
GEID-AD	0.3431	0.6733	0.0803	0.1529	0.3379	0.0288	0.4616	−10.3990

	Relation 5		Relation 6			Relation 7		Relation 8	
IIV	−52.9063	−2.1699	0.1711	−0.2394	−0.0289	0.3996	0.3083	−0.0155	0.64
FP	−28.8266	−1.5656	0.2138	−0.1584	−0.0491	0.4748	0.1698	−0.0145	0.74
IIV-ACT1	−62.6071	−2.3968	0.1624	−0.1598	−0.0116	0.4111	0.2868	−0.0186	0.48
IIV-ACT2	−16.1630	−1.4534	0.1743	−0.1173	−0.0212	0.4157	0.2783	−0.0185	0.48
GEID-AD	−31.1447	−1.5907	0.2070	−0.1944	−0.0499	0.5483	0.0386	−0.0170	0.61

	Relation 9		Relation 10		Relation 11		
IIV	0.8560	−0.6254	0.0206	0.7498	0.0473	0.3891	0.9537
FP	0.7836	−0.4461	0.0221	0.7347	0.0475	0.3828	0.9540
IIV-ACT1	0.8493	−0.6060	0.0237	0.7210	0.0507	0.4803	0.9446
IIV-ACT2	0.8545	−0.6080	0.0252	0.7059	0.0506	0.4800	0.9448
GEID-AD	0.4172	−0.2048	0.0281	0.6731	0.0511	0.4629	0.9427

TABLE 24
Durbin–Watson statistic for IIV and FP and estimates of ρ_{ii} by three methods.

D–W		ρ_{ii}		
IIV	FP	IIV-ACT1	IIV-ACT2	GEID-AD
1.70	1.73	0.1325	0.1583	0.1486
1.44	1.44	0.1616	0.1616	0.2067
1.75	1.52	0.2909	0.2276	0.0163
2.27	2.25	−0.1378	−0.1230	−0.1169
1.81	1.12	0.0417	0.4480	0.1834
2.20	2.42	−0.2001	−0.2523	−0.1375
1.73	1.00	0.1842	0.2102	0.8009
1.81	1.83	0.0775	0.0772	0.0685
1.96	1.49	0.0303	0.0268	0.6546
1.88	1.83	0.0915	0.1170	0.1664
1.67	1.67	0.0449	0.0448	0.0726

When using GEID-AD we obtain two startling ρ_{ii} values: 0.80 in relation 7 and 0.65 in relation 9. For the former relation we had a very small D–W value so this was not quite unexpected. On the other hand for relation 5 with almost as small a D–W value we obtained a ρ_{ii} estimate of 0.18. The parameter estimates of these two relations also differ considerably from those given by other methods.

In Chapter 5, FP and IIV were found to give the best ex post forecasts. In Table 25 the ex post forecasts of the methods considered here are included. If we compare IIV-ACD and IIV-ACT2 we find that they are practically equal except for the variable y_6 where IIV-ACT2 is considerably better. Compared with IIV we usually notice an improved performance but this is not obtained in all cases. Marked improvements are obtained for y_2 (25%), y_4 (16%), y_{11} (26%), and y_{14} (14%). When we compare GEID-AD with FP we obtain improved ex post forecasts in all cases but two. More marked improvements can be noticed for y_2 (26%), y_4 (19%), y_6 (23%), y_7 (22%), y_{11} (26%), and y_{14} (25%). GEID-AD is in most cases better than IIV-ACT2.

TABLE 25
Ex post forecasts for the Klein–Goldberger model.
The entries are $10^4 \cdot \Sigma(y_{it} - \hat{y}_{it})^2/\Sigma(y_{it} - \bar{y}_{it})^2$.

	OLS	IIV	FP	IIV-ACD	IIV-ACT2	GEID-AD
y_1	75	60	55	59	58	49
y_2	527	546	529	410	408	388
y_3	92	92	89	86	85	82
y_4	313	311	307	262	261	249
y_5	4116	3259	3555	3561	3552	3380
y_6	3794	3172	2172	3936	3171	1673
y_7	53	45	41	47	47	32
y_8	4912	4803	4516	4417	4363	3992
y_9	1735	1841	1948	1996	1961	2044
y_{10}	645	654	646	642	638	619
y_{11}	234	234	234	173	173	173
y_{12}	42	36	32	36	36	30
y_{13}	199	176	196	178	175	240
y_{14}	77	70	59	60	60	45

Chapter 8

ALGORITHMS FOR REORDERING INTERDEPENDENT SYSTEMS

LENNART BODIN

1. Introduction

The specification of each structural equation of the interdependent system is based on economic theory and scientific hypothesis. The structural equations express either some aspect of the behaviour of an individual, sector or market, or some non-behavioural relation such as equilibrium relations and technical identities. The totality of all structural relations, the structural form of the system, expresses the composed economic hypothesis concerning, for instance, a national economy.

In the construction of this hypothesis, in the stage of the model building, it seems to be a well-established practice to start with a set of hypotheses concerning consumption and consumption behaviour, and to formulate structural equations explaining consumption. Other economic variables or blocks of variables are successively analysed in the logical order determined by the model builder. A set of technical identities often complete the construction of the structural form.

The order in which the structural equations, and the endogenous variables, appear in the structural form is determined by the order in which the model builder formulates his hypothesis. This order may be consistent with a logical order in which economic hypotheses successively develop and interrelate, but the order is almost never determined with other criteria in mind. In the analysis and estimational work of large economic models it may however be a valuable instrument of the analysis to reconsider the order in which the structural equations appear and to formulate criteria and principles for reordering the structural equations. It will be argued that this analysis, and the results of the reordering algorithms, may give important information about the structure of the complete model.

Our reordering analysis takes its origin from the analysis of the optimal iterative performance of the Recursive Fix-Point method, but reordering may accordingly be called for with other criteria in mind. These include the analysis of block-recursiveness and the definition of a causal ordering in the model. The need for reordering analysis is the more obvious the larger the model and the more complex its structure.

2. Principles Used for Selecting Orderings and Constructing Algorithms

In the previous section three incentives for reordering the structural form of the interdependent system were suggested. These are:

(i) Reorder to improve the convergence properties of the iterative techniques of the Gauss–Seidel family.

(ii) Reorder to accomplish the decomposition of the interdependent system into the blocks that form the structure of the block-recursive specification; cf. F.M. Fisher (1965).

(iii) Reorder to derive a better understanding of the causal structure of the complete model and, if possible, to trace a causal ordering of the structural relations.

In the sequel the implications of the three reordering incentives will be discussed.

As the analysis of reordering should be applicable in actual econometric work and result in instructions for empirical work, we aim at computer-oriented algorithms. This is so because the number of different orderings in a model of n relations is $n!$. It is therefore possible only in very small models to analyse all orderings. In other models criteria for selecting orderings must be formulated and these criteria should allow for computer programming.

All analyses aim at the selection of a very small subset of orderings which can be used for detailed studies in various respects. Although our analysis is directed towards computer applications it is valuable if at least some of the constructed algorithms can be applied without the use of a computer. Some of our algorithms fulfill this property.

2.1. Convergence Improvements

The convergence properties of the Recursive Fix-Point method are dependent on the order in which the relations of the structural form of the ID system are processed. This property is a reflexion of the fact that the RFP method is based on the Gauss–Seidel principle with successive and relation-wise recalculations of iterates. In the convergence analysis of RFP in Chapter 2 it was stated that $(n-1)!$ different orderings of the relations may lead to different convergence performance with respect to the local convergence criterion. A subset of these orderings can be described as optimal orderings in the sense of equations (5.13) and (7.7) in Chapter 2.

The two equations defining optimal orderings for RFP estimation are based on knowledge of the complete structure of the model. They are in particular dependent on the numerical values of the parameters of the model. From the point of view of RFP estimation this implies that the optimal ordering needed for optimal iterative estimation cannot be determined until convergence is obtained and the estimation is completed, that is, too late for the optimal ordering to be used in the estimation itself. Accordingly the information contained in (5.13) and (7.7) of Chapter 2 cannot be used directly in the ordering algorithms. The fact that some essential numerical quantities are missing when the choice of optimal ordering is to be made, that is, when the RFP estimation is to begin, leads to an important modification in the search for orderings. We are forced to search for optimal orderings, conditional on the information available *before* the structural parameter set is known.

The information which has been used in the construction of the reordering algorithms is that of the structure of the position matrix $P(b)$ defined in Section 8 of Chapter 2. In some empirical investigations the orderings selected on the basis of the restricted knowledge has been compared with the optimal orderings determined on the basis of the complete knowledge of the model structure. It has been found that for every investigated model the $P(b)$ matrix gives sufficient information for the selection of optimal or near-optimal orderings with respect to the convergence of RFP.

2.2. Block-Recursive Decomposition

Large econometric models sometimes consist of different blocks of variables, recursive and/or interdependent, which together specify what Fisher (1965) defines as a block-recursive structure. It is one specific feature of a block-recursive structure that its B matrix can be transformed into a block-triangular form

$$B = \begin{pmatrix} B_{11} & 0 & \cdots & 0 \\ B_{21} & B_{22} & \ddots & \vdots \\ \vdots & & \ddots & 0 \\ B_{k1} & \cdots & \cdots & B_{kk} \end{pmatrix}, \tag{2.1}$$

where the B_{ij} are submatrices of different orders.[1]

[1] Some B_{ij} matrices, with $i > j$, may be zero matrices.

The ordering process must be able to identify the k different blocks of (2.1), and it must also produce the specific order ***between*** these blocks. In order to accomplish these goals one need not know the numerical values of the parameters of the B matrix. It is sufficient if the position matrix $P(b)$ is known, since this matrix specifies which variables occur in the interrelations between the endogenous variables.

Comment: In the block-recursive model the ordering *within* each block is not specified uniquely. The n_i relations of block i can be permuted in $n_i!$ different ways, and each of these orderings is consistent with the block-recursive specification of the model.

2.3. Information about the Causal Structure

In a recursive system the structural relations, and the endogenous variables, can be reordered to form a causal chain between the relations and the ensuing endogenous variables. This chain has no current feed-backs. The ordering which produces the causal chain can be defined as the causal ordering of the system; Simon (1957). In the interdependent system it is not possible to specify an ordering of the structural relations without any current feed-backs. It is therefore impossible to define a causal ordering in the sense referred to above. On the other hand information and knowledge of the inherent causal structure is valuable in the evaluation of the complete model structure. By reordering the structural form information about the positions of the primary feed-backs of the system can be extracted and attempts can be made to define approximate causal orderings.[2] Much information can be obtained from the $P(b)$ matrix in itself — additional information about for instance the strength of the feed-back may be based on the parameters of the B matrix.

2.4. Framework for the Ordering Algorithms

The principal design of the complete ordering process is outlined in Figure 1. For reasons outlined in Sections 2.1–2.3 the position matrix $P(b)$ is used as input in the ordering process. This matrix is specified along with the formulation of the model and is therefore available before the

[2] In the present state of research we have only begun to analyse these concepts. As approximate causal orderings we use orderings which minimize the number of feed-backs between the endogenous variables.

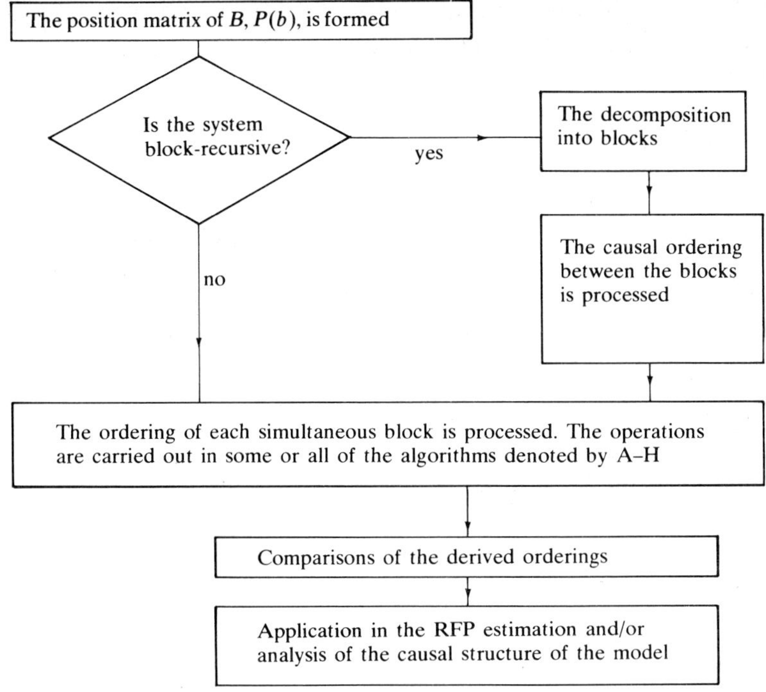

FIGURE 1. The principal design of the process for the selection of orderings.

parameter estimation starts. It is one of the quantities of the model specification which is extremely easy to derive; as stated in the definition (iv) of Section 8 in Chapter 2, it specifies zero and non-zero entries of the B matrix.

3. An Algorithm that Produces the Block-Triangular Structure of the *B* Matrix of a Block-Recursive System

For those cases where the B matrix can be reformulated in the block-triangular form (2.1) the following algorithm produces the decomposition into blocks, had this not been specified along with the model formulation. The technique is proposed by Steward (1962). The process starts by forming a matrix $Q(b)$ defined as

$$Q(b) = I + P(b), \tag{3.1}$$

with I an identity matrix of order $n \times n$. $Q(b)$ is raised to the nth power, $Q(b)^n$. The matrix multiplication is performed by Boolean arithmetics. If and only if

$$Q(b)^n_{ij} = Q(b)^n_{ji} = 1, \tag{3.2}$$

the equations i and j belong to the same unique block.

The criterion (3.2) implies that a system where all relations constitute one simultaneous interdependent block will have all entries of $Q(b)^n$ equal to unity. A block-recursive system will have some entries equal to zero.

When the different blocks have been identified a position matrix $P_B(b)$ for the interrelations of the different blocks is defined as

$$P_B(b)_{ij} = 1 \quad \text{if the endogenous variables of block } i \text{ are dependent on the endogenous variables of block } j,\ i \neq j,$$
$$= 0 \quad \text{otherwise.}$$

The $P_B(b)$ matrix is subsequently used to determine the ordering between the different blocks.

4. Algorithms for Ordering the Relations of a Simultaneous Block

Each one of the eight ordering algorithms A–H of Figure 1 aims at producing an ordering vector $(i_1, i_2, \cdots, i_n)$ of the n relations of the simultaneous block under study. A reordered $P(b)$ matrix, where the rows and columns have been permuted to appear analogously to the ordering vector, is optionally produced as output. In the sequel some principles of the basic arithmetic of the algorithms will be discussed.

Since one of the main incentives for the reordering process is that of iterative efficiency, the algorithms have been developed with reference to the iterative scheme of the RFP method. For the case $\alpha = 1.0$ the computation of the new iterates $y^{(s+1)}$ in RFP is given by

$$y^{(s+1)} = E^{(s+1)}y^{(s+1)} + F^{(s+1)}y^{(s)} + G^{(s+1)}z, \tag{4.1}$$

where the basic definitions are given in Section 4 of Chapter 2.

The approximate convergence condition developed for RFP states that all roots of the equation

$$|F + \lambda E - \lambda I| = 0 \tag{4.2}$$

should be less than unity in absolute value in order for (4.1) to converge. Extensive mathematical and numerical investigations of (4.2) for many models, theoretical constructs as well as applied models, have shown that for the optimal ordering the number of non-zero roots of (4.2) is minimum.

Transferring this conclusion to the selection of orderings implies that the ordering algorithms must produce orderings that bear the following properties:

(i) The F matrix of the reordered system must contain a minimum number of rows with non-zero entries, and/or a minimum number of columns with non-zero entries.

(ii) The ideal, but unattainable, ordering is the causal ordering which can be produced in a recursive system. For this system and its causal ordering the F matrix is equal to the zero matrix and the roots of (4.2) are all zero.

Comment: The first criterion implies that a minimum number of $y^{(s+1)}$ iterates are directly dependent on $y^{(s)}$ and/or that a minimum number of $y^{(s)}$ iterates have direct influence on $y^{(s+1)}$. The second criterion applied in a recursive system implies that no direct relations exist between the $y^{(s)}$ and $y^{(s+1)}$ iterates.

The two criteria can both be evaluated with the $P(b)$ matrix as the source of information. We note that without knowledge of the parameters of the B matrix we cannot find the roots of (4.2), on the other hand we may find an upper limit for the number of non-zero roots of (4.2). The upper limit is given by the smaller of the two numbers defined in paragraph (i) above.

The basic arithmetic of the ordering algorithms is the following:

The start. The ordering vector appears as the zero vector $(0, 0, \cdots, 0)$.

Step 1. The following row sums and column sums of $P(b)$ are calculated:

$$r(i) = \sum_j P(b)_{ij}, \tag{4.3}$$

$$c(i) = \sum_j P(b)_{ji}. \tag{4.4}$$

For all indices i with $r(i) = 0$ apply the forward allocation and for all indices i with $c(i) = 0$ apply the backward allocation according to the following definitions.

Forward allocation. The index i, $1 \leqq i \leqq n$, replaces the zero component of the ordering vector with the smallest (leftmost) position number. All elements of row i and column i of $P(b)$ are set equal to zero. The index i will not be used in any of the operations in the rest of the algorithm.

Backward allocation. The index i, $1 \leqq i \leqq n$, replaces the zero component of the ordering vector with the largest (rightmost) position number. The operations of the backward allocation are otherwise those of the forward allocation.

Step 2. If the repeated use of the arithmetic of Step 1 does not result in the selection of an index i, several different criteria are used to select an index subject to forward allocation.

In algorithms A–E the selection is based on the maximum value of the unweighted column sum (4.4) or the maximum value of a weighted column sum where differents weights can be used. In algorithms F–H a technique proposed by van der Giessen (1970) is employed. Algorithm F is an adaptation of the technique, algorithms G and H are extensions. In these algorithms successive substitutions among the endogenous variables are applied on the $P(b)$ matrix until one variable becomes dependent on itself. In the $P(b)$ matrix this is manifested by $P(b)_{ii}$ being different from zero. For this index forward allocation is applied.

The forward allocation of Step 2 is followed by the arithmetic of Step 1. The algorithm switches between Steps 1 and 2 until the ordering vector is complete.

The orderings produced by different algorithms may sometimes coincide, sometimes differ substantially. None of the ordering algorithms is *a priori* expected to produce an ordering which is superior to the orderings produced by the other algorithms. Empirical investigations have shown, on the other hand, that algorithms G and H seem to produce orderings which are somewhat better, according to the iterative evaluation, than the other orderings. This is however a rule with exceptions.

Comment: All ordering algorithms are able to find the causal ordering of a recursive system and the optimal ordering of the one-loop model described in Section 10.1 of Chapter 2.

5. Case Studies

In three different case studies reorderings of interdependent systems and applications of the reordering algorithms will be examined.

5.1. An Extensive Analysis of a Small ID System

In Section 10.3 of Chapter 2 a small ID system in seven relations referred to as the US I model was analysed with respect to some convergence properties of the RFP method. In this section we will give results of a more complete analysis of all possible orderings of this model and of additional convergence characteristics.

The B matrix of this model is written as

$$B = \begin{pmatrix} 0 & 0 & 0 & 0 & b_{15} & 0 & 0 \\ 0 & 0 & 0 & 0 & 0 & b_{26} & 0 \\ 0 & 0 & 0 & 0 & 0 & b_{36} & 0 \\ 0 & 0 & 0 & 0 & 0 & 0 & b_{47} \\ 0 & 0 & 0 & -1 & 0 & 1 & 0 \\ 1 & 1 & 0 & 0 & 0 & 0 & 0 \\ 0 & 0 & -1 & 1 & 1 & 0 & 0 \end{pmatrix}. \tag{5.1}$$

The seven relations of the model can be reordered in $n! = 5040$ different ways. All these orderings have been derived and an analysis of some of the properties of the orderings has been carried through. A few characteristics of the B matrices corresponding to the 5040 orderings are given in Table 1. The table shows classifications of the B matrices according to:

(i) N_F = the number of non-zero coefficients in the F matrix of (4.7) in Chapter 2;

(ii) N_R = the number of rows of the F matrix which possess non-zero coefficients;

(iii) N_c = the number of columns of the F matrix which possess non-zero coefficients;

(iv) N_{CR} = the minimum number of the two criteria in (ii) and (iii).

TABLE 1
Distribution of 5040 reorderings of the US I model with regard to four classification criteria.[a]

	Numerical value of the criterion								
	1	2	3	4	5	6	7	8	9
(i) N_F	0	0	140	630	1750	1750	630	140	0
(ii) N_R	0	129	1134	2166	1410	201	0	0	0
(iii) N_C	0	148	1118	2114	1486	174	0	0	0
(iv) N_{CR}	0	277	2005	2344	412	2	0	0	0

[a] The classification criteria are specified in the text above.

In Section 4 it was argued that the general principles for the selection of orderings for optimal RFP estimation state that those orderings should be selected which have a minimum value of the number of rows and/or columns in the F matrix which possesses non-zero entries. For this model 277 orderings out of the 5040 different orderings obtain the minimum value of criterion (iv) of 2. The actual orderings produced by the eight ordering algorithms are presented in Table 2. Of these five different orderings four belong to the 277 potentially optimal orderings according to criterion (iv). The first ordering produced by algorithm A has the value 3 defined by criterion (iv).

In this small model it is possible to enter deeply into the analysis of the different orderings. It has earlier been stated that $(n-1)!$ different orderings may effect the convergence properties of RFP. In practice this means that the first relation need not take part in the reordering process whereas relations 2 to n do. In this model all 720 permutations of relations 2 to 7 have been analysed with respect to the characteristic equation of $L(1.0, v)$. It has been found that many of these permutations yield the same equation, and in all only 12 different characteristic equations have been found.[3] The analysis showed that the 12 equations were distributed as shown in Table 3. The mathematical analysis of the 12 equations showed that their general formula can be written as

TABLE 2
Ordering vectors produced by the ordering algorithms of Figure 1.

Algorithm	Ordering vector
A	4, 1, 2, 6, 5, 3, 7
B–E	6, 2, 3, 4, 5, 7, 1
F	2, 3, 4, 5, 1, 6, 7
G	2, 3, 4, 5, 1, 7, 6
H	2, 3, 4, 5, 7, 1, 6

TABLE 3
The US I model: Distribution of 720 orderings with respect to the 12 different characteristic equations of $L(1.0, v)$.

	Equation											
	1	2	3	4	5	6	7	8	9	10	11	12
Orderings	132	66	132	66	108	24	108	24	24	24	6	6

[3] We expect this result not to be restricted to just this model, that is, different orderings may often given identical characteristic equations, however the number 12 may be specific for this model.

$$(1-\alpha-\lambda)\{(1-\alpha-\lambda)^6-(1-\alpha-\lambda)^4(b_{26}+b_{47})\alpha^2\lambda$$
$$+(1-\alpha-\lambda)^3(b_{15}\lambda^a-b_{47}\lambda^b)\alpha^3+(1-\alpha-\lambda)^2b_{26}b_{47}\alpha^4\lambda^2$$
$$-(1-\alpha-\lambda)(b_{15}b_{47}\lambda^c-b_{26}b_{47}\lambda^d)\alpha^5-b_{15}b_{36}b_{47}\alpha^6\lambda^e\}=0. \tag{5.2}$$

The exponential parameters *a, b, c, d* and *e* of (5.2) assume the values given in Table 4, in the 12 characteristic equations.

In the next step of the analysis the convergence properties of the 12 equations were analysed, that is, the spectral radii of the 12 different versions of $L(\alpha, v)$. In this analysis the characteristic equations of the iteration matrices $K(\alpha)$ and $R(\alpha)$ of the FFP and SFP methods were included. These equations are, respectively,

$$K(\alpha):\quad (1-\alpha-\lambda)[(1-\alpha-\lambda)^6-(1-\alpha-\lambda)^4(b_{26}+b_{47})\alpha^2$$
$$+(1-\alpha-\lambda)^3(b_{15}-b_{47})\alpha^3+(1-\alpha-\lambda)^2b_{26}b_{47}\alpha^4$$
$$-(1-\alpha-\lambda)(b_{15}b_{47}-b_{26}b_{47})\alpha^5-b_{15}b_{36}b_{47}\alpha^6]=0, \tag{5.3}$$

$$R(\alpha):\quad (1-\alpha-\lambda)^4[(1-\alpha-\lambda)^3-(1-\alpha-\lambda)^2(b_{15}+b_{26})(1-\lambda)$$
$$+(1-\alpha-\lambda)b_{15}b_{47}(1-\lambda)^2-b_{15}b_{36}b_{47}(1-\lambda)^3]=0. \tag{5.4}$$

TABLE 4
Numerical values of the exponential parameters *a* − *e* of (5.2).

Equation	Parameters				
	a	*b*	*c*	*d*	*e*
1	1	2	2	3	3
2	2	2	3	3	3
3	2	1	3	2	3
4	1	1	2	2	3
5	1	1	2	2	2
6	2	1	3	2	2
7	2	2	3	3	4
8	1	2	2	3	4
9	1	2	2	3	2
10	2	1	3	2	2
11	1	1	2	2	1
12	2	2	3	3	5

Using the numerical values of the B parameters given by the RFP estimation, $b_{15} = 0.370$, $b_{26} = 0.175$, $b_{36} = 0.461$ and $b_{47} = 0.328$, an evaluation of (5.2), (5.3) and (5.4) was performed. The main results concerning spectral radii and optimal α are given in Table 5.

In this model $\rho(L(\alpha_{opt}, v)) < \rho(K(\alpha_{opt}))$ for all the 12 different equations of $L(\alpha, v)$. On the other hand $\rho(L(\alpha_{opt}, v)) < \rho(R(\alpha_{opt}))$ for only 3 of the 12 equations. The choice of ordering is thus of great importance should RFP perform better than SFP in this model. It is therefore important to note that all orderings produced by the algorithms A–H correspond to equation number seven, that is, the optimal class of orderings. Hence the use of RFP combined with the use of any of the ordering algorithms is expected to result in optimal Fix-Point estimation of this model.

We note that the actual estimation results, given in Table 6 in Chapter 2, somewhat contradict this conclusion. It was found that SFP converged in 17 iterations, whereas RFP converged in 19 iterations. Two explanations are plausible: (i) the approximate convergence criteria may sometimes differ exceptionally much from the exact convergence criteria, and (ii) optimal RFP estimation requires a more accurately specified value of α than the one used here. As observed in Table 7 of Chapter 2, RFP is more sensitive than the other methods with respect to the accuracy of α.

Another conclusion of the analysis of this model concerns the superiority of the ordering with the lowest order of the characteristic equation of $L(\alpha, v)$. The statement may be extended to include the FFP and SFP methods as well. FFP with the slowest convergence has the highest order, whereas SFP has a low order.

TABLE 5
Convergence characteristics of the FFP, SFP and RFP methods for the US I model.

Method		$\rho(A(1.0))$	α_{opt}	$\rho(A(\alpha_{opt}))$	Order of the char. eq. of $A(1.0)$
FFP		0.7929	0.956	0.7146	6
SFP		1.0788	0.687	0.4280	3
RFP	1	0.6090	0.999	0.6076	3
	2	0.5189	1.081	0.4355	3
	3	0.5689	0.890	0.5398	3
	4	0.4213	1.080	0.2836	3
	5	0.5761	1.040	0.5426	4
	6	0.6796	0.868	0.6164	4
	7	0.3665	1.080	<u>0.1846</u>	2
	8	0.6927	0.962	0.5729	3
	9	0.7210	0.980	0.6642	4
	10	0.5735	0.871	0.5360	3
	11	0.6465	1.051	0.6235	5
	12	0.3484	1.069	0.2996	2

5.2. The Structure of the Wharton EFU Model

The Wharton EFU model has been analysed with respect to (i) the decomposition into blocks of equations and the creation of a block-triangular structure of the B matrix, and (ii) reorderings between and within the blocks created under (i). In this study no convergence analysis has been performed since the Fix-Point estimates are not at our disposal due to lack of data.

The model specification has been taken from Evans (1969). In our analysis minor modifications have been introduced in order to assure that each endogenous variable appears once and only once as a left-hand variable in the structural form.[4]

With reference to the principal design of the ordering process given in Figure 1 the ordering analysis of the Wharton EFU model can be described in five different steps.

Step 1. The $P(b)$ matrix of the model was derived. In the present specification the first p rows of $P(b)$ refer to the behavioural relations of the model, the remaining $n-p$ rows to the identities. In this model $p = 47$ and $n-p = 35$. The total number of non-zero coefficients of $P(b)$ is 185 of which 69 correspond to the coefficients of the original F matrix. These 69 coefficients were distributed in the F matrix in 41 rows and 37 columns.

Step 2. The model was analysed with respect to the block-triangularity of the B matrix. The algorithm of Section 3 showed that 6 different blocks of equations and variables could be recognized.

Step 3. The model was decomposed into the six blocks derived in the preceding step. A position matrix $P_B(b)$ showing the interrelations between the blocks was specified as the following matrix:

$$P_B(b) = \begin{bmatrix} 0 & 0 & 0 & 0 & 0 & 0 \\ 1 & 0 & 0 & 0 & 0 & 0 \\ 1 & 0 & 0 & 0 & 0 & 0 \\ 1 & 1 & 1 & 0 & 0 & 0 \\ 1 & 0 & 1 & 1 & 0 & 0 \\ 1 & 1 & 1 & 1 & 1 & 0 \end{bmatrix}. \tag{5.5}$$

[4] At present the ordering algorithms require that each endogenous variable appears once and only once as a left-hand variable in the structural form. In order to analyse relations that are basically symmetric, e.g. identities, we must formulate them asymmetrically. Modifications of the ordering algorithms are however being tested. These modifications allow for some relations to be specified symmetrically.

It is immediately seen that in this decomposition the model has a blocktriangular structure. The ordering between the blocks is given by (5.5).

Step 4. For each one of the six blocks the ordering within the block itself was analysed with all of the ordering algorithms A–H.

Step 5. By a synthesis of the preceding steps two $P(b)$ matrices were outlined. Figure 2 shows the $P(b)$ matrix of the original ordering of the

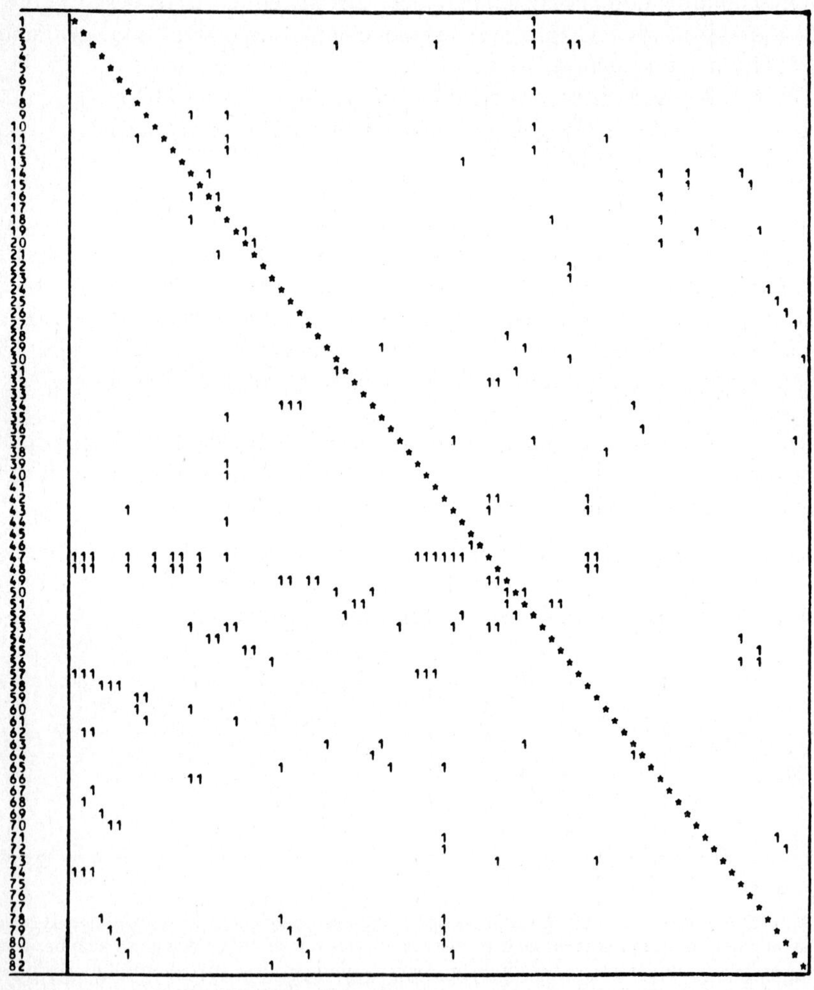

FIGURE 2. The position matrix $P(b)$ of the original ordering of the Wharton EFU model.

model. Figure 3 shows the complete result of the ordering process, where algorithm H has been used to produce the ordering within the blocks.

In summary the reordered model shows a B matrix with only 14 non-zero coefficients of the corresponding F matrix, that is, 14 coefficients above the main diagonal of the B matrix. These 14 coefficients are distributed in 13 rows and 10 columns of the F matrix. Furthermore the B matrix has been partitioned into 36 submatrices B_{ij} of which all matrices

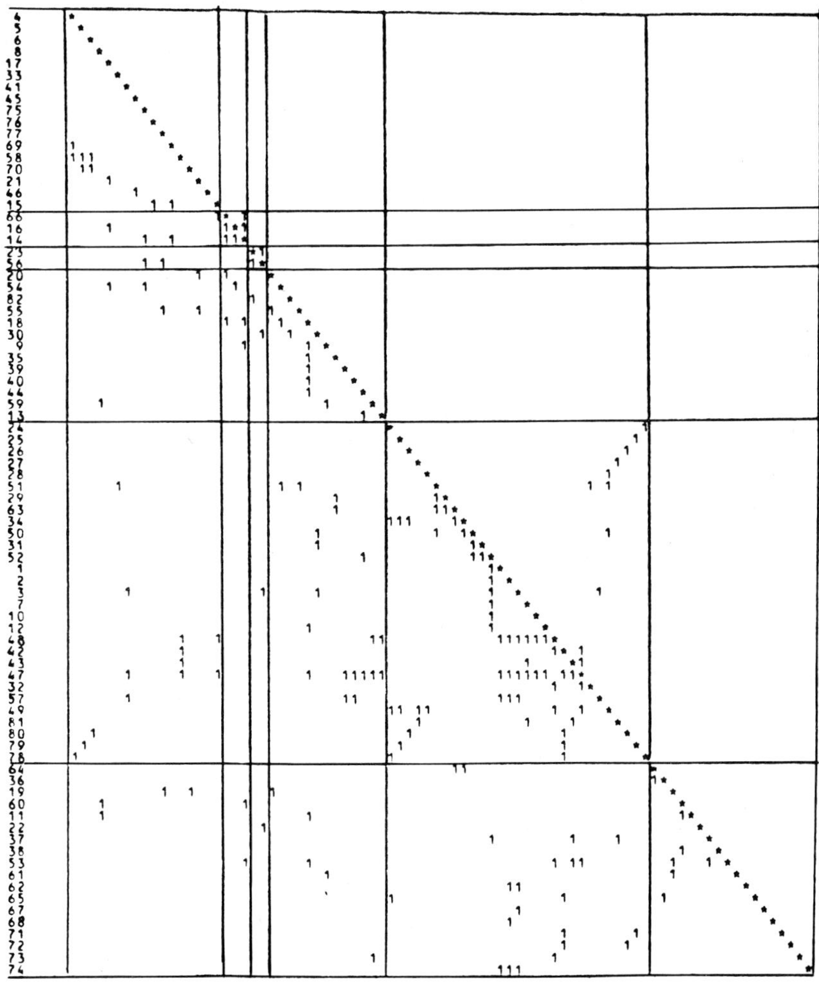

FIGURE 3. The position matrix $P(b)$ of the reordered version of the Wharton EFU model; the ordering given by algorithm H.

where $j > i$ are zero matrices. The submatrices B_{32} and B_{52} are equal to zero matrices of order 2×3 and 29×3, respectively.

The partitioned and decomposed model is now in a form suitable for RFP estimation. The estimation may proceed block-wise, thus ensuring that the actual dimension of the estimational work is set by the actual block-size, not by the dimension of the whole model. When convergence is obtained in one block the estimation proceeds with the next block to come, using the estimates of the preceding blocks.

Analysis of the model on the basis of the reordered version may continue with analysis of the causal ordering of the model, and analysis of the degree of interdependence in the whole system. Other developments may utilize the partitioning in order to specify the system into a block-recursive form and explicitly incorporate the block-recursive specification in the estimation procedure.

5.3. Reorderings of Models of National and Regional Economies

The third case study deals with a comparison of the results of the ordering algorithms in the eight models of national and regional economies introduced in Section 10.3 of Chapter 2. Two criteria have been used in the evaluation of the orderings, that is the minimum values of N_F and N_{CR} according to the definitions given in Section 5.1 of this chapter.

These two criteria do not explicitly relate to the convergence analysis and the iterative performance. It has been shown, however, in Section 5.1 and by extensive empirical investigations that a strong connection exists between the two criteria on the one hand and optimal iterative performance on the other. As an example the RFP estimations analysed in Section 10.3 of Chapter 2 are all based on orderings which show minimum values of N_F and N_{CR} and minimum values of *NOIT*, the number of iterations necessary for convergence. The results given by Bodin (1974) indicate a strong positive correlation between N_{CR} and *NOIT* when different orderings are tested in RFP estimation of one and the same model.

In Table 6 some of the comparisons are summarized. In these eight models the two algorithms G and H showed somewhat better results according to the defined criteria. Our experience with applications of the ordering algorithms in actual RFP estimations shows that these two algorithms tend to produce the best orderings.

An additional conclusion concerns the great reduction in N_F and N_{CR} accomplished by all of the ordering algorithms. The reduction is greater the larger the model. The gain in reordering seems to be greater in the larger models.

TABLE 6
Comparisons of the ordering algorithms A–H in eight models of national and regional economies.[a]

Model	Best algorithms, criterion min N_F	min N_F	Best algorithms, criterion min N_{CR}	min N_{CR}	Criterion values original ordering N_F	N_{CR}
US I	A–E	3	B–H	2	5	3
US II	A–H	2	F–H	1	4	3
Greece	A, C–H	3	C–H	2	10	6
US III	A	5	B–H	4	14	10
Taiwan	B–E	5	B–E, G, H	2	21	7
Ohio	F	1	F–H	1	17	11
Czechoslovakia	C–F	7	B–H	6	34	19
Puerto Rico	G, H	3	G, H	1	26	15

[a] The criterion values N_F and N_{CR} are defined in Section 5.1 of this chapter.

Comment: A complete reordering, using any of the algorithms A–H, applied on a model of size 30–50 relations takes about 1 second CPU-time on the IBM 370/155 of the University Computer Centre, Uppsala, Sweden. Computer programs are available at nominal charge to cover costs from The Department of Data Analysis, University of Örebro, P.O. Box 923, S-701 30 Örebro, Sweden.

Chapter 9

AN ANALYSIS OF THE NONLINEAR KLEIN–GOLDBERGER MODEL USING FIX-POINT ESTIMATION AND OTHER METHODS

DAVID EDGERTON

1. Introduction

Whilst economists have been building nonlinear models for a great many years, it is only in the past decade that econometricians have begun to study in any detail the problems concerned with estimation and prediction in nonlinear interdependent (ID) systems. There now exists a fair amount of material on the theoretical problems concerned with such systems, but reports on the empirical application of the various methods suggested are very scarce. One of the few papers of any length which take up the estimation of an empirical model is that due to Klein (1969), where a nonlinear version of Klein–Goldberger's model was estimated using FIML, OLS and various versions of TSLS.

In this article the author shows how the methods, developed in his thesis [Edgerton (1973c)] and a series of other research reports, can be applied to the Klein–Goldberger model. This model was chosen in the hope that the FP and IIV methods which we present here could be compared with the Classical methods given by Klein.

In the next section we give a brief description of the classical specification (CLID) of a nonlinear ID system, and show how Wold's reformulation principle can be applied to yield REID and GEID systems. In contrast to the CLID system these specifications yield unbiased predictors. In this section we also take up various estimation techniques, especially the GEID and IIV estimators and the iterative methods used to obtain these estimates (the FP and IIV methods).

In Section 3 we describe the nonlinear Klein–Goldberger model and give a brief account of other investigations of this model and its linear predecessors. A description of the REID and GEID versions of the model is also given. In Section 4 the results of the investigation are given. Special attention is paid to parameter estimation, prediction inside and outside the sampling period, and to the convergence of the various iterative methods. Finally various conclusions are given, and the good results yielded by the FP method are stressed.

2. Nonlinear Interdependent Systems

2.1. *The Classic Specification* (*CLID*)

Consider a system of nonlinear stochastic equations which has n endogenous variables (denoted by the column vector y_t) and m predetermined variables (z_t) connected by n behavioural equations. If the error terms δ_t occur in an additive manner, the system can be written in the *structural form* (SF)

$$y_{it} = f_i(y_t, z_t; \theta_i) + \delta_{it}, \qquad i = 1, \cdots, n, \quad t = 1, \cdots, T, \tag{2.1}$$

where θ_i is a row vector of unknown parameters. If we now attempt to obtain the *reduced form* (RF) by solving (2.1) for the endogenous variables, it is clear that in general multiple (let us say K) solutions can occur, which we denote

$$y_{it} = h_{(k)i}(z_t, \delta_t; \Theta), \qquad k = 1, \cdots, K, \tag{2.2}$$

where some or all of these may be non-analytic.

Now, it is clear that at any one time only one set of endogenous variables can actually be observed, that is only one of the solutions (2.2) can be the *true* reduced form. To avoid problems with identification, we will assume that the model definition states which of the RF's is the true one.[1] The problem of choice of reduced form thus becomes a choice between models, and Edgerton (1973c) has shown that a consistent decision process is to take the solution which maximises ΣR^2 for the FP estimates. In practice problems with multiple solutions have not occurred.

The main reason we are interested in the reduced form is that we wish to be able to obtain predictions of the endogenous variables for given values of the predetermined variables. By analogy with linear systems this is done by setting the error terms equal to zero in the true RF, which we denote in what follows as $h_i(.)$. This RF is, however, a nonlinear function of δ_t, and since the expectation operator is only invariant under linear transformations we have in general

$$E(y_{it} \mid z_t) \neq h_i(z_t, 0; \Theta), \tag{2.3}$$

that is, we do not obtain *unbiased predictors*.

We are here interested in models which only contain nonlinearities in the variables. Such systems have a SF that can be written

[1] Goldfeld and Quandt (1972) use a similar definition.

$$y_{it} = \sum_{j \neq i}^{n} \beta_{ij} y_{jt} + \sum_{j=1}^{p} \beta_{ij}^{F} g_j(y_t, z_t) + \sum_{j=1}^{m} \gamma_{ij} z_{jt} + \delta_{it}, \tag{2.4}$$

where $g_j(y_t, z_t)$ are functions that contain no unknown parameters, there being p such functions in the system. The matrix Θ has been decomposed into $(\beta \; \beta^F \; \Gamma)$ associated with the endogenous variables, functions and predetermined variables respectively.

For the sake of brevity we introduce the notation

$$y_{jt}^{F} = g_j(y_t, z_t), \qquad j = 1, \cdots, p, \quad t = 1, \cdots, T, \tag{2.5}$$

and writing (2.4) in vector form we obtain

$$y_t = \beta y_t + \beta^F y_t^F + \Gamma z_t + \delta_t. \tag{2.6}$$

An alternative way of writing the system which sometimes proves useful is to transform (2.6) into a set of n linear behavioural relations and p nonlinear identities [see Christ (1966, p. 115)]. We do this by the simple device of defining p new endogenous variables

$$_{P}y_t = y_t^F. \tag{2.7}$$

Defining $\tilde{y}_t' = (y_t' \; _{P}y_t')$ and $\tilde{\beta} = (\beta \; \beta^F)$ then we can rewrite the SF as

$$y_t = \tilde{\beta} \tilde{y}_t + \Gamma z_t + \delta_t, \tag{2.8a}$$

$$_{P}y_t = y_t^F. \tag{2.8b}$$

The system (2.8) is sometimes called the *pseudo-linearized SF.*

The Classical methods of estimation and prediction in nonlinear systems are either (i) to take the first-order Taylor expansion of the SF (2.4), or (ii) to estimate (2.4) directly but make predictions using $h_i(Z_t, 0; \Theta)$. Since the right-hand side of (2.3) can be interpreted as a Taylor series approximation of the left-hand side, we can see that both Classical methods are based on expansions, and neither yield unbiased predictors.

2.2. Reformulated (REID) and General (GEID) Systems

To obtain a system which yields unbiased predictors we can use Wold's reformulation principle, see Mosbaek and Wold et al. (1970) where further references can be found. Here we define the conditional predictor

$$\eta_t^* = E(y_t \mid z_t), \tag{2.9}$$

and introduce the notation

$$y_t = \eta_t^* + \varepsilon_t. \tag{2.10}$$

Equation (2.10) defines the error term ε_t, which has the property $E(\varepsilon_t \mid z_t) = 0$. If we make the classical assumption that $E(\delta_t \mid z_t) = 0$, we can take conditional expectations on both sides of (2.6), and obtain

$$\eta_t^* = \beta\eta_t^* + \beta^F E(y_t^F \mid z_t) + \Gamma z_t. \tag{2.11}$$

What is required, therefore, is an expression for the expectation in (2.11), and this we get by taking a Taylor expansion *around* η_t^*.[2]

Consider an element of $E(y_t^F \mid z_t)$, that is $E(g_j(y_t, z_t) \mid z_t)$. Using (2.10) and the Taylor expansion we obtain

$$E(g_j(y_t, z_t) \mid z_t) = g_j(\eta_t^*, z_t) + \sum_{r=2}^{\infty} \sum_{\mu_r} \left(E\left(\prod_{k=1}^{n} (\varepsilon_{kt})^{r_k} \mid z_t \right) \Big/ \prod_{k=1}^{n} r_k! \right) \times \Delta_j(r_1, \cdots, r_n, \eta_t^*), \tag{2.12}$$

where

$$\mu_r = (r_1, \cdots, r_n; r_1 + \cdots + r_n = r),$$

and

$$\Delta_j(r_1, \cdots, r_n, \eta_t^*) = \left(\frac{\partial^r g_j(y_t, z_t)}{\partial y_{1t}^{r_1} \cdots \partial y_{nt}^{r_n}} \right)_{y_t = \eta_t^*}.$$

Note that the summation in (2.12) begins at $r = 2$, since $E(\varepsilon_t \mid z_t) = 0$ a priori.

Now the partial derivatives Δ are known functions of η_t^* and z_t which we shall denote as $\eta_t^{S*} = g^S(\eta_t^*, z_t)$, and if we let $\eta_t^{F*} = g(\eta_t^*, z_t)$, we can express (2.12) as

$$E(y_t^F \mid z_t) = \eta_t^{F*} + \beta^C \eta_t^{S*}, \tag{2.13}$$

where the β^C are linear combinations of the moments of ε_t (which are assumed constant for all t and z_t). We can therefore write (2.11) as

[2] In the Classic approach any expansions are around $E(y_t)$ or $\bar{y}$.

$$\eta_t^* = \beta\eta_t^* + \beta^F\eta_t^{F*} + \beta^S\eta_t^{S*} + \Gamma z_t, \tag{2.14}$$

where $\beta^S = \beta^F\beta^C$. Using (2.10) we can rewrite this as

$$y_t = \beta\eta_t^* + \beta^F\eta_t^{F*} + \beta^S\eta_t^{S*} + \Gamma z_t + \varepsilon_t, \tag{2.15}$$

which is known as the *reformulated (REID) structural form.*

Equation (2.15) is clearly a generalisation of the result for linear systems [Mosbaek and Wold et al. (1970), Lyttkens (1973a)].

If we now define

$$_P\eta_t^* = E(y_t^F \mid z_t) = \eta_t^{F*} + \beta^C\eta_t^{S*}, \tag{2.16}$$

then we can write the pseudo-linearized REID SF as

$$y_t = \tilde{\beta}\tilde{\eta}_t^* + \Gamma z_t + \varepsilon_t, \tag{2.17a}$$

$$_Py_t = \eta_t^{F*} + \beta^C\eta_t^{S*} + {}_P\varepsilon_t, \tag{2.17b}$$

where $\tilde{\eta}_t^{*\prime} = (\eta_t^{*\prime}\ {}_P\eta_t^{*\prime})$ and $_P\varepsilon_t = {}_Py_t - {}_P\eta_t^*$. Note that nonlinear identities of the CLID SF now include parameters to be estimated in the REID SF.

Whilst some forms of nonlinearities (e.g. polynomial functions) have Taylor expansions which contain only a finite number of terms, in general the exact REID SF (2.15) may contain an infinite series. In practice this means that we must *truncate* the Taylor expansion (2.12) after, say, S terms, and use this truncated series as an approximation. One of the differences between the REID system and the Classic methods, however, is that now we can use as many terms of the Taylor series as desired.

Predictions using the REID system are found by solving (2.14) for η_t^*. We can observe that this equation can be rewritten

$$\begin{aligned}\eta_t^* &= f(\eta_t^*, z_t; \theta) + \beta^S\eta_t^{S*}\\ &= \phi(\eta_t^*, z_t; \theta^*) \quad \text{say,}\end{aligned} \tag{2.18}$$

where θ^* is the expanded matrix $(\beta\ \beta^F\ \beta^S\ \Gamma)$. Equation (2.18) is solved to yield the unbiased predictor

$$\eta_t^* = \psi(z_t; \theta^*), \tag{2.19}$$

and the REID RF is thus

$$y_t = \psi(z_t; \theta^*) + \varepsilon_t. \tag{2.20}$$

Now, the zero correlation assumptions implied by the REID specification can be greatly in excess of the number of parameters to be estimated. Wold [see for example Ågren and Wold (1969)] has proposed a *General* (GEID) specification which obeys the parity principle. To use GEID in nonlinear systems we define the expanded vector $\xi'_t = (\eta_t^{*\prime}\ \eta_t^{F*\prime}\ \eta_t^{S*\prime}\ z'_t)$ and let $\xi_{(i)t}$ be the vector of terms actually present in the ith equation of (2.15). We can also define $\theta^*_{(i)}$, which is the ith row of θ^* excluding a priori zero terms, and write the reformulated SF as

$$y_{it} = \theta^*_{(i)}\xi_{(i)t} + \varepsilon_{it}, \qquad i = 1, \cdots, n. \tag{2.21}$$

In the GEID specification we now assume that $E(\varepsilon_{it} \mid \xi_{(i)t}) = 0$, that is we define the ith element of η_t^* as

$$\eta^*_{it} = E(y_{it} \mid \xi_{(i)t}), \qquad i = 1, \cdots, n. \tag{2.22}$$

The SF and RF of the GEID system will now be identical to that of the REID system except that the conditions in the expectations in the Taylor expansion (2.12) will now be $\xi_{(i)t}$ instead of z_t, and the expansion will now begin at $k = 1$ since $E(\varepsilon_{jt} \mid \xi_{(i)t}) \neq 0$.

If we wish to use a GEID specification in the pseudo-linearized SF then we can define

$$\eta^*_{it} = E(y_{it} \mid \tilde{\xi}_{(i)t}), \qquad i = 1, \cdots, n, \tag{2.23a}$$

$${}_P\eta^*_{it} = E({}_Py_{it} \mid \eta^{F*}_{it}, \eta^{S*}_{[i]t}), \qquad i = 1, \cdots, p, \tag{2.23b}$$

where $\tilde{\xi}'_t = (\tilde{\eta}_t^{*\prime}\ z'_t)$ and $\eta^{S*}_{[i]t}$ is those elements of η_t^{S*} present in the ith equation of (2.17b). This definition of the pseudo-linearized GEID SF avoids the difficulties with ambiguities mentioned in Edgerton (1973c, pp. 72–73).

2.3. *Classical Estimation Methods*

The Classical methods we shall consider in this article are those which are based on direct estimation of (2.6). The aim of these methods is to obtain consistent estimates C of θ, and then use these estimates to get predictors $h_i(z_t, 0; C)$. These predictors consistently estimate $h_i(z_t, 0; \theta)$ but not $E(y_{it} \mid z_t)$; see (2.3).

The simplest Classical method is Ordinary Least Squares (OLS), which is not consistent. The most commonly used consistent method for linear systems is the Two-Stage Least Squares (TSLS) method. For nonlinear systems we build $\tilde{Y} = (Y\ Y^F)$ and take the regression of $\tilde{Y}$ on Z. In the second stage, predictors $\hat{\tilde{Y}}$ of $\tilde{Y}$ are formed from the first regression, and used in a regression of y_i on $\hat{\tilde{Y}}_{(i)}$ and $Z_{(i)}$.[3] This method is consistent [see Edgerton (1972)], but difficulties occur in the first stage if the number of observations T is not somewhat larger than the number of predetermined variables m. One of the most common approaches in the above situation is to use a small number of principal components of Z in the first stage. A number of varieties of this approach are possible [see for example Hirvonen (1975)], and in Section 3 we shall take up the methods used in our study. Note that these principal component methods are small sample methods, for large samples T must be considerably larger than m and ordinary TSLS can be used. Discussions concerning consistency are therefore irrelevant.

Various other classical methods are also applicable. Klein (1969) takes up the use of Full Information Maximum Likelihood (FIML) in considerable detail, and a number of other methods are briefly dealt with in Edgerton (1973c). Our main interest here, however, is centered on the estimators to be taken up in what follows.

2.4. The GEID Estimator and Fix-Point (FP) Iterative Method

Wold (1965) proposed a new method for estimating ID systems, the Fix-Point method. This method, however, is iterative and therefore might not converge, or converge to different solutions depending on the starting values. Ågren (1972a, 1975) defined the GEID estimator, which is a set of nonlinear equations that can be solved using the FP method. Using this definition he showed that for linear models the GEID estimator yields a set of roots, one of which belongs to a sequence that converges in probability to the true parameter values as $T \to \infty$. In Edgerton (1973c) we can find a definition of the GEID estimator for nonlinear ID systems. For the REID/GEID SF (2.15) we define the GEID estimator as the real solutions of the set of equations

$$c^*_{(i)} = y_i X'_{(i)} (X_{(i)} X'_{(i)})^{-1}, \qquad i = 1, \cdots, n, \tag{2.24a}$$

$$y^*_t = \psi(z_t; C^*), \tag{2.24b}$$

$$y^{F*}_t = g(y^*_t, z_t), \tag{2.24c}$$

$$y^{S*}_t = g^S(y^*_t, z_t), \qquad t = 1, \cdots, T. \tag{2.24d}$$

[3] $Y_{(i)}$ and $Z_{(i)}$ are those variables actually present in the ith equation of (2.6).

where $X' = (Y^{*\prime}\ Y^{F*\prime}\ Y^{S*\prime}\ Z')$ is the estimate of ξ', and $C^* = (\beta\ \beta^F\ \beta^S\ G)$ is the estimate of Θ^*. In system (2.24) we use the notation $X_{(i)}$ to indicate that only those variables actually present in the ith equation are used; $c^*_{(i)}$ is the ith row of C^* excluding those terms a priori equal to zero.

If we eliminate (2.24b–d) from (2.24a) we obtain a system of equations that is nonlinear in C, and we can therefore obtain multiple solutions. The ΣR^2 criterion can be used to distinguish between the different solutions,[4] but in fact problems with multiple solutions have not occurred. The asymptotic properties of the GEID estimator are discussed at length in Edgerton (1973c), here we shall merely point out the following results:

(1) If there are only a finite number of terms in (2.15) then under weak regularity conditions, there exists a root of (2.24) that is consistent and asymptotically normal.

(2) If we have used a truncated system containing S terms, then there exists a root of (2.24), denoted C^*_S, such that

$$\operatorname*{plim}_{T\to\infty} C^*_S = \bar{\Theta}^*_S \quad \text{and} \quad \lim_{S\to\infty} \| \bar{\Theta}^*_S - \Theta^*_S \| = 0,$$

where Θ^*_S denotes the subset of Θ^* present when we use S terms of the Taylor expansion; C^*_S is also asymptotically normal.

(3) The asymptotic standard error of the parameters is a complicated expression [see Edgerton (1973a, 1973c)], but a reasonable approximation can be obtained from

$$s(c^*_{(i)j}) \approx s^*_i [(X_{(i)} X'_{(i)})^{-1}]^{1/2}_{jj}, \tag{2.25}$$

where s^*_i is residual standard error from the ith REID/GEID SF equation.

The GEID estimator for the pseudo-linearized SF of a REID or GEID system is defined as the real solutions of

$$c_{(i)} = y_i \tilde{X}'_{(i)} (\tilde{X}_{(i)} \tilde{X}'_{(i)})^{-1}, \qquad i = 1, \cdots, n, \tag{2.26a}$$

$$b^C_{[j]} = ({}_PY_j - y^{F*}_j) Y^{S*\prime}_{[j]} (Y^{S*}_{[j]} Y^{S*\prime}_{[j]})^{-1}, \qquad j = 1, \cdots, p, \tag{2.26b}$$

$${}_Py^*_t = y^{F*}_t + B^C y^{S*}_t, \qquad t = 1, \cdots, T, \tag{2.26c}$$

[4] $R^2_i = 1 - k \cdot \Sigma (y_{it} - y^*_{it})^2 \cdot [\Sigma (y_{it} - \bar{y}_i)^2]^{-1}$, where k is either one or some suitable correction for degrees of freedom. The maximum ΣR^2 criterion works independently of the choice of k.

together with (2.24b–d); y_i^{S*} is the estimate of η_i^{S*}, and C is the estimate of $\Theta = (\tilde{\beta}\ \Gamma)$.

Asymptotically the two GEID estimators have the same properties, but in small samples they may lead to different estimates. In our empirical studies we have used (2.26), since the pseudo-linearized system is considerably simpler to write down. Eliminating all the identities to form a SF which merely contains behavioural relations leads to many compound variables.

The systems (2.24) and (2.26) are highly nonlinear, and some form of iterative method is required. We shall use Bodin's Recursive Fix-Point (RFP) method, which is a variant of the usual FP method which has improved convergence properties; see Bodin (1970, 1974) and Mosbaek and Wold et al. (1970).

The RFP method for nonlinear systems can be described as follows. Choose initial proxies for Y^*, $Y^{(0)}$ say. For the GEID estimator (2.24) we obtain the $(s+1)$st proxies in two steps:

Step 1. Obtain new parameter proxies from the least squares regression

$$y_{it} = \phi_i(y_{it}^{(s+1)}, \cdots, y_{i-1,t}^{(s+1)}, y_{i+1,t}^{(s)}, \cdots, y_{nt}^{(s)}, z_t; c_{(i)}^{(s+1)}) + e_{it}^{(s+1)}. \tag{2.27}$$

Step 2. Calculate new predictor proxies from

$$y_{it}^{(s+1)} = \alpha(y_{it} - e_{it}^{(s+1)}) + (1-\alpha)y_{it}^{(s)}, \tag{2.28}$$

with α in the range (0,2). For this method we alternate between Step 1 and Step 2 as we work from $i = 1$ to $i = n$. Note that the function ϕ is given by the right-hand side of (2.14), and merely represents the REID SF. Equation (2.27) is thus the regression of y_i on the proxies for Y^*, Y^{F*}, Y^{S*} and Z. Note also that the most common start values are $Y^{(0)} = Y$ (the so-called OLS start) and $Y^{(0)} = YZ'(ZZ')^{-1}Z$ (TSLS start). In the case of undersized samples we would use principal components of Z in the TSLS start. We can also see that the ordering of the variables is very important for RFP, and Bodin (1974) gives various algorithms to obtain good orderings.

For the pseudo-linearized SF we obtain very similar results for RFP. The essential difference is that i varies between 1 and $n+p$, and that the regression (2.27) would be of y_i on the proxies for $\tilde{X}$ for $i = 1, \cdots, n$ and of ${}_Py_i - y_i^{F*}$ on the proxy for Y^{S*} for $i = n+1, \cdots, n+p$. Note that for linear identities we would use merely Step 2, that is form new predictor proxies. This is true for both the GEID estimators.

Iteration of the FP methods is continued until the parameters have converged, a usual criterion being that the relative difference between the parameter values in two successive iterations should be less than Δ for all parameters. We used a value of $\Delta = 10^{-6}$.

As we shall report further on, we had few problems concerning convergence for RFP. The computer program used can be obtained on request from the author; Edgerton (1977).

2.5. *The Iterated Instrumental Variable (IIV) Method*

The IIV method was suggested by Lyttkens [see, for example, Mosbaek and Wold et al. (1970)] and has been investigated by Bergström (1974). A nonlinear version was suggested by Edgerton (1971) but not further developed in later articles. Basically the IIV methods are the same as the FP methods except that new parameter proxies are obtained by using the Y^* terms as instrumental variables instead of as least squares regressors. If we wish to develop an IIV estimator for the nonlinear case we can proceed as follows. Let

$$X'_{1(i)} = (Y'_{(i)}\ Y^{F\prime}_{(i)}\ Z'_{(i)}),$$

and

$$\hat{X}'_{1(i)} = (\hat{Y}^{*\prime}_{(i)}\ \hat{Y}^{F*\prime}_{(i)}\ Z'_{(i)}),$$

then the IIV estimator is defined as the real solutions of

$$c_{(i)} = y_i\hat{X}'_{1(i)}(X_{1(i)}\hat{X}'_{1(i)})^{-1}, \tag{2.29a}$$

$$\hat{y}^*_t = h(z_t, 0; C), \tag{2.29b}$$

$$\hat{y}^{F*}_t = g(y^*_t, z_t). \tag{2.29c}$$

This method is clearly based on the CLID SF, and as explained in Edgerton (1971) it is difficult to see how a GEID specification which yields unbiased predictors could be defined so as to be estimable by IIV. The consistency of the parameter estimates can be established, however, by similar techniques to those in Edgerton (1973c).

The original IIV iterative method solved (2.29) using a technique which inverted the system at every iteration. This is clearly impractical for a nonlinear system, and we shall here describe a variant called RSIIV by Bergström, which is analogous to RFP. This proceeds in two steps:

Step 1. Obtain new parameter proxies using IV on

$$y_{it} = f_i(y_{1t}^{(s+1)}, \cdots, y_{i-1,t}^{(s+1)}, y_{i+1,t}^{(s)}, \cdots, y_{nt}^{(s)}, z_t; c_{(i)}^{(s+1)}) + d_{it}^{(s+1)}. \tag{2.30}$$

Step 2. Calculate new predictor proxies from

$$y_{it}^{(s+1)} = \alpha(y_{it} - d_{it}^{(s+1)}) + (1-\alpha)y_{it}^{(s)}. \tag{2.31}$$

An approximation to the asymptotic standard error can be obtained from

$$s(c_{(i)j}) = s_i[(\hat{X}_{1(i)}X'_{1(i)})^{-1}\hat{X}_{1(i)}\hat{X}'_{1(i)}(X_{1(i)}\hat{X}'_{1(i)})^{-1}]_{jj}^{1/2}, \tag{2.32}$$

where s_i is the residual standard error from the ith equation of the CLID SF.

2.6. *Non-Aligned Systems*

The nonlinear systems we have described so far have all been aligned, that is each endogenous variable has appeared as the left-hand variable in one and only one SF equation. Whilst this is the usual way of writing ID systems it is not the only way, and in fact the Klein–Goldberger model is non-aligned. In two reports [Edgerton (1974, 1975)] the author has taken up various problems in connection with GEID/FP estimation of non-aligned models, and various conditions for applicability have been given. These conditions were presented as necessary and sufficient, and whilst the necessity has been supported by our empirical investigations the sufficiency has to some extent been contradicted. As we shall report later on, no estimation proved possible in the non-aligned model in spite of the above conditions being satisfied.

3. The Nonlinear Klein–Goldberger Model

3.1. *Description of the Model*

The Klein–Goldberger model is a well-known model of the economy of the USA which has been presented in different forms by the above authors over a number of years. The version we shall consider here is that presented in Klein (1969, 1974), which is nonlinear due to the fact that the deflator variable is considered as endogenous. Earlier references to linear versions of the model can be found in the above references.

The model described by Klein consists of 16 behavioural relations, 3 linear identities and 1 nonlinear identity. Many of the variables, however, are of an extremely compound character which makes the formal manipulation of the model rather intricate. We have therefore added a number of variable definitions as identities so as to simplify the presentation of the model; one can see that we are using a pseudo-linearized SF. Altogether our system contains 16 linear behavioural relations, 17 linear identities and 5 nonlinear identities, a total of 38 equations. Furthermore an extra 4 nonlinear identities are used for prediction purposes.

In the Appendix a full definition of the variables is presented, both in the form given by Klein and as y_i, z_j variables. In Table 1 we give the (aligned) system we have used for estimation, which we shall now discuss.

We can see that equations 14–16 merely contain predetermined variables as explanatory variables, and thus OLS is consistent here. If we furthermore assume that the error terms for these equations are independent of the errors in all the other behavioural relations, then the variables y_{14}, y_{15} and y_{16} can themselves be considered predetermined. This in turn would imply that equation 10 contained only predetermined explanatory variables, and under the assumption of independent errors y_{10} could also be considered as predetermined. While both Klein (1969), and more specifically Bergström (1974), make such assumptions, we have not done so since a priori there is no reason to believe that the said errors are independent. The practical difference between the two approaches is that for the above variable we shall use $\hat{y}$ and y^* for the TSLS and FP estimation instead of the y values themselves, and that a slightly different base is used for the first stage of the TSLS calculations.

An interesting equation is equation 6. Klein here makes the model non-aligned by letting the non-government GNP (y_{21}) be explained in terms of the privately employed (y_6), capital stock (y_{22}) and hours worked (y_{23}). Now, the usual Keynesian assumption is that the production function determines the demand for labour given the total demand and the capital stock. It does not seem unreasonable therefore to also consider the aligned system given in Table 1. We shall in fact analyse both models.

A further point is that four variables of interest, π, P_c, S_c and π_r, are not directly included amongst the 38 endogenous variables which define the ID system. This means that predictions for these variables can be obtained after one has inverted the 38 equation ID system. One can also see that these variables are nonlinear functions of the other endogenous variables, and thus the methods described in Section 2.2 can be used to reformulate these identities and so obtain better predictions.

3.2. *Discussion of Other Investigations of the Model*

Klein (1969) gives an extensive report of an investigation of the non-aligned model using FIML, OLS and various versions of TSLS. In that

TABLE 1

CLID SF for the aligned Klein–Goldberger model.

Behavioural relations

	Endogenous variables[a]	Predetermined variables
1	19	1, 3
2	38	1, 4
3	38	1, 5, 6
4	20	1, 7
5	17, 31	1, 8
6	21, 22, 23	1
7	9, 24	1
8	25	1, 16
9	24, 32	1
10	16	1, 5
11	33	1, 18
12	35	1, 20
13	26, 36	1, 21
14		1, 5, 11, 22
15		1, 23, 24
16		1, 24, 25, 26

Linear identities

17	$y_{17} = y_1 + y_2 + y_3 + y_4 - y_5 + y_{14} - z_7 + z_{27}$
18	$y_{18} = -y_{11} - y_{15} + y_{35} - z_{19} - z_{28} - z_{29}$
19	$y_{19} = y_{38} - 0.7z_2$
20	$y_{20} = -y_4 + y_{17} + z_7$
21	$y_{21} = y_{25} - 0.95z_{11}$
22	$y_{22} = y_3 + y_{14}$
23	$y_{23} = y_7 - 0.95z_{13}$
24	$y_{24} = -y_{29} + z_{15}$
25	$y_{25} = y_{17} - z_{10}$
26	$y_{26} = y_{10} - z_5$
27	$y_{27} = y_8 + z_{10}$
28	$y_{28} = y_9 + z_{14}$
29	$y_{29} = y_6 + z_{12}$
30	$y_{30} = -y_{13} - y_{15} + y_{35} - y_{37} - z_{28}$
31	$y_{31} = -y_{34} + z_9$
32	$y_{32} = y_{34} - z_{17}$
33	$y_{33} = -y_{12} + y_{30} - z_{19}$

Nonlinear identities

34	$y_{34} = y_{37}/y_{27}$
35	$y_{35} = y_{17}y_{34}$
36	$y_{36} = y_{22}y_{34}$
37	$y_{37} = y_7y_{28}y_{29}$
38	$y_{38} = y_{18}/y_{34}$

Extra nonlinear identities

39	$y_{39} = y_{30}/y_{34}$
40	$y_{40} = y_{39} - y_{12}/y_{34}$
41	$y_{41} = y_{11}/y_{34}$
42	$y_{42} = y_{13}/y_{34}$

[a] These are the endogenous variables on the right-hand side of the respective equations. The left-hand side endogenous variable is the same as the equation number.

paper a data list is given for the years 1928–1941, 1946–1965. Due to the presence of many lagged variables the number of time periods used is reduced somewhat, and Klein has also used the values for 1965 for prediction purposes. The observation period is thus 1929–1941, 1947–1964, a total of 31 observations.

The total number of predetermined variables in the model is 29, which is only two less than the number of observations. This means that direct TSLS estimation becomes problematical, and Klein has instead replaced the usual first stage with a regression of the endogenous variables on a certain number of principal components of the predetermined variables. This is only one of a number of possible methods of using principal components but for the sake of compatibility we will restrict ourselves to this.

Klein, however, fails to state which base he uses for the principal components, and also whether these are based on the correlation matrix (R) or the covariance matrix (S). In the latter case a knowledge of the scalings of the variables is also necessary. In our calculations we have used the 28 non-constant predetermined variables as base, used both R and S, and for the latter we have used the data given by Klein (using h instead of $100 \times h$, however). In the first stage we have thus regressed on a constant term plus certain numbers of principal components. We have not been able to reproduce Klein's results, however.

A further ambiguity is that Y_{1965} is given as 371.2 in Klein's table IV, but as 374.2 in the Appendix. We have used the latter figure in our evaluation of the predictive power, but since all the predictions given are less than 371, this ambiguity should not be too serious. An exception to this is the FIML prediction given by Klein, but for reasons given below we shall not take up these values to further analysis here.[5]

As a check on the internal consistency of Klein's OLS and FIML results we performed various numerical tests. A duplication of the OLS calculations showed that whilst nearly all the equations yielded identical values (excepting rounding error), the wage rate equation (equation 9) showed quite marked differences. In a private communication Professor Klein has explained that the model is incorrectly given in Klein (1969, 1974), and that the correct explanatory variable should be $p_{-1} - p_{-2}$ instead of $p - p_{-1}$. This communication did not reach the author until the computational results

[5] In a private communication Klein has explained that the 1963 figures have been calculated by himself using certain base period valuations he had available. He is not certain which figure is correct, but thinks that it is 371.2. Note also that the variable denoted as Y by Klein is given as y_{38} in the article (see Appendix, Table A.2), and thus Y_{1965} could in our notation be written as $y_{38,\,1965}$.

presented in this article had already been obtained, and thus the analysis given here is based on the model given in Klein's articles, and is therefore not directly comparable with the results Klein actually obtained.

A further check was performed on the FIML coefficients given by Klein by using them to calculate the residual standard error of each equation, and also the predictions for 1965. As expected we obtained different s_e results for equation 9, but more surprisingly also for equations 5 and 7; for the latter equation a value of 0.092 was obtained instead of 0.043. The predictions we calculated were also quite different from those given by Klein. It seems reasonable to suppose that some signs have been incorrectly given for the FIML coefficients [cf. the constant term in Klein's equations (3.11) and (3.11a)].

For the reasons given above we have not used Klein's results further in our study; all comparisons are thus based on our own computations. Due to the amount of computer time necessary for the calculation of FIML estimates we have not been able to give such results here. We hope, however, that the results given will prove of interest.

3.3. The REID and GEID Specifications Applied to the Klein–Goldberger Model

Looking at Table 1 we can see that equations 1–33 are linear, and can thus be reformulated in the usual way, that is

$$y_{it} = \beta_i \eta_t^* + \gamma_i z_t + \varepsilon_{it}. \tag{3.1}$$

For the behavioural relation 1–16 the coefficients β, γ must be estimated, whilst for linear identities 17–33 they are known and will not be estimated.

Equations 34–42 are nonlinear identities, and contain three different types of nonlinearities: (i) y_1y_2, (ii) $y_1y_2y_3$, and (iii) y_1/y_2. We can use (2.12) directly to obtain the reformulated form of these functions, although it is usually easier in specific cases to use the polynomial of inverse function expansions; see, for example, Edgerton (1973c, pp. 72–80). Using these results we obtain

(i)

$$\text{REID: } E(y_1y_2 \mid Z) = \eta_1^*\eta_2^* + E(\varepsilon_1\varepsilon_2 \mid Z), \tag{3.2a}$$

$$\text{GEID: } E(y_1y_2 \mid \xi_{(i)}) = \eta_1^*\eta_2^* + E(\varepsilon_2 \mid \xi_{(i)}) \cdot \eta_1^* + E(\varepsilon_1 \mid \xi_{(i)}) \cdot \eta_2^* + E(\varepsilon_1\varepsilon_2 \mid \xi_{(i)}), \tag{3.2b}$$

(ii)

$$E(y_1y_2y_3 \,|\, .) = \eta_1^*\eta_2^*\eta_3^* + \sum_{j=k}^{3} \sum_{\substack{a=0 \\ a+b+c=j}}^{1} \sum_{b=0}^{1} \sum_{c=0}^{1} (\eta_1^*)^a(\eta_2^*)^b(\eta_3^*)^c \cdot E(\varepsilon_1^{1-a}\varepsilon_2^{1-b}\varepsilon_3^{1-c} \,|\, .), \tag{3.3}$$

(iii)

$$E(y_1/y_2 \,|\, .) = \eta_1^*/\eta_2^* + \sum_{j=k}^{\infty} (-1)^j [E(\varepsilon_1\varepsilon_2^{j-1} \,|\, .) \cdot (\eta_2^*)^{-j} - E(\varepsilon_2^j \,|\, .) \cdot \eta_1^*(\eta_2^*)^{-j-1}]. \tag{3.4}$$

For (ii) and (iii) we obtain REID from setting $k = 2$ and $. = Z$, whilst GEID comes from setting $k = 1$ and $. = \xi_{(i)}$. For the ratio function (iii) some conditions on either the distribution of y_2 or on the range of inference in the model must be given if the Taylor series in (3.4) is to converge; see Edgerton (1973c, pp. 56, 75, 153–156).

It should be remarked that in all the nonlinear identities some of the y variables are themselves defined in other nonlinear identities. Strictly speaking this means that if the errors in the behavioural relations are stationary, the moments given in (3.2)–(3.4) may not be. Since we do not know which errors are stationary, and since the Monte Carlo study in Edgerton (1973c) indicated that divergence from stationarity had only a minor effect for estimation and prediction, it was decided to ignore this complication in our study.

Note now that when we come to estimate the model using the GEID estimator then the equations 34–38 will be of the form

$$y_{it} = \eta_{i-33,t}^{F*} + \beta_{[i]}^{C*}\eta_{[i]t}^{S*} + \varepsilon_{it}, \tag{3.5}$$

where β^C and η^{S*} are to be estimated. The FP iterations will thus include a regression of $y_i - y_{i-33}^{F*}$ on $Y_{[i]}^{S*}$.

The same sort of regression is needed for equations 39–42, but since these endogenous variables do not occur anywhere else in the model we can wait until the iterations are complete and then use the *known* values of y_i^{F*} and $Y_{[i]}^{S*}$ in a single regression to estimate $\beta_{[i]}^C$.

3.4. The Estimation Methods Used

Of the Classical methods OLS can be used as usual in both the aligned and non-aligned models. For TSLS we used a first-stage comprising of a regression of the first I principal components of S or R. These estimates were denoted TSLS:SI and TSLS:RI, $I = 4, \cdots, 9$, and were obtained for both the aligned and non-aligned models.

As a first approximation FP was applied to the model using *no* Taylor expansions in its formulations. This method was called FP(0), and can be interpreted as FP applied to a model *defined* in terms of η^* instead of y.

For all other methods the complete Taylor expansion was used for the nonlinearities of types (i) and (ii), but for the ratio identities various truncations of the infinite series were used. Setting $k = 1$ (GEID) and $k = 2$ (REID) we used 0, 1, 2 or 3 terms of the expansion (3.4). These methods were called FP:RI and FP:GI for $I = 0, 1, 2, 3$ and also FP:$R0^*$ and FP:$G0^*$.

The results given in this article for FP all refer to the aligned model. Attempts to estimate the non-aligned model using a modified GEID estimator did not prove succesful, as will be reported in the next section. Similarly it did not prove possible to obtain convergence for IIV.

4. Results from the Empirical Investigation

4.1. Applicability of the Different Estimation Methods

As discussed in the previous section, we have used various principal component methods in applying TSLS. We hope, naturally, that a few components will provide sufficient information about the predetermined variables to yield good estimates. In the following tables we give, for each component of the covariance matrix (S) and the correlation matrix (R), (i) the eigenvalue (λ), (ii) the variance explained by the component ($= \lambda / \Sigma \lambda$), (iii) the cumulative variance explained, and (iv) the average R^2_{SF} for TSLS based on the number of components applied to the aligned model. The average R^2_{SF} measures the fit of the whole model to the sampled data,[6] see also Sections 4.2 and 4.3.

It is very difficult to draw any definite conclusions from these tables. A few components evidently explain nearly all the variation, and there seems little reason to use more than the minimum number of components from this point of view. The average R^2_{SF}, however, shows that at least for the S matrix we do gain something by using more components. This is somewhat surprising since it is for S that the most variation is explained by a few components. Since none of the TSLS methods can be unequivically denoted as 'best', we have analysed all components from 4 to 9.

[6] Here we have taken the average for the 20 most important variables given in Klein (1969).

TABLE 2
Principal components using the covariance matrix S.

Component	(i)	(ii)	(iii)	(iv)
1	88840.9	95.88	95.88	
2	3678.9	3.97	99.85	
3	58.3	0.06	99.92	
4	35.9	0.04	99.96	0.8417
5	11.3	0.01	99.97	0.8401
6	7.7	0.01	99.98	0.9052
7	5.9	0.01	99.98	0.9125
8	5.2	0.01	99.99	0.9128
9	3.3	——	99.99	0.9049

TABLE 3
Principal components using the correlation matrix R.

Component	(i)	(ii)	(iii)	(iv)
1	22.94	81.92	81.92	
2	2.43	8.66	90.58	
3	1.66	5.93	96.51	
4	0.37	1.33	97.84	0.9120
5	0.21	0.75	98.60	0.9164
6	0.11	0.38	98.98	0.9024
7	0.07	0.27	99.24	0.9082
8	0.07	0.23	99.48	0.9092
9	0.04	0.16	99.63	0.9054

As mentioned earlier in Section 2.6 we also attempted to estimate the non-aligned system using the variants of GEID/FP given in Edgerton (1974, 1975). In each case the Y^* proxies converged, but in such a way that the $X'X$ matrix in equation 6 was singular. The parameter estimates thus converged for all equations except the sixth, where they grew without bound. At first we thought that it was the presence of the constant term in the sixth equation that caused the trouble (it is due to the constant term that the number of 'normal equations' for the GEID estimator is not sufficient), but even when the model was re-estimated without the constant term in equation 6 the same problem occurred. It is thus evident that either the theorems given in the above papers are necessary but not sufficient, or that we have not applied these theorems correctly to the Klein–Goldberger model.[7] In both cases more research is necessary.

[7] A further possibility is, of course, that the computer program is incorrect. Every effort has been made to ensure that this is not the case, but we can not guarantee that this has not happened.

It can also be remarked in passing that certain nonlinear identities gave rise to very small determinants in the FP estimation of the aligned system. This was due, however, to the fact that the expansion variable in these equations were themselves very small, see for example (3.4) in the case where η_2^* is large. The $X'X$ matrix is thus not singular in these cases (otherwise the parameter estimates would not have converged), but inappropriately scaled. Our inversion procedure did not use these determinents, however, and use of more accurate procedures showed that rounding error was negligible.[8]

Finally we must report that we were unable to obtain convergence for the IIV method. Bergström (1974) has also reported that the RSIIV technique does not converge as often as, for example, RFP and that he obtained no convergence for Dutta–Su's model. In a private communication Professor Klein has suggested that the instruments in successive iterations should be filtered from trend to aid convergence, an idea which deserves further attention.

4.2. *Analysis of the Parameter Estimates*

The computer program we have used [see Edgerton (1977)] produces for each equation and method the parameter estimates, the asymptotic standard errors (approximate values in the case of FP and IIV) and asymptotic t-values. If we denote by d_t the empirical estimate of the SF error term δ_t,

$$d_t = y_t - By_t - B^F y_t^F - Gz_t, \tag{4.1}$$

and by e_t the empirical estimate of the RF (or prediction) error ε_t,

$$e_t = y_t - y_t^* = y_t - \psi(z_t\,;C^*) \quad \text{FP methods,} \tag{4.2a}$$

$$= y_t - h(z_t, 0; C) \quad \text{Non-FP methods,} \tag{4.2b}$$

then we also obtain the following quantities:

$$s_i^2 = f_{1i}^{-1}\Sigma d_{it}^2 \quad \text{Estimate of} \quad \sigma_i^2 = E(\delta_i^2),$$

$$s_i^{*2} = f_2^{-1}\Sigma e_{it}^2 \quad \text{Estimate of} \quad \sigma_i^{*2} = E(\varepsilon_i^2),$$

[8] The estimates of the Taylor expansion parameters are not of interest as such and are not presented here. There are large variations in the estimates depending on the number of terms used, but for finite Taylor series the estimation can be good [see Edgerton (1973d)].

where $f_{1i} = T -$ (number of CLID parameters in the ith SF equation), and $f_2 = T -$ (average number of CLID parameters per SF equation),

$$R^2_{RF:i} = 1 - s^{*2}_i(T-1)[\sum(y_{it} - \bar{y}_i)^2]^{-1} \quad \text{Measure of predictive ability,}$$
$$R^2_{SF:i} = 1 - s^2_i(T-1)[\sum(y_{it} - \bar{y}_i)^2]^{-1}$$

$$D = \sum e_t e_{t-1} / \sum e^2_t \qquad \text{Durbin–Watson statistic,} \qquad \text{FP methods,}$$
$$= \sum d_t d_{t-1} / \sum d^2_t \qquad \qquad \text{Non-FP methods.}$$

We can note that for nonlinear models $\bar{d}_t \neq 0$ for FP methods, and thus s^2_i could therefore be adjusted appropriately. The Durbin–Watson statistics are given as applied to those error terms for which zero autocorrelation is assumed, and not (as is sometimes given for TSLS) for the last stage regression. The same applies to s^2_i, see also Johnston (1972, p. 384).

The R^2_{SF} statistics measure, at least for the Classical methods, the appropriateness of the SF equations. For the FP methods it can be argued that since e_t appears as the error even in the SF of a REID/GEID system, that it is R^2_{RF} that should be used even in this connection. We shall, in fact, interpret R^2_{SF} with caution for all the methods. Note finally that, apart from B^2_{SF} applied to OLS, all the R^2 quantities can be less than zero.

Let us now proceed to examine the parameter estimates we obtained. The full computer output can be obtained from the author; in this section we present in Table 4 a summary of the results for the SF equations for certain of the estimation methods. To save space we have not included all methods here. Those excluded do not in any way change the conclusions we reach, however.

We agree with Klein (1969, 1974) that it is difficult to draw any long going conclusions from these estimates, except that they are quite different for different methods! If we attempt to summarize the results, we can draw some tentative conclusions, however. We can see, for example, that the TSLS methods and the FP methods are both rather clustered, and are often separated both from each other and from the OLS estimates. In many cases it appears that FP is further from OLS than the TSLS methods, and that TSLS:S is further from OLS than TSLS:R. It is also fairly generally evident that TSLS tends to OLS as the number of components increases, a not very surprising result since we expect TSLS to degenerate to OLS when all the variables are included in the first stage. No tendency to OLS can be noted in the FP methods. As a final point here we can note that TSLS:$S4$ give some very peculiar results in some equations, which tends to confirm our analysis in Section 4.1.

TABLE 4
Parameter estimates.[a]

Equation 1

	$\beta_{1,19}$	$\gamma_{1,1}$	$\gamma_{1,3}$	t_1	t_2	t_3	R^2_{SF}	D–W
OLS	0.239	−4.75	0.579	6.7	4.7	7.8	0.984	2.46
TSLS: *R4*	0.208	−4.10	0.639	3.7	3.0	5.6	0.983	2.52
TSLS: *R6*	0.238	−4.70	0.582	4.6	3.7	5.6	0.984	2.46
TSLS: *R8*	0.248	−4.83	0.558	5.4	4.2	5.9	0.984	2.43
TSLS: *S4*	0.252	−5.14	0.560	4.7	3.9	5.3	0.984	2.43
TSLS: *S6*	0.238	−4.73	0.581	4.4	3.6	5.3	0.984	2.46
TSLS: *S8*	0.256	−4.99	0.541	5.2	4.1	5.3	0.984	2.40
FP: *0*	0.160	−2.53	0.714	2.8	1.9	5.7	0.980	2.34
FP: *R1*	0.181	−3.89	0.705	2.8	2.3	5.6	0.982	2.41
FP: *R3*	0.153	−3.05	0.747	2.4	1.8	5.7	0.981	2.42
FP: *G1*	0.180	−3.82	0.706	2.9	2.3	5.8	0.982	2.45
FP: *G3*	0.167	−3.32	0.720	2.6	2.0	5.6	0.981	2.44

Equation 2

	$\beta_{2,38}$	$\gamma_{2,1}$	$\gamma_{2,4}$	t_1	t_2	t_3	R^2_{SF}	D–W
OLS	0.332	−0.38	0.616	6.5	0.3	9.2	0.999	0.79
TSLS: *R4*	0.185	−1.78	0.808	2.9	1.1	9.7	0.998	1.24
TSLS: *R6*	0.193	−1.72	0.797	3.1	1.1	9.9	0.998	1.23
TSLS: *R8*	0.299	−0.71	0.659	5.3	0.5	9.0	0.998	0.90
TSLS: *S4*	0.198	−1.55	0.789	2.0	0.9	6.1	0.998	1.21
TSLS: *S6*	0.246	−1.16	0.728	3.5	0.8	8.1	0.998	1.07
TSLS: *S8*	0.260	−0.70	0.663	4.8	0.5	8.2	0.998	0.91
FP: *0*	0.101	−1.84	0.913	1.4	0.8	9.4	0.997	1.42
FP: *R1*	0.136	−2.47	0.872	1.7	1.2	8.3	0.998	1.41
FP: *R3*	0.176	−1.86	0.818	2.3	0.9	8.2	0.998	1.47
FP: *G1*	0.139	−2.40	0.869	1.8	1.1	8.6	0.998	1.45
FP: *G3*	0.191	−1.70	0.798	2.4	0.8	7.8	0.998	1.48

Equation 3

	$\beta_{3,38}$	$\gamma_{3,1}$	$\gamma_{3,5}$	$\gamma_{3,6}$	t_1	t_2	t_3	t_4	R^2_{SF}	D–W
OLS	0.059	−2.64	−0.353	0.252	6.9	1.9	1.7	2.3	0.971	2.13
TSLS: *R4*	0.048	−1.21	−0.476	0.385	5.6	0.9	2.2	3.5	0.969	2.30
TSLS: *R6*	0.049	−1.30	−0.479	0.368	5.8	0.9	2.3	3.4	0.970	2.29
TSLS: *R8*	0.055	−2.09	−0.412	0.290	6.5	1.5	2.0	2.7	0.971	2.20
TSLS: *S4*	0.046	−1.00	−0.498	0.413	5.7	0.7	2.3	4.0	0.968	2.32
TSLS: *S6*	0.049	−1.61	−0.426	0.365	5.9	1.1	2.0	3.4	0.970	2.29
TSLS: *S8*	0.053	−1.91	−0.428	0.308	6.4	1.4	2.0	2.8	0.971	2.22
FP: *0*	0.051	−2.32	−0.259	0.342	5.4	1.4	1.0	2.8	0.970	2.27
FP: *R1*	0.052	−2.31	−0.336	0.347	5.5	1.4	1.4	2.9	0.970	2.27
FP: *R3*	0.051	−1.89	−0.393	0.348	5.4	1.2	1.6	2.9	0.970	2.30
FP: *G1*	0.052	−2.46	−0.299	0.349	5.4	1.5	1.2	2.9	0.970	2.31
FP: *G3*	0.051	−1.86	−0.398	0.348	5.5	1.2	1.7	2.9	0.970	2.30

Equation 4

	$\beta_{4,20}$	$\gamma_{4,1}$	$\gamma_{4,7}$		t_1	t_2	t_3		R^2_{SF}	$D-W$
OLS	0.130	−23.5	0.426		6.5	6.1	4.5		0.992	1.78
TSLS:*R4*	0.134	−24.2	0.407		5.9	5.6	3.8		0.992	1.73
TSLS:*R6*	0.142	−25.7	0.370		6.3	−5.9	3.4		0.992	1.63
TSLS:*R8*	0.135	−24.3	0.405		6.4	6.1	4.1		0.992	1.73
TSLS:*S4*	0.129	−23.2	0.432		5.5	5.1	3.9		0.992	1.80
TSLS:*S6*	0.133	−23.9	0.415		6.1	5.8	4.0		0.992	1.75
TSLS:*S8*	0.137	−24.7	0.396		6.4	6.1	3.9		0.992	1.70
FP:*0*	0.142	−25.6	0.371		5.5	5.2	3.0		0.992	1.90
FP:*R1*	0.141	−25.6	0.373		5.4	5.1	3.0		0.992	1.89
FP:*R3*	0.142	−25.7	0.369		5.5	5.2	3.0		0.992	1.87
FP:*G1*	0.140	−25.3	0.380		5.4	5.1	3.1		0.992	1.91
FP:*G3*	0.141	−25.5	0.374		5.5	5.2	3.1		0.992	1.88

Equation 5

	$\beta_{5,17}$	$\beta_{5,31}$	$\gamma_{5,1}$	$\gamma_{5,8}$	t_1	t_2	t_3	t_4	R^2_{SF}	$D-W$
OLS	0.028	−8.71	−0.901	0.480	4.7	2.7	2.0	3.8	0.980	2.02
TSLS:*R4*	0.027	−9.95	−0.911	0.490	4.0	2.6	1.9	3.3	0.980	2.05
TSLS:*R6*	0.026	−8.52	−0.865	0.511	3.9	2.3	1.8	3.5	0.980	2.12
TSLS:*R8*	0.028	−9.48	−0.915	0.474	4.4	2.7	2.0	3.4	0.980	2.01
TSLS:*S4*	0.026	−10.47	−0.915	0.510	3.9	2.8	1.9	3.6	0.979	2.07
TSLS:*S6*	0.027	−9.94	−0.907	0.495	4.1	2.8	1.9	3.5	0.980	2.06
TSLS:*S8*	0.027	−9.33	−0.905	0.488	4.3	2.6	1.9	3.6	0.980	2.05
FP:*0*	0.022	−5.92	−0.835	0.606	3.1	1.8	1.5	4.1	0.979	2.22
FP:*R1*	0.021	−5.14	−0.680	0.627	3.1	1.6	1.3	4.3	0.979	2.25
FP:*R3*	0.020	−4.64	−0.722	0.657	3.1	1.5	1.4	4.8	0.978	2.32
FP:*G1*	0.021	−5.30	−0.717	0.623	3.2	1.8	1.4	4.5	0.979	2.17
FP:*G3*	0.019	−4.20	−0.700	0.666	3.1	1.4	1.3	5.0	0.978	2.30

Equation 6 (non-aligned)

	$\beta_{6,6}$	$\beta_{6,22}$	$\beta_{6,23}$	$\gamma_{6,1}$	t_1	t_2	t_3	t_4	R^2_{SF}	$D-W$
OLS	5.05	0.269	92.9	−6.80	5.8	3.6	2.5	2.3	0.827	2.42
TSLS:*R4*	4.41	0.257	158.9	−7.54	0.8	1.8	0.7	2.2	0.807	2.37
TSLS:*R6*	4.90	0.239	170.4	−8.70	3.0	2.7	2.5	2.5	0.794	2.27
TSLS:*R8*	4.64	0.247	165.9	−8.13	3.2	2.9	2.5	2.4	0.801	2.32
TSLS:*S4*	−15.1	0.660	99.6	−6.44	0.3	0.6	0.5	0.3	−3.85	2.21
TSLS:*S6*	3.85	0.257	193.7	−7.53	0.9	2.1	1.0	2.1	0.781	2.36
TSLS:*S8*	4.65	0.246	172.1	−8.37	2.1	2.6	1.8	2.5	0.796	2.31

Equation 6 (aligned)

	$\beta_{6,21}$	$\beta_{6,22}$	$\beta_{6,23}$	$\gamma_{6,1}$	t_1	t_2	t_3	t_4	R^2_{SF}	$D-W$
OLS	0.109	−0.012	−0.362	0.868	5.7	0.9	0.1	2.0	0.720	1.99
TSLS:*R4*	0.028	0.013	30.78	0.269	0.3	0.4	1.0	0.3	0.431	2.11
TSLS:*R6*	0.099	−0.009	−2.50	1.05	3.1	0.5	0.2	2.0	0.709	1.80
TSLS:*R8*	0.108	−0.016	−2.43	0.974	3.6	0.8	0.2	2.0	0.718	1.93
TSLS:*S4*	−0.065	0.043	65.42	−0.421	0.3	0.6	0.9	0.2	−0.590	2.21
TSLS:*S6*	0.029	0.012	33.84	0.153	0.4	0.4	1.2	0.2	0.387	1.44
TSLS:*S8*	0.062	−0.003	16.46	0.570	1.6	0.1	1.0	0.9	0.632	2.00

FP:*0*	0.196	−0.050	−12.16	0.990	4.7	2.3	1.5	1.9	0.485	1.91
FP:*R1*	0.176	−0.043	−9.26	1.02	4.0	1.9	1.0	1.8	0.577	1.84
FP:*R3*	0.170	−0.036	−13.87	1.09	4.5	1.8	1.4	1.9	0.609	1.95
FP:*G1*	0.232	−0.063	−19.71	1.04	5.2	2.9	2.4	2.1	0.264	1.91
FP:*G3*	0.178	−0.039	−16.96	1.17	4.6	1.9	1.7	2.1	0.576	1.95

Equation 7

	$\beta_{7,9}$	$\beta_{7,24}$	$\gamma_{7,1}$	t_1	t_2	t_3	R^2_{SF}	$D\text{-}W$
OLS	−0.331	−0.018	1.13	6.2	11.2	82.0	0.814	1.16
TSLS:*R4*	−0.521	−0.021	1.17	4.1	6.7	38.7	0.731	1.69
TSLS:*R6*	−0.358	−0.018	1.14	4.8	8.5	59.6	0.813	1.25
TSLS:*R8*	−0.363	−0.018	1.14	5.0	8.8	61.2	0.812	1.26
TSLS:*S4*	−0.490	−0.021	1.16	3.3	5.4	32.1	0.755	1.63
TSLS:*S6*	−0.521	−0.021	1.17	4.0	6.6	38.0	0.731	1.69
TSLS:*S8*	−0.449	−0.020	1.16	5.5	8.9	56.9	0.782	1.53
FP:*0*	1.02	0.010	0.836	2.0	1.0	7.6	−3.43	1.61
FP:*R1*	4.23	0.074	0.147	2.7	2.4	0.4	−47.19	1.82
FP:*R3*	−1.27	−0.035	1.33	4.2	5.7	20.4	−1.23	1.97
FP:*G1*	0.645	0.002	0.919	0.5	0.1	3.1	−1.39	1.35
FP:*G3*	−1.30	−0.036	1.33	3.6	5.0	17.3	−1.40	1.98

Equation 8

	$\beta_{8,25}$	$\gamma_{8,1}$	$\gamma_{8,16}$	t_1	t_2	t_3	R^2_{SF}	$D\text{-}W$
OLS	0.422	−10.8	0.266	18.4	10.6	6.3	0.999	1.49
TSLS:*R4*	0.452	−11.5	0.210	13.3	9.4	3.4	0.999	1.18
TSLS:*R6*	0.443	−11.3	0.228	14.9	9.9	4.2	0.999	1.28
TSLS:*R8*	0.430	−11.0	0.252	16.1	10.2	5.1	0.999	1.41
TSLS:*S4*	0.528	−13.4	0.071	10.0	7.7	0.7	0.998	0.85
TSLS:*S6*	0.419	−10.7	0.270	14.5	9.6	5.1	0.999	1.53
TSLS:*S8*	0.417	−10.7	0.275	15.8	9.9	5.7	0.999	1.56
FP:*0*	0.466	−11.9	0.184	5.5	4.0	1.2	0.999	1.98
FP:*R1*	0.466	−11.9	0.185	5.6	4.0	1.2	0.999	2.02
FP:*R3*	0.463	−11.8	0.190	5.6	4.0	1.3	0.999	2.13
FP:*G1*	0.456	−11.6	0.203	5.5	3.9	1.3	0.999	2.04
FP:*G3*	0.458	−11.7	0.201	5.6	4.0	1.4	0.999	2.14

Equation 9

	$\beta_{9,24}$	$\beta_{9,32}$	$\gamma_{9,1}$	t_1	t_2	t_3	R^2_{SF}	$D\text{-}W$
OLS	−0.014	1.78	0.158	4.1	4.4	6.6	0.705	1.96
TSLS:*R4*	−0.017	1.75	0.173	4.4	2.9	6.3	0.697	1.93
TSLS:*R6*	−0.016	2.02	0.165	4.3	4.2	6.3	0.691	1.89
TSLS:*R8*	−0.016	1.76	0.170	4.4	3.9	6.6	0.700	1.95
TSLS:*S4*	−0.019	1.22	0.196	4.7	2.0	6.7	0.671	1.88
TSLS:*S6*	−0.017	1.22	0.188	4.5	2.1	6.6	0.680	1.92
TSLS:*S8*	−0.016	1.66	0.172	4.3	3.2	6.4	0.700	1.96
FP:*0*	−0.022	−0.712	0.236	4.4	0.8	6.0	0.296	1.41
FP:*R1*	−0.020	−0.169	0.219	4.2	0.2	6.6	0.457	1.58
FP:*R3*	−0.018	0.612	0.195	3.9	1.1	6.3	0.616	1.93
FP:*G1*	−0.019	−0.146	0.217	4.6	0.2	7.3	0.461	1.48
FP:*G3*	−0.018	0.492	0.201	4.2	1.0	6.7	0.597	1.90

Equation 10[b]

	$\beta_{10,16}$	$\gamma_{10,1}$	$\gamma_{10,5}$	t_1	t_2	t_3	R^2_{SF}	$D-W$
OLS	0.172	0.320	0.823	3.4	1.2	12.7	0.869	1.57
TSLS: *R4*	0.176	0.284	0.836	3.3	1.0	12.8	0.869	1.57
TSLS: *R6*	0.152	0.353	0.833	2.9	1.3	12.6	0.869	1.59
TSLS: *R8*	0.152	0.361	0.831	2.9	1.3	12.6	0.869	1.58
TSLS: *S4*	0.177	0.278	0.837	3.1	1.0	12.8	0.869	1.57
TSLS: *S6*	0.189	0.284	0.829	3.5	1.0	12.6	0.869	1.54
TSLS: *S8*	0.171	0.321	0.830	3.2	1.2	12.6	0.869	1.57
FP	0.160	0.418	0.813	2.8	1.4	11.4	0.869	1.54

Equation 11

	$\beta_{11,33}$	$\gamma_{11,1}$	$\gamma_{11,18}$	t_1	t_2	t_3	R^2_{SF}	$D-W$
OLS	0.795	−0.069	−0.687	15.9	0.1	7.0	0.909	2.28
TSLS: *R4*	0.837	0.081	−0.781	14.8	0.1	7.2	0.906	2.47
TSLS: *R6*	0.811	−0.013	−0.724	15.0	0.2	7.0	0.909	2.37
TSLS: *R8*	0.811	−0.130	−0.707	15.7	0.2	7.0	0.909	2.34
TSLS: *S4*	0.817	−0.068	−0.726	15.0	0.1	7.0	0.909	2.38
TSLS: *S6*	0.827	−0.015	−0.752	15.2	0.2	7.2	0.907	2.43
TSLS: *S8*	0.805	−0.084	−0.702	15.6	0.1	7.0	0.909	2.32
FP: *0*	0.525	0.640	−0.322	4.9	0.4	1.4	0.813	1.26
FP: *R1*	0.487	1.44	−0.341	4.6	1.0	1.4	0.779	1.20
FP: *R3*	0.437	−0.367	−0.010	5.9	0.2	0.1	0.725	1.49
FP: *G1*	0.561	1.02	−0.416	5.2	0.8	1.8	0.835	1.30
FP: *G3*	0.412	0.570	−0.092	4.7	0.4	0.5	0.718	1.26

Equation 12

	$\beta_{12,35}$	$\gamma_{12,1}$	$\gamma_{12,20}$	t_1	t_2	t_3	R^2_{SF}	$D-W$
OLS	0.013	0.754	0.877	1.7	0.9	10.8	0.983	2.28
TSLS: *R4*	0.008	0.587	0.923	1.1	0.7	11.4	0.983	2.05
TSLS: *R6*	0.007	0.674	0.899	1.5	0.8	11.1	0.983	1.99
TSLS: *R8*	0.011	0.707	0.889	1.6	0.8	11.0	0.983	1.96
TSLS: *S4*	0.009	0.604	0.916	1.3	0.7	11.6	0.983	2.04
TSLS: *S6*	0.008	0.577	0.926	1.1	0.7	11.4	0.983	2.06
TSLS: *S8*	0.012	0.713	0.889	1.6	0.8	10.9	0.983	1.96
FP: *0*	0.010	0.642	0.905	1.3	0.7	10.8	0.983	1.98
FP: *R1*	0.010	0.648	0.909	1.3	0.7	10.9	0.983	1.98
FP: *R3*	0.011	0.689	0.892	1.5	0.8	10.6	0.983	1.96
FP: *G1*	0.010	0.662	0.900	1.5	0.8	11.3	0.983	1.97
FP: *G3*	0.011	0.681	0.895	1.5	0.8	11.0	0.983	1.97

Equation 13

	$\beta_{13,26}$	$\beta_{13,36}$	$\gamma_{13,1}$	$\gamma_{13,21}$	t_1	t_2	t_3	t_4	R^2_{SF}	$D-W$
OLS	−0.243	0.062	−0.388	0.937	1.1	6.8	2.1	38.2	0.998	1.50
TSLS: *R4*	−0.535	0.066	−0.432	0.932	1.2	6.2	2.2	34.9	0.998	1.66
TSLS: *R6*	−0.358	0.062	−0.408	0.938	0.9	6.3	2.2	36.8	0.998	1.56
TSLS: *R8*	−0.442	0.064	−0.418	0.935	1.4	6.7	2.2	37.0	0.998	1.61
TSLS: *S4*	−0.534	0.065	−0.438	0.934	1.1	6.2	2.2	35.2	0.998	1.65
TSLS: *S6*	−0.670	0.065	−0.459	0.933	1.5	6.1	2.3	34.0	0.997	1.70

TSLS:*S8*	−0.612	0.065	−0.445	0.934	1.7	6.6	2.3	35.6	0.997	1.68
FP:*0*	0.487	0.056	−0.250	0.942	0.7	4.3	1.1	33.6	0.997	1.17
FP:*R1*	0.555	0.055	−0.221	0.943	0.8	4.3	1.0	33.4	0.997	1.16
FP:*R3*	0.548	0.054	−0.255	0.947	0.8	4.4	1.1	35.6	0.997	1.20
FP:*G1*	0.439	0.057	−0.247	0.938	0.6	4.5	1.1	33.5	0.997	1.24
FP:*G3*	0.515	0.054	−0.261	0.947	0.8	4.5	1.1	35.8	0.997	1.24

Equation 14[c]

	$\gamma_{14,1}$	$\gamma_{14,5}$	$\gamma_{14,11}$	$\gamma_{14,12}$	t_1	t_2	t_3	t_4	R^2_{SF}	$D\text{–}W$
	9.33	−2.11	0.066	0.360	3.1	3.8	4.1	2.4	0.958	1.59

Equation 15[c]

	$\gamma_{15,1}$	$\gamma_{15,23}$	$\gamma_{15,24}$		t_1	t_2	t_3		R^2_{SF}	$D\text{–}W$
	−1.41	0.049	8.56		3.2	39.4	13.5		0.993	0.75

Equation 16[c]

	$\gamma_{16,1}$	$\gamma_{16,24}$	$\gamma_{16,25}$	$\gamma_{16,26}$	t_1	t_2	t_3	t_4	R^2_{SF}	$D\text{–}W$
	−0.511	0.533	1.14	−0.815	1.7	2.9	13.9	2.4	0.922	0.95

[a] In this table the figures in the columns t_i refer to the asymptotic t-values of the ith parameter estimate.

[b] For equation 10 all FP methods have the same estimates.

[c] For equations 14, 15 and 16 all estimation methods give the same results.

Great care must be taken in the interpretation of the t-values. For OLS this quantity has very little meaning due to the asymptotic bias. For TSLS the values are merely asymptotically correct, for FP both approximate and asymptotic, and our sample size is only 31. A general tendency, however, is that FP yields smaller t-values than TSLS. Which of the values is more 'correct' is difficult to say; see also Edgerton (1973c).

If we look at each equation in turn we see that there are five which are dubious. Equation 6 has low R^2_{SF} values, large variations in the coefficient values for the different methods and many non-significant t-values. This is true for both the aligned and non-aligned versions. Equation 7 shows much the same tendencies, except that most parameters are significant, with the addition that the FP methods give different signs for $\beta_{7,9}$. In equation 9 the FP methods tend to have the wrong sign for $\beta_{9,32}$, but these estimates are non-significant. Even here the R^2_{SF} values are low. Equations 12 and 13 have non-significant estimates of $\beta_{13,35}$ and $\beta_{13,26}$. For the last mentioned it is only the FP methods which give the correct sign. We can thus agree with Klein (1969) that these equations ought to be respecified.[9]

[9] On the basis of FIML estimation Klein also suggests respecification of the first equation.

The presence of autocorrelation in the error terms leads to a large increase in the variance of the estimation methods, and in the case of dynamic models also leads to inconsistency. We have therefore calculated the Durbin–Watson statistic for each equation and method. It should be noted that this statistic is not strictly appropriate for ID systems, especially dynamic ones, but can still be used as an indicator of autocorrelation; see for example Selén (1975).

Looking at the different equations we can see, for the SF errors δ, that it is 2, 7, 15 and 16 that are dubious, maybe also 1 and 8. For the FP methods, where it is autocorrelation in ε that is important, we can see that 11, 13, 15 and 16 are dubious, maybe also 1 and 2. In both cases we suspect equation 1 of negative autocorrelation and all the others of positive autocorrelation.

Selén (1975) has suggested various ways of estimating linear ID systems which contain autocorrelated errors. The estimation of nonlinear systems in such situations is, as far as the author is aware, at present unexplored, but should not provide too many problems in generalization.

4.3. Analysis of Prediction Results

The analysis of prediction results can proceed more explicitly than our analysis of the parameter estimates. We have obtained results both for the R^2_{RF} values calculated inside the sampling period,[10] and for the *ex post* forecasts for 1965. We have analysed these quantities both by taking averages for the 20 most important variables as given by Klein (1969, 1974), for the *ex post* forecasts using the absolute percentage error of prediction, and also by ranking the methods for each of these variables.[11] The sum of the ranks has then been calculated for each method. Note that for the percentage errors for Y_{1965} we used the (probably) incorrect value of 374.2. This does not affect the rankings as all methods gave predictions under 371.2, and increases the prediction error merely from a little under 1% to a little over.

Looking at Table 5 we can see that inside the sampling period the FP methods clearly give the best results, followed by the TSLS and OLS methods for the aligned model and finally the TSLS and OLS methods for the non-aligned model. This is true for both criteria. For the *ex post* predictions the ordering varies depending upon which criteria is used, and

[10] These figures measure the same effect as Klein's one-period simulations.

[11] Three variables give the same results for all methods and have thus not been included in the rankings. For R^2_{RF} we rank as one the method with the largest value, for the absolute percentage error the method with the smallest value.

TABLE 5
Prediction results inside the sample period and *ex post*.[a]

	Sample period		*Ex post*	
	Average R^2_{RF}	Ranking R^2_{RF}	Average % error	Ranking % error
Aligned model				
OLS	0.9056 (18)	347½(21)	9.1215 (19)	287½(16½)
TSLS: *R4*	0.9120 (14)	207 (12)	9.1923 (21)	216½(8)
TSLS: *R5*	0.9164 (10)	171½(10)	8.9722 (14)	182½(4)
TSLS: *R6*	0.9024 (22)	244½(13)	9.0003 (16)	213½(6)
TSLS: *R7*	0.9082 (17)	304½(20)	9.4325 (27)	436½(34)
TSLS: *R8*	0.9092 (16)	275½(17)	9.2412 (22)	333½(21)
TSLS: *R9*	0.9054 (19)	350 (22)	9.1558 (20)	287½(16½)
TSLS: *S4*	0.8417 (24)	386½(24)	10.1418 (32)	418½(31)
TSLS: *S5*	0.8401 (25)	410½(26)	10.1552 (34)	416½(30)
TSLS: *S6*	0.9052 (20)	292½(18)	9.6289 (31)	362½(24)
TSLS: *S7*	0.9125 (13)	271½(16)	9.5652 (30)	437½(35)
TSLS: *S8*	0.9128 (12)	255½(14)	9.5344 (29)	428½(33)
TSLS: *S9*	0.9049 (21)	293½(19)	9.4383 (28)	314½(19)
FP: *0*	0.9200 (6½)	130 (4)	8.3068 (8)	379 (25)
FP: *R0**	0.9178 (8)	143 (6½)	8.3262 (9)	392 (27)
FP: *R1*	0.9253 (5)	134 (5)	8.0349 (6)	315 (20)
FP: *R2*	0.9336 (3)	113 (3)	7.3109 (4)	252 (12)
FP: *R3*	0.9367 (1)	108 (1½)	8.0588 (7)	220 (9)
FP: *G0**	0.9166 (9)	164½(9)	7.2520 (3)	274 (14)
FP: *G1*	0.9200 (6½)	143 (6½)	7.5045 (5)	224 (10)
FP: *G2*	0.9289 (4)	151 (8)	5.1872 (1)	209 (5)
FP: *G3*	0.9346 (2)	108 (1½)	5.3361 (2)	238 (11)
Non-aligned model				
OLS	0.8898 (23)	377½(23)	9.4094 (26)	354½(22)
TSLS: *R4*	0.6367 (34)	493½(31)	8.5259 (10)	158½(2)
TSLS: *R5*	0.9144 (11)	200½(11)	8.8816 (13)	156½(1)
TSLS: *R6*	0.4838 (35)	539½(35)	8.6963 (12)	168½(3)
TSLS: *R7*	0.7078 (32)	523½(33)	9.3174 (24)	405½(28)
TSLS: *R8*	0.7598 (30)	486½(30)	9.0894 (18)	296½(18)
TSLS: *R9*	0.7031 (33)	538½(34)	9.0358 (17)	257½(13)
TSLS: *S4*	0.7974 (28)	400½(25)	10.1448 (33)	420½(32)
TSLS: *S5*	0.8387 (26)	425½(28)	10.1609 (35)	383½(26)
TSLS: *S6*	0.8181 (27)	413½(27)	8.5814 (11)	264½(15)
TSLS: *S7*	0.9114 (15)	266 (15)	9.4082 (25)	412½(29)
TSLS: *S8*	0.7685 (29)	464½(29)	9.2672 (23)	358½(23)
TSLS: *S9*	0.7132 (31)	518½(32)	8.9831 (15)	215½(7)

[a] The figures in brackets after each entry are the ranks of the methods for that column.

for neither case is it as clear as for the sampling period predictions. For the average percentage error we can see, however, that the FP methods are still clearly best followed by TSLS:*R* for the non-aligned model, TSLS:*R* for the aligned model, OLS and finally TSLS:*S*. If we use the rankings of the percentage errors there is no really clear pattern, but the TSLS:*R* methods with few components seem to be best followed by the FP methods with most terms (especially the FP:*G* methods). The other methods seem to be fairly mixed, with the TSLS:*S* methods being the worst.

We are, of course, hoping that the results inside the sampling period will give some indication of the performance of the methods in *ex post* prediction. This hope is not really supported by this study. Spearman's rank correlation coefficient between the average R^2 and the average percentage error is only 0.55, and between the ranking of R^2 and the percentage error is as low as 0.13. Further examination shows that the two criteria give very similar rankings for R^2 (0.97), but a greater difference for the *ex post* predictions (0.68).

If we now look at Table 6 the reason for the difference between the two criteria in the *ex post* forecasts becomes apparent. For many variables all methods give very similar results, where maybe the low TSLS:*R* methods give very slightly the best results. For those variables where the difference is large between the methods, however, it is most often the FP methods which give the best results. This is especially apparent for variable y_{41} (S_c, the corporate savings) where the FP methods are the only reasonable ones, see particularly the good result for FP:*G3*.

We are thus led to suspect that the distribution of the percentage errors has a shorter tail for the FP methods, and further analysis supports this conclusion. If we describe the distribution of the percentage errors of prediction for each method by calculating how many of the 17 important variables which give different results fall into the ranges (0,1), (1,5), (5,20), (20,70), $(70,\infty)$ then we obtain a quintuple for each method.[12] Altogether 11 distinct quintuples were observed, which can be grouped as follows:

A: Error distributions with few large errors and many small errors: $(3,7,7,0,0)$, $(3,7,6,1,0)$, $(4,6,6,0,1)$, $(4,6,5,2,0)$.

B: Error distributions with some large errors and many small errors: $(4,6,5,1,1)$, $(3,7,6,0,1)$, $(3,8,4,1,1)$, $(3,7,5,1,1)$.

C: Error distributions with some large errors and few small errors: $(2,9,4,1,1)$, $(2,8,5,1,1)$, $(1,9,5,1,1)$.

[12] The intervals given were chosen so as to characterize the different methods and to avoid empty cells.

TABLE 6
Forecasts for 1965.[a]

	$Y_1(C_d)$	$Y_2(C_n)$	$Y_3(R)$	$Y_4(H)$	$Y_5(I_m)$	$Y_7(h)$	$Y_{10}(r)$	$Y_{17}(X)$	$Y_{27}(W)$
Aligned model									
Actual	59.6	308.1	20.6	76.5	32.7	1.038	4.64	539.2	315.1
OLS	55.2	303.0	22.8	75.6	29.7	1.023	4.91	530.7	311.1
TSLS:*R4*	55.6	303.6	22.4	75.6	29.8	1.024	4.92	531.1	311.3
TSLS:*R6*	55.2	303.5	22.5	75.5	29.7	1.022	4.86	530.9	311.3
TSLS:*R8*	54.9	303.1	22.6	75.5	29.7	1.022	4.86	530.2	311.0
TSLS:*S4*	55.2	303.2	22.5	75.5	29.8	1.022	4.94	530.4	310.9
TSLS:*S6*	55.2	303.3	22.5	75.5	29.8	1.022	4.95	530.6	311.2
TSLS:*S8*	54.8	303.0	22.6	75.5	29.7	1.023	4.91	530.0	311.0
FP:*0*	54.7	303.1	22.5	75.4	29.7	1.021	4.87	529.8	310.8
FP:*R1*	55.0	303.1	22.5	75.5	29.7	1.016	4.87	530.3	311.0
FP:*R3*	55.7	303.4	22.6	75.6	29.7	1.028	4.87	531.3	311.5
FP:*G1*	55.4	303.4	22.6	75.6	29.7	1.019	4.87	531.1	311.3
FP:*G3*	55.6	303.4	22.6	75.6	29.6	1.031	4.87	531.4	311.5
Non-aligned model									
OLS	55.2	303.0	22.8	75.6	29.7	1.023	4.91	530.8	311.3
TSLS:*R4*	55.4	303.5	22.4	75.5	29.9	1.021	4.92	530.9	311.3
TSLS:*R6*	55.2	303.5	22.5	75.5	29.8	1.021	4.86	530.7	311.2
TSLS:*R8*	54.9	303.0	22.6	75.5	29.7	1.021	4.86	530.2	311.0
TSLS:*S4*	55.2	303.3	22.4	75.5	29.8	1.022	4.92	530.4	310.9
TSLS:*S6*	55.1	303.2	22.5	75.5	29.9	1.020	4.95	530.2	311.0
TSLS:*S8*	54.8	303.0	22.6	75.5	29.8	1.022	4.91	529.9	310.9

	$Y_{28}(w)$	$Y_{29}(N_w)$	$Y_{34}(p)$	$Y_{38}(Y)$	$Y_{39}(\pi)$	$Y_{40}(P_c)$	$Y_{41}(S_c)$	$Y_{42}(\pi_r)$
Aligned model								
Actual	5.492	68.0	1.228	374.2	95.3	51.5	12.9	33.6
OLS	5.484	67.5	1.216	369.6	85.2	40.4	1.7	34.2
TSLS:*R4*	5.479	67.3	1.193	370.1	85.2	40.7	1.1	34.2
TSLS:*R6*	5.484	67.5	1.216	369.8	85.3	40.6	1.6	34.2
TSLS:*R8*	5.484	67.4	1.215	369.4	84.9	40.2	1.3	34.2
TSLS:*S4*	5.467	66.9	1.202	369.3	83.8	38.9	−0.2	34.4
TSLS:*S6*	5.479	67.2	1.210	369.6	84.5	40.0	0.7	34.2
TSLS:*S8*	5.479	67.3	1.213	369.2	84.5	39.7	0.9	34.2
FP:*0*	5.504	67.3	1.218	366.8	84.9	40.4	3.8	34.2
FP:*R1*	5.499	67.4	1.218	364.6	86.4	42.6	3.7	33.8
FP:*R3*	5.492	67.5	1.210	368.8	81.7	36.6	5.3	33.8
FP:*G1*	5.504	67.6	1.215	366.4	88.0	44.6	4.1	33.7
FP:*G3*	5.489	67.5	1.200	369.1	83.5	44.3	10.8	35.2
Non-aligned model								
OLS	5.475	67.4	1.213	369.7	84.9	39.9	1.2	34.3
TSLS:*R4*	5.500	67.7	1.221	369.9	86.0	41.8	2.3	34.0
TSLS:*R6*	5.494	67.6	1.220	369.7	85.6	41.1	2.1	34.1
TSLS:*R8*	5.489	67.5	1.217	369.3	85.1	40.4	1.6	34.1
TSLS:*S4*	5.467	66.9	1.202	369.3	83.8	38.9	−0.2	34.4
TSLS:*S6*	5.505	67.8	1.223	369.3	85.8	41.7	2.4	33.9
TSLS:*S8*	5.487	67.5	1.216	369.2	84.9	40.2	1.4	34.1

[a] All methods give the same predictions for $Y_{14}(I)$, $Y_{15}(D)$ and $Y_{16}(r_S)$, namely 46.7, 59.1 and 4.63. The actual values are 50.0, 55.7 and 4.38.

The methods fall into these groups as follows:

A: All the FP methods except FP:*0* and FP:*R0**.
B: Non-aligned TSLS:*R*, Non-aligned TSLS:*S6, 8, 9,* Aligned TSLS:*R9*, and Aligned OLS.
C: Aligned TSLS:*R* except *R9*, Aligned TSLS:*S*, FP:*0, R0**, Non-aligned OLS, and Non-aligned TSLS:*S4, 5, 7.*

Inside group A one can note that it is FP:*G3* which has the excellent (3, 7, 7, 0, 0), and that the other FP:*G* methods have (3, 7, 6, 1, 0).

The results given so far indicate that the FP methods give the best predictions both inside and (probably) outside the sampling period. We are also interested, however, in a more detailed comparison where we can both identify the best method within each group of methods and then compare these with each other. To identify the best method within each group we have used four criteria, the averages and overall ranking described earlier and also the internal rankings and pairwise comparisons within each group of methods.[13] In Tables 7 and 8 we give the best two or three methods inside each group for each criterion, where the use of a / indicates equivalence.

For the predictions in the sampling period one can see that the best methods inside the respective groups are Aligned TSLS:*R5,* TSLS:*S8,* FP:*R3* and FP:*G3,* Non-aligned TSLS:*R5* and TSLS:*S7.* For the *ex post* forecasts we have Aligned TSLS:*R5,* TSLS:*S9,* FP:*R3* and FP:*G2,* Non-aligned TSLS:*R4* and TSLS:*S9.* We can thus see that for the aligned TSLS:*R* and FP:*R* we have the same method best for both periods, for non-aligned TSLS:*R* and FP:*G* the best R^2 method is the second best

TABLE 7
The best methods inside the sampling period.

Group	Internal rankings	Overall rankings	Averages	Pairwise comparisons
Aligned				
TSLS:*R*	*R5–R4*	*R5–R4*	*R5–R4*	*R5–R4*
TSLS:*S*	*S7–S8*	*S8–S7*	*S8–S7*	*S8–S7*
FP:*R*	*R3–R2*	*R3–R2*	*R3–R2*	*R3–R2*
FP:*G*	*G3–G2*	*G3–0*	*G3–G2*	*G3–G2*
Non-aligned				
TSLS:*R*	*R5–R4*	*R5–R8*	*R5–R8*	*R5–R8*
TSLS:*S*	*S7–S4*	*S7–S4*	*S7–S5*	*S7–S4*

[13] The overall rankings for all methods and the rankings for just one particular group of methods can, when added over all variables, lead to different results.

TABLE 8
The best methods for the *ex post* forecasts.

Group	Internal rankings	Overall rankings	Averages	Pairwise comparisons
Aligned				
TSLS:*R*	*R5–R4/R6*	*R5–R6–R4*	*R5–R6–R4*	*R4–R5–R6*
TSLS:*S*	*S9–S6*	*S9–S6*	*S9–S8*	*S9–S6*
FP:*R*	*R3/R2–R1*	*R3–R2–R1*	*R2–R1–R3*	*R3–R2–R1*
FP:*G*	*G2–G3*	*G2–G1*	*G2–G3*	*G3–G2*
Non-aligned				
TSLS:*R*	*R4–R6–R5*	*R5–R4–R6*	*R4–R6–R5*	*R4–R5–R6*
TSLS:*S*	*S9–S6*	*S9–S6*	*S6–S9*	*S6–S9*

percentage error method, whilst for TSLS:*S* the best R^2 method is a bad method for the *ex post* forecasts.

From Tables 7 and 8 we can see quite clearly that using the additional Taylor expansion terms in the FP estimation leads to a marked improvement in prediction ability, both inside and outside the sampling period. The FP:*0* method does not really give very satisfactory results, whilst using two or three terms yields a marked improvement. In Edgerton (1973c, p. 151) the results of a Monte Carlo study indicated that one or two terms were sufficient, and that even FP:*0* performed adequately. The point of truncation thus seems to vary from model to model, but the use of some terms seems to be recommended.

For the TSLS methods it is apparent that merely a few components are sufficient when using the correlation matrix, which agrees with the results in Klein (1969, 1974). For the covariance matrix one needs considerably more components.

In Tables 9–11 we compare the best methods for each group with each other. In Table 11 we use the best method given from inside the sampling period for comparisons *ex post*.

From Table 9 one can see that inside the sampling period FP is best followed by TSLS:*R*, TSLS:*S* and OLS. In each case the aligned model is superior to the non-aligned. For the *ex post* forecasts the internal rankings give almost exactly the same results for the four best methods, which explains the discrepencies between Tables 10 and 11 for that column. In general one can see in these two tables that the FP methods and TSLS:*R* give the best results, and that these are very similar. Using the error distribution given earlier one would probably consider the FP methods best, with the very large reduction in the worst errors for FP:*G3* being the deciding factor. Note also that for the *ex post* forecasts the non-aligned model seems to be superior for TSLS.

TABLE 9
Rankings of the best methods inside the sampling period.

	Internal rankings	Overall rankings	Averages	Pairwise comparisons
OLS[a]	7	7	7	7
TSLS:*R5*[a]	3	3	3	3
TSLS:*S8*[a]	5	5	5	5
FP:*R3*	2	$1\frac{1}{2}$	1	2
FP:*G3*	1	$1\frac{1}{2}$	2	1
OLS[b]	8	8	8	8
TSLS:*R5*[b]	4	4	4	4
TSLS:*S7*[b]	6	6	6	6

[a] Aligned.
[b] Non-aligned.

TABLE 10
Rankings of the best methods for *ex post* forecasts.

	Internal rankings	Overall rankings	Averages	Pairwise comparisons
OLS[a]	$6\frac{1}{2}$	6	6	6
TSLS:*R5*[a]	4	2	4	4
TSLS:*S9*[a]	$6\frac{1}{2}$	7	8	7
FP:*R3*	1	5	2	1
FP:*G2*	3	3	1	2
OLS[b]	8	8	7	8
TSLS:*R4*[b]	2	1	3	3
TSLS:*S9*[b]	5	4	5	5

[a] Aligned.
[b] Non-aligned.

TABLE 11
Rankings for *ex post* forecasts using the best methods from inside the sampling period.

	Internal rankings	Overall rankings	Averages	Pairwise comparisons
OLS[a]	5	5	5	5
TSLS:*R5*[a]	$1\frac{1}{2}$	2	4	$3\frac{1}{2}$
TSLS:*S8*[a]	8	8	8	8
FP:*R3*	3	3	2	1
FP:*G3*	4	4	1	2
OLS[b]	6	6	7	6
TSLS:*R5*[b]	$1\frac{1}{2}$	1	3	$3\frac{1}{2}$
TSLS:*S7*[b]	7	7	6	7

[a] Aligned.
[b] Non-aligned.

4.4. Convergence Properties

In the analysis of nonlinear interdependent models we meet two kinds of convergence difficulties. Firsly we have the problem of convergence of the parameter estimates in FP and IIV estimation. If these methods converge then we automatically obtain the sample period predictions at the same time (that is we can calculate R^2_{RF} without further iteration). For the Classical methods, however, we must solve the estimated model to obtain these predictions. For the *ex post* predictions we must solve the estimated system for all methods. If we are interested in R^2_{RF} it therefore follows that the Classical methods are almost as time consuming as the FP methods.[14]

The numerical methods we have used to solve these problems are related. For the GEID estimates we have used the RFP method [see (2.27) and (2.28)], whilst for the predictions we have used the Successive Over-Relaxation (SOR) method, which essentially is (2.28). The choice of these methods is based on the experience of Edgerton (1973c), Bodin (1974) and Klein (1969),[15] and also enables us to use the same algorithm for both sets of computations.

There are two factors of vital importance for both RFP and SOR estimation, that is the ordering of the equations and the choice of relaxation factor, α. Bodin (1974, ch. 12) has thoroughly discussed the choice of orderings, and given a number of different algorithms which can yield near-optimal orderings prior to estimation. These methods all use a position matrix which has (i, j)th element equal to 1 if variable j appears in equation i, and zero otherwise. One then attempts to minimize the number of positive terms above the main diagonal, and also use a number of other refinements given by Bodin. We have used a computer program SORT5 which Dr. Bodin has been kind enough to provide us with.[16]

Figure 1 gives the position matrix of the original ordering, where we can see that there exists 28 positive elements above the main diagonal. In the near-optimal ordering given in Figure 2 there only exists 9 positive elements above the main diagonal. We can also see that the equations 14, 15, 16, 10 and 26 form a recursive block, whilst the other equations form one interdependent block.

We have used the near-optimal ordering in our estimation of the model and also in our analysis of the other convergence properties of the system.

[14] In practice we have often found that the Classical methods take longer than FP, a result which may partly be due to the fact that the convergence criteria for R^2 is based on the predictions, whilst for FP it is based on the parameter estimates.

[15] Klein recommends Gauss–Seidel iterations, which is SOR with relaxation factor equal to 1.

[16] A small error on input has forced us to slightly modify the result given by this program.

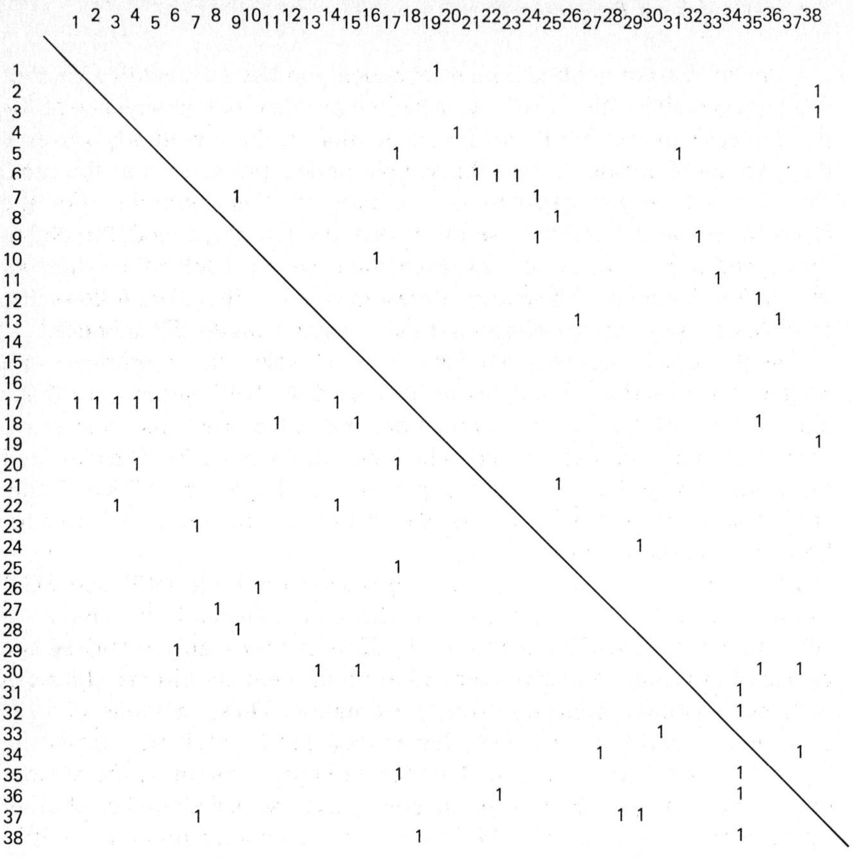

FIGURE 1. Position matrix using the original ordering.

Using OLS start and $\alpha = 0.9$ we obtained convergence to 10^{-6} for FP:*0* in 47 iterations using the near-optimal ordering, but after 400 iterations no convergence had been obtained using the original ordering.

In our analysis of the relaxation factor we have mainly used FP:*0* estimation so as to keep our study within reasonable limits. In Table 12 we give the number of iterations needed and time used (in seconds) for FP:*0* estimation using OLS and TSLS start and a number of convergence criteria. The time used is for the whole process, that is of convergence to 10^{-6}. The TSLS start used five components of the correlation matrix since our results had shown this to give satisfactory R^2 properties.

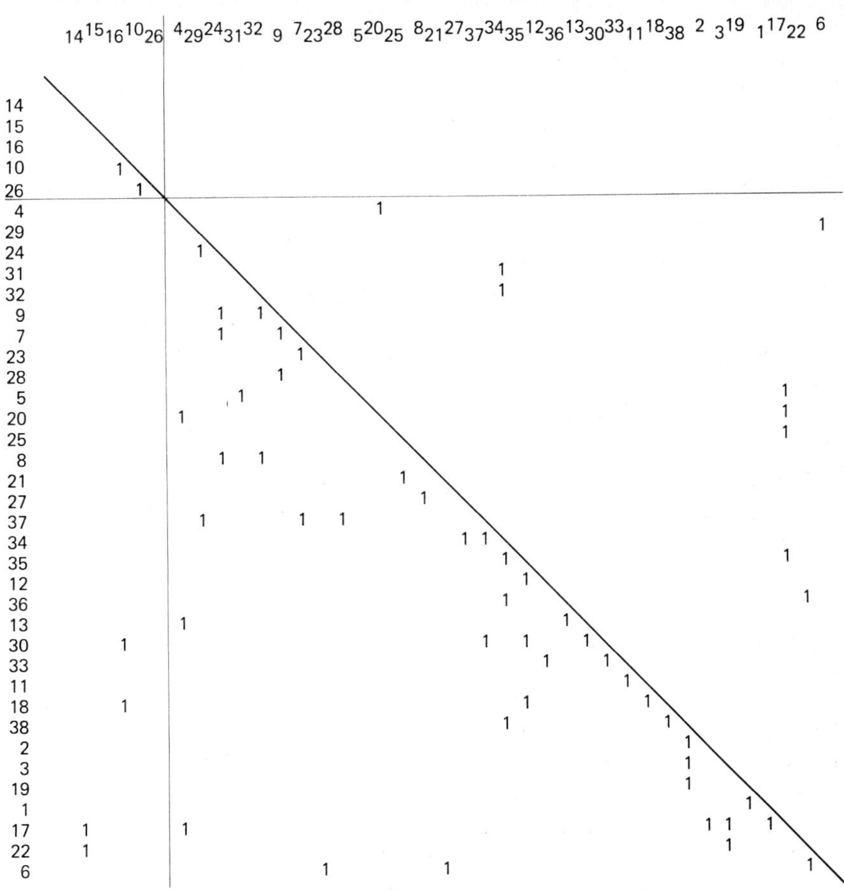

FIGURE 2. Position matrix using a near-optimal ordering.

TABLE 12
Convergence properties of FP:*0*, near-optimal ordering.

	OLS start					TSLS start				
α	10^{-3}	10^{-4}	10^{-5}	10^{-6}	Time	10^{-3}	10^{-4}	10^{-5}	10^{-6}	Time
0.5	70	93	111	127	33.1	79	107	136	164	44.5
0.6	55	70	82	96	25.3	60	81	101	121	33.5
0.7	43	54	63	73	19.2	46	61	76	91	24.2
0.8	33	40	46	60	15.9	35	46	56	66	17.9
0.9	24	28	37	47	12.5	25	32	39	46	12.4
1.0	>200					>200				

Our results confirm many of the results given previously for RFP in Bodin (1974) and Edgerton (1973c). There exists a maximum value of α over which convergence does not occur, and for many cases of RFP this α_{max} is equal to the optimum value of α (more correctly one can say that α_{opt} and α_{max} are so close that increments of α of the order used in practice do not detect any difference). For nonlinear models the use of TSLS start does not give any advantages over OLS start, a difference compared with linear models, again confirming the results given in Edgerton (1973c). One can note that convergence is quick and problem-free for this model.

In Table 13 we give the number of iterations and time used for the various FP methods,[17] using $\alpha = 0.9$ and convergence criterion 10^{-6}. We have used OLS start and the near-optimal ordering. Note that the times vary somewhat from the results given in the postscript to Edgerton (1973c) due to a modification in the Univac 1108 since that monograph was published. We also give in this table the number of iterations needed for convergence of the *ex post* forecasts; see also Table 14.

Note that the times are not linear in the number of iterations (*NOIT*) in Table 13 since slightly more complicated subroutines must be used as the number of FP Taylor terms increases. Note also that for FP:*G2* we obtained convergence in 72 iterations taking 34 seconds when $\alpha = 1.0$. We did not obtain any forecasts here, however, using 100 iterations.

In Table 14 we give the convergence results for the predictions using the Classical methods. We calculated the predictions inside the sample period time-point by time-point, and thus the columns 'Max iter' and 'Min iter' refer to the number of iterations for the slowest and fastest time-point. As we can see the maximum number of iterations lies well above the FP methods in many cases. More detailed examination of the time-points reveals that it is in the pre-war period that the greatest number of iterations are used. This is interesting, since the iterations are started using the observed values of the endogenous variables, y_t, and converge to the predictions, $\hat{y}_t$. The number of iterations used is thus a measure of

TABLE 13
Convergence properties of the different FP methods.

	0	*R0**	*R1*	*R2*	*R3*	*G0**	*G1*	*G2*	*G3*
NOIT (sample)	47	41	68	55	52	56	57	125	59
Time (seconds)	12	13	24	20	21	20	22	53	27
NOIT (*ex post*)	30	31	36	35	45	29	30	39	46

[17] We used double precision on Lund's Computer Centre's Univac 1108.

TABLE 14
Convergence properties of the Classical methods for prediction.

	Aligned model			Non-aligned model		
	Sample period		*Ex post*	Sample period		*Ex post*
	Max iter	Min iter		Max iter	Min iter	
OLS	58	24	28	78	34	37
TSLS:*R4*	112	38	39	173	31	37
TSLS:*R5*	50	18	21	56	31	37
TSLS:*R6*	57	23	26	266	35	39
TSLS:*R7*	58	24	28	201	34	42
TSLS:*R8*	56	24	27	159	33	41
TSLS:*R9*	57	24	30	169	33	41
TSLS:*S4*	641	91	109	>600	93	109
TSLS:*S5*	746	88	103	>600	98	113
TSLS:*S6*	67	32	35	89	32	39
TSLS:*S7*	52	25	30	46	22	27
TSLS:*S8*	45	21	29	140	34	41
TSLS:*S9*	51	23	27	177	33	40

$\|y_t - \hat{y}_t\|$, that is the goodness of fit of the model for that time-point. Since the same pattern is observed in all methods one can conclude that the model is less applicable in the pre-war period. For the non-aligned TSLS:*S4* we obtained a max iteration of 567 using $\Delta = 10^{-5}$, and for TSLS:*S5* we obtained a max iteration of 338 using the same Δ and $\alpha = 0.8$.

5. Conclusion

The main conclusion of this article is that the theoretical results given in Edgerton (1973c) are well supported by the empirical results we have obtained. The use of Taylor expansions around the unbiased predictor yields better predictions with the GEID estimator when applied to the nonlinear Klein–Goldberger model, and the use of two or three terms yields very satisfactory *ex post* forecasts. It can also be seen that the use of the first term of the Taylor series (which is used in a GEID specification) seems to be superior to the exclusion of that term (which is implied by the REID specification). We have thus obtained some evidence in favour of a GEID specification for this model.

The use of principal components with TSLS estimation is not at all problem free. The best results were obtained using only a few components calculated from the correlation matrix. The use of the unnormalized covariance matrix seems unadvisable, especially when using only a few components. TSLS:*S4* and TSLS:*S5* provided very unsatisfactory results for both the parameter estimates and the predictions. In general the choice of the number of components to use seems very problematical.

This study has provided no firm evidence in support of either the aligned or the non-aligned model. For the TSLS estimators the aligned model seems best for predictions inside the sample period, whilst the non-aligned model seems superior for the *ex post* forecasts. For OLS the aligned model seems slightly better in both cases. Equation 6 seems highly unsatisfactory in both models, however. It is evident that further research in the development of FP methods for non-aligned models would be of help.

The convergence properties of RFP proved very satisfactory in this model. The same cannot be said for the IIV method used, RSIIV, which did not converge for any choice of relaxation parameter. The convergence of the predictions inside the sample period also proved difficult for some of the TSLS methods.

Finally one can say that the model seems to be quite severely mis-specified, both in the fact that several equations give very dubious parameter estimates, R^2_{SF} and Durbin–Watson statistics for some or all estimation methods, and also in the fact that there are indications that the model is not appropriate in the pre-war period.

Appendix

TABLE A.1
Definition of the variables.

C_d =	Consumption of durables, billions of 1954 dollars.
C_n =	Consumption of non-durables, billions of 1954 dollars.
Y =	Personal disposable income, billions of 1954 dollars.
I =	Investment in plant and equipment, billions of 1954 dollars.
X =	Gross national product, billions of 1954 dollars.
W_1 =	Private employee wages and salaries, billions of 1954 dollars.
W_2 =	Public employee wages and salaries, billions of 1954 dollars.
r =	Average yield on corporate bonds, percent.
R =	Residential construction, billions of 1954 dollars.
r_S =	Yield on prime commercial paper, 4–6 months, percent.
H =	Stock of inventories, billions of 1954 dollars.
I_m =	Imports, billions of 1954 dollars.
p_m =	Implicit price deflator for imports, 1954 = 1.00.
N_w =	Wage and salary workers, millions.
N_G =	Government employees, millions.
N_S =	Self-employed, millions.
N_L =	Total labour force, millions.
h =	Index of hours worked per week, 1954 = 1.00.
w =	Annual earnings, thousands of current dollars.
p =	Implicit GNP deflator, 1954 = 1.00.
S_c =	Corporate saving, including inventory valuation adjustment, billions of 1954 dollars.
P_c =	Corporate profits, including inventory valuation adjustment, billions of 1954 dollars.
T_c =	Corporate profit taxes, billions of current dollars.
π_c =	Proprietors income, billions of 1954 dollars.
π_r =	Rental income, billions of 1954 dollars.
D =	Capital consumption allowances, billions of current dollars.
D_u =	Dummy variable, 0 for 1929–1946, 1 for 1947–1965.
r_d =	Average discount rate at all Federal Reserve Banks, percent.
R_e =	Year-end ratio of members bank's excess to required reserves.
G =	Government expenditures, billions of 1954 dollars.
E =	Exports, billions of 1954 dollars.
T_i =	Reconciling item between net national product and income, billions of current dollars.
T =	Personal taxes plus social service contribution less government business transfer payments less interest on government debt, billions of 1954 dollars.

TABLE A.2
Definition of model variables.

Endogenous variables	Predetermined variables
$y_1 = C_d$	$z_1 = 1$
$y_2 = C_n$	$z_2 = y_{-1}$
$y_3 = R$	$z_3 = (C_d)_{-1}$
$y_4 = H$	$z_4 = (C_n)_{-1}$
$y_5 = I_m$	$z_5 = r_{-1}$
$y_6 = N_w - N_G + N_S - 0.95(N_w - N_G + N_S)_{-1}$	$z_6 = R_{-1}$
$y_7 = h$	$z_7 = H_{-1}$
$y_8 = W_1$	$z_8 = (I_m)_{-1}$
$y_9 = w - w_{-1}$	$z_9 = p_m$
$y_{10} = r$	$z_{10} = W_2$
$y_{11} = pS_c$	$z_{11} = (X - W_2)_{-1}$
$y_{12} = p\pi_c$	$z_{12} = N_G - N_S + 0.95(N_w - N_G + N_S)_{-1}$
$y_{13} = p\pi_r$	$z_{13} = h_{-1}$
$y_{14} = I$	$z_{14} = w_{-1}$
$y_{15} = D$	$z_{15} = N_L - N_S$
$y_{16} = r_S$	$z_{16} = (W_1)_{-1}$
$y_{17} = X$	$z_{17} = p_{-1}$
$y_{18} = pY$	$z_{18} = (pP_c - T_c - pS_c)_{-1}$
$y_{19} = Y - 0.7Y$	$z_{19} = T_c$
$y_{20} = X - (H - H_{-1})$	$z_{20} = (p\pi_c)_{-1}$
$y_{21} = X - W_2 - 0.95(X - W_2)_{-1}$	$z_{21} = (p\pi_r)_{-1}$
$y_{22} = I + R$	$z_{22} = I_{-1}$
$y_{23} = h - 0.95h_{-1}$	$z_{23} = \Sigma_{i=1}^{20} [p(I + R)]_{-1}$
$y_{24} = N_L - N_w - N_S$	$z_{24} = D_u$
$y_{25} = X - W_2$	$z_{25} = r_d$
$y_{26} = r - r_{-1}$	$z_{26} = (R_e)_{-1}$
$y_{27} = W_1 + W_2$	$z_{27} = G + E$
$y_{28} = w$	$z_{28} = T_i$
$y_{29} = N_w$	$z_{29} = T$
$y_{30} = p\pi$	
$y_{31} = p_m - p$	
$y_{32} = p - p_{-1}$	
$y_{33} = pP_c - T_c$	
$y_{34} = p$	
$y_{35} = pX$	
$y_{36} = p(I + R)$	
$y_{37} = p(W_1 + W_2)$	
$y_{38} = Y$	
$y_{39} = \pi = P_c + \pi_c$	
$y_{40} = P_c$	
$y_{41} = S_c$	
$y_{42} = \pi_r$	

Chapter 10

ON FIX-POINT ESTIMATION IN INTERDEPENDENT SYSTEMS WITH SPECIFICATION ERRORS

ANDERS WESTLUND

1. Introduction

Economists and econometricians often claim that the problem to choose technique for estimating econometric models is of minor importance, at least in comparison with problems of model specification and data collection. In principle, this seems to be a reasonable judgement. However, it must be emphasized that if attempts to specify the econometric model and collect data are not completely successful (the model will be mis-specified and/or quality of data will be unsatisfactory), the basis for argument will change. Then, the choice of estimation technique will probably often be decisive of the possibilities to at all apply the results given by the econometric work. It is a well-known fact that different estimation approaches are based on various assumptions concerning the econometric model, and perhaps more important, the different estimation approaches are more or less robust against departures from such assumptions. The concept of specification error within econometrics should in fact be related to the techniques applied for analysis. Consequently, whether the purpose of econometric model building is structural estimation, prediction, or planning and control, the reliability in application depends on choice of estimation technique, besides on the qualities of model specification and data.

In evaluating econometric estimators various approaches have been used. That evaluation work is partly directed towards assessing the effects of structural specification errors on structural estimation and prediction. However, there is still much work to be done in order to obtain enough knowledge concerning robustness of different estimators. The ultimate goal here is to learn about the exact distributions of the estimators. Due to the great complexities involved in the exact analytical small-sample technique, it has not to a great extent been used for analysing the specification problems. Exceptions known to the author are Richardson (1970), which gives an analysis of robustness of Ordinary Least Squares (OLS) estimation, and Hale (1976) and Hale et al. (1976), where effects of mis-specification of the exact sampling distributions of the k-class estimators are studied. The specification errors considered are wrong exclusion of relevant exogenous variables and wrong inclusion of irrelevant exogenous variables.

One way to overcome some of the mathematical complexities is to release the small-sample restrictions. The large-sample asymptotic approach is applied in Fisher (1966),[1] where comparisons of asymptotic behaviour between the Limited Information Maximum Likelihood (LIML) and Two-Stage Least Squares (TSLS) estimators are given. Cases of wrong omission of exogenous variables are examined (the specification errors remain fixed), when time series length increases. The results are somewhat discouraging as, by the criterion used, there is no possibility to discriminate between the two estimators. Further similar comparisons are given in Fisher (1967).

Another way of simplifying the exact theoretical small-sample approach, still assuming small samples, is the small-σ method. This approach is introduced in Kadane (1971) and then applied by Ramage (1971) to study, in the context of single equation k-class estimation, the effects of three types of mis-specification, viz.

(i) omission of system variables from a single equation;

(ii) omission of variables from the entire system;

(iii) mis-classification of endogenous variables as exogenous.

Ramage compares the relative sensitivity of the estimators to specification errors, and determines the relative seriousness for estimation of the three types of specification errors under investigation. In particular the comparisons show that, with respect to mean squared error approximations, the TSLS estimator dominates LIML to the order of approximations, when the degree of overidentification in the actually used equation does not exceed 6. Furthermore, OLS seems to dominate TSLS under more restrictive conditions, and both types of omission of variable errors become increasingly more serious than comparable mis-classification of variable errors, as the relative size of the specification errors increases.

Most studies of the mis-specification problem in ID system analysis are done according to the Monte Carlo principle. Although this approach faces several inherent difficulties, e.g. the problem of generalization of results from such studies, most knowledge of robustness within econometric analysis is probably to be taken from Monte Carlo studies. One way to partially overcome the difficulty of misleading generalizations is, furthermore, to systematically combine theoretical analysis and numerical simula-

[1] Cf. Nagar (1959).

tion. Results obtained in a majority of such Monte Carlo studies are summarized in Smith (1973) and in Sowey (1973).

Evaluation of the Fix-Point (FP) technique, originally introduced by Wold (1965), is so far to a very small extent directed towards aspects concerning robustness against defects in structural specification. Thus, the purpose of this paper is mainly to indicate some robustness properties of FP estimation. The results are based on a small Monte Carlo study. Before introducing design and presenting results of the study, we will give some short comments on the concept of specification error.

The general framework within which estimation, prediction and control are carried out usually includes several assumptions concerning the residuals. These are assumed (i) not to be correlated with the exogenous variables, (ii) to be serially, and sometimes mutually independent, (iii) to have first- and second-order moments (characterized by homoscedasticity), and furthermore (iv) often to be normally distributed. The concept of specification error is generally introduced as errors that will cause departures from such assumptions. Thus, specification errors might be

- essential variables (exogenous or endogenous) have been wrongly omitted, or replaced by insufficient substitutes;
- incorrect functional forms have been used in a number of system relations;
- wrong a priori restrictions have been used on some parts of the structural form;
- a wrong assumption of structural stability has been formulated.

We will refer to these four situations as the errors of specification, and the consequent departures from the residual assumptions as primary effects (rather than errors of specification). To these problems should be added certain problems of data; e.g. errors of measurement (which may influence the residual distributions), co-variations of different exogenous variables as far as trend, business-cycle and seasons are concerned (which will cause multicollinearity and problems of analytical precision). Specification errors may be deliberately introduced in such situations, as variables or equations may be omitted in order to combat the multicollinearity problem.

As econometric ID systems only are approximations of reality, and of necessity, they abstract from the real world by limiting the number of variables included in each equation and in the system as a whole, there are in reality always more variables in each equation, than are assumed in practical approximations. Furthermore, outside equations always exist, either relating variables in the model alone, or relating them to unincluded variables. Thus, there are always in principle specification errors due to wrong omission of variables [cf. the discussion in Liu (1960) and in Fisher (1961)]. But as the 'apparent hypothesis' of an ID structure includes residuals, just the fact that the model is an approximation of reality does not mean that it is wrongly specified. This illustrates the realitivity of the concept of specification errors.

The common assumption of normally distributed residuals representing sums of impacts from a large number of variables, each following a distribution with finite variance is, however, probably rather restrictive. Of course, observed distributions of economic variables will never display infinite second-order moments, but only such moments sufficiently large to be regarded as actually infinite. There is, however, considerable evidence that many economic variables are represented by distributions that may be characterized by infinite variances. As the residuals are interpreted to represent the complete impact of several omitted variables, it is certainly sometimes likely that part of the residuals of econometric models will possess infinite variances. Based on a general form of the central limit theorem [see Gnedenko-Kolmogorov (1954)], the residuals will thus probably often follow a symmetric stable distribution.

The Monte Carlo study given here, thus includes robustness analysis for the Fix-Point technique and some alternative estimators, within cases characterized by wrong omission of variables and wrong assumption of residual normality.

2. The Design of a Monte Carlo Study

One approach for obtaining information on the small sample properties of different methods for structural and reduced form estimation is thus the Monte Carlo technique. This technique is based on a frame of reference under control of the experimentor. The properties of a given estimator may be found for different sample sizes, error structures, and structural conditions, different techniques may be compared for a given frame of reference, as well as performances of a given technique for different frames of reference. The main draw-back of the Monte Carlo technique is that generalizations beyond the framework used require extensive testing procedures and also applications of experimental designs. However, by some kind of analytical confirmation, hypothesis generated by Monte Carlo studies may be placed in general theory.

The present Monte Carlo study involves just one main structure, but furthermore several, in different ways, wrongly specified modifications of that structure. The main structure is the following overidentified three-relation system:

$$\begin{aligned}
\text{(S-0):}\quad y_{1t} &= \beta_{12}y_{2t} + \beta_{13}y_{3t} + \gamma_{11}z_{1t} + \gamma_{12}z_{2t} + \delta_{1t},\\
y_{2t} &= \beta_{21}y_{1t} + \gamma_{23}z_{3t} + \gamma_{24}z_{4t} + \gamma_{25}z_{5t} + \delta_{2t},\\
y_{3t} &= \beta_{31}y_{1t} + \gamma_{33}z_{3t} + \gamma_{34}z_{4t} + \gamma_{36}z_{6t} + \delta_{3t}.
\end{aligned} \tag{2.1}$$

System (2.1) will be used as the 'theoretically true' structure of the study.[2] The parameter input matrix is given by

$$\beta_{ij},\quad i,j = 1,2,3;\qquad \gamma_{ij},\quad i = 1,2,3,\quad j = 1,\cdots,6.$$

0	0.1	0.9	−0.5	0.5	0	0	0	0
−0.2	0	0	0	0	2.1	−0.3	0.6	0
0.2	0	0	0	0	−1.9	0.1	0	−0.5

With structure (S-1) effects are studied when one endogenous variable (and consequently one relation) is wrongly omitted. Three alternatives are here analyzed:

(S-1, 1): the first relation in (2.1) is omitted, and $\beta_{21} = \beta_{31} = 0$,

(S-1, 2): the second relation in (2.1) is omitted, and $\beta_{12} = 0$,

(S-1, 3): the third relation in (2.1) is omitted, and $\beta_{13} = 0$.

As $|\beta_{12}| \simeq |\beta_{21}| \simeq |\beta_{31}| < |\beta_{13}|$ is used, there are some possibilities to study effects of 'essential' vs 'less essential' wrongly omitted endogenous variables, i.e., y_{3t} has been given the position of being an 'essential' endogenous variable.

In structure (S-2), aspects of wrongly omitted 'essential' vs 'less essential' exogenous variables are elucidated. Thus,

(S-2, 1): $\gamma_{23} = \gamma_{33} = 0$

[2] $E(\delta_t\delta_t') = \begin{bmatrix} 1 & 0.15 & 0.15 \\ & 1 & 0.15 \\ & & 1 \end{bmatrix}.$

and

$$(\text{S-2}, 2): \; \gamma_{24} = \gamma_{34} = 0$$

are estimated. It is seen that $|\gamma_{23}| \simeq |\gamma_{33}| > |\gamma_{24}| \simeq |\gamma_{34}|$, i.e., z_{3t} is a 'more essential' exogenous variable than z_{4t}.

In structure (S-3) the above mentioned effects of specification errors as serially correlated residuals are studied. The exogenous variable z_{5t} is chosen to be accentuatedly serially correlated.

Thus,

$$(\text{S-3}, 1): \; \gamma_{25} = 0$$

and

$$(\text{S-3}, 2): \; \gamma_{36} = 0$$

are estimated within the present Monte Carlo study.

The problems of collinearity are partly computational and partly problems of reliability of individual coefficients. The collinearity pattern problem is usual in applied econometrics, as it arises when basic trends and cycles pervade many economic time series in a similar way. That causes the great interrelationships among e.g. the exogenous variables, and moment matrices will be almost singular, and therefore difficult to invert. Thus, it has been considered important to shed some light on that essential problem in this Monte Carlo study. The time series values z_{1t}, $t = 1, 2, \cdots, 30$, are therefore permuted in order to become highly correlated to z_{2t}, $t = 1, 2, \cdots, 30$, which corresponds to structure (S-C). One proposed solution to a collinearity problem will be to use principal components instead of all separate exogenous variables. In the case of just one highly disturbing correlation (as in the actual situation), it may be suitable to exclude one variable and thus inaugurate a specification error. That situation is studied in structure (S-4), where z_{1t} will be excluded,

$$(\text{S-4}): \; \gamma_{11} = 0.$$

Another problem regarded in this study is residual heteroscedasticity, which is likely to occur when the quality of structure gradually aggravates. One part of the study thus includes a successive increase of the residual variance in the third structural relation. The following assumptions are made:

$$\begin{aligned}
&\text{var}(\delta_{1t}) = \text{var}(\delta_{2t}) = \sigma_\delta^2, \\
&\text{var}(\delta_{3t}) = \sigma_\delta^2, \qquad t = 1, \cdots, 10, \\
&\text{var}(\delta_{3t}) = 4\sigma_\delta^2, \qquad t = 11, \cdots, 20, \\
&\text{var}(\delta_{3t}) = 9\sigma_\delta^2, \qquad t = 21, \cdots, 30,
\end{aligned}$$

and the structure is here denoted (S-H).

So far, the residuals have been assumed normally distributed. There is, however, a mounting evidence that residuals of econometric systems display distributional characteristics different from those of normal distributions. Thus, residuals generated from the symmetric stable distribution class are applied. This class of distributions has been chosen because if the elements of an econometric time series (as the residuals) are considered to be sums of a large number of independent elements, the distribution of the series should also belong to that class. The distributions may be defined by the characteristic function with a location parameter of zero and a scale parameter of unity,

$$\begin{aligned}
f(t;\alpha,\beta) &= \exp(-|t|^\alpha \exp(-\tfrac{1}{2}\pi i\beta k(\alpha)\text{sign}(t))), \quad \alpha \neq 1, \quad 0 < \alpha \leq 2, \\
&= \exp(-|t|(1 + (2/\pi)i\beta \ln|t|\,\text{sign}(t))), \quad \alpha = 1,
\end{aligned} \tag{2.2}$$

where α is the characteristic exponent, and β a skewness parameter $(-1 \leq \alpha \leq 1,\ k(\alpha) = 1 - |1 - \alpha|)$.

The normal distribution is stable with $\alpha = 2$. Another special case is the Cauchy distribution ($\alpha = 1$). Properties of the class of stable distributions are reviewed in Feller (1966).

Unfortunately, density functions can not be given explicitly for the members of this class (the normal and the Cauchy distributions are of course exceptions). The computer program used in this study in order to generate stable symmetrically distributed residuals is given in Chambers et al. (1976). The characteristic exponent is varied as $\alpha = 1.0(0.2)2.0$, and $\beta = 0$.

The exogenous variables used in the simulation process are all uniformly distributed random drawings with the density function

$$\begin{aligned}
f(z) &= 1/(b_i - a_i) \qquad a_i < z < b_i, \\
&= 0 \qquad \text{elsewhere}.
\end{aligned} \tag{2.3}$$

The ranges of those distributions are chosen as presented in Table 1.

TABLE 1

Exogenous variables	Range	
	a_i	b_i
z_1	5	10
z_2	15	30
z_3	0.5	50
z_4	2	8
z_5	8	22
z_6	10	14

For each residual distribution and sample size, the estimates of the structural form parameters are calculated by the (i) Fix-Point (FP) technique, and furthermore by (ii) Ordinary Least Squares (OLS), (iii) Two-Stage Least Squares (TSLS), (iv) Direct L_1-Norm[3] estimator (OLA), and finally (v) Two-Stage L_1-Norm estimator (2SLA). In addition, reduced form estimation and conditional predictions are made within the study. The reduced form is estimated directly by two methods, viz. (i) Least Squares No Restriction (LSNR), and (ii) L_1-Norm Estimation and No Restriction (LANR).

In this Monte Carlo study, the number of replications is 100. The reason for that is mainly that in numerous other Monte Carlo studies, that number of replications has been found to be reasonably sufficient. Furthermore, some comments should be given concerning the sample sizes used. The main purpose of such Monte Carlo studies is to investigate the small-sample properties of structural estimators and predictions. The concept 'small sample' is, of course, relative. For practical purposes, the studies usually choose time series length $T \leq 50$. This is a realistic bound for most samples dealing with annual time series or grouped cross-section data. Monthly and quarterly time series are often longer, but small sample investigations are often not relevant in these instances. (Furthermore, serial correlation will cut down the effective sample size.) The present study is based on relatively short time series, viz. $T = 10$ and $T = 20$.

In econometric applications the best test for evaluating different estimators is dictated by the particular decisions, which will be based upon the estimated structure. This is due to the fact that it is much easier to select a relevant criterion for evaluation in specific applications when the

[3] The L_1-norm is defined as follows: given the data y_i and assuming it is of the form $y_i = a^* + e_i$ where e_i are the random variables, then the number a_1 is the L_1-norm estimate of a^*, if a_1 minimizes $\sum_{i=1}^{n} |y_i - a_1|$.

model builder is in possession of a priori experience of the approximate structure, sample size used, the relative importance of bias and precision properties, etc. If thus, the choice of estimation principle is to be made relative to specific applications, it is not possible to follow that line in these evaluation circumstances. The basic criteria for selection will therefore be non-committal in relation to loss functions of underlying decision processes.

An examination of the means and standard deviations of the estimators of the structural parameters is made in terms of summary statistics. These permit evaluations on the basis of criteria as smallest bias and smallest standard deviation. A combined measure of these two criteria is the Root Mean Square Error (RMSE). In the Monte Carlo evaluation, we will thus study

$$\text{Observed bias}\,(\hat{\alpha}) = \frac{1}{S}\sum_{s=1}^{S} a_s - \alpha, \tag{2.4}$$

where a_s is the estimate of the parameter α in the sth sample replication, and S is the number of replications,

$$\text{Observed stand.dev.}(\hat{\alpha}) = \left(\frac{1}{S-1}\sum_{s=1}^{S}\left(a_s - \frac{1}{S}\sum_{s=1}^{S} a_s\right)^2\right)^{1/2}, \tag{2.5}$$

$$\text{Observed RMSE}(\hat{\alpha}) = \left(\frac{1}{S}\sum_{s=1}^{S}(a_s - \alpha)^2\right)^{1/2}. \tag{2.6}$$

The criteria described in (2.4)–(2.6) will furthermore be used in evaluating predictions of endogenous variables for different prediction horizons. Unless there is a specific interest in individual structural or reduced form parameters or in predictions on individual prediction horizons, the predictive power test according to Ball's (1963) Q^2-measure is a simple summary measure of the entire set of estimates and predictions by the model

$$Q_i^2 = 1 - \left(\sum_{t=1}^{T}(y_{it}^p - y_{it})^2\right) \Big/ \left(\sum_{t=1}^{T}(y_{it} - \bar{y}_{it})^2\right). \tag{2.7}$$

Q^2 is determined for each endogenous variable, within the sample period, as well as within the prediction period.

Different criteria, of course, lead to different selections of preferred methods of estimation. Furthermore, it should be observed that different types of structure will influence the estimation methods in different ways through different criteria.

3. Some Results of the Study

The main results of the Monte Carlo study, designed according to the presentation above, are given in this section and supplemented with certain tables and figures. First, some comments on the structural estimation are given, and then prediction abilities by different reduced form estimation approaches are illustrated.

In estimating the structural form of the system, besides the FP technique four estimators are applied (OLS, TSLS, OLA and 2SLA). For the different structures and residual distribution cases and each estimator various summary statistics are prepared, viz. mean biases, root mean squared errors and standard deviations. Furthermore, results from the individual replicates are available, and so it is possible to make pairwise comparisons and to estimate the sampling distributions of each estimator. We will, however, concentrate the discussion on results concerning the RMSE and bias criterions.

The first and most simple comparison is here based on just the number of times that one specific estimator gives the best results. Table 2 gives a summary according to the RMSE criterion. The picture is very clear. Thus, the OLS method is dominating for the structures where residuals are normally distributed. The second best technique is evidently the FP

TABLE 2
Frequencies of best results for structural parameter estimates on smallest RMSE criterion.

Structure	$T = 10$ Estimators					$T = 20$ Estimators				
	OLS	OLA	TSLS	2SLA	FP	OLS	OLA	TSLS	2SLA	FP
(S-0)	10	0	0	0	2	7	0	2	0	3
(S-1, 1)	—	—	—	—	—	—	—	—	—	—
(S-1, 2)	6	0	1	0	0	3	0	3	0	1
(S-1, 3)	3	1	1	0	2	4	0	0	0	3
(S-2, 1)	8	0	0	0	2	6	1	0	1	2
(S-2, 2)	7	0	1	0	2	6	0	2	0	2
(S-3, 1)	10	0	0	0	1	8	0	1	1	1
(S-3, 2)	6	1	1	0	3	7	0	1	1	2
(S-4)	7	0	1	0	3	9	0	0	0	2
(S-C)	6	0	2	0	4	9	0	0	0	3
(S-H)	10	0	0	0	2	10	0	0	2	0
(S-0, $\alpha = 2.0$)	8	0	1	0	3	9	0	2	0	1
(S-0, $\alpha = 1.8$)	3	7	0	1	1	4	7	0	1	0
(S-0, $\alpha = 1.6$)	3	6	1	2	0	2	9	0	1	0
(S-0, $\alpha = 1.4$)	3	6	1	2	0	0	8	0	4	0
(S-0, $\alpha = 1.2$)	4	4	0	4	0	0	7	0	5	0
(S-0, $\alpha = 1.0$)	0	7	0	5	0	0	2	0	10	0

method. There are no clear differences in results between the two alternative sample sizes, and furthermore no clear differences between the structure (S-0) and the mis-specified cases. Contrary to the results given by Hunt et al. (1974), the results in the normal cases are here clear in favour of the L_2-norm estimators. The FP technique is apparently not robust against incorrect normality assumptions for residual distributions. OLS loses its leading position and the L_1-norm estimators tend to give more 'best' results as the residual distribution will be more non-normal. There is also a tendency that 2SLA is relatively better than OLA, when the sample size is increasing.

The next question is whether it is possible to obtain a consistent ranking of the five estimators based on the RMSE summary measure. The sum of the ranks for each estimator and each residual distribution are consequently determined and are here given in Table 3. The ranks will range from 1 for the best estimator to 5 for the worst one. These ranks mainly confirm the results given in Table 2, i.e., that OLS is the best estimator for normally distributed cases (mis-specified, or not), that L_1-norm estimators outperform L_2-norm estimators as soon as α is less than 2, and that the FP technique is clearly less good as residuals are non-normal. The above formulated hypothesis that FP is the second-best technique in the normal cases is not confirmed by the ranking results. That position is here taken by the TSLS method, which leaves FP to be the third best technique.

TABLE 3
Structural parameter estimates; rankings by smallest RMSE.

Structure	$T = 10$ Estimators					$T = 20$ Estimators				
	OLS	OLA	TSLS	2SLA	FP	OLS	OLA	TSLS	2SLA	FP
(S-0)	15	42	27.5	58	37.5	18.5	48.5	26.5	56.5	30
(S-1, 1)	—	—	—	—	—	—	—	—	—	—
(S-1, 2)	8.5	23.5	14.5	35	23.5	12.5	26	12	33	21.5
(S-1, 3)	13	22.5	18	33.5	18	11	25.5	17.5	34	17
(S-2, 1)	14	27	26	46	37	21	31	27	41	30
(S-2, 2)	12.5	38	21	48	30.5	19	36.5	20.5	46	28
(S-3, 1)	13	31.5	30.5	52	38	19	37.5	27.5	49	32
(S-3, 2)	20	30.5	28.5	50.5	35.5	18	36	29.5	48	33.5
(S-4)	16	37	34	51	27	16	35.5	33	50.5	30
(S-C)	21	47.5	25	58.5	28	17.5	41	31.5	58	32
(S-H)	14	32	45	48	41	17	35.5	33.5	45	49
(S-0, $\alpha = 2.0$)	18	46	24	58	34	18	47	24	57	34
(S-0, $\alpha = 1.8$)	29	25	41.5	43	41.5	30	22	36	42	50
(S-0, $\alpha = 1.6$)	29	24	42	34	51	41	17	40	27	55
(S-0, $\alpha = 1.4$)	31	21	42	31	55	40	20	43	21	56
(S-0, $\alpha = 1.2$)	24	23	48	33	52	40	17	48	19	56
(S-0, $\alpha = 1.0$)	31	17	51	28	53	42	22	50	14	52

The question is, however, whether the rankings are consistent enough, i.e., if rankings are similar for different parameters to be estimated. In order to test for that consistency, Kendall's W test statistic is computed. It is then found that all cases lead to acceptable consistency (significancy at 0.05 or 0.01 levels). The main conclusion to be drawn is therefore that there is a certain confidence in the rankings given in Table 3 according to the RMSE criterion.

As the RMSE measure is a function of bias and standard deviation it is interesting to evaluate the relative contributions of these measures to RMSE. We have here limited ourselves to some comments on the bias criterion. As is well-known from earlier studies, according to the bias criterion, TSLS clearly dominates OLS. Similarly 2SLA dominates OLA. Consequently, TSLS gives smaller bias than OLA as far as for $\alpha = 1.4$ in the non-normal residual specifications. Table 4 furthermore shows that the FP technique is relatively better here than according to the RMSE criterion, and seems to be the second best method in normal as well as non-normal cases.

TABLE 4a
Frequencies of best results for structural parameter estimates based on the smallest bias criterion.

Structure	$T = 10$ Estimators					$T = 20$ Estimators				
	OLS	OLA	TSLS	2SLA	FP	OLS	OLA	TSLS	2SLA	FP
(S-0)	2	1	5	4	0	1	1	7	1	2
(S-0, $\alpha = 2.0$)	1	0	2	4	5	1	0	6	1	4
(S-0, $\alpha = 1.8$)	0	1	6	2	3	2	1	4	3	2
(S-0, $\alpha = 1.6$)	1	2	0	3	6	2	0	3	5	2
(S-0, $\alpha = 1.4$)	0	1	1	5	5	1	1	1	7	2
(S-0, $\alpha = 1.2$)	0	3	0	6	3	1	1	0	9	1
(S-0, $\alpha = 1.0$)	1	3	1	4	3	1	1	0	9	1

TABLE 4b
Structural parameter estimates; rankings by smallest bias.

Structure	$T = 10$ Estimators					$T = 20$ Estimators				
	OLS	OLA	TSLS	2SLA	FP	OLS	OLA	TSLS	2SLA	FP
(S-0)	40.5	42	23	35	39.5	44	51	18.5	34.5	32
(S-0, $\alpha = 2.0$)	43	50	27	26	34	42	49	21	42	26
(S-0, $\alpha = 1.8$)	56	40	33	26	25	48	39	29	29	35
(S-0, $\alpha = 1.6$)	52	39	39	22	28	51	39	31	23	36
(S-0, $\alpha = 1.4$)	54	41	38	20	27	50	33	36	19	42
(S-0, $\alpha = 1.2$)	50	37	45	18	30	51	33	44	16	36
(S-0, $\alpha = 1.0$)	46	35	44	25	30	50	29	45	17	39

The relative differences between estimators according to RMSE and bias criterions are illustrated in Figures 1 and 2. The curves given there typically represent most structural parameters estimated within the study.

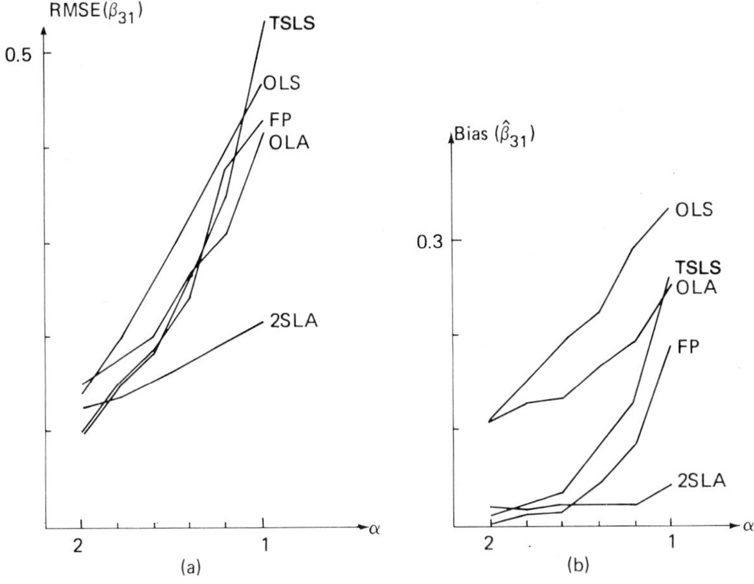

FIGURE 1. (a) RMSE($\hat{\beta}_{31}$), $\alpha = 1(0.2)2$, $T = 20$; (b) bias ($\hat{\beta}_{31}$), $\alpha = 1(0.2)2$, $T = 20$.

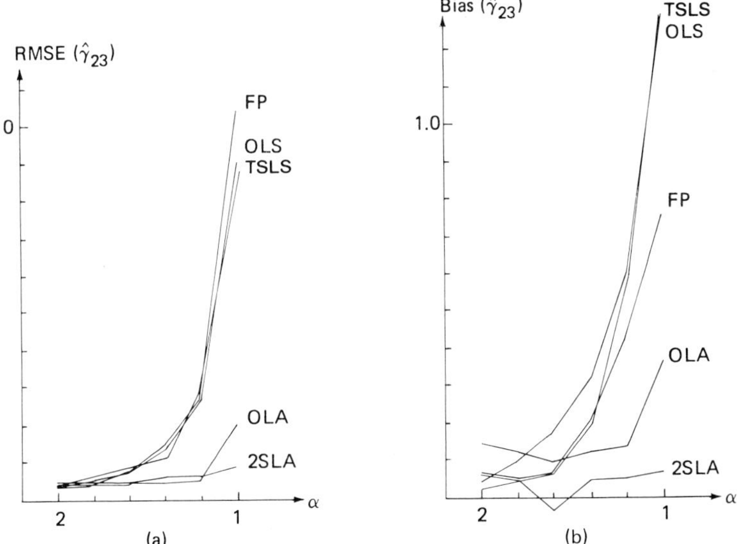

FIGURE 2. (a) RMSE ($\hat{\gamma}_{23}$), $\alpha = 1(0.2)2$, $T = 20$; (b) bias($\hat{\gamma}_{23}$), $\alpha = 1(0.2)2$, $T = 20$.

As was mentioned earlier the estimation results obtained in each single replicate are available. In ranking the five estimators within each replicate it is possible to further evaluate the summary rankings given above. There is in several cases, however, no clear consistency in rankings between the different replicates. What is then to explain the clear differences between estimators observed e.g. in Table 3? The reason is apparently significant differences in the sampling distributions of different estimators. As an example, it is above observed that TSLS is clearly better than 2SLA for the normal case, for $\alpha = 1.8$ they will almost be equally good, and then 2SLA will be the leading technique, and the difference is increasing with decreasing α. In examining the number of times TSLS is better than 2SLA for the 100 replicates, there is for different α some tendency in accordance with earlier results. In Table 5 some of these results are presented, and it is apparently seen that these results are more mixed. Most cases in that table will probably lead to insignificancy if testing for differences. If matching Table 5a with the results given in Table 5b, the situation is further

TABLE 5a
Number of times TSLS is better than 2SLA according to the smallest squared error criterion (100 replicates); $T = 20$.

Structure	Parameters				
	β_{12}	β_{13}	β_{21}	β_{31}	Σ_β
(S-0, $\alpha = 2.0$)	64	69	62	59	254
(S-0, $\alpha = 1.8$)	62	64	58	57	241
(S-0, $\alpha = 1.6$)	58	59	46	52	215
(S-0, $\alpha = 1.4$)	52	55	43	39	189
(S-0, $\alpha = 1.2$)	42	43	43	32	160
(S-0, $\alpha = 1.0$)	48	43	46	35	172

TABLE 5b
Number of times TSLS is within the 5 worst cases according to smallest squared error criterion (within 200 cases; 100 replicates for each of TSLS and 2SLA); $T = 20$.

Structure	Parameters				
	β_{12}	β_{13}	β_{21}	β_{31}	Σ_β
(S-0, $\alpha = 2.0$)	0	0	2	2	4
(S-0, $\alpha = 1.8$)	2	1	3	3	9
(S-0, $\alpha = 1.6$)	4	2	5	4	15
(S-0, $\alpha = 1.4$)	5	4	5	4	18
(S-0, $\alpha = 1.2$)	5	5	5	5	20
(S-0, $\alpha = 1.0$)	5	5	5	5	20

explained. These results will to some extent illustrate the relative differences in sampling distributions of TSLS and 2SLA, respectively, for different residual distributions.

The overall impressions obtained are the following. For the normal distribution cases, OLS is the best technique followed by FP and TSLS methods. For non-normal cases, OLA and 2SLA are the best techniques. The FP method by and large seems to be the worst alternative. However, if bias is the most interesting criterion of evaluation, the FP technique is better than OLS and TSLS. It should be noticed that the FP technique is to some extent treated in an unfair way. The FP algorithm used has not always converged within 50 iterations. That is the case especially for small α and $T = 10$. This observed difficulty in convergence of the iteration process, however, partly concerns the matter of cost and is one aspect that must be considered when relatively evaluating estimation approaches. Another drawback due to the evaluation of the FP method is, however, the fact that the present Monte Carlo study is concentrated on the classical assumptions of residual correlations. The more general GEID specification, for which just the FP technique still leads to consistent estimation, is not applied at all.

In estimating the reduced form and deriving conditional predictions seven estimators are used. Besides indirect estimation by the five techniques discussed above, direct estimation in reduced form is performed by the LSNR and LANR techniques. In evaluating prediction abilities by the different approaches several measures are determined, e.g. bias and precision of the predictions. We will, however, restrict our comments on prediction abilities by presenting results on just the Ball's Q^2 measure for prediction and sample periods, respectively. Q^2 results for prediction period are given in Table 6. As is seen, we have not written out all the Q^2 measures. Cases where Q^2 is too small, corresponding to extremely bad prediction abilities are marked by an *.

In the normal distribution cases TSLS and FP seem to be the best alternatives, and in opposition to the structural estimation situation clearly better than OLS. Direct estimation by LSNR (or LANR) is a relatively better alternative in mis-specification cases than in prediction based on structure (S-0). That is the case especially for $T = 20$ and the severe mis-specification cases, e.g. (S-1, 3) and (S-2, 1), and in the heteroscedasticity case (S-H). For the non-normal cases and $T = 10$, the FP technique is probably the best alternative. However, predictions here will very soon be of very bad quality. Therefore, it is unfortunately not possible to draw any wide conclusions from these results. For $T = 20$, however, some interesting results are given. As said before, for $\alpha = 2$, TSLS will be the best alternative. Then for $\alpha = 1.8$–1.2, 2SLA is apparently the leading alterna-

TABLE 6a
Ball's Q^2, prediction period, $T = 10$.

Structure	Estimators						
	OLS	OLA	TSLS	2SLA	FP	LSNR	LANR
	0.634	0.543	0.682	0.544	0.633	0.377	0.243
(S-0)	0.862	0.826	0.866	0.819	0.863	0.756	0.686
	0.529	0.419	0.605	0.449	0.572	0.357	0.156
(S-1, 1)	0.825	0.789	0.825	0.789	0.825	0.825	0.789
	0.580	0.486	0.580	0.486	0.580	0.580	0.486
(S-1, 2)	0.592	0.458	0.679	− 1.944	0.656	0.542	0.381
	0.499	0.373	0.607	− 4.491	0.581	0.540	0.444
(S-1, 3)	0.522	0.407	0.508	0.416	0.476	0.290	0.097
	0.851	0.817	0.846	0.785	0.828	0.787	0.722
	0.217	0.043	0.358	0.104	0.241	0.211	0.054
(S-2, 1)	− 0.348	− 0.591	− 0.202	− 0.416	− 0.572	− 0.404	− 0.852
	− 0.806	− 1.129	− 0.509	− 0.731	− 1.013	− 0.838	− 1.312
	0.644	0.537	0.694	0.345	0.632	0.424	0.241
(S-2, 2)	0.844	0.795	0.847	0.810	0.843	0.719	0.620
	0.537	0.414	0.623	0.407	0.588	0.377	0.179
	0.612	0.327	− 1.003	*	− 4.135	0.542	0.381
(S-3, 1)	− 0.189	− 1.411	− 1.207	*	*	− 1.158	− 2.364
	0.538	0.367	0.515	*	*	0.540	0.444
	*	*	− 6.514	*	0.127	0.290	0.097
(S-3, 2)	0.453	− 0.019	0.378	− 1.592	0.799	0.787	0.722
	*	*	− 9.133	*	− 2.402	− 0.194	− 0.313
	0.179	− 0.837	0.443	− 2.613	0.346	0.025	− 0.342
(S-4)	0.850	0.797	0.862	0.764	0.781	0.782	0.720
	0.359	− 0.166	0.591	− 3.070	0.579	0.423	0.187
	0.090	− 0.517	0.349	− 0.916	0.300	− 0.070	− 0.463
(S-C)	0.848	0.807	0.860	0.749	0.860	0.758	0.696
	0.319	− 0.320	0.547	− 0.992	0.530	0.370	0.077
	− 8.881	*	− 1.609	− 5.833	− 2.318	− 0.584	− 0.888
(S-H)	− 0.458	− 1.486	0.422	− 1.422	0.204	0.500	0.420
	− 8.063	*	− 1.350	− 7.246	− 2.126	− 0.599	− 0.840
	0.030	− 0.323	0.373	*	0.338	− 0.062	− 0.487
(S-0, $\alpha = 2.0$)	0.594	0.565	0.696	*	0.713	0.519	0.352
	− 0.084	− 0.382	0.281	*	0.301	− 0.213	− 0.516
	*	− 8.160	*	*	− 0.532	− 1.895	− 2.076
(S-0, $\alpha = 1.8$)	− 1.386	0.273	*	− 3.621	0.409	− 0.048	0.095
	*	*	*	*	− 1.170	− 1.715	− 2.281
	*	*	*	*	− 6.231	*	− 7.051
(S-0, $\alpha = 1.6$)	*	− 7.426	*	− 0.501	− 0.694	− 1.724	− 0.575
	*	*	*	*	− 8.793	− 9.357	*
	*	*	*	*	*	*	*
(S-0, $\alpha = 1.4$)	*	*	*	− 7.409	− 5.872	− 8.758	− 3.177
	*	*	*	*	*	*	*
(S-0, $\alpha = 1, 1.2$)	*	*	*	*	*	*	*

TABLE 6b

Ball's Q^2, prediction period, $T = 20$.

Structure	Estimators						
	OLS	OLA	TSLS	2SLA	FP	LSNR	LANR
(S-0)	0.759	0.723	0.782	0.734	0.778	0.748	0.691
	0.899	1.887	0.899	0.885	0.900	0.893	0.867
	0.722	0.691	0.763	0.710	0.760	0.739	0.699
(S-1, 1)	0.852	0.844	0.852	0.844	0.852	0.852	0.844
	0.705	0.686	0.705	0.686	0.705	0.705	0.686
(S-1, 2)	0.752	0.721	0.774	0.737	0.772	0.750	0.713
	0.723	0.694	0.763	0.723	0.759	0.751	0.717
(S-1, 3)	0.551	0.513	0.552	0.506	0.573	0.702	0.651
	0.887	0.873	0.879	0.855	0.896	0.892	0.876
(S-2, 1)	−0.355	−0.374	0.492	0.141	0.519	0.511	0.458
	−1.126	−1.066	0.050	0.059	0.059	0.242	0.211
	−2.267	−2.234	−0.144	−0.153	−0.148	−0.050	−0.095
(S-2, 2)	0.731	0.720	0.780	0.735	0.774	0.760	0.720
	0.878	0.863	0.876	0.862	0.878	0.869	0.855
	0.707	0.685	0.764	0.726	0.761	0.742	0.705
(S-3, 1)	0.720	0.643	0.724	0.429	0.764	0.750	0.713
	−0.241	−0.937	−0.236	−1.049	−0.212	0.198	0.043
	0.708	0.662	0.754	0.658	0.756	0.751	0.717
(S-3, 2)	0.549	0.482	0.657	0.586	0.716	0.702	0.651
	0.891	0.879	0.895	0.882	0.898	0.892	0.876
	0.287	0.225	0.470	0.409	0.488	0.621	0.568
(S-4)	0.506	0.439	0.610	0.527	0.606	0.558	0.490
	0.897	0.881	0.896	0.877	0.899	0.894	0.877
	0.675	0.642	0.761	0.710	0.759	0.742	0.705
(S-C)	0.500	0.429	0.593	0.466	0.569	0.515	0.428
	0.897	0.880	0.896	0.875	0.899	0.887	0.867
	0.676	0.646	0.756	0.702	0.751	0.711	0.675
(S-H)	−0.445	−0.416	−0.063	−0.092	−0.045	−0.053	−0.079
	0.637	0.640	0.677	0.647	0.678	0.670	0.645
	−0.108	−0.375	−0.115	−0.123	−0.123	−0.105	−0.119
(S-0, $\alpha = 2.0$)	0.607	0.545	0.663	0.533	0.653	0.615	0.544
	0.782	0.757	0.786	0.736	0.785	0.761	0.724
	0.550	0.478	0.624	0.537	0.626	0.575	0.514
(S-0, $\alpha = 1.8$)	−5.550	*	−0.639	0.461	0.395	0.324	0.445
	0.484	0.247	0.621	0.658	0.658	0.577	0.643
	*	*	−2.003	0.484	0.308	0.237	0.443
(S-0, $\alpha = 1.6$)	*	*	*	0.307	−0.724	−0.903	0.309
	−3.912	−7.262	−0.930	0.565	0.414	0.152	0.540
	*	*	*	0.390	−1.429	−1.535	0.339
(S-0, $\alpha = 1.4$)	*	*	*	0.184	−9.214	−9.713	0.124
	*	*	*	0.434	−0.342	−1.235	0.390
	*	*	*	0.269	*	*	0.202
(S-0, $\alpha = 1.2$)	*	*	*	0.043	*	*	−0.110
	*	*	*	0.278	−5.483	−8.514	0.237
	*	*	*	0.137	*	*	0.033
(S-0, $\alpha = 1.0$)	*	*	*	−0.274	*	*	−0.309
	*	*	*	−0.026	*	*	−0.005
	*	*	*	−0.998	*	*	−0.143

tive, closely followed by direct estimation through LANR. The L_2-norm techniques are certainly not to be recommended, when $\alpha \leq 1.6$. The FP method, however, is the best L_2-norm alternative. For extremely small α, the LANR technique seems to be more robust than 2SLA. This is not surprising as these cases certainly will be similar to cases with bad quality in structural specification. Consequently, techniques based partly on structural information will be handicapped in relation to direct estimation techniques as LANR. It is, however, to some extent surprising that 2SLA and LANR are doing so well for these extreme non-normal cases. In Figure 3, these results are illustrated by the y_{2t} variable (y_{1t} and y_{3t} provide similar figures). The overall impression is here that the FP technique seems to be the L_2-norm technique most robust against different specification errors.

When considering Ball's Q^2, determined within the sample period, the FP method is besides LSNR the best technique, and clearly better than other methods for structural estimation. It is even better than 2SLA and slightly better than LANR. The results obtained for the stable distributed residual cases are given in Table 7, and furthermore illustrated by Figure 4 (the case y_{2t} and $T = 20$).

In the next section we will summarize this presentation of results by some conclusive comments.

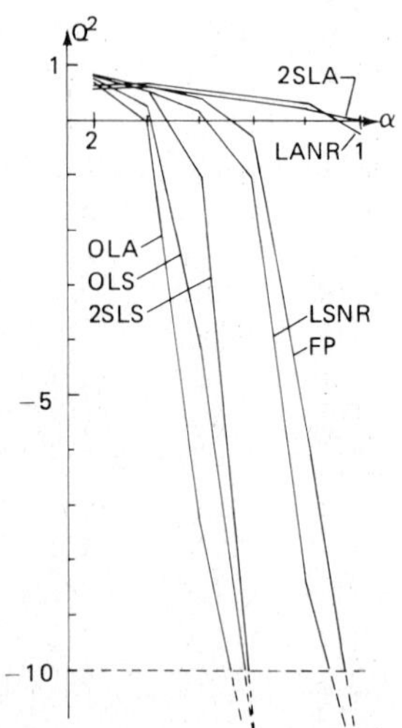

FIGURE 3. Ball's $Q^2(y_{2t})$, prediction period.

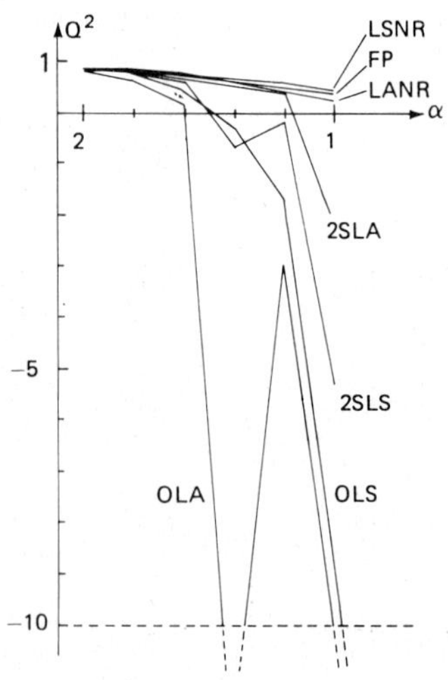

FIGURE 4. Ball's $Q^2(y_{2t})$, sample period.

TABLE 7a
Ball's Q^2, sample period, $T = 10$.

Structure	Estimators						
	OLS	OLA	TSLS	2SLA	FP	LSNR	LANR
	0.596	0.420	0.697	*	0.781	0.833	0.726
(S-0, $\alpha = 2.0$)	0.682	0.613	0.726	*	0.741	0.823	0.718
	0.398	0.112	0.541	*	0.627	0.750	0.592
	0.169	0.088	−1.338	−4.126	0.741	0.803	0.684
(S-0, $\alpha = 1.8$)	0.412	0.505	−0.476	−3.672	0.690	0.794	0.673
	−0.031	−0.271	−1.536	−2.871	0.598	0.738	0.562
	−0.650	−4.790	−8.000	0.224	0.671	0.761	0.615
(S-0, $\alpha = 1.6$)	−0.065	−0.290	−7.596	0.383	0.654	0.768	0.637
	−0.770	−5.027	−7.339	0.035	0.565	0.712	0.528
	−9.658	−8.617	*	−0.490	0.608	0.718	0.535
(S-0, $\alpha = 1.4$)	0.032	−1.495	−2.180	0.265	0.595	0.733	0.576
	−9.462	−7.925	*	−0.524	0.522	0.678	0.468
	*	−6.830	−3.742	−1.693	0.565	0.672	0.460
(S-0, $\alpha = 1.2$)	*	−3.358	−1.224	−0.367	0.551	0.689	0.495
	*	−6.225	−3.653	−2.270	0.476	0.640	0.396
	*	*	*	*	0.361	0.629	0.367
(S-0, $\alpha = 1.0$)	*	−5.807	*	−2.637	−0.342	0.639	0.389
	*	−9.780	*	*	0.073	0.608	0.338

TABLE 7b
Ball's Q^2, sample period, $T = 20$.

Structure	Estimators						
	OLS	OLA	TSLS	2SLA	FP	LSNR	LANR
	0.694	0.651	0.735	0.611	0.753	0.769	0.716
(S-0, $\alpha = 2.0$)	0.857	0.838	0.860	0.834	0.861	0.877	0.851
	0.683	0.634	0.734	0.673	0.746	0.773	0.720
	0.442	0.090	0.634	0.570	0.686	0.706	0.637
(S-0, $\alpha = 1.8$)	0.750	0.633	0.788	0.767	0.800	0.823	0.782
	0.444	0.094	0.648	0.613	0.694	0.724	0.653
	−0.101	−0.474	0.424	0.460	0.598	0.623	0.530
(S-0, $\alpha = 1.6$)	0.401	0.087	0.622	0.675	0.728	0.760	0.696
	−0.084	−0.452	0.455	0.510	0.616	0.653	0.557
	−2.427	*	−1.110	0.349	0.495	0.529	0.408
(S-0, $\alpha = 1.4$)	−0.348	*	−0.699	0.550	0.628	0.666	0.573
	−2.314	*	−1.034	0.402	0.526	0.569	0.444
	−4.584	−3.730	−0.422	0.209	0.387	0.432	0.272
(S-0, $\alpha = 1.2$)	−1.769	−2.953	−0.115	0.386	0.497	0.546	0.410
	−4.367	−3.518	−0.317	0.269	0.425	0.474	0.312
	*	*	−7.620	*	0.298	0.346	0.146
(S-0, $\alpha = 1.0$)	*	*	−5.374	−2.172	0.373	0.423	0.234
	*	*	−6.459	*	0.324	0.378	0.177

4. Conclusions

The choice of technique for estimation of econometric systems should be actuated by the field of application (structural estimation, prediction, etc.) as well as by the loss function (relative weighting of bias, precision, etc.). If first considering structural estimation, the present study shows OLS to be a technique very robust against partial mis-specifications according to the RMSE criterion. OLS is here closely followed by FP and TSLS methods. OLS, however, loses its leading position in robustness to FP and TSLS if just regarding the bias criterion. Furthermore, if the usual residual normality assumption is not correct, L_1-norm estimators seem to be clearly preferable to L_2-norm estimators, at least according to RMSE. However, the FP technique shows a remarkable robustness against residual non-normality due to the bias criterion. One conclusion may then be that if searching for a technique for structural estimation characterized by a common robustness against specification problems studied in this work, the FP technique seems to be a reasonable alternative.

The picture concerning reduced form estimation and prediction is similar. According to the Ball's Q^2 criterion, TSLS, FP and LSNR techniques are best for the residual normality cases. When residual distributions are non-normal, LSNR and FP methods are leading if measured within the sample period. In prediction period, however, 2SLA and LANR are extremely robust compared to the L_2-norm techniques.

Finally, it should be emphasized that if one has a priori knowledge concerning problems of data and model specification, that should certainly increase the possibilities to select an estimator that protects against consequencies of the special problems. It is then perhaps not relevant to choose a technique characterized by a common robustness against problems in model specification.

Chapter 11

FIX-POINT ESTIMATES OF THE STRUCTURE OF A MODEL USING DIFFERENT *Y* PROXY STARTS

SYDNEY MAY

1. Introduction[1]

We report here on experiments carried out to explore the implications of multiple, distinct feasible solutions for the Fix-Point (FP) estimators of the structure of stochastic linear equations, in the context of a particular ten-equation model. This question of the possibility of multiple distinct feasible FP solutions ('plural parameter sets' as described by Bodin) has been addressed in Ågren (1972a) and Bodin (1974), both of whom refer also to a paper by Lyttkens.[2] Since general analytic results are not feasible, their treatment is restricted to special (small) tractable models, but the presence of plural FP parameter sets has been established as a possibility, nonetheless.

The motivation for the experiments springs from the implied practical considerations facing the model builder, as journeyman estimator, who is desirous of invoking the FP estimator as a practical alternative to other simultaneous estimators, for example, Two-Stage Least Squares [due to Theil (1958) and Basmann (1957)], Limited-Information Maximum Likelihood [due to Anderson and Rubin (1949)], Full-Information Maximum Likelihood [due to Koopmans et al. (1950)], and Three-Stage Least Squares [due to Zellner and Theil (1962)].

Since many, if not most of the models being specified for estimation currently are large relative to the sample size, direct application of the usual full-information methods are ruled out automatically, and the limited-information methods must be modified, in order to meet this difficulty. The Fix-Point estimator does not share this disability, so that one might wish to give serious consideration to FP, when estimation of a large model is being undertaken.

[1] During several years of experimentation with the Fix-Point and other methods, the writer has been the fortunate recipient of the advice and encouragement of Professor Herman Wold; advice patiently given, and gratefully received. The author wishes also to acknowledge support provided by the Canada Council, Grant S71–0386, for earlier phases of this research.

[2] University of Uppsala, Institute of Statistics Seminar Paper "On the direct estimation of the constants of Summer's model by GEID-specification", 1966.

It is perhaps worth mentioning at this point that in the writer's experience serious problems of convergence with the FP estimator were never encountered using larger models, whereas with small models (4–5 equations) very slow convergence, or oscillating values, were often encountered when the noise content of the equations was 5 percent, or more. One might offer the conjecture that larger models have B structures that are characteristically sparse, compared to smaller models. The presence of a relatively large number of restricted parameters (zero-restricted), together with a diagonal-dominated $(I-\beta)$ structure, appears to make the FP iterative process less sensitive to the changes in the values determined in successive iterations.

Another potential advantage of the FP method is that it requires less in the way of restrictions in the specification of the statistical model to be used for estimation, than is the case for the well-known classical methods. For these latter, it is assumed that the error component of any given endogenous variable is uncorrelated with *all* the predetermined variables in the model.

This assumption could be interpreted as being unduly restrictive for practical model building, if we consider that in specifying a structural equation we do not try to include *all* the variables that could conceivably contribute something to the generation of the left-hand variable. Consequently, there may be variables omitted for practical purposes, some of them predetermined variables, and given the approximate nature of the specification, their omission implies that the resultant error term in the equation will be correlated with predetermined variables that are not included in the equation. Thus, in practical model building the FP method seems to provide the possibility of *some* accommodation of the statistical implications of approximate specification, in contrast to the classical methods.

In the case of FP, all that is required for consistency is that the error component of a given endogenous variable be uncorrelated with certain regressor variables in the structural equation that is specified to determine the endogenous variable. For example, if we assume the ith equation to be given by

$$y_i = \beta_{i3}\eta_3^* + \beta_{i6}\eta_6^* + \gamma_{i1}z_1 + \gamma_{i8}z_8 + \varepsilon_i, \tag{1.1}$$

where the η^* variables are y proxies taken from

$$\eta^* = \beta\eta^* + \Gamma z + \varepsilon \quad \text{or} \quad \eta^* = (I-\beta)^{-1}\Gamma z; \tag{1.2}$$

then the assumption that ε_{it} is uncorrelated with z_{1t}, z_{8t}, η_{3t}^*, η_{6t}^* and η_{it}^*, ensures the consistency of the FP estimator, given that $|I-\beta| \neq 0$; cf. Wold (1965b).

Wold has given the name GEID (Generalized Interdependent system) to distinguish this less restrictive statistical model from the Classical one (CLID).

A potential disadvantage of the FP method is that, for a given data sample, the estimator is not necessarily unique, the sample being consistent with more than one set of estimators, B^*, G^*, Y^*, satisfying

$$Y^* = Y^*B^{*\prime} + ZG^{*\prime}, \tag{1.3}$$

where B^*, C^*, Y^* correspond to a FP estimate for B, Γ, H^*, in the 'true' system specified as

$$Y = H^*B' + Z\Gamma' + \varepsilon, \tag{1.4}$$

$$H^* = H^*B' + Z\Gamma', \tag{1.5}$$

where Y, Y^*, H^*, and ε are $T \times n$, Z is $T \times m$; T is the sample size.

In the following sections, we describe an experiment that explores the practical consequences of estimating the structure of a synthetic system of ten equations by the FP method, using a variety of Y proxy starts ($Y^{(0)}$), the aim being to compare the structural estimates obtained from the differing Y proxy starts, with given data samples. Within the context of this ten-equation model at least, it could be considered encouraging to find that the FP estimation process converged to essentially the same FP estimates, even when the process was initiated from very different regions of the parameter space.

Following this, we describe procedures for generating data samples (Y, Z, ε) that honour the assumptions of the GEID statistical model, procedures suggested by Professor Wold in private communications. These are useful for generating data required for sampling experiments designed to investigate the finite-sample performance of FP, and other estimators, when one wishes to invoke the GEID statistical model.

2. A Typical Experiment

The FP method is initiated using a starting set of Tn values, $Y^{(0)}$ to obtain the first estimates of the structure, $B^{(1)}$, $G^{(1)}$ in

$$Y = Y^{(0)}B^{(1)\prime} + ZG^{(1)\prime} + \varepsilon^{(1)}. \tag{2.1}$$

These estimates are then used to compute the next set of Y proxies, $Y^{(1)}$, from

$$Y^{(1)} = Y^{(0)}B^{(1)\prime} + ZG^{(1)\prime}. \tag{2.2}$$

This procedure is repeated until, at some stage s, all the elements of $B^{(s)}$, $G^{(s)}$ satisfy a convergence criterion

$$|(\alpha_{ij}^{(s)} - \alpha_{ij}^{(s-1)})/\alpha_{ij}^{(s-1)}| < \zeta,$$

where α_{ij} corresponds to some element of B, or G, and where ζ is selected according to the degree of precision required to satisfy one's idea of 'convergence' for the model being estimated.

In addition, for defining convergence, the elements of $Y^{(s)}$ and $YRF^{(s)}$, $(y_{it}^{(s)}/yrf_{it}^{(s)})$, are made to satisfy an ζ- or related criterion, where

$$Y^{(s)} = Y^{(s-1)}B^{(s)\prime} + ZG^{(s)\prime}, \tag{2.3}$$

$$YRF^{(s)} = ZG^{(s)\prime}(I - B^{(s)\prime})^{-1}. \tag{2.4}$$

The criterion $\zeta = 0.005$ was used for both α_{ij} and $Y^{(s)}$, in the reported experiment.

For other versions of the experiment described, but not reported here, the convergence criterion used for the Y proxies was sometimes relaxed to 0.01, a more generous criterion being used to avoid a great many extra iterations which, in the cases analyzed in detail, had no significant effect on the final FP estimates of β and Γ. A data sample of 50 observations requires the convergence of no less than 500 elements in $Y^{(s)}$, and since the computations were carried out in single precision (at most, seven significant digits) the prolongation of the iterative procedure as a result of six or so of these 500 not meeting a stricter ζ criterion (after all the elements of B, G had already converged, according to the stricter ζ criterion) was felt to be wasteful, since this seemed to add little in the way of precision for the model being used.

The nature of the experiment is to start with a given system

$$Y = H^*\beta' + Z\Gamma' + \varepsilon, \tag{2.5}$$

a given sample (Y, Z, ε) that satisfies the GEID restrictions,[3] and to

[3] In the experiments, correlations were permitted between z's and errors, so long as these satisfied the GEID assumptions. The non-zero correlations ranged between -0.51 and

estimate the structure, repeatedly, using different Y proxy starts, $Y^{(0)}$, for each of 10 variations.

The different sets of $Y^{(0)}$ for each variation are selected from different eligible subsets of the predetermined variables, Z. In order to judge if these Y proxy starts are sufficiently 'different', from one variation to the next, the first iterates, $B^{(1)}$, $G^{(1)}$, from each variation are compared to ascertain if the FP process was initiated from appropriately 'different' regions of the parameter space. These first iterates are reproduced below in Table 1, and suggest at least modest success in achieving some variability in the starting values for the structural estimates.

The model used for the experiment consists of ten equations, two of which, equations 9 and 10, are accounting identities. Apart from the ten endogenous variables, the model contains seventeen predetermined variables. B contains eleven unrestricted parameters in the eight behavioural equations, and G contains thirty unrestricted parameters. The data set (Y, Z, ε) was generated with the noise components, ε, satisfying approximately

$$\varepsilon_i'\varepsilon_i / T = 0.05\bar{y}_i, \qquad i = 1, 2, \cdots, 8,$$

where $\bar{y}_i$ = sample average of $\bar{y}_i$. That is, a target of five percent was used for the coefficient of variation for the true error term, in generating a set of joint normal (Z, ε) variates, for the predetermined variables, and total errors associated with the eight behavioural equations

$$y_i = \beta_i\eta^* + \gamma_i z + \varepsilon_i, \qquad i = 1, 2, \cdots, 8. \tag{2.6}$$

The final iterates, i.e., the FP estimators for each of the ten different Y

+0.58. In terms of *absolute* values, these were distributed in the population, and for comparison in the sample used for the experiment reported:

Absolute correlation values	Number of correlations	
	Population	Sample
0.00–0.10	41	24
0.10–0.20	22	32
0.20–0.30	18	16
0.30–0.40	15	20
Greater than 0.40	10	14

Naturally, some of the GEID zero-correlations were violated by the sample used.

TABLE 1
Summary of first iterates in FP by variation.

Variation	1	2	3	4	5
B (1, 7)	−0.3453E–03	0.6835E–01	0.1769E–01	−0.8609E–02	−0.1935E–01
B (2, 7)	0.4705E–01	0.1910E–02	0.6193E–01	−0.1677	−0.2091
B (3, 9)	0.1704	0.4189	0.9046	−0.2669	−0.4099
B (4, 8)	0.3551E–01	−0.5796E–02	0.8654E–01	0.3664E–01	−0.1062
B (5, 10)	0.6027	1.013	0.6276	0.1406	0.6009
B (6, 1)	1.422	1.452	−0.3097	0.1740	0.3110E–01
B (6, 2)	0.7788	0.7821	0.8500	0.4502	1.382
B (6, 4)	0.7151	0.8108E–01	−1.220	0.7699	1.014
B (7, 5)	0.3622E–01	−0.8618E–02	0.7323E–01	−0.1832E–01	0.2114E–01
B (8, 3)	0.3011	0.3258	0.4502	0.9202E–01	−0.3531
B (8, 5)	0.3874	−0.2441E–01	0.2454	−0.2753	0.5004E–02
G (1, 1)	−0.9648	−1.027	−0.9791	−0.9523	−0.9401
G (1, 2)	1.127	1.118	1.119	1.119	1.110
G (1, 3)	1.149	1.168	1.149	1.155	1.165
G (1, 4)	1.132	1.115	1.136	1.130	1.127
G (2, 1)	1.420	1.452	1.412	1.715	1.771
G (2, 2)	1.327	1.333	1.309	1.196	1.186
G (2, 3)	1.148	1.159	1.162	1.244	1.288
G (2, 5)	1.513	1.509	1.511	1.468	1.419
G (3, 1)	2.334	2.374	1.295	3.103	3.226
G (3, 6)	1.282	1.209	1.679	1.180	1.227
G (3, 7)	1.642	1.577	1.458	1.419	1.463
G (3, 8)	1.461	1.310	1.552	1.454	1.382
G (4, 1)	1.720	1.760	1.685	1.731	1.858
G (4, 8)	1.532	1.530	1.519	1.517	1.528
G (4, 9)	−1.500	−1.505	−1.498	−1.510	−1.451
G (4, 10)	1.465	1.473	1.459	1.477	1.423
G (5, 1)	4.796	5.058	4.813	5.379	4.880
G (5, 10)	1.714	1.079	1.519	1.685	1.548
G (5, 11)	−1.334	−1.408	−1.375	−1.580	−1.398
G (5, 12)	0.5928	0.6314	0.7887	0.7471	0.7412
G (6, 1)	2.475	2.338	5.436	4.470	3.095
G (6, 8)	−1.017	−0.3132	−0.4261	−0.9044	−1.016
G (6, 13)	0.4175E–01	−0.9908	−0.5461	−0.6102	−0.2410E–02
G (6, 14)	−0.2251	0.8413	0.4072	−0.1580	−0.3122
G (7, 1)	0.7876	0.8173	0.7789	0.8206	0.7877
G (7, 5)	0.7473	0.7604	0.7502	0.7654	0.7609
G (7, 15)	0.5128E–01	0.5327E–01	0.2014E–01	0.5478E–01	0.5271E–01
G (8, 1)	1.930	2.475	2.250	2.643	3.065
G (8, 15)	0.1626	0.1538	0.2988E–02	0.2401	0.1222
G (8, 16)	0.2983	0.1490	0.1311	0.3800	0.2404
B (1, 7)	−0.1896E–01	0.2858E–01	0.1317E–01	0.1441E–01	−0.1968E–01
B (2, 7)	0.2554E–01	0.1391	0.3243E–01	0.8704E–01	−0.1105
B (3, 9)	0.6984E–01	0.2643E–02	0.9046	0.2345	−0.2669
B (4, 8)	0.5845E–01	−0.3213E–01	−0.3684E–01	−0.7349E–01	−0.1252E–01
B (5, 10)	1.864	−0.3600	−0.1855	1.301	0.7863E–01
B (6, 1)	1.633	−0.2643	−1.216	0.7841	1.706
B (6, 2)	1.756	−0.4174	0.2920	0.1462	0.8466
B (6, 4)	0.9654	0.5077	−0.2818	2.081	0.9322
B (7, 5)	−0.2511E–01	0.8426E–01	0.5650E–01	0.3622E–01	−0.8618E–02

TABLE 1
(continued)

Variation	6	7	8	9	10
$B(8, 3)$	−0.2381E–01	0.7308E–01	0.5753	0.3011	0.3258
$B(8, 5)$	−0.2569	0.5433	−0.6018E–02	0.3874	−0.2441E–01
$G(1, 1)$	−0.9562	−0.9753	−0.9676	−0.9797	−0.9517
$G(1, 2)$	1.131	1.131	1.119	1.120	1.136
$G(1, 3)$	1.156	1.138	1.151	1.152	1.153
$G(1, 4)$	1.131	1.120	1.127	1.137	1.126
$G(2, 1)$	1.432	1.373	1.439	1.360	1.573
$G(2, 2)$	1.322	1.350	1.314	1.282	1.410
$G(2, 3)$	1.155	1.092	1.162	1.193	1.147
$G(2, 5)$	1.521	1.501	1.508	1.534	1.437
$G(3, 1)$	2.400	2.454	1.295	2.095	3.103
$G(3, 6)$	1.375	1.359	1.679	1.440	1.180
$G(3, 7)$	1.629	1.634	1.458	1.676	1.419
$G(3, 8)$	1.414	1.439	1.552	1.444	1.454
$G(4, 1)$	1.692	1.788	1.816	1.861	1.765
$G(4, 8)$	1.524	1.528	1.520	1.524	1.529
$G(4, 9)$	−1.490	−1.513	−1.516	−1.530	−1.503
$G(4, 10)$	1.468	1.481	1.468	1.470	1.473
$G(5, 1)$	3.297	6.000	5.648	4.241	5.420
$G(5, 10)$	1.750	1.583	1.695	1.681	1.655
$G(5, 11)$	−0.9602	−1.396	−1.549	−1.539	−1.509
$G(5, 12)$	0.4210	0.5452	0.7638	0.6882	0.7269
$G(6, 1)$	−0.6677E–01	5.939	5.649	2.296	1.958
$G(6, 8)$	−0.3953	−0.5126	−0.3033	−1.258	−0.9542
$G(6, 13)$	−0.6117	−1.045	−0.7688	0.1587	−0.6561
$G(6, 14)$	0.8993	−0.1652E–01	0.8199	−0.1640E–01	0.3581
$G(7, 1)$	0.8475	0.8033	0.7629	0.7876	0.8173
$G(7, 5)$	0.7475	0.7283	0.7586	0.7473	0.7604
$G(7, 15)$	0.5251E–01	0.6461E–02	0.4443E–01	0.5128E–01	0.5327E–01
$G(8, 1)$	2.850	2.252	2.351	1.930	2.475
$G(8, 15)$	0.3208	0.3539E–01	0.5949E–01	0.1626	0.1538
$G(8, 16)$	0.1894	0.1761	0.9934E–01	0.2983	0.1490

proxy starts, are reproduced in Table 2. In all ten cases, the FP procedure converged to structural estimates that are virtually indistinguishable, for practical purposes. The experiment was repeated using different data samples (Y, Z, ε), with comparable results.

Table 3 contains indexes of the z subsets used for the Y proxy starts in each of the ten variations used. For example, the first set used for $Y^{(0)}$ consisted of

$$z_2, z_3, z_6, z_4, z_7, z_1, z_8, z_5, z_9, z_{17}.$$

TABLE 2
Summary of FP estimation by variation.

Variation	1	2	3	4	5
B (1, 7)	0.8093E–01	0.8093E–01	0.8093E–01	0.8093E–01	0.8093E–01
B (2, 7)	0.9446	0.9415	0.9404	0.9382	0.9395
B (3, 9)	0.2144	0.2144	0.2144	0.2143	0.2143
B (4, 8)	0.3451E–02	0.3436E–02	0.3445E–02	0.3444E–02	0.3462E–02
B (5, 10)	0.3705	0.3705	0.3705	0.3705	0.3705
B (6, 1)	0.5565	0.5566	0.5565	0.5567	0.5566
B (6, 2)	0.4069	0.4069	0.4070	0.4068	0.4069
B (6, 4)	0.2465	0.2465	0.2466	0.2465	0.2465
B (7, 5)	0.2620E–01	0.2620E–01	0.2620E–01	0.2620E–01	0.2620E–01
B (8, 3)	0.2057	0.2057	0.2057	0.2057	0.2057
B (8, 5)	0.1072	0.1072	0.1072	0.1072	0.1072
G (1, 1)	– 1.087	– 1.087	– 1.087	– 1.087	– 1.087
G (1, 2)	1.097	1.097	1.097	1.097	1.097
G (1, 3)	1.168	1.168	1.168	1.168	1.168
G (1, 4)	1.133	1.133	1.133	1.133	1.133
G (2, 1)	0.6840	0.6894	0.6881	0.6886	0.6889
G (2, 2)	1.279	1.279	1.280	1.280	1.279
G (2, 3)	1.140	1.140	1.140	1.140	1.140
G (2, 5)	0.8177	0.8198	0.8193	0.8239	0.8223
G (3, 1)	1.278	1.279	1.278	1.278	1.278
G (3, 6)	1.355	1.355	1.355	1.355	1.355
G (3, 7)	1.391	1.391	1.391	1.391	1.391
G (3, 8)	1.266	1.266	1.266	1.266	1.266
G (4, 1)	1.749	1.749	1.749	1.749	1.749
G (4, 8)	1.526	1.527	1.526	1.526	1.527
G (4, 9)	– 1.507	– 1.507	– 1.507	– 1.507	– 1.507
G (4, 10)	1.473	1.473	1.473	1.473	1.473
G (5, 1)	– 1.342	– 1.342	– 1.342	– 1.342	– 1.343
G (5, 10)	1.574	1.574	1.574	1.574	1.574
G (5, 11)	– 0.8513E–01	– 0.8507E–01	– 0.8507E–01	– 0.8502E–01	– 0.8504E–01
G (5, 12)	0.6136E–02	0.6115E–02	0.6126E–02	0.6103E–02	0.6108E–02
G (6, 1)	1.349	1.348	1.349	1.350	1.349
G (6, 8)	– 1.447	– 1.447	– 1.447	– 1.447	– 1.447
G (6, 13)	– 0.7160E–01	– 0.7164E–01	– 0.7158E–01	– 0.7171E–01	– 0.7167E–01
G (6, 14)	– 0.2043E–01	– 0.2037E–01	– 0.2052E–01	– 0.2029E–01	– 0.2039E–01
G (7, 1)	0.7389	0.7389	0.7389	0.7389	0.7389
G (7, 5)	0.7155	0.7155	0.7155	0.7155	0.7155
G (7, 15)	0.1033E–02	0.1038E–02	0.1031E–02	0.1040E–02	0.1039E–02
G (8, 1)	1.010	1.010	1.010	1.010	1.010
G (8, 15)	– 0.1078E–01	– 0.1070E–01	– 0.1075E–01	– 0.1066E–01	– 0.1070E–01
G (8, 16)	– 0.2049E–01	– 0.2043E–01	– 0.2047E–01	– 0.2041E–01	– 0.2043E–01
B (1, 7)	0.8093E–01	0.8093E–01	0.8093E–01	0.8094E–01	0.8093E–01
B (2, 7)	0.9418	0.9427	0.9431	0.9441	0.9419
B (3, 9)	0.2144	0.2143	0.2143	0.2143	0.2143
B (4, 8)	0.3468E–02	0.3439E–02	0.3471E–02	0.3453E–02	0.3456E–02
B (5, 10)	0.3705	0.3705	0.3705	0.3705	0.3705
B (6, 1)	0.5565	0.5566	0.5567	0.5566	0.5566
B (6, 2)	0.4070	0.4069	0.4067	0.4069	0.4068
B (6, 4)	0.2466	0.2465	0.2465	0.2465	0.2465

TABLE 2
(continued)

Variation	6	7	8	9	10
B(7, 5)	0.2620E–01	0.2620E–01	0.2620E–01	0.2620E–01	0.2620E–01
B(8, 3)	0.2057	0.2057	0.2057	0.2057	0.2057
B(8, 5)	0.1072	0.1072	0.1072	0.1072	0.1072
G(1, 1)	– 1.087	– 1.087	– 1.087	– 1.087	– 1.087
G(1, 2)	1.097	1.097	1.097	1.097	1.097
G(1, 3)	1.168	1.168	1.168	1.168	1.168
G(1, 4)	1.133	1.133	1.133	1.133	1.133
G(2, 1)	0.6866	0.6871	0.6869	0.6856	0.6857
G(2, 2)	1.279	1.279	1.279	1.279	1.279
G(2, 3)	1.140	1.140	1.140	1.140	1.140
G(2, 5)	0.8199	0.8186	0.8209	0.8190	0.8215
G(3, 1)	1.278	1.278	1.279	1.278	1.279
G(3, 6)	1.355	1.355	1.355	1.355	1.355
G(3, 7)	1.391	1.391	1.391	1.391	1.391
G(3, 8)	1.266	1.266	1.266	1.266	1.266
G(4, 1)	1.749	1.749	1.749	1.749	1.749
G(4, 8)	1.527	1.527	1.526	1.526	1.526
G(4, 9)	– 1.507	– 1.507	– 1.507	– 1.507	– 1.507
G(4, 10)	1.473	1.473	1.473	1.473	1.473
G(5, 1)	– 1.342	– 1.343	– 1.342	– 1.342	– 1.342
G(5, 10)	1.574	1.574	1.574	1.574	1.574
G(5, 11)	– 0.8510E–01	– 0.8505E–01	– 0.8497E–01	– 0.8505E–01	– 0.8504E–01
G(5, 12)	0.6116E–02	0.6120E–02	0.6108E–02	0.6100E–02	0.6114E–02
G(6, 1)	1.349	1.349	1.349	1.349	1.349
G(6, 8)	– 1.447	– 1.447	– 1.447	– 1.447	– 1.447
G(6, 13)	– 0.7158E–01	– 0.7165E–01	– 0.7173E–01	– 0.7162E–01	– 0.7168E–01
G(6, 14)	– 0.2049E–01	– 0.2041E–01	– 0.2022E–01	– 0.2040E–01	– 0.2032E–01
G(7, 1)	0.7389	0.7389	0.7389	0.7389	0.7389
G(7, 5)	0.7155	0.7155	0.7155	0.7155	0.7155
G(7, 15)	0.1039E–02	0.1035E–02	0.1037E–02	0.1038E–02	0.1035E–02
G(8, 1)	1.010	1.010	1.010	1.010	1.010
G(8, 15)	– 0.1067E–01	– 0.1075E–01	– 0.1067E–01	– 0.1067E–01	– 0.1070E–01
G(8, 16)	– 0.2042E–01	– 0.2047E–01	– 0.2041E–01	– 0.2041E–01	– 0.2044E–01

TABLE 3
Index of Z used for indicated Y proxy start.

Variation	$y_1^{(0)}$	$y_2^{(0)}$	$y_3^{(0)}$	$y_4^{(0)}$	$y_5^{(0)}$	$y_6^{(0)}$	$y_7^{(0)}$	$y_8^{(0)}$	$y_9^{(0)}$	$y_{10}^{(0)}$
1	2	3	6	4	7	1	8	5	9	17
2	5	6	8	7	9	1	10	2	3	16
3	9	10	2	11	3	1	12	4	5	15
4	12	15	4	16	10	1	13	3	11	14
5	17	2	11	3	12	1	14	6	13	4
6	4	5	13	6	14	1	15	7	16	3
7	7	9	17	10	2	1	16	11	4	13
8	11	12	3	15	4	1	17	13	5	9
9	16	17	6	2	7	1	9	14	10	8
10	3	4	8	5	9	1	6	12	11	7

The endogenous variable, y_6, does not appear as an explanatory variable in any of the behavioural equations, so that a proxy start is not really required for this variable. However, since it is convenient to mechanically assemble y_6 proxies along with the others, rather than to recognize its special status in this model, z_1, the term used for the intercepts, was allocated to $y_6^{(0)}$ in all repetitions.

An additional, eleventh variation was carried out in which a *zero* start was used for the y proxies. The FP estimates obtained using this y proxy start are given in Table 4, and it may be noted that these are essentially the same as for the other ten y proxy starts.

These results do not lay to rest the potential implications of multiple, distinct permissible FP solutions from a given sample, but along with other evidence (e.g., comparison of FP estimates with TSLS, LIML, and other estimators), they do seem to indicate that the FP process can be expected to converge to sensible estimates of the structures of well-specified models.

If there is a puzzling, albeit agreeable aspect to the results of the experiment described, it is the absence of *any* evidence of convergence to plural FP estimators with given data samples, when we start with Y proxies from ten different subspaces of the space spanned by the seventeen z's. The results, of course, are specific to the model used, and the ten variations comprise only a small fraction of all the possible Y proxy starts that could be selected from combinations of eligible z's. Further experiments with additional Y proxy starts, and with alternative models, can be expected to shed further light and, it might be hoped, to fortify the practical implications of the results reported here.

3. The Generation of Synthetic Data for GEID Experiments

First to simplify the exposition, define a vector w, whose components are a typical observation from a sample (Z, ε),

$$w' = (z_{1t}, \ldots, z_{mt}, \quad \varepsilon_{1t}, \ldots, \varepsilon_{nt}), \tag{3.1}$$

and a variance–covariance matrix, for all t,

$$E(ww') \equiv \begin{pmatrix} E(z_t z_t') & E(z_t \varepsilon_t') \\ E(\varepsilon_t z_t') & E(\varepsilon_t \varepsilon_t') \end{pmatrix}. \tag{3.2}$$

In order to carry out Monte Carlo experiments with systems that conform to the GEID statistical model, it is useful to be able to invoke a simple procedure to produce a variance–covariance matrix $E(ww')$ approp-

TABLE 4
Summary of FP estimation with zero start.

$B(1, 7)$	0.8093E–01
$B(2, 7)$	0.9436
$B(3, 9)$	0.2142
$B(4, 8)$	0.3444E–02
$B(5, 10)$	0.3705
$B(6, 1)$	0.5571
$B(6, 2)$	0.4062
$B(6, 4)$	0.2464
$B(7, 5)$	0.2620E–01
$B(8, 3)$	0.2057
$B(8, 5)$	0.1072
$G(1, 1)$	– 1.087
$G(1, 2)$	1.097
$G(1, 3)$	1.168
$G(1, 4)$	1.133
$G(2, 1)$	0.6864
$G(2, 2)$	1.279
$G(2, 3)$	1.140
$G(2, 5)$	0.8227
$G(3, 1)$	1.278
$G(3, 6)$	1.355
$G(3, 7)$	1.391
$G(3, 8)$	1.266
$G(4, 1)$	1.749
$G(4, 8)$	1.527
$G(4, 9)$	– 1.507
$G(4, 10)$	1.473
$G(5, 1)$	– 1.343
$G(5, 10)$	1.574
$G(5, 11)$	– 0.8470E–01
$G(5, 12)$	0.6096E–02
$G(6, 1)$	1.349
$G(6, 8)$	– 1.447
$G(6, 13)$	– 0.7194E–01
$G(6, 14)$	– 0.1988E–01
$G(7, 1)$	0.7389
$G(7, 5)$	0.7155
$G(7, 15)$	0.1041E–02
$G(8, 1)$	1.010
$G(8, 15)$	– 0.1066E–01
$G(8, 16)$	– 0.2041E–01

riate for generating the samples (Y, Z, ε) for experimentation. The following ingenious procedure was suggested by Professor Wold in private communications.

First, generate a sample (Y, Z, ε) using an 'approximate' structure, $B^{\neq}, G^{\neq}$, and an 'approximate' variance–covariance matrix, $E^{\neq}(ww')$. Use this sample to compute B^*, G^*, Y^*, ε^* by Fix-Point so that

$$Y = Y^*B^{*\prime} + ZG^{*\prime} + \varepsilon^*, \qquad Y^* = Y^*B^{*\prime} + ZG^{*\prime}. \tag{3.3}$$

If we define the second-order moments involving the variables Y^*, Z, ε^*, as *population* moments corresponding to some true system, then these moments, plus B^*, G^*, corresponding now to asymptotic FP estimates, provide a 'true' structure β, Γ, that satisfies the GEID statistical model. This can then be used to generate the samples required for the experiments. This was the method used for the experiment reported here.

As an illustration of the 'before-and-after' structures, $(B^{\neq}, G^{\neq})$ and (B, Γ), Table 5 contains the structures that were used as the basis of the reported experiment.

Table 6 permits a comparison of the true structure with the asymptotic values for certain k-class estimators, Two-Stage Least Squares (TSLS), Ordinary Least Squares (OLS), Minimum Second Moment k (LVK), and Unbiased k (UBK), the latter two both due to Nagar (1959). The OLS estimator, of course, is not a consistent estimator in a Classic ID statistical model, as well.[4]

An alternative, more difficult procedure, but one that permits retention of the initial β, Γ involves the prescription of $E(ww')$ whose elements are made to satisfy specific conditions. Let a typical structural equation be characterized by

$$y_i = \beta_i \eta^* + \gamma_i z + \varepsilon_i, \tag{3.4}$$

and the corresponding (solved-for) reduced form equation by

$$y_i = \omega_i z + \varepsilon_i, \tag{3.5}$$

where ω_i is the ith row of $\Omega = (I - \beta)^{-1}\Gamma$.

Let y_h^* denote a typical member of η^*, with a corresponding reduced form equation

$$y_h = w_h z + \varepsilon_h. \tag{3.6}$$

Then the (Z, ε) data required for GEID experiments must satisfy

$$E(y_i^* \quad \varepsilon_i) = E(w_i z, \varepsilon_i) = 0, \qquad i = 1, 2, \ldots, n, \tag{3.7a}$$

[4] The hypothetical 'asymptotic' moments used to compute the classical estimators are of course obtained from a particular sample, as described, for convenience in carrying out GEID experiments. Thus asymptotic classical estimates in Table 6 are in part accidental, and a curiosity; nothing *general* can be inferred. For the particular set of moments used, the large sample errors of the classical methods appear modest in size, and there is not much difference between the results from the different classical estimators, including OLS.

TABLE 5
'Approximate' and 'true' structures used.

	'Approximate'	'True'
$B(1, 7)$	0.100	0.099
$B(2, 7)$	0.340	0.349
$B(3, 9)$	0.230	0.242
$B(4, 8)$	0.130	0.102
$B(5, 10)$	0.410	0.409
$B(6, 1)$	0.650	0.570
$B(6, 2)$	0.290	0.414
$B(6, 4)$	0.350	0.248
$B(7, 5)$	0.020	0.028
$B(8, 3)$	0.200	0.196
$B(8, 5)$	0.130	0.131
$G(1, 1)$	− 1.110	− 1.104
$G(1, 2)$	1.120	1.103
$G(1, 3)$	1.130	1.152
$G(1, 4)$	1.140	1.131
$G(2, 1)$	1.210	1.166
$G(2, 2)$	1.220	1.279
$G(2, 3)$	1.230	1.177
$G(2, 5)$	1.250	1.267
$G(3, 1)$	1.310	1.239
$G(3, 6)$	1.360	1.341
$G(3, 7)$	1.370	1.377
$G(3, 8)$	1.380	1.366
$G(4, 1)$	1.410	1.505
$G(4, 8)$	1.480	1.491
$G(4, 9)$	− 1.490	− 1.514
$G(4, 10)$	1.400	1.457
$G(5, 1)$	− 1.510	− 1.587
$G(5, 10)$	1.500	1.499
$G(5, 11)$	− 1.510	− 1.421
$G(5, 12)$	1.520	1.523
$G(6, 1)$	1.610	1.176
$G(6, 8)$	− 1.680	− 1.441
$G(6, 13)$	1.630	1.617
$G(6, 14)$	1.640	1.693
$G(7, 1)$	0.710	0.738
$G(7, 5)$	0.750	0.708
$G(7, 15)$	0.750	0.709
$G(8, 1)$	0.810	0.893
$G(8, 15)$	0.850	0.808
$G(8, 16)$	0.860	0.839

$$E(y_h^* \quad \varepsilon_i) = E(w_h z, \varepsilon_i) = 0, \qquad \text{for applicable } h, i, \tag{3.7b}$$

$$E(w \quad w') \qquad \text{non-negative definite.} \tag{3.7c}$$

An example of a four-equation model with one identity that could be used with this procedure is the following:

$$I - \beta = \begin{pmatrix} 1.0 & 0 & 0 & -0.5 \\ -0.5 & 1.0 & 0 & 0 \\ 0 & -0.5 & 1.0 & 0 \\ 0 & 0 & -1.0 & 1.0 \end{pmatrix}, \tag{3.8}$$

TABLE 6
Summary of asymptotic estimators.

	TRUE	TSLS	OLS	LVK	UBK
B (1, 7)	0.9883E–01	0.9131E–01	0.9031E–01	0.9140E–01	0.9152E–01
B (2, 7)	0.3487	0.3361	0.3421	0.355	0.3348
B (3, 9)	0.2425	0.2396	0.2394	0.2395	0.2396
B (4, 8)	0.1015	0.1004	0.1010	0.1004	0.1003
B (5, 10)	0.4092	0.4081	0.4073	0.4065	0.4083
B (6, 1)	0.5699	0.5474	0.5588	0.5479	0.5452
B (6, 2)	0.4140	0.4417	0.4288	0.4410	0.4441
B (6, 4)	0.2478	0.2464	0.2449	0.2463	0.2466
B (7, 5)	0.2776E–01	0.2764E–01	0.2777E–01	0.2767E–01	0.2761E–01
B (8, 3)	0.964	0.1733	0.1651	0.1733	0.1751
B (8, 5)	0.1308	0.1402	0.1426	0.1402	0.1396
G(1, 1)	− 1.104	− 1.088	− 1.099	− 1.088	− 1.089
G(1, 2)	1.103	1.109	1.110	1.109	1.109
G(1, 3)	1.152	1.151	1.151	1.151	1.151
G(1, 4)	1.131	1.128	1.128	1.128	1.128
G(2, 1)	1.166	1.151	1.172	1.182	1.183
G(2, 2)	1.279	1.289	1.286	1.290	1.290
G(2, 3)	1.177	1.176	1.177	1.176	1.176
G(2, 5)	1.267	1.273	1.270	1.273	1.274
G(3, 1)	1.230	1.258	1.250	1.258	1.258
G(3, 6)	1.341	1.358	1.358	1.358	1.358
G(3, 7)	1.377	1.373	1.374	1.373	1.373
G(3, 8)	1.366	1.357	1.357	1.357	1.357
G(4, 1)	1.505	1.497	1.495	1.497	1.497
G(4, 8)	1.491	1.490	1.490	1.490	1.490
G(4, 9)	− 1.514	− 1.507	− 1.507	− 1.507	− 1.507
G(4, 10)	1.457	1.464	1.464	1.464	1.464
G(5, 1)	− 1.587	− 1.435	− 1.419	− 1.424	− 1.438
G(5, 10)	1.499	1.427	1.428	1.429	1.427
G(5, 11)	− 1.421	− 1.475	− 1.478	− 1.481	− 1.474
G(5, 12)	1.523	1.515	1.516	1.517	1.515
G(6, 1)	1.176	1.027	1.082	1.030	1.017
G(6, 8)	− 1.441	− 1.453	− 1.452	− 1.453	− 1.454
G(6, 13)	1.617	1.582	1.581	1.582	1.582
G(6, 14)	1.693	1.793	1.788	1.792	1.793
G(7, 1)	0.7377	0.7392	0.7388	0.7391	0.7393
G(7, 5)	0.7079	0.7073	0.7070	0.7072	0.7073
G(7, 15)	0.7091	0.7089	0.7087	0.7089	0.7090
G(8, 1)	0.8932	0.9944	1.029	0.9941	0.9866
G(8, 15)	0.8082	0.8222	0.8272	0.8222	0.8211
G(8, 16)	0.8389	0.8228	0.8241	0.8228	0.8225

$$\Gamma = \begin{pmatrix} 20.0 & 1.0 & 0 & 0 & 0 \\ 2.0 & 0 & 1.0 & 0 & 0 \\ 2.0 & 0 & 0 & 1.0 & 0 \\ 0 & 0 & 0 & 0 & 1.0 \end{pmatrix}. \tag{3.9}$$

If we convene to define all the predetermined variables apart from z_1, in units such that their variances are equal, then we need only specify a correlation matrix, R, that can be used as the basis for generating a sample (Z, ε, Y), that contains non-zero correlations between some components Z and ε. An example of such an R that satisfies the assumptions of the GEID statistical model is

$$R = \left(\begin{array}{c|c} R(z, z) & R(z, \varepsilon) \\ \hline R(\varepsilon, z) & R(\varepsilon, \varepsilon) \end{array}\right) \tag{3.10}$$

$$= \begin{array}{c} \\ z_1 \\ z_2 \\ z_3 \\ z_4 \\ z_5 \\ \varepsilon_1 \\ \varepsilon_2 \\ \varepsilon_3 \end{array} \begin{array}{c} \begin{array}{cccccccc} z_1 & z_2 & z_3 & z_4 & z_5 & \varepsilon_1 & \varepsilon_2 & \varepsilon_3 \end{array} \\ \begin{pmatrix} 1.0 & 0 & 0 & 0 & 0 & 0 & 0 & 0 \\ 0 & 1.0 & 0.38 & 0.32 & 0.55 & 0 & 0 & -0.30 \\ 0 & 0.38 & 1.00 & -0.20 & 0.22 & -0.36 & 0 & 0.15 \\ 0 & 0.32 & -0.20 & 1.00 & -0.14 & 0.18 & -0.20 & 0 \\ 0 & 0.55 & 0.22 & -1.40 & 1.00 & 0 & 0.20 & 0 \\ 0 & 0 & -0.36 & 0.18 & 0 & 1.00 & -0.43 & 0.30 \\ 0 & 0 & 0 & -0.20 & 0.20 & -0.43 & 1.00 & 0.20 \\ 0 & -0.30 & 0.15 & 0 & 0 & 0.30 & 0.20 & 1.00 \end{pmatrix} \end{array}$$

This can be verified as follows. The reduced form structure for the model is

$$\Omega = \begin{pmatrix} 24.5700 & 1.1428 & 0.2857 & 0.5714 & 0.5714 \\ 14.2900 & 0.5714 & 1.1428 & 0.2857 & 0.2857 \\ 9.1430 & 0.2857 & 0.5714 & 1.1428 & 0.14285 \\ 9.1430 & 0.2857 & 0.5714 & 1.1428 & 1.1428 \end{pmatrix}. \tag{3.11}$$

If we eliminate terms that involve zero covariances, the conditions corresponding to (3.7a–c) reduce to

$$\begin{aligned} E(\varepsilon_1, y_1^*) &= E(\varepsilon_1, \omega_{13}z_3 + \omega_{14}z_4) = 0, \\ E(\varepsilon_2, y_2^*) &= E(\varepsilon_2, \omega_{24}z_4 + \omega_{25}z_5) = 0, \\ E(\varepsilon_3, y_3^*) &= E(\varepsilon_3, \omega_{32}z_2 + \omega_{33}z_3) = 0, \\ E(\varepsilon_4, y_4^*) &= E(\varepsilon_3, \omega_{42}z_2 + \omega_{43}z_3) = 0; \end{aligned} \tag{3.12a}$$

$$E(\varepsilon_1, y_4^*) = E(\varepsilon_1, \omega_{43}z_3 + \omega_{44}z_4) = 0,$$

$$E(\varepsilon_2, y_1^*) = E(\varepsilon_2, \omega_{14}z_4 + \omega_{15}z_5) = 0, \tag{3.12b}$$

$$E(\varepsilon_3, y_2^*) = E(\varepsilon_3, \omega_{22}z_2 + \omega_{23}z_3) = 0.$$

Correlation matrix R, as in (3.10), augmented by a row and column for ε_4, is non-negative definite.

Since in this model $\varepsilon_4 = \varepsilon_3$, R as in (3.10) with the first row and column deleted, was used to generate the sample (Z, ε). This reduced R has eigenvalues (rounded here to 4 figures):

$$0.4400,\ 1.547,\ 0.3719,\ 1.542,\ 1.235,\ 0.8934,\ 0.9701. \tag{3.12c}$$

It can be verified that conditions (3.12a–c) are satisfied. If the predetermined variables have the same variance, then each equation in (3.12a–b) will have a common factor of the type

$$\text{var}(\varepsilon_i)\cdot\text{var}(z),$$

where var(z) denotes the variance common to the predetermined variables. Thus the expected values, $E(\varepsilon_i, z_k)$, can be replaced by $r(\varepsilon_i, z_k)$, where r denotes the simple, true correlation between the variables indicated by the arguments. By way of illustration, we can verify the first relation in (3.12a),

$$E(\varepsilon_1, y_1^*) = \omega_{13}\cdot r(\varepsilon_1, z_3) + \omega_{14}\cdot r(\varepsilon_1, z_4)$$

$$= 0.2857(-0.36) + 0.5714(0.18) = 0,$$

and the first relation in (3.12b),

$$E(\varepsilon_1, y_4^*) = \omega_{43}\cdot r(\varepsilon_1, z_3) + \omega_{44}\cdot r(\varepsilon_1, z_4)$$

$$= 0.5714(-0.36) + 1.1428(0.18) = 0.$$

The eigenvalues of R in (3.10) are all positive, so that the last of the GEID conditions also is satisfied.

LIST OF ABBREVIATIONS AND NOTATIONS

Variables, residuals and parameters are denoted by Greek letters for theoretical concepts, and by corresponding Roman letters for empirical concepts.

Systems (Models or Parts of Models)

ID	Interdependent
CLID	Classic ID (abbreviation used only in tables)
REID	Reformulated ID
GEID	General ID
SF	Structural form
RF	Reduced form
RRF	Restricted reduced form
URF	Unrestricted reduced form

Variables and Residuals	*Theoretical*	*Empirical*
Endogenous variables		y_i $(i = 1, n)$
Ditto, vector notation		y
Ditto, conditional expectation	η^*	y^*
Ditto, individual variables	η_i^*	y_i^*
$n \times T$ data matrix for endogenous variables		Y
$m \times T$ " " " predetermined "		Z
Residuals, in SF	δ	d
Ditto, in RF	ε	e

Matrices and Vectors

Matrix $$Y = \begin{bmatrix} y_{11} \cdots y_{1T} \\ \cdots\cdots\cdots \\ y_{n1} \cdots y_{nT} \end{bmatrix}$$

Column vector $$y = \begin{bmatrix} y_1 \\ \vdots \\ y_n \end{bmatrix} = (y_1, \cdots, y_n)$$

Ditto, with time index $$y_t = \begin{bmatrix} y_{1t} \\ \vdots \\ y_{nt} \end{bmatrix} = (y_{1t}, \cdots, y_{nt})$$

Row vector over time	$y_i = [y_{i1}, \cdots, y_{iT}]$	
Relations	*Theoretical*	*Empirical*
Classic ID, in SF	$y = \beta y + \Gamma z + \delta$	$y = By + Gz + d$
Ditto, with time specified	$y_t = \beta y_t + \Gamma z_t + \delta_t$	$y_t = By_t + Gz_t + d_t$
REID and GEID, in SF	$y = \beta\eta^* + \Gamma z + \varepsilon$	$y = By^* + Gz + e$
Ditto, ith relation, either:	$y_i = \beta_i\eta^* + \gamma_i z + \varepsilon_i$	$y_i = b_i y^* + g_i z + e_i$
or, equivalently:	$y_i = \beta_{(i)}\eta^*_{(i)} + \gamma_{(i)}z_{(i)} + \varepsilon_i$	$y_i = b_{(i)}Y^*_{(i)} + g_{(i)}z_{(i)} + e_i$
Ditto, behavioral relations	${}_1y = \beta_1\eta^* + \Gamma_1 z + {}_1\varepsilon$	${}_1y = B_1 y^* + G_1 z + {}_1e$
Ditto, identities	${}_2y = \beta_2\eta^* + \Gamma_2 z + {}_2\varepsilon$	${}_2y = B_2 y^* + G_2 z + {}_2e$
Parameters		
In SF	$\beta = [\beta_{ik}], \quad \Gamma = [\gamma_{ik}]$	$B = [b_{ik}], \quad G = [g_{ik}]$
In RF	$\Omega = [\omega_{ik}] = [I - \beta]^{-1}\Gamma$	$W = [w_{ik}] = [I - B]^{-1}G$
In URF	$\Pi = [\pi_{ik}]$	$P = [p_{ik}]$

Integer Notations for Size

T	Number of observations
n	Number of endogenous variables
m	Number of predetermined variables
p	Number of behavioural relations
q	Number of identities
n_i	Number of explanatory endogenous variables in ith relation
m_i	Number of predetermined variables in ith relation
$NOIT$	Number of iterations

Estimation methods

OLS	Ordinary Least Squares
TSLS	Two-Stage Least Squares
3SLS	Three-Stage Least Squares
LIML	Limited Information Maximum Likelihood
FIML	Full Information Maximum Likelihood
FIMD	Ditto, with Diagonal covariance matrix for the residuals
IIV	Iterative Instrumental Variables
FP	Fix-Point

AFP Algebraic FP
FFP Fractional FP
PFP Parametric FP
RFP Recursive FP
SFP Solved system FP (earlier called RFFP: Reduced Form FP)

Steps for the iterative FP procedures: $s = 0, 1, 2, \cdots$
Iterative proxies for y^*: $y^{(s)}$

Estimators

GEID For ordinary GEID systems, covering REID systems as a special case
GEID-A For Geid systems with autocorrelated residuals

There are also other estimators for GEID systems with autocorrelated residuals

Various Notations

I Identity matrix
I_p Identity matrix of order p
Kronecker product, $A \otimes B = [a_{ij} B]$
Q_i^2 $1 - \Sigma_t (y_{it} - y_{it}^*)^2 / \Sigma_t (y_{it} - \bar{y}_i)^2$ with $y_{it}^* = W_i z_t$

K $= [k_{ij}]$ Matrix that specifies the SF residuals as a moving summation process of first order: $\delta_t = \upsilon_t + K\upsilon_{t-1}$
R $= [r_{ij}]$ Matrix that specifies the SF residuals as an autoregressive process of first order: $\delta_t = R\delta_{t-1} + \upsilon_t$
MSE Mean square error
RMSE Root mean square error

Note: For more specific notations, see the text of the various chapters.

LIST OF REFERENCES

Ågren, A., 1967, The fractional Fix-Point method, FL Thesis (University Institute of Statistics, Uppsala).

Ågren, A., 1969, Fractional Fix-Point (FFP) estimation, in: Wold and Lyttkens, eds. (1969) Section 10, 37–38.

Ågren, A., 1970, Fractional Fix-Point (FFP) estimation, in: Mosbaek and Wold et al. (1970) Chapter 3.6, 129–136.

Ågren, A., 1972a, Extensions of the Fix-Point method, Published Doctoral Thesis (University of Uppsala, Uppsala).

Ågren, A., 1972b, Convergence analysis of the Fix-Point method based on pseudo-variables, Seminar Paper (University Institute of Statistics, Uppsala).

Ågren, A., 1973a, Extensions of the Fix-Point method I: The GEID estimates and the fractional Fix-Point method, Economie Appliquée XXVI, 561–582.

Ågren, A., 1973b, A short note on the GEID specification and the GEID estimator, in: Lyttkens and Wold, eds. (1973).

Ågren, A., 1975, The consistency of the GEID (FP) estimates, Journal of the Royal Statistical Society B 37, 293–295.

Ågren, A. and H. O. Wold, 1969, On the structure and estimation of general interdependent systems, in: P. R. Krishnaiah, ed., Multivariate analysis II (Academic Press, New York) 543–565.

Amemiya, T., 1966, Specification analysis in the estimation of parameters of a simultaneous equation model with autoregressive parameters, Econometrica 34, 283–306.

Anderson, T. W. and H. Rubin, 1949, Estimation of the parameters of a single stochastic difference equation in a complete system of stochastic equations, Annals of Mathematical Statistics 20, 46–63.

Ball, R. J., 1963, The significance of simultaneous methods of parameter estimation in econometric models, Applied Statistics 12, 14–25.

Basmann, R. L., 1957, A generalized classical method of linear estimation of coefficients in a structural equation, Econometrica 25, 77–83.

Basmann, R. L., 1963, Remarks concerning the application of exact finite sample distribution functions of CCL estimates in econometric statistical inference, Journal of the American Statistical Association 58, 619–636.

Basmann, R. L., 1965, On the application of the identifiability test statistic in predictive testing of explanatory economic models, The Econometric Annal of the Indian Econometric Journal 13, 387–423.

Bentzel, R. and B. Hansen, 1954, On recursiveness and interdependency in economic models, Review of Economic Studies 22, 153–168.

Bentzel, R. and H. Wold, 1946, On statistical demand analysis from the view-point of simultaneous equations, Skandinavisk Aktuarietidskrift 29, 95–114.

Bergström, R., 1970, Dutta–Su's model: A study of the estimates of the IIV and FP methods, Seminar Paper (University Institute of Statistics, Uppsala).

Bergström, R., 1971, Estimation of Pavlopoulos' model by IIV and other methods, Seminar Paper (University Institute of Statistics, Uppsala).

Bergström, R., 1972, An investigation of the Reduced Fix-Point method, Seminar Paper (University Institute of Statistics, Uppsala).

Bergström, R., 1973, Investigations of Fix-Point and Iterative Instrumental Variables methods: Convergence properties, comparative studies, and applications, Economie Appliquée XXVI, 505–526.

Bergström, R., 1974, Studies in the estimation of interdependent systems: Especially the Fix-Point and Iterative Instrumental Variables methods, Published Doctoral Thesis (University of Uppsala, Uppsala).

Bergström, R., 1975a, Estimation of a model explaining wages and prices by methods for simultaneous equation systems, Seminar Paper (University Institute of Statistics, Uppsala).

Bergström, R., 1975b, Estimation of a macroeconomic model with autocorrelated residuals by consistent methods of the IIV and FP type, Seminar Paper (University Institute of Statistics, Uppsala).

Bergström, R., 1975c, Modifications of the IIV and GEID estimators in the case of lagged endogenous variables and autocorrelated residuals, Seminar Paper (University Institute of Statistics, Uppsala).

Bergström, R., 1976, Estimation of a model of the Czechoslovak economy, Ekonomicko-Matematický Obzor 12, 1–29.

Bergström, R., 1979, Computer program for the FP methods used in Chapter 5 of this volume (University Institute of Statistics, Uppsala).

Bergström, R., 1980, Estimation of large econometric models by consistent methods: The case of the Polish W–3 model, Research Report (Department of Statistics, University of Uppsala).

Bodin, L., 1968, Studies of explicit and fractional Fix-Point estimation of interdependent systems, FL Thesis (University of Uppsala, Uppsala).

Bodin, L., 1969, Recursive Fix-Point (RFP) estimation, in: Wold and Lyttkens, eds. (1969) Section 11, 38–39.

Bodin, L., 1970, Recursive Fix-Point (RFP) estimation, in: Mosbaek and Wold et al. (1970) Chapter 3.7, 136–142.

Bodin, L., 1973a, Improved FP estimation of GEID systems by the RFP method, in: Lyttkens and Wold, eds. (1973) Chapter 4.

Bodin, L., 1973b, Extension of the Fix-Point method II: The recursive Fix-Point method, Economie Appliquée XXVI, 583–607.

Bodin, L., 1974, Recursive Fix-Point estimation: Theory and applications, Published Doctoral Thesis (University of Uppsala, Uppsala).

Brown, T. M., 1960, Simultaneous least squares: A distribution free method of equation system structure estimation, International Economic Review 1, 173–191.

Chambers, J. M., C. L. Mallows and B. W. Stuck, 1976, A method for simulating stable random variables, Journal of the American Statistical Association 71, 340–344.

Chow, G. C. and R. C. Fair, 1973, Maximum likelihood estimation of linear equation systems with autoregressive residuals, Annals of Economic and Social Measurement 2, 17–28.

Christ, C., 1966, Econometric models and methods (Wiley, New York).

Christ, C., C. Hildreth and T.-Ch. Liu, 1960, A symposium on simultaneous equation estimation, Econometrica 28, 835–865.

Cochrane, D. and G. H. Orcutt, 1950, Application of least squares regression to relationships containing autocorrelated error terms, Journal of the American Statistical Association 44, 32–61.

Cramér, H., 1946, Mathematical methods of statistics (Princeton University Press, Princeton, NJ). Previously published in 1945 (Almqvist and Wiksell, Uppsala).

Dhrymes, Ph. J., 1970, Econometrics, statistical foundations and applications (Harper & Row, Evanston, IL).

Dhrymes, Ph. J. and H. Erlat, 1974, Asymptotic properties of full information estimators in dynamic autoregressive simultaneous equation models, Journal of Econometrics 2, 247–259.

Dhrymes, Ph. J. and J. Taylor, 1976, On an efficient two-step estimator for dynamic simultaneous equations models with autoregressive errors, International Economic Review 17, 362–376.

Dhrymes, Ph. J., R. Berner and D. Cummins, 1974, A comparison of some limited information estimators for dynamic simultaneous equation models with autocorrelated errors, Econometrica 42, 313–332.

Dicks-Miraux, L. A., 1961, The interrelationship between cost and price changes, 1946–1959: A study of inflation in post-war Britain, Oxford Economic Papers 13, 267–292.
Duesenberry, J. S., G. Fromm, L. R. Klein and E. Kuh, 1965, The Brookings quarterly econometric model of the United States (Rand-McNally, Chicago, IL).
Duncan, O. D., 1966, Path analysis: Sociological examples, American Journal of Sociology 72, 1–16.
Durbin, J., 1960, Estimation of parameters in time series regression models, Journal of the Royal Statistical Society B 22, 139–153.
Dutta, M. and V. Su, 1969, An econometric model of Puerto Rico, Review of Economic Studies 36, 319–333.
Edgerton, D. L., 1971, Prediction and estimation in nonlinear economic models, Seminar Paper (University Institute of Statistics, Uppsala).
Edgerton, D. L., 1972, Some properties of two stage least squares as applied to nonlinear models, International Economic Review 13, 26–32.
Edgerton, D. L., 1973a, The combined use of predictors and Taylor series in nonlinear interdependent systems, Economie Appliquée XXVI, 537–559.
Edgerton, D. L., 1973b, Nonlinear interdependent systems and other problems, European meeting of the Econometric Society (Oslo).
Edgerton, D. L., 1973c, Nonlinear interdependent systems, Published Doctoral Thesis (University of Uppsala, Uppsala).
Edgerton, D. L., 1973d, Detailed results of a Monte Carlo study, Seminar Paper (University Institute of Statistics, Lund).
Edgerton, D. L., 1974, Use of the GEID estimator and the Fix-Point method in nonaligned asymmetric ID systems, Research Report 74:3 (University Institute of Statistics, Lund).
Edgerton, D. L., 1975, A further note on the GEID estimator and FP method in nonaligned ID systems, Research Report 75:12 (University Institute of Statistics, Lund).
Edgerton, D. L., 1977, ABCNL: A computer program for nonlinear interdependent systems, Research Report (University Institute of Statistics, Lund).
Evans, M. K., 1969, Macroeconomic activity (Harper & Row, New York).
Fair, R. C., 1970, A short-run forecasting model of the United States economy (Heath and Co., Lexington, MA).
Fair, R. C., 1972, Efficient estimation of simultaneous equations with autoregressive errors by instrumental variables, Review of Economics and Statistics LIV, 444–449.
Fair, R. C., 1973, A comparison of alternative estimators of macroeconomic models, International Economic Review 14, 261–277.
Fair, R. C., 1974, An evaluation of a short-run forecasting model, International Economic Review 15, 285–303.
Feller, W., 1966, An introduction to probability theory and its applications, Vol. 2 (Wiley, New York).
Fisher, F. M., 1961, On the cost of approximate specification in simultaneous equations estimation, Econometrica 29, 139–170.
Fisher, F. M., 1965, Dynamic structure and estimation in economy-wide econometric models, in: Duesenberry et al., eds. (1965) 589–636.
Fisher, F. M., 1966, The relative sensitivity to specification error of different k-class estimators, Journal of the American Statistical Association 61, 345–356.
Fisher, F. M., 1967, Approximate specification and the choice of a k-class estimator, Journal of the American Statistical Association 62, 1265–1276.
Fisher, R. A., 1925, Statistical methods for research workers (Oliver and Boyd, Edinburgh).
Fisher, R. A., 1935, The design of experiments (Oliver and Boyd, Edinburgh).
Fromm, G. and L. R. Klein, 1969, Solutions of the complete system, in: J. S. Duesenberry et al., eds., The Brookings model: Some further results (North-Holland, Amsterdam) 362–421.
Girshick, M. A. and T. Haavelmo, 1947, Statistical analysis of the demand for food: Examples of simultaneous estimation of structural equations, Econometrica 15, 79–110.
Gnedenko, B. V. and Z. N. Kolmogorov, 1954, Limit distributions for sums of independent random variables (Addison-Wesley, Cambridge).

Goldberger, A. S., 1959, Impact multipliers and dynamic properties of the Klein–Goldberger model (North-Holland, Amsterdam).
Goldfeld, S. M. and R. E. Quandt, 1972, Nonlinear methods in econometrics (North-Holland, Amsterdam).
Grether, D. M. and G. S. Maddala, 1972, On the asymptotic properties of some two step procedures for estimating distributed lag models, International Economic Review 13, 737–744.
Haavelmo, T., 1943, The statistical implications of a system of simultaneous equations, Econometrica 11, 1–12.
Haavelmo, T., 1949, The probability approach in econometrics, Econometrica 12, Suppl.
Hale, C., 1976, The moments of some k-class estimators of a structural coefficient in a mis-specified equation, European meeting of the Econometric Society (Helsinki).
Hale, C., R. S. Mariano and J. G. Ramage, 1976, Finite sample analysis of mis-specification in simultaneous equation models, Discussion Paper 357 (Department of Economics, University of Pennsylvania, Philadelphia, PA).
Hatanaka, M., 1976, Several efficient two-step estimators for the dynamic simultaneous equations model with autoregressive disturbances, Journal of Econometrics 4, 189–204.
Hendry, D. F., 1971, Maximum likelihood estimation of systems of simultaneous regression equations with errors generated by a vector autoregressive process, International Economic Review 12, 257–272.
Hendry, D. F., 1974, Maximum likelihood estimation of systems of simultaneous regression equations with errors generated by a vector autoregressive process: A correction, International Economic Review 15, 260.
Hirvonen, J., 1975, On the use of two stage least squares with principal components, Bank of Finland Publications D 36 (Helsinki).
Hood, W. C. and T. C. Koopmans, eds., 1973, Studies in econometric method (Wiley, New York).
Hui, B. S., 1978, The partial least squares approach to path models of indirectly observed variables with multiple indicators, Doctoral Thesis (University of Pennsylvania, Philadelphia, PA).
Hui, B. S., 1979, On building PLS models with interdependent inner relations, Conference on Systems under Indirect Observation, 18–20 Oct. (Cartigny near Geneva).
Hunt, J. G., J. M. Dowling and F. R. Glahe, 1974, L_1 estimation in small samples with Laplace error distributions, Decision Sciences 5, 22–29.
Johnston, J., 1972, Econometric methods, 2nd ed. (McGraw-Hill, New York). Earlier version published in 1963.
Kadane, J. B., 1971, Comparison of k-class estimators when the disturbances are small, Econometrica 39, 723–737.
Klein, L. R., 1950, Economic fluctuations in the United States 1921–41 (Wiley, New York).
Klein, L. R., 1960, Single equation vs. equation system methods of estimation in econometrics, Econometrica 28, 866–871.
Klein, L. R., 1964, Problems in the estimation of interdependent systems, in: Peltier and Wold, eds. (1966) 51–87.
Klein, L. R., 1966a, The Keynesian revolution (Macmillan, London).
Klein, L. R., 1966b, Problems in the estimation of interdependent systems, in: Peltier and Wold, eds. (1966) 140–155.
Klein, L. R., 1969, Estimation of interdependent systems in macroeconometrics, Econometrica 37, 171–191.
Klein, L. R., 1974, A textbook of econometrics, 2nd ed. (Prentice-Hall, Englewood Cliffs, NJ).
Klein, L. R., 1975, Research contributions of the SSRS–Brookings econometric model project: A decade in review, in: G. Fromm and L. R. Klein, eds., The Brookings model: Perspective and recent developments (North-Holland, Amsterdam) 13–34.
Klein, L. R. and A. S. Goldberger, 1955, An econometric model of the United States (North-Holland, Amsterdam).
Kloek, T. and L. B. M. Mennes, 1960, Simultaneous equation estimation based on principal components of predetermined variables, Econometrica 28, 45–61.

Koopmans, T. C., ed., 1950, Statistical inference in dynamic economic models (Wiley, New York).

Koopmans, T. C., H. Rubin and R. B. Leipnik, 1950, Statistical inference in dynamic economic models, in: Koopmans, ed. (1950) Chapter II.

L'Esperance, L., G. Fromm and G. Nestel, 1969, Gross state product and an econometric model of a state, Journal of the American Statistical Association 64, 787–807.

Liu, T. C., 1960, Underidentification, structural estimation and forecasting, Econometrica 28, 855–865.

Lyttkens, E., 1966, A modification of the symmetric iterative method for estimating interdependent systems, Seminar Paper (University Institute of Statistics, Uppsala).

Lyttkens, E., 1967, On the Fix-Point method and related problems, including an explicit treatment of the estimation problem of Girshick–Haavelmo's model, Part I–II, First Blaricum meeting of the Econometric Society.

Lyttkens, E., 1968, The Fix-Point method with iterated reduced form coefficients and the Fix-Point method with pseudovariables, Seminar Paper (University Institute of Statistics, Uppsala).

Lyttkens, E., 1969a, Two devices for reducing the rounding errors of the FP procedures, in: Wold and Lyttkens, eds. (1969) Section 13.

Lyttkens, E., 1969b, Algebraic Fix-Point (AFP) estimation, in: Wold and Lyttkens, eds. (1969) Section 14.

Lyttkens, E., 1970a, Algebraic FP (AFP) estimation of Summers' model, in: Mosbaek and Wold et al. (1970) Chapter 3.8.

Lyttkens, E., 1970b, Algebraic FP (AFP) estimation of Girshick–Haavelmo's model, in: Mosbaek and Wold et al. (1970) Chapter 9.3.

Lyttkens, E., 1970c, Symmetric and asymmetric estimation methods, in: Mosbaek and Wold et al. (1970) Chapter 11.

Lyttkens, E., 1970d, Maximum likelihood aspects of the FP estimation of GEID models, in: Mosbaek and Wold et al. (1970) Chapter 3.10.

Lyttkens, E., 1973a, The Fix-Point method for estimating interdependent systems with the underlying model specification, Journal of the Royal Statistical Society A 136, 353–394.

Lyttkens, E., 1973b, Investigation of the Fix-Point (FP) and Interative Instrumental Variables (IIV) and related estimation methods: Various theoretical aspects, Economie Appliquée XXVI, 425–470.

Lyttkens, E., 1974, The Iterative Instrumental Variables method for estimating interdependent systems where lagged endogenous variables occur and the residuals are autocorrelated, Seminar Paper (Rutgers University, New Brunswick, NJ).

Lyttkens, E., 1975, The Iterative Instrumental Variables method when the residuals are autocorrelated and lagged endogenous variables occur in the structural equations, Third World Congress of the Econometric Society (Toronto).

Lyttkens, E. and H. Wold, 1970, Reference to more general ID systems, in: Mosbaek and Wold et al. (1970) Chapter 3.2.

Lyttkens, E. and H. Wold, eds., 1973, FP (Fix-Point), IIV (Iterative Instrumental Variables) and related approaches to ID (Interdependent) systems: Theory and applications, European meeting of the Econometric Society (Oslo).

Madansky, A., 1976, Foundations of econometrics (North-Holland, Amsterdam).

Malinvaud, E., 1964, Méthodes statistiques de l'econométrie (Dunod, Paris). English revised 2nd edition published in 1970 (North-Holland, Amsterdam).

May, S., 1973, Choosing an estimator: A comparison of k-class and Fix-Point estimators, European meeting of the Econometric Society (Oslo).

Mitchell, B., 1970, Estimation of large econometric models, Ph.D. Thesis (M.I.T.).

Mosbaek, E. J., 1968, Book review of Duesenberry et al. (1965), Econometrica 36, 194–196.

Mosbaek, E. J. and H. Wold, with contributions by E. Lyttkens, A. Ågren and L. Bodin, 1970, Interdependent systems: Structure and estimation (North-Holland, Amsterdam).

Nagar, A. L., 1959, The bias and moment matrix of the general k-class estimators of the parameters in simultaneous equations, Econometrica 27, 575–595.

Ostrowski, A. M., 1960, Solution of equations and systems of equations (Academic Press, New York).
Pavlopoulos, P., 1966, A statistical model for the Greek economy 1949–59 (North-Holland, Amsterdam).
Peltier, R. and H. Wold, eds., 1966, La technique des modèles dans les sciences humaines, Entretiens de Monaco en sciences humaines, Session 1964 (Union Européenne d'Editions, Monaco).
Ramage, J. G., 1971, A perturbation study of the k-class estimators in the presence of specification error, Doctoral Thesis (Yale University, New Haven, CT).
Richardson, D. H., 1970, On the robustness of ordinary least squares, Seminar Note (University of Kansas, Lawrence, KS).
Salviucci, P., ed., 1965, Semaine d'étude sur le rôle de l'analyse économétrique dans la formulation de plans de développement, Scripta Varia 28 (Pontifical Academy of Science, Vatican City).
Sargan, J. D., 1961, The maximum likelihood estimation of economic relationships with autoregressive residuals, Econometrica 29, 414–426.
Sargan, J. D., 1964, Wages and prices in the United Kingdom, in: Econometric analysis for national economic planning, Colston Papers XVI (Butterworths, London).
Schönfeld, P., 1971, A useful central limit theorem for m-dependent variables, Metrika 17, 116–128.
Selén, J., 1973, Autocorrelated residuals in ID-systems, in: Lyttkens and Wold, eds. (1973) Chapter 8.
Selén, J., 1974, On the properties of some estimation methods for regression models containing autocorrelated error terms, Research Report 74–6 (University Institute of Statistics, Uppsala).
Selén, J., 1975, Interdependent systems with serially correlated errors, Published Doctoral Thesis (University of Uppsala, Uppsala).
Simon, H., 1957, Causal ordering and identifiability, in: H. Simon, ed., Models of man (Wiley, New York) 10–36.
Smith, V. K., 1973, Monte Carlo methods: Their role for econometrics (Lexington Books, Toronto).
Sowey, E. R., 1973, A classified bibliography of Monte Carlo studies in econometrics, Journal of Econometrics 1, 377–395.
Steward, D., 1962, On an approach to techniques for the analysis of the structure of large systems of equations, SIAM Review 4, 321–342.
Sujan, I. and M. Tkáč, 1973, The econometric forecasting model of Czechoslovakia, European meeting of the Econometric Society (Oslo).
Sujan, I. et al., 1972, Dynamický krátkodobý prognostický model ekonomiky CSSR, Research Report CRC/UNDP/ (Bratislava).
Summers, R., 1965, A capital intensive approach to the small sample properties of various simultaneous equation estimators, Econometrica 33, 1–41.
Theil, H., 1953, Estimation and simultaneous correlation in complete equation systems, Mimeo. (Central Planning Bureau, The Hague).
Theil, H., 1958, Economic forecasts and policy (North-Holland, Amsterdam).
Tinbergen, J., 1937, An econometric approach to business cycles problems (Hermann, Paris).
Tinbergen, J., 1939, Statistical testing of business-cycle theories, Vol. 2: Business cycles in the United States of America: 1919–1932 (United Nations, Geneva).
van der Giessen, A. A., 1970, Solving nonlinear systems by computer: A new method, Statistica Neerlandica 24, 41–50.
Westlund, A., 1976, Estimation and prediction in interdependent systems in the presence of specification errors, Unpublished Doctoral Thesis (Department of Statistics, University of Umea).
Wilks, S. S., 1962, Mathematical statistics (Wiley, New York).
Wold, H., 1938, A study in the analysis of stationary time series (Almqvist and Wiksell, Uppsala). 2nd edition with an appendix by P. Whittle published in 1954 (Almqvist and Wiksell, Uppsala).

Wold, H., 1940, The demand for agricultural products and its sensitivity to price and income changes (in Swedish), Statens Offentliga Utredningar 1940:16 (Stockholm).

Wold, H., 1947, Statistical estimation of economic relationships, Proceedings of the International Statistical Institute Conference, Vol. 5 (Washington, DC) 1–22.

Wold, H., 1954, Causality and econometrics, Econometrica 22, 62–174.

Wold, H., 1955, Possibilités et limitations des systèmes à chaîne causale, Cahiers du Séminaire d'Econométrie de R. Roy 3 (Centre National de la Recherche Scientifique, Paris) 81–101.

Wold, H., 1958, A case study of interdependent versus causal chain systems, Review of the International Statistical Institute 5, 5–25.

Wold, H., 1960, Ends and means in econometric model building: Basic considerations reviewed, in: Probability and statistics, The Harald Cramér volume (Wiley, New York) 355–434. Previously published in 1959 (Almqvist and Wiksell, Uppsala).

Wold, H., 1961a, Construction principles of simultaneous equations models in econometrics, Bulletin of the International Statistical Institute 38, no. 4, 111–138.

Wold, H., 1961b, Unbiased predictors, Proceedings of the Fourth Berkeley Symposium of Mathematical Statistics and Probability 1, 719–761.

Wold, H., 1963a, On the consistency of least squares regression, Sankyā A 25, no. 2, 211–215.

Wold, H., 1963b, Toward a verdict on macroeconomic simultaneous equations, in: Salviucci, ed. (1965) 115–166.

Wold, H., 1964a, The approach of model building: Crossroads of probability theory, statistics and theory of knowledge, in: Peltier and Wold, eds. (1966) 1–38.

Wold, H., 1964b, On the definition and meaning of causal concepts, in: Peltier and Wold, eds. (1966) 265–295.

Wold, H., 1965, A Fix-Point theorem with econometric background, I–II, Arkiv för Matematik 6, 209–240.

Wold, H., 1966, Nonlinear estimation by iterative least squares procedures, in: Research papers in statistics: Festschrift for J. Neyman (Wiley, New York) 411–444.

Wold, H., 1969a, The Fix-Point (FP) method, in: Wold and Lyttkens, eds. (1969) Section 9.

Wold, H., 1969b, Mergers of econometrics and philosophy of science, Synthese 20, 427–482.

Wold, H., 1979a, Model construction and evaluation when theoretical knowledge is scarce: An example of the use of partial least squares, Cahier 1979:06 (Department of Econometrics, University of Geneva).

Wold, H., 1979b, Soft modeling: The basic PLS design, and some extensions, in: K. Jöreskog and H. Wold, eds., Systems under indirect observation: Causality, structure, prediction (North-Holland, Amsterdam) forthcoming.

Wold, H. in association with L. Juréen, 1953, Demand analysis: A study in econometrics (Wiley, New York). Previously published in 1952 (Geber, Uppsala).

Wold, H. and E. Lyttkens, eds., 1969, Nonlinear iterative partial least squares (NIPALS) estimation procedures, Bulletin of the International Statistical Institute 42, 29–51.

Wright, S., 1934, The method of path coefficients, Annals of Mathematical Statistics 5, 161–215.

Yearbook of National Account Statistics (United Nations, New York).

Young, D. M., 1971, Iterative solution of large linear systems (Academic Press, New York).

Yu, Tzong-Shian, 1970, A short-term macroeconomic model of Taiwan, Second World Congress of the Econometric Society (Cambridge).

Zellner, A., 1962, An efficient method of estimating seemingly unrelated regressions and tests for aggregation bias, Journal of the American Statistical Association 57, 348–368.

Zellner, A. and H. Theil, 1962, Three-stage least squares: Simultaneous estimation of simultaneous equations, Econometrica 30, 54–78.

AUTHOR INDEX

SUBJECT INDEX